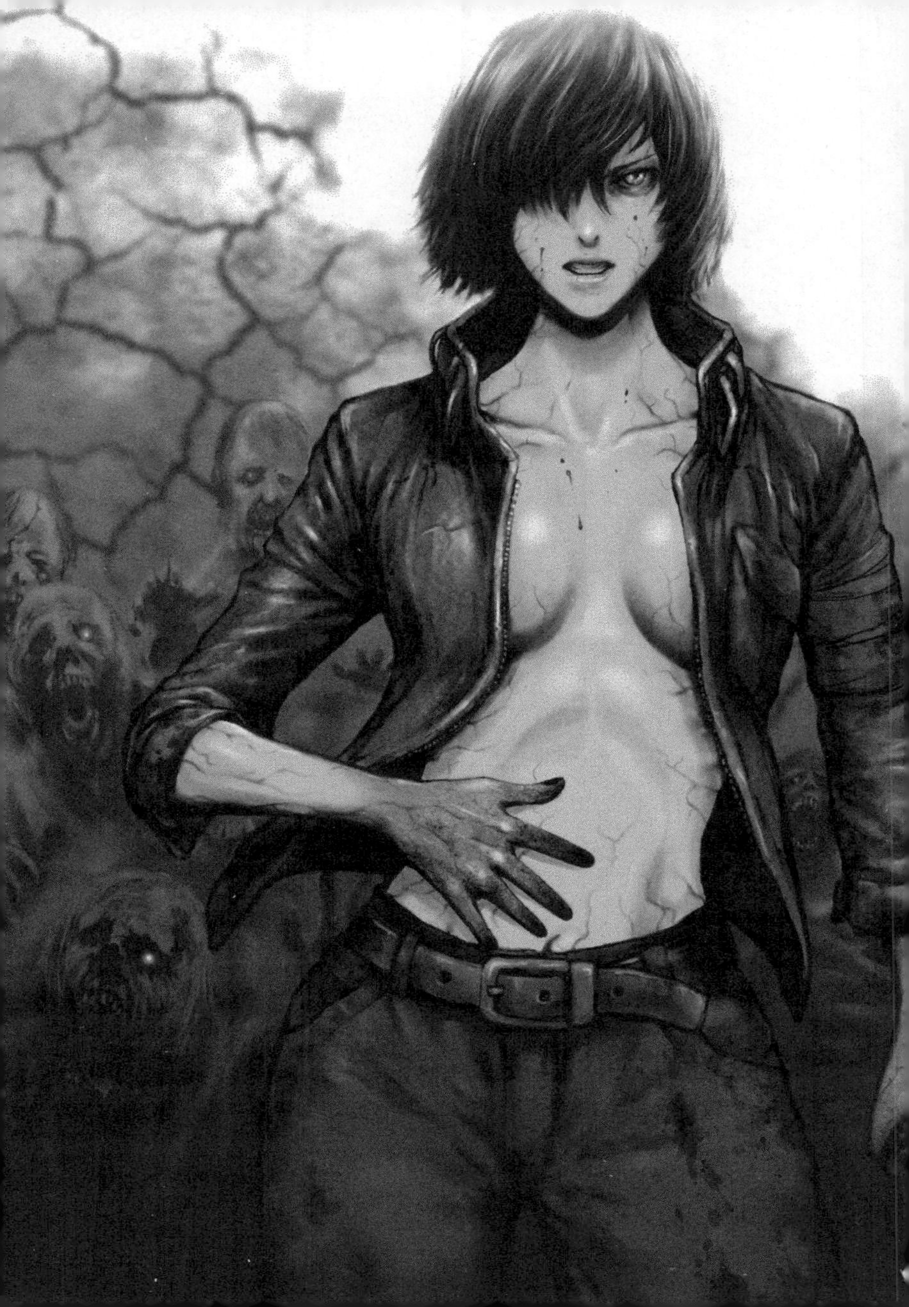

CONTENTS

CHAPTER 5

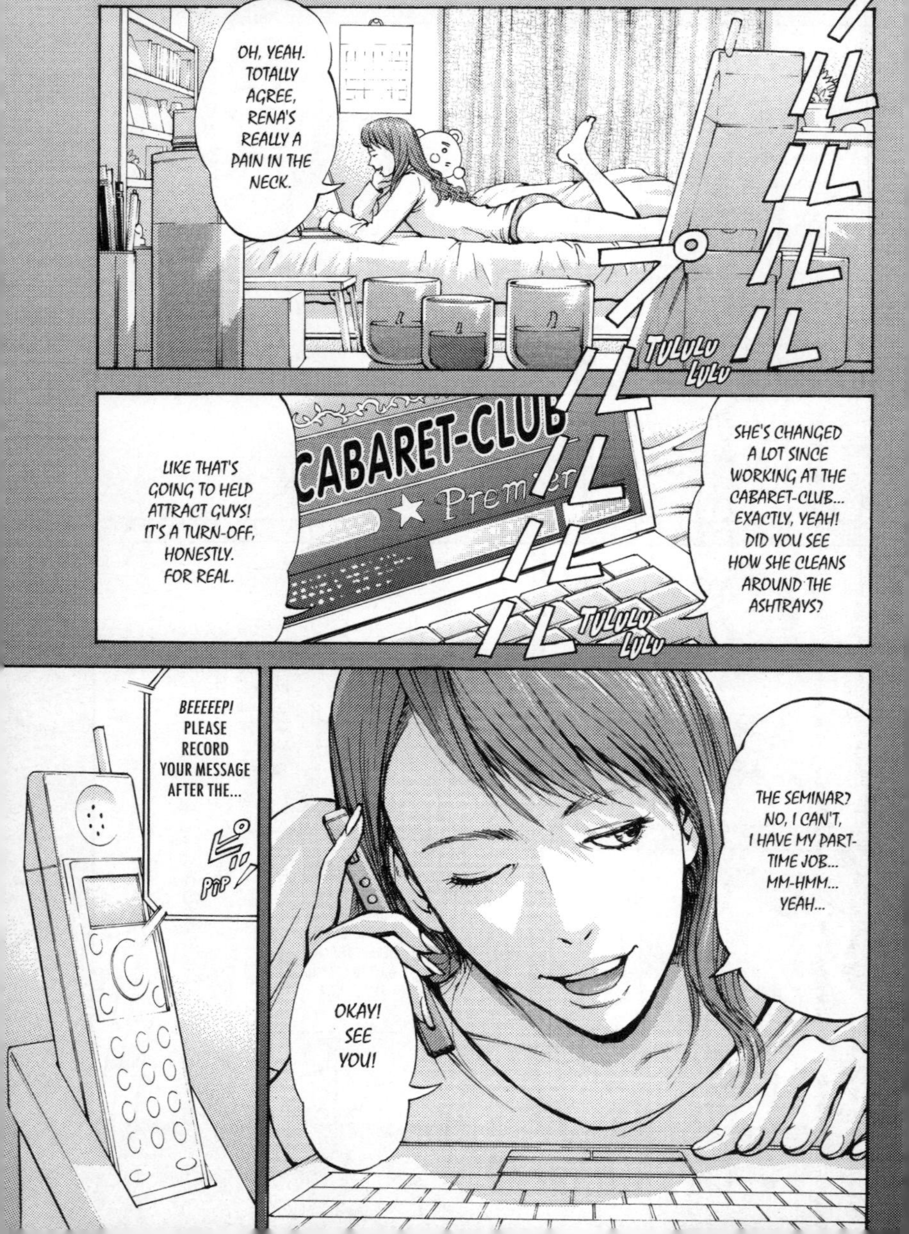
TULULU LULU
OH, YEAH. TOTALLY AGREE, RENA'S REALLY A PAIN IN THE NECK.
SHE'S CHANGED A LOT SINCE WORKING AT THE CABARET-CLUB... EXACTLY, YEAH! DID YOU SEE HOW SHE CLEANS AROUND THE ASHTRAYS?
TULULU LULU
CABARET-CLUB
LIKE THAT'S GOING TO HELP ATTRACT GUYS! IT'S A TURN-OFF, HONESTLY. FOR REAL.
THE SEMINAR? NO, I CAN'T, I HAVE MY PART-TIME JOB... MM-HMM... YEAH...
OKAY! SEE YOU!
BEEEEEP! PLEASE RECORD YOUR MESSAGE AFTER THE...
PIP

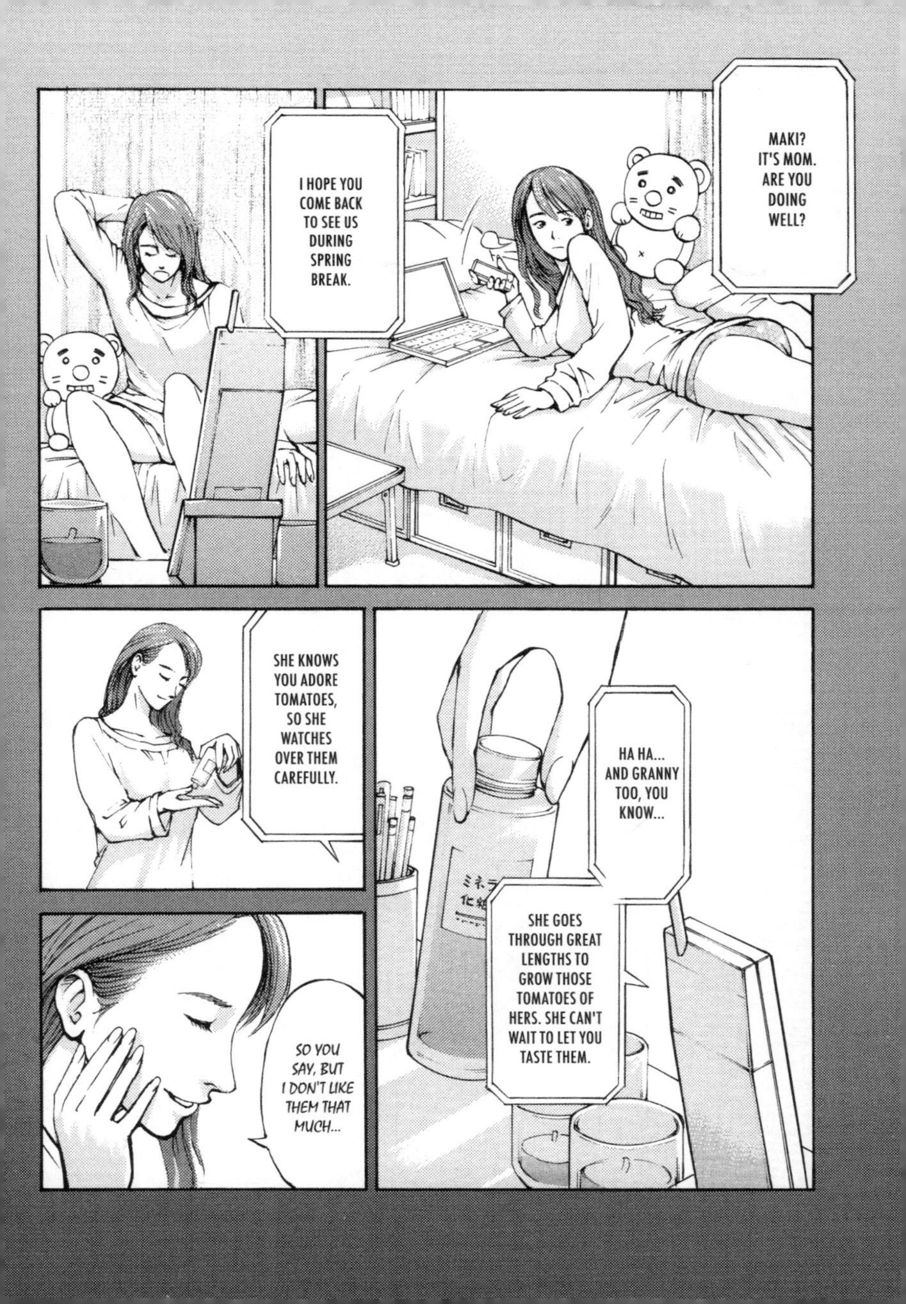
MAKI? IT'S MOM. ARE YOU DOING WELL?
I HOPE YOU COME BACK TO SEE US DURING SPRING BREAK.
HA HA... AND GRANNY TOO, YOU KNOW...
SHE GOES THROUGH GREAT LENGTHS TO GROW THOSE TOMATOES OF HERS. SHE CAN'T WAIT TO LET YOU TASTE THEM.
SHE KNOWS YOU ADORE TOMATOES, SO SHE WATCHES OVER THEM CAREFULLY.
SO YOU SAY, BUT I DON'T LIKE THEM THAT MUCH...

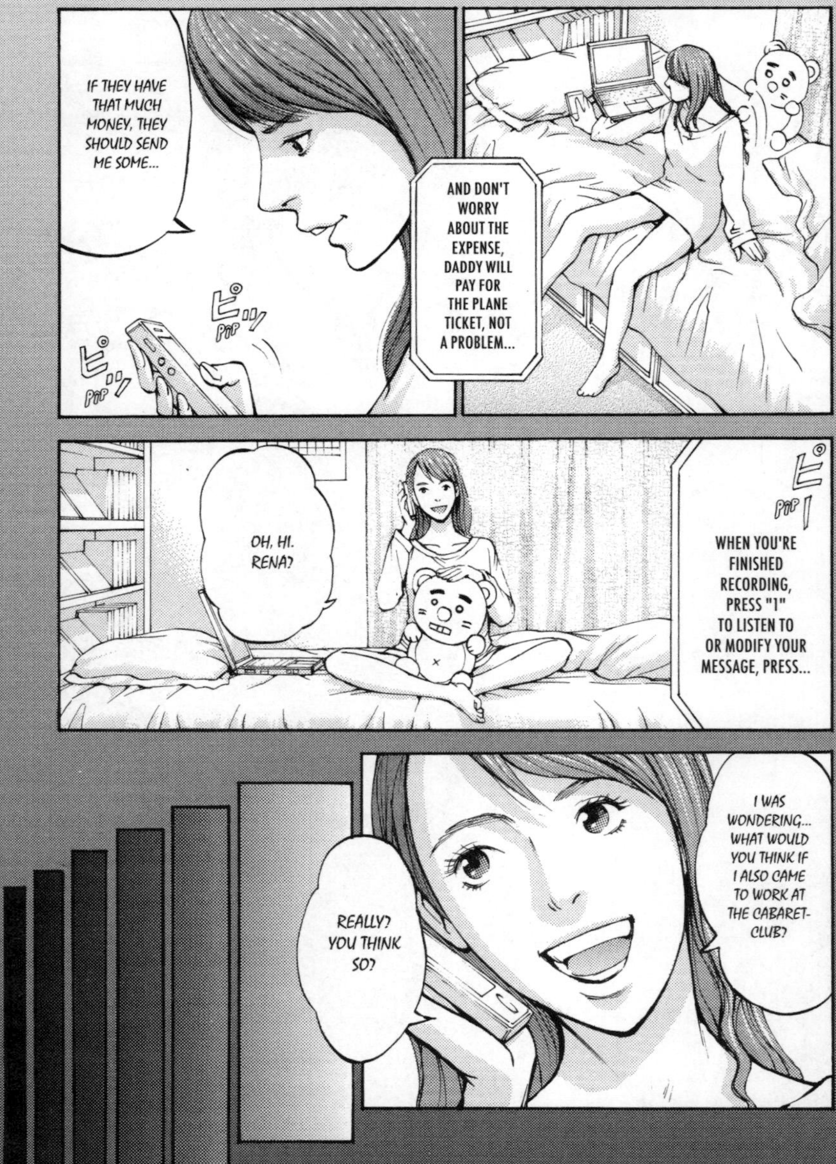
AND DON'T WORRY ABOUT THE EXPENSE, DADDY WILL PAY FOR THE PLANE TICKET, NOT A PROBLEM...
IF THEY HAVE THAT MUCH MONEY, THEY SHOULD SEND ME SOME...
ピッ PIP
ピッ PIP
ピ PIP
WHEN YOU'RE FINISHED RECORDING, PRESS "1" TO LISTEN TO OR MODIFY YOUR MESSAGE, PRESS...
OH, HI. RENA?
I WAS WONDERING... WHAT WOULD YOU THINK IF I ALSO CAME TO WORK AT THE CABARET-CLUB?
REALLY? YOU THINK SO?

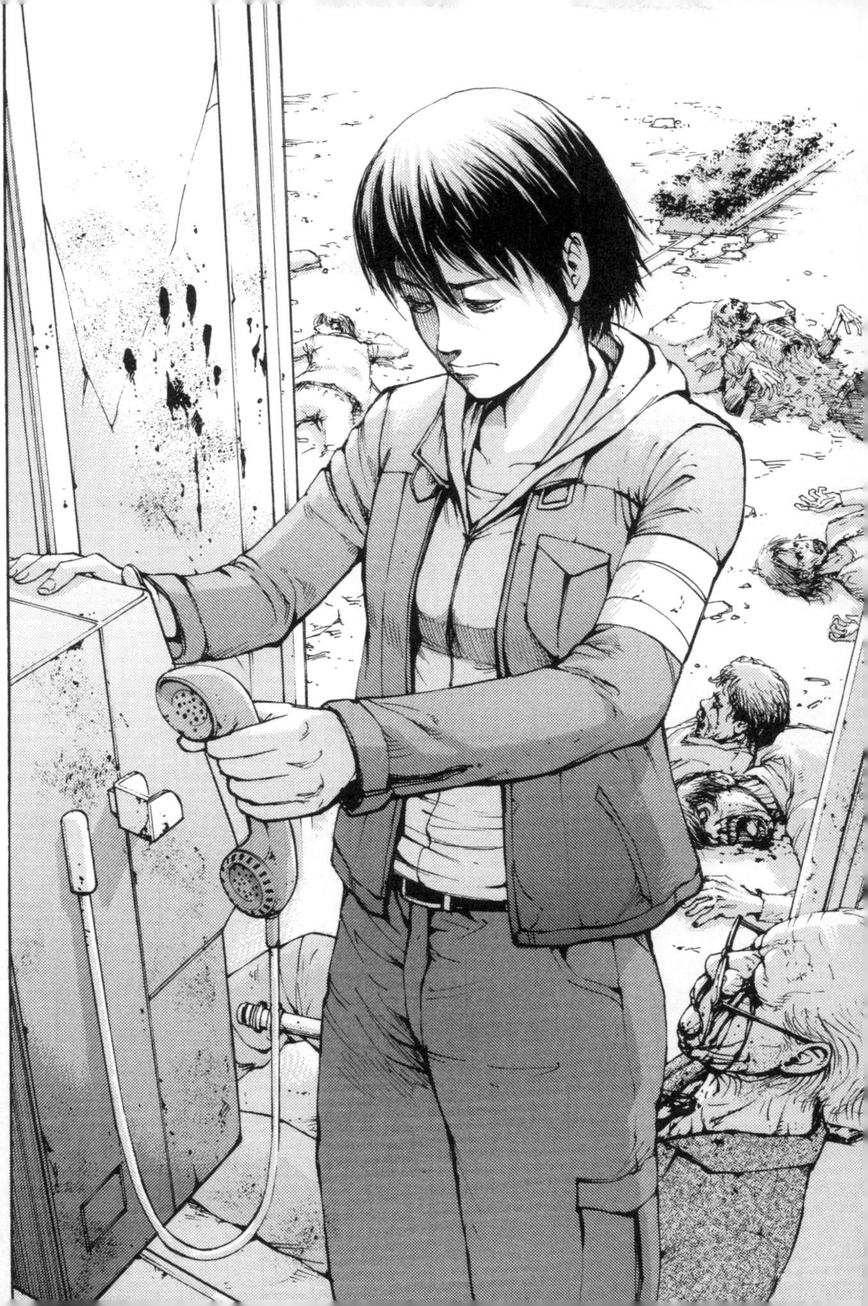

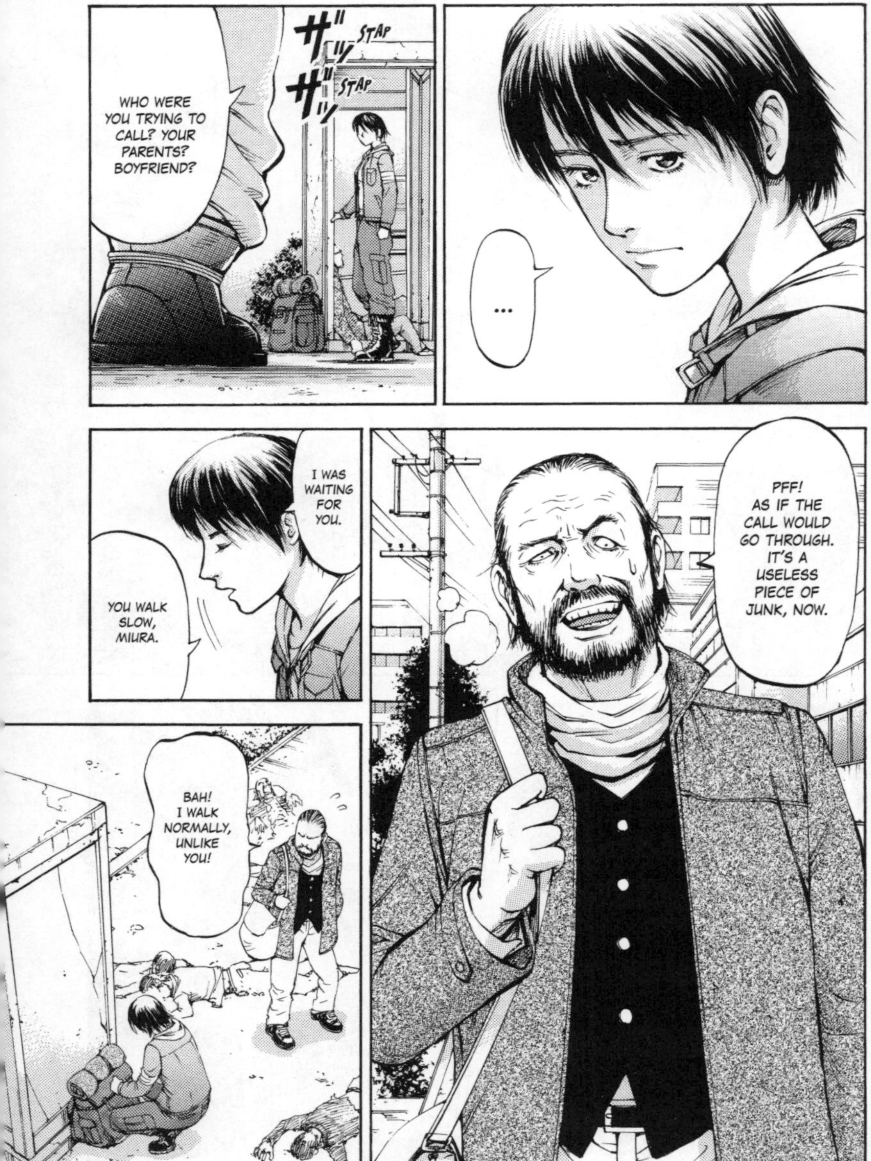
...
ザッ STAP
ザッ STAP
WHO WERE YOU TRYING TO CALL? YOUR PARENTS? BOYFRIEND?
PFF! AS IF THE CALL WOULD GO THROUGH. IT'S A USELESS PIECE OF JUNK, NOW.
I WAS WAITING FOR YOU.
YOU WALK SLOW, MIURA.
BAH! I WALK NORMALLY, UNLIKE YOU!

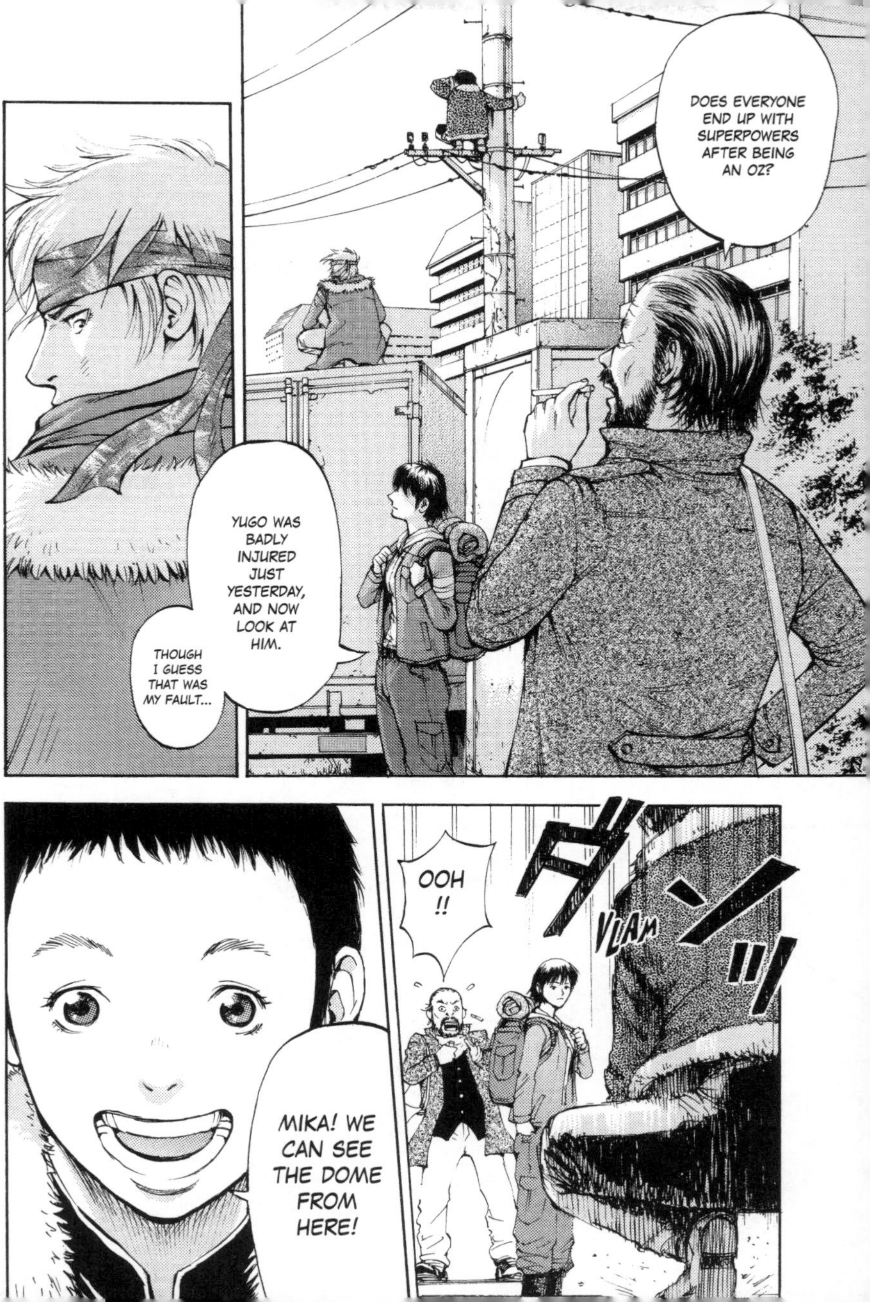
DOES EVERYONE END UP WITH SUPERPOWERS AFTER BEING AN OZ?
YUGO WAS BADLY INJURED JUST YESTERDAY, AND NOW LOOK AT HIM.
THOUGH I GUESS THAT WAS MY FAULT...
OOH !!
VLAM
MIKA! WE CAN SEE THE DOME FROM HERE!

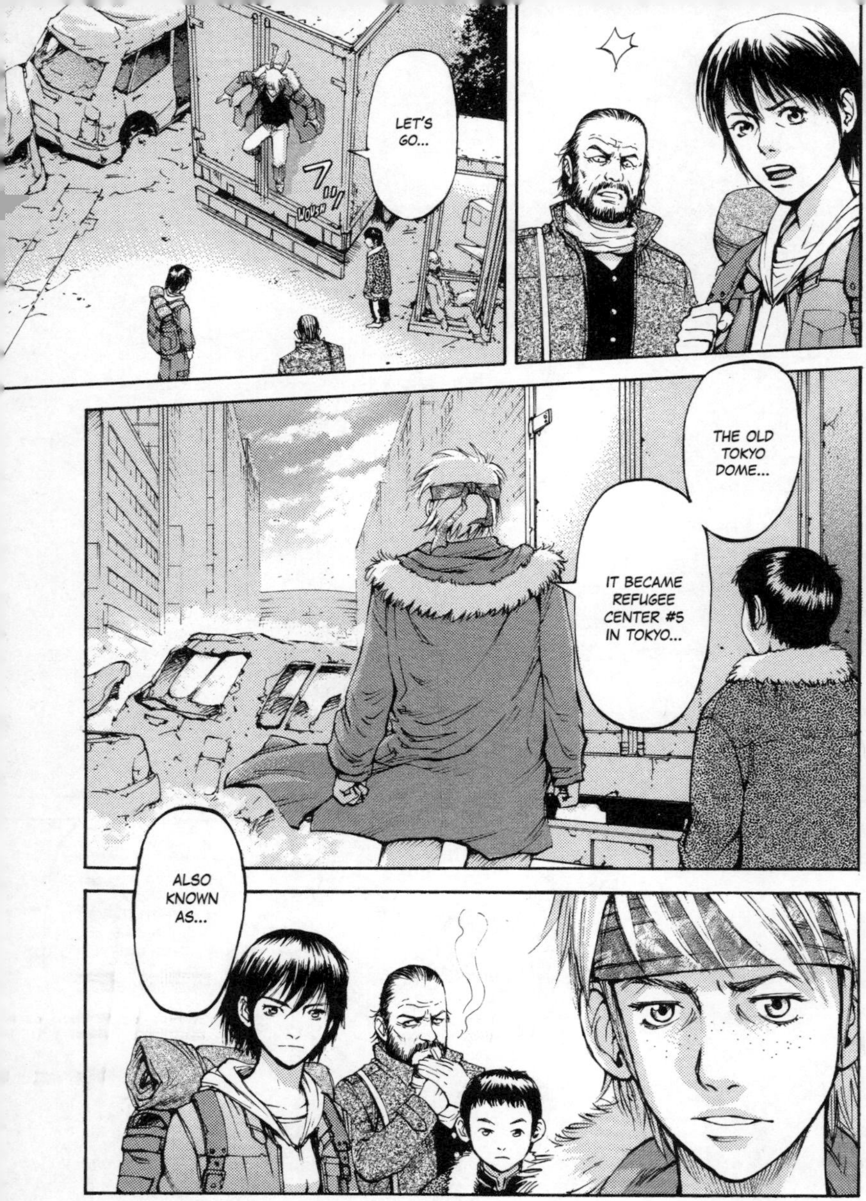
LET'S GO...
WOUSH
THE OLD TOKYO DOME...
IT BECAME REFUGEE CENTER #5 IN TOKYO...
ALSO KNOWN AS...

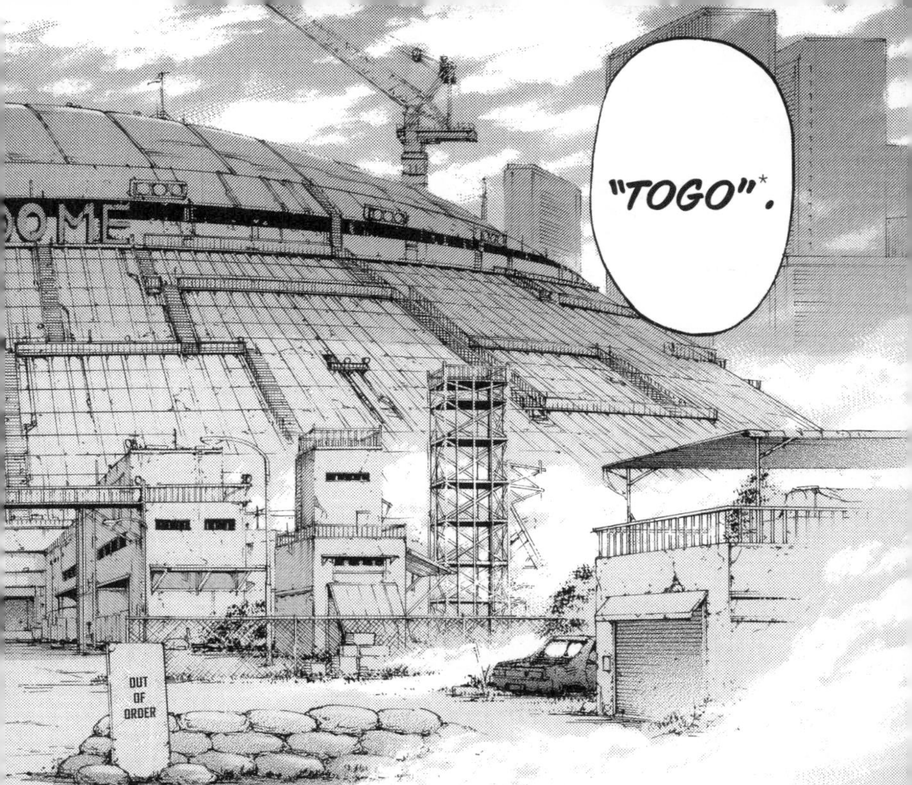
"TOGO"*.
DOME
OUT OF ORDER

*A.N. : From "Tokyo" and "go" (five, in Japanese).

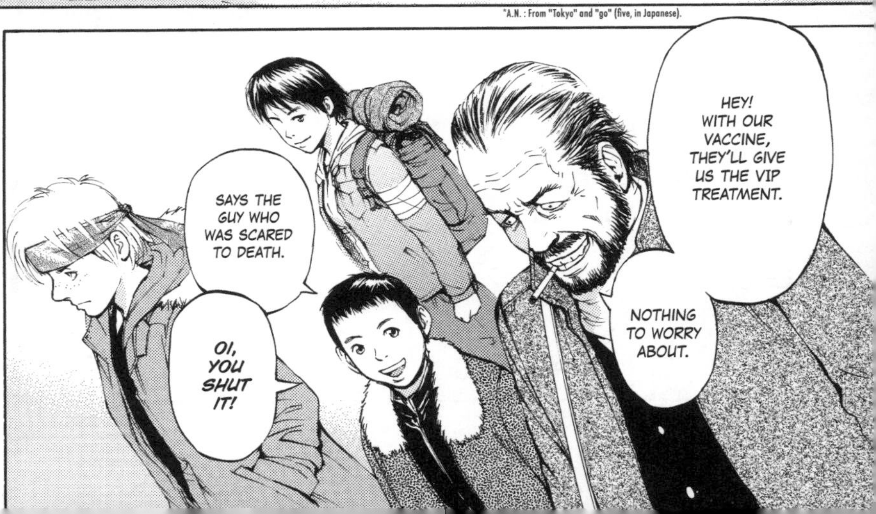
HEY! WITH OUR VACCINE, THEY'LL GIVE US THE VIP TREATMENT.
NOTHING TO WORRY ABOUT.
SAYS THE GUY WHO WAS SCARED TO DEATH.
OI, YOU SHUT IT!

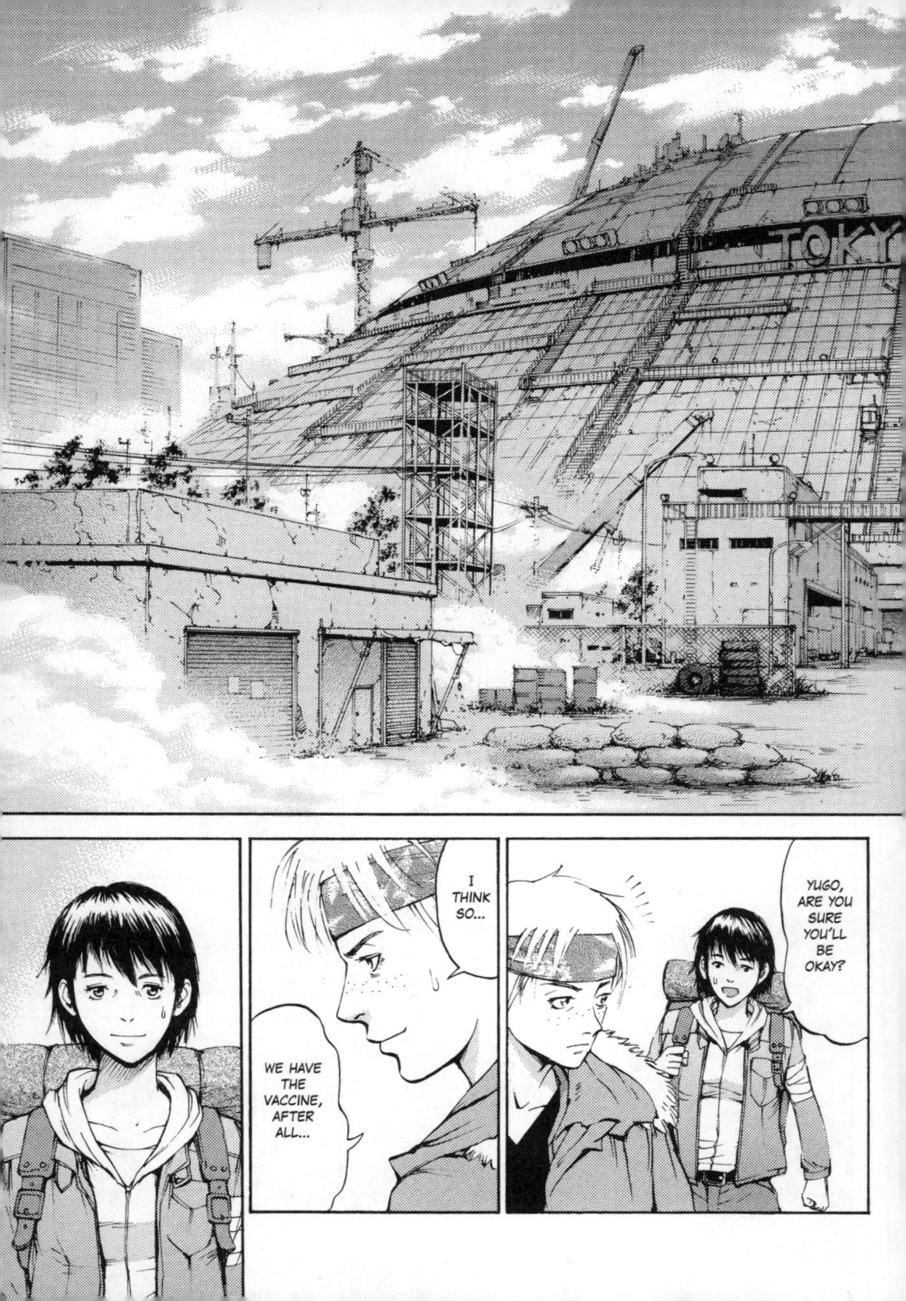
TOKY
YUGO, ARE YOU SURE YOU'LL BE OKAY?
I THINK SO...
WE HAVE THE VACCINE, AFTER ALL...

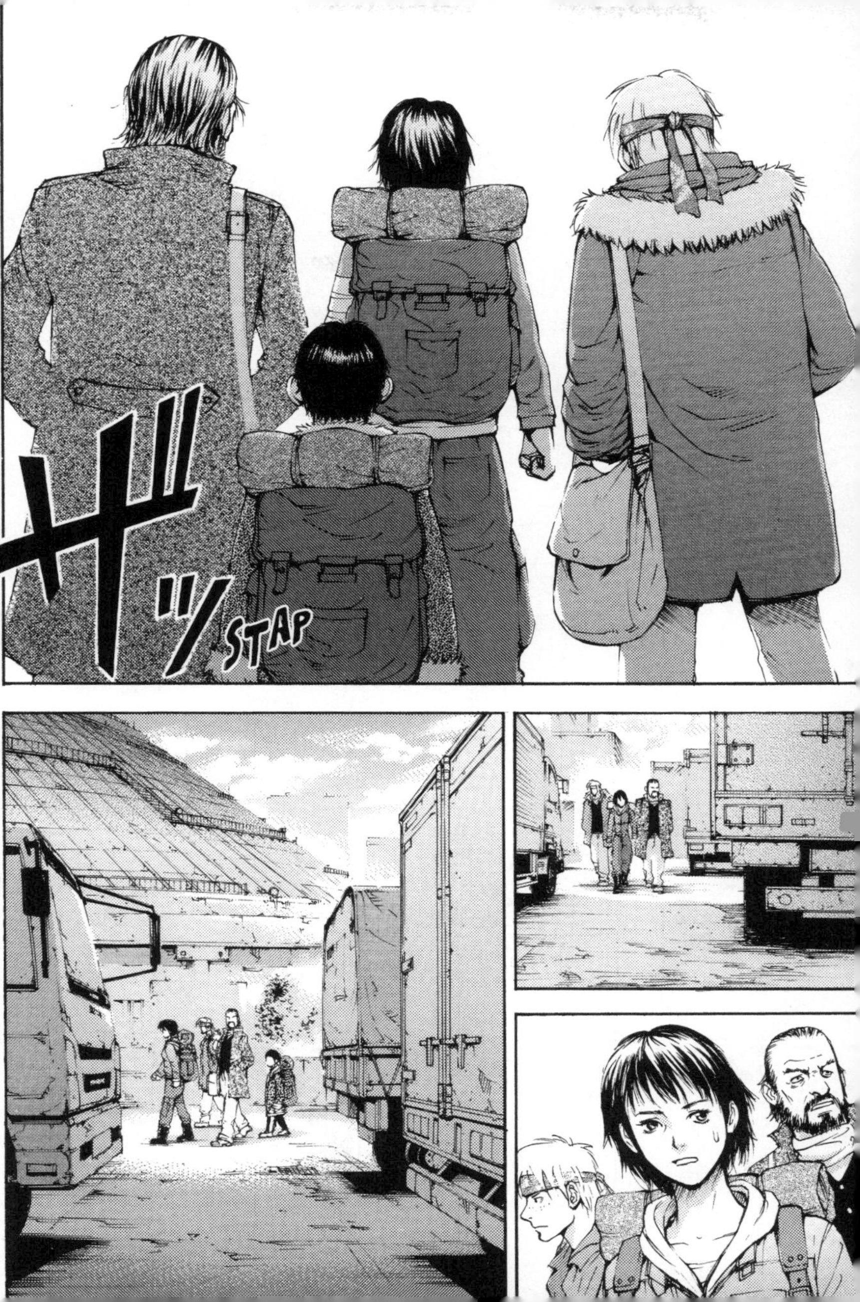
ザッ
STAP

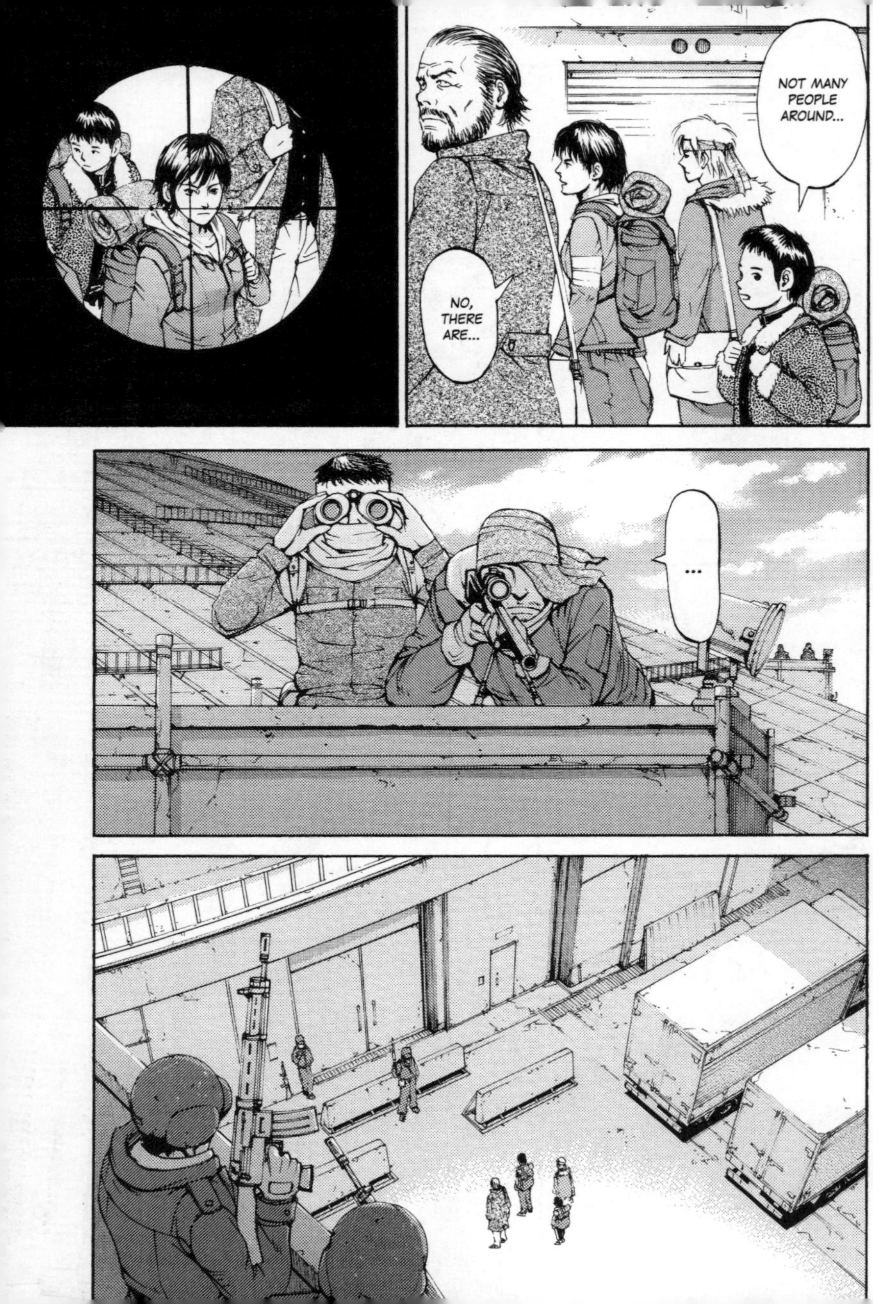
NOT MANY PEOPLE AROUND...
NO, THERE ARE...
...

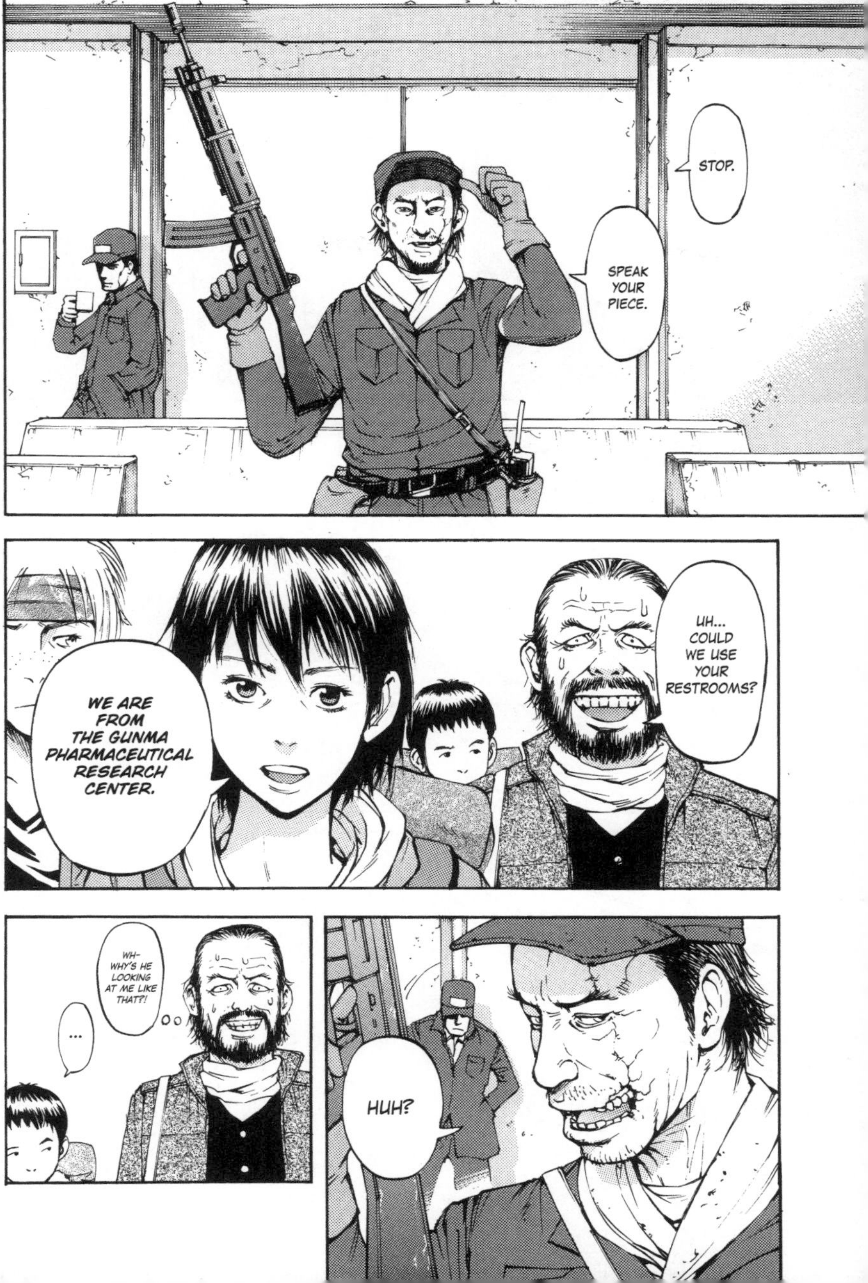
STOP.
SPEAK YOUR PIECE.
UH... COULD WE USE YOUR RESTROOMS?
WE ARE FROM THE GUNMA PHARMACEUTICAL RESEARCH CENTER.
HUH?
WH- WHY'S HE LOOKING AT ME LIKE THAT?!
...

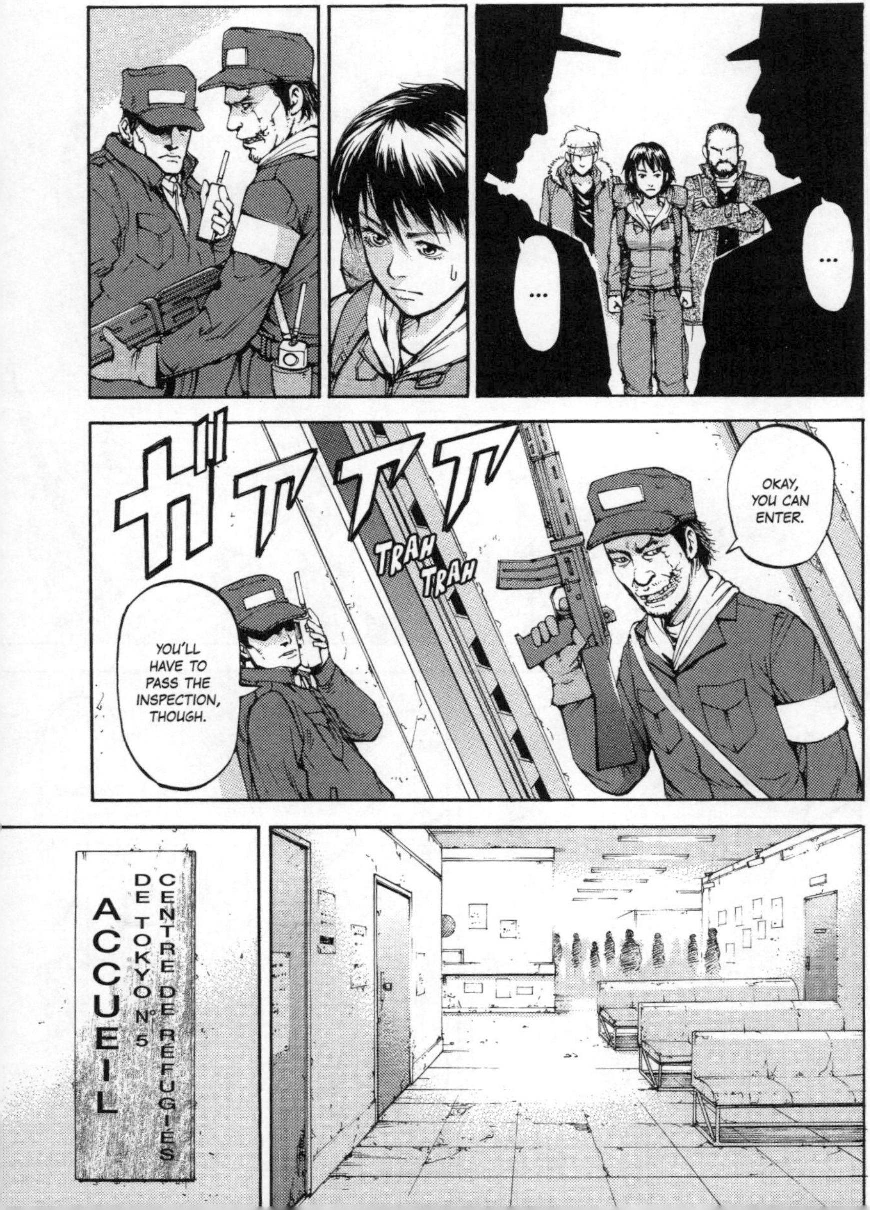
...
...
ガァァァ
TRAH TRAH
OKAY, YOU CAN ENTER.
YOU'LL HAVE TO PASS THE INSPECTION, THOUGH.
CENTRE DE RÉFUGIÉS DE TOKYO N° 5
ACCUEIL

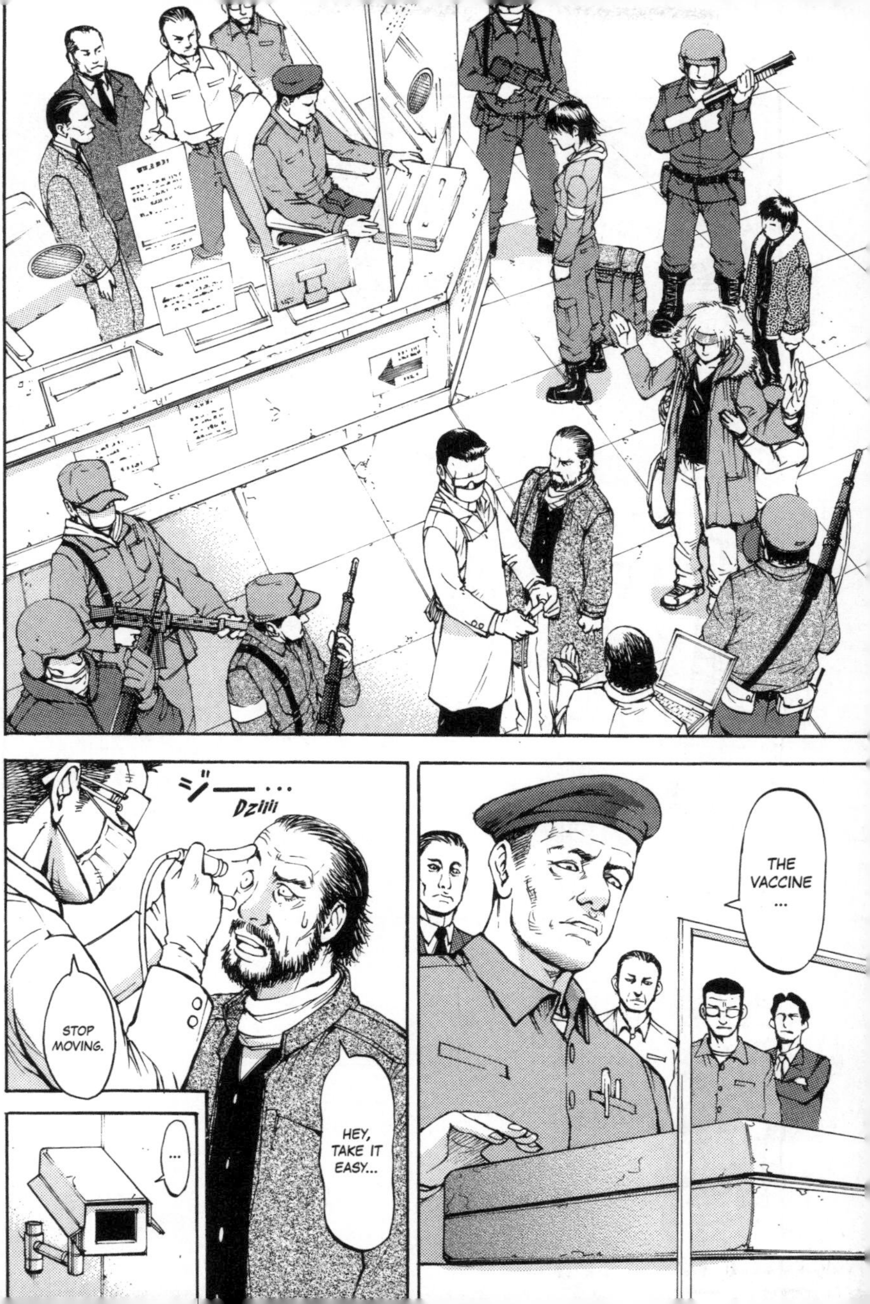
THE VACCINE ...
ジー…
Dziiii
HEY, TAKE IT EASY...
STOP MOVING.
...

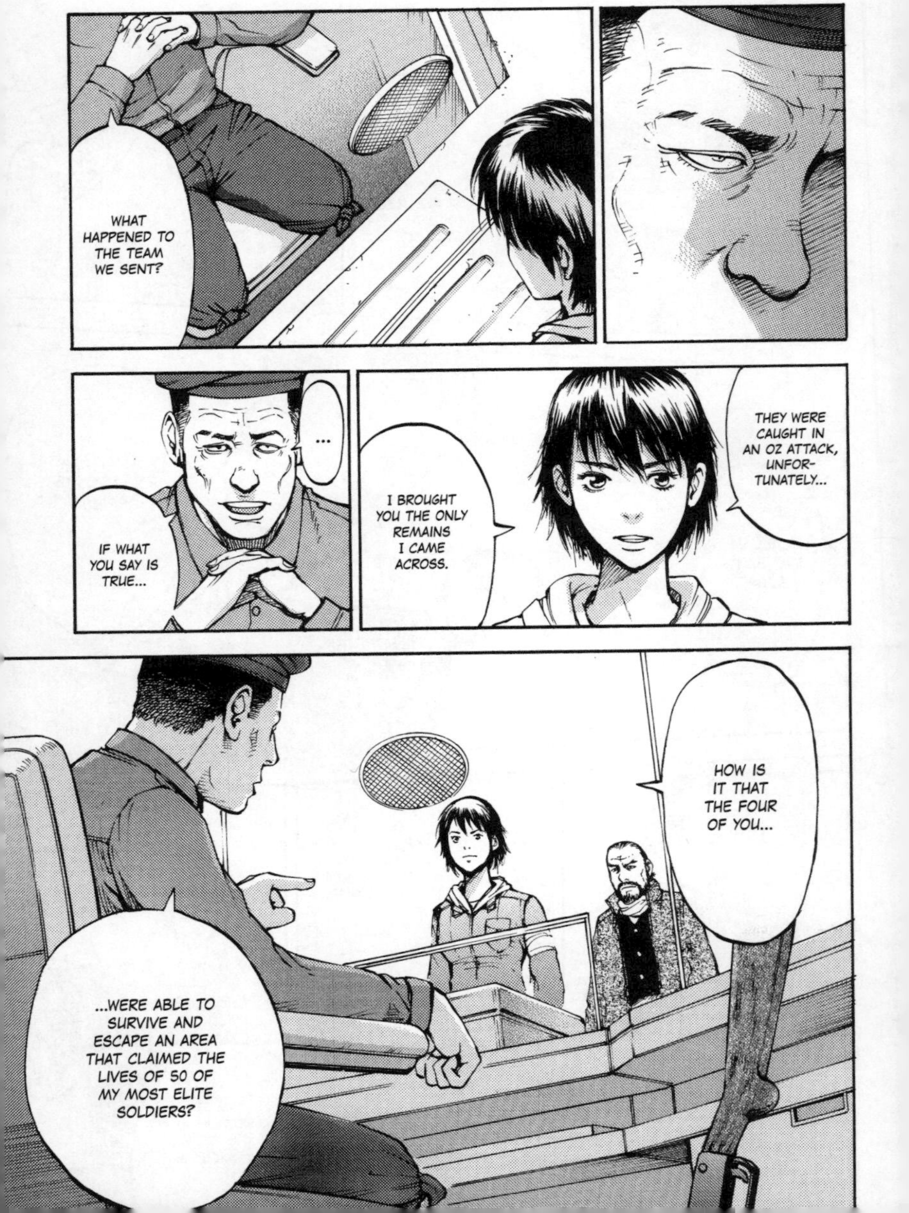
WHAT HAPPENED TO THE TEAM WE SENT?
THEY WERE CAUGHT IN AN OZ ATTACK, UNFORTUNATELY...
I BROUGHT YOU THE ONLY REMAINS I CAME ACROSS.
...
IF WHAT YOU SAY IS TRUE...
HOW IS IT THAT THE FOUR OF YOU...
...WERE ABLE TO SURVIVE AND ESCAPE AN AREA THAT CLAIMED THE LIVES OF 50 OF MY MOST ELITE SOLDIERS?

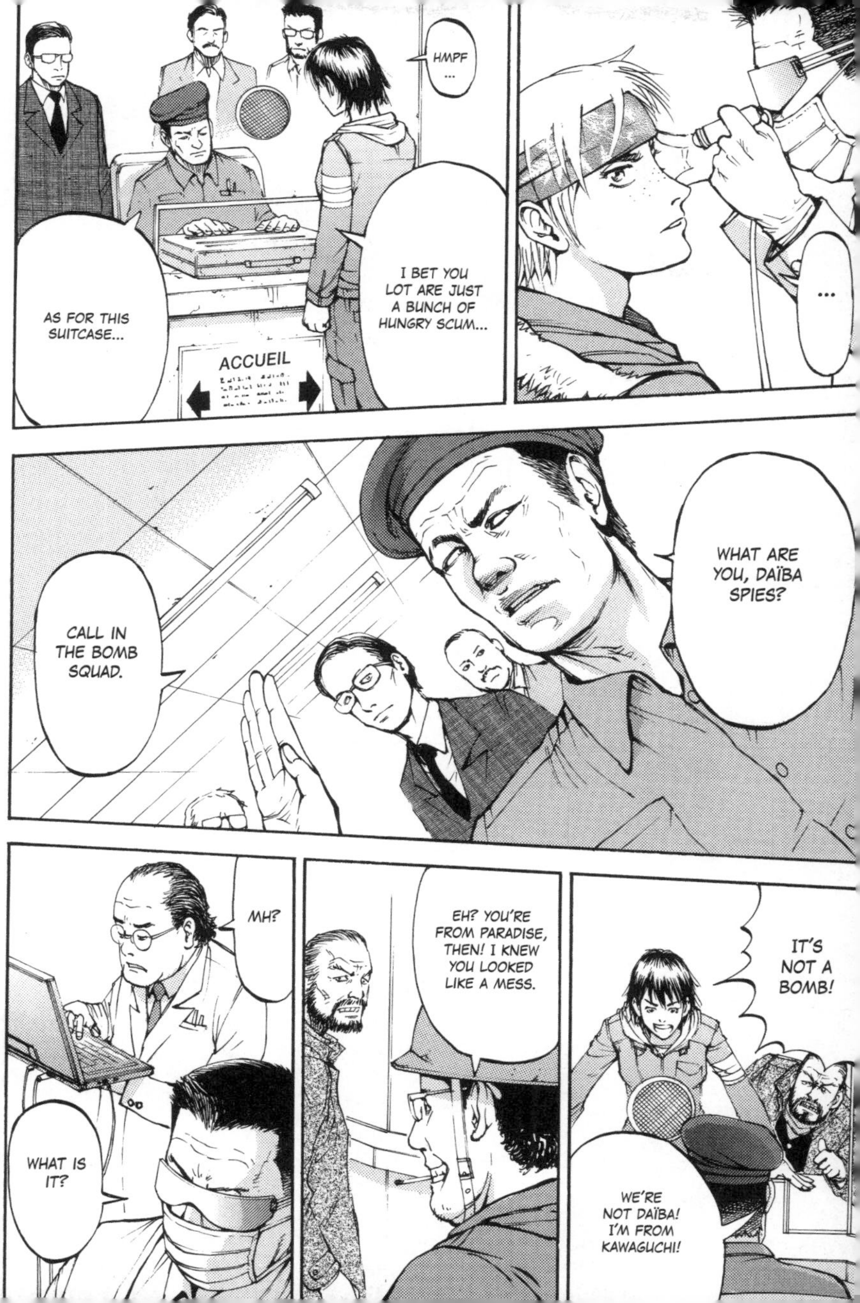
...
HMPF ...
I BET YOU LOT ARE JUST A BUNCH OF HUNGRY SCUM...
AS FOR THIS SUITCASE...
ACCUEIL
WHAT ARE YOU, DAÏBA SPIES?
CALL IN THE BOMB SQUAD.
IT'S NOT A BOMB!
WE'RE NOT DAÏBA! I'M FROM KAWAGUCHI!
EH? YOU'RE FROM PARADISE, THEN! I KNEW YOU LOOKED LIKE A MESS.
MH?
WHAT IS IT?

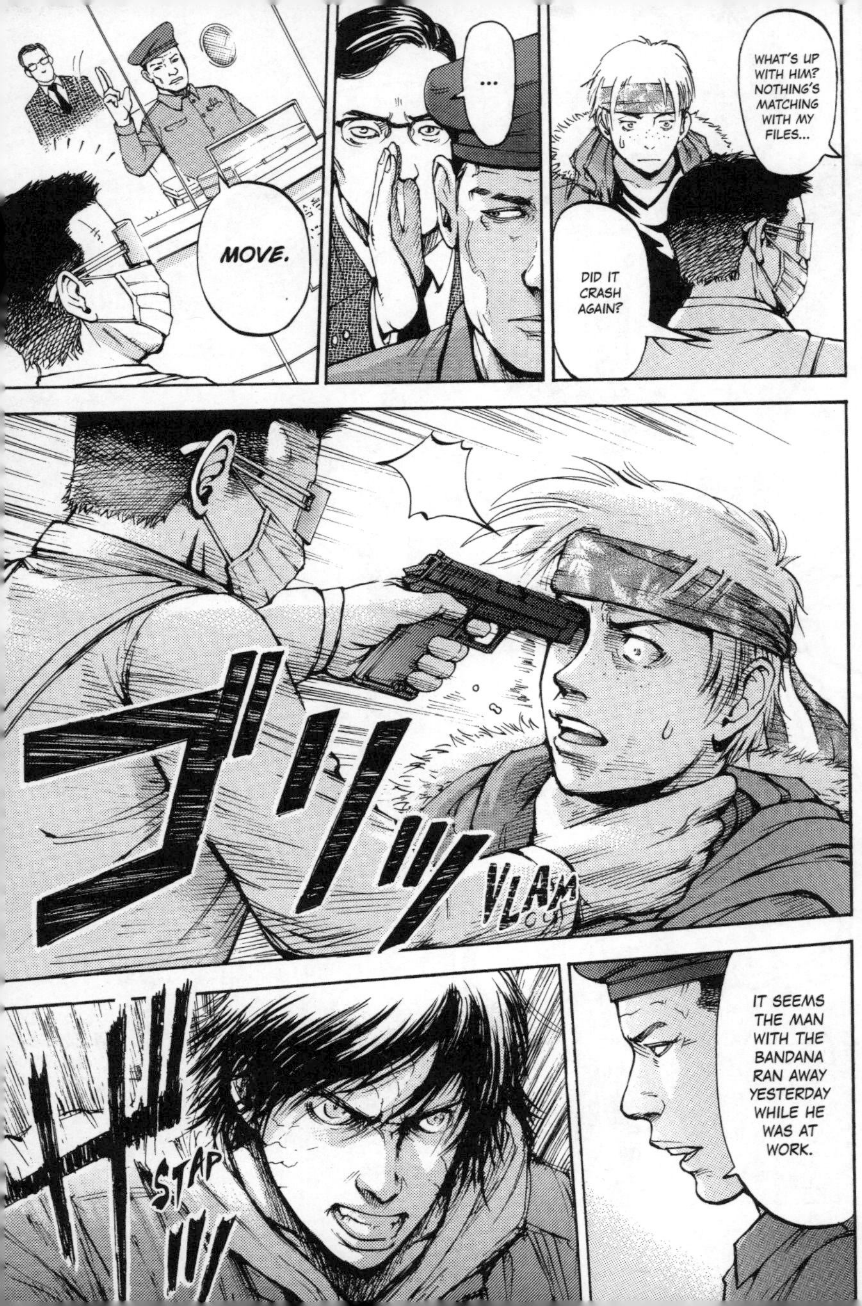
WHAT'S UP WITH HIM? NOTHING'S MATCHING WITH MY FILES...
DID IT CRASH AGAIN?
...
MOVE.
VLAM
IT SEEMS THE MAN WITH THE BANDANA RAN AWAY YESTERDAY WHILE HE WAS AT WORK.
STAP

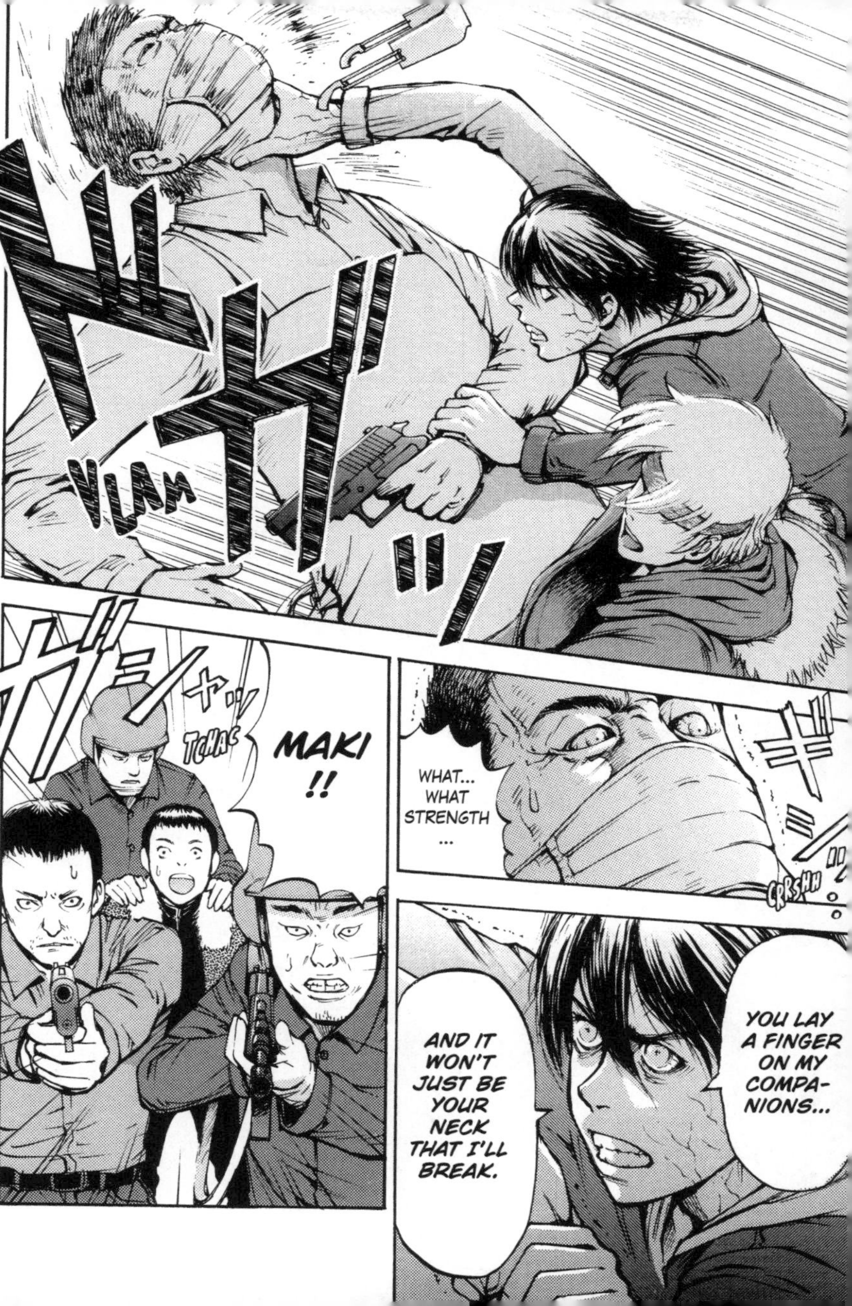
VLAM
WHAT... WHAT STRENGTH ...
CRRSHH
YOU LAY A FINGER ON MY COMPANIONS...
AND IT WON'T JUST BE YOUR NECK THAT I'LL BREAK.
TCHAC
MAKI !!

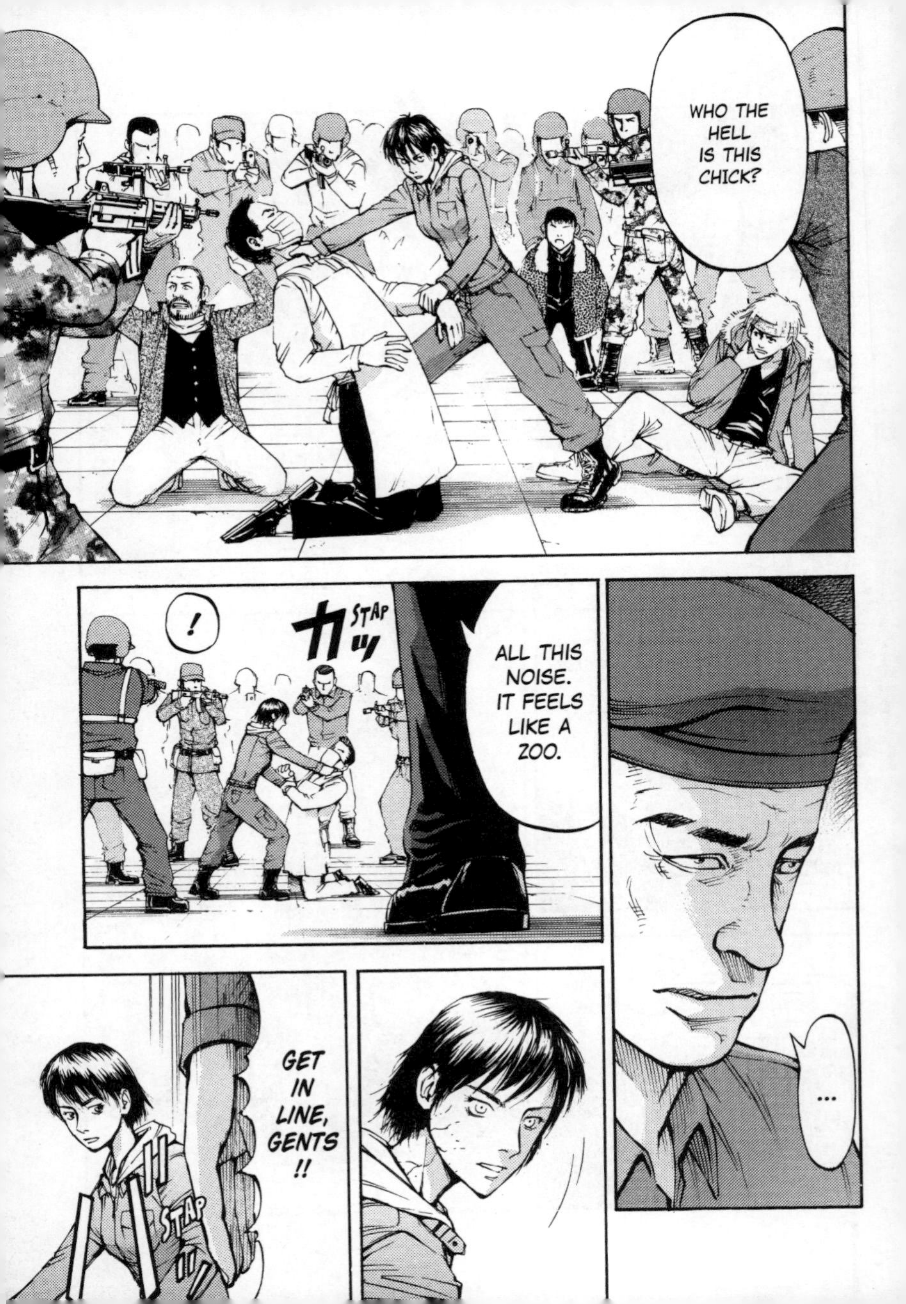
WHO THE HELL IS THIS CHICK?
...
ALL THIS NOISE. IT FEELS LIKE A ZOO.
カッ STAP
!
GET IN LINE, GENTS!!
STAP!!

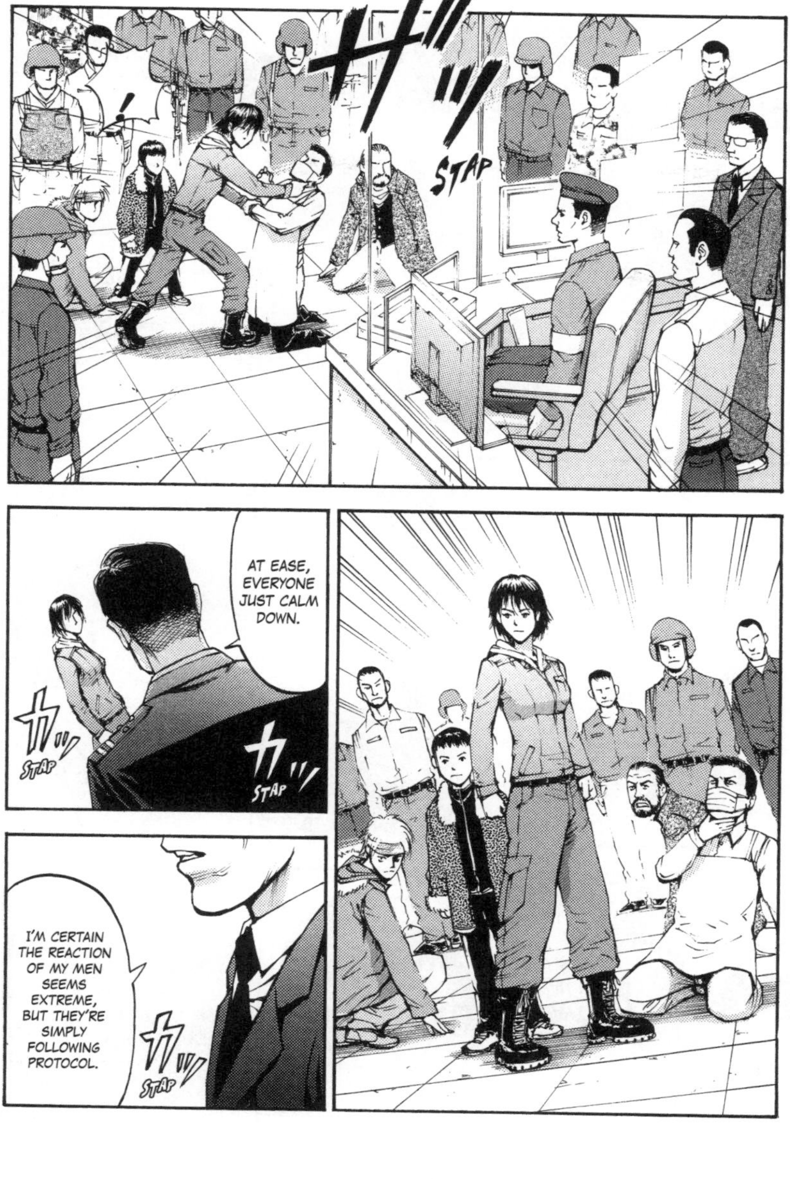
ザッ
STAP
AT EASE, EVERYONE JUST CALM DOWN.
カッ
STAP
カッ
STAP
I'M CERTAIN THE REACTION OF MY MEN SEEMS EXTREME, BUT THEY'RE SIMPLY FOLLOWING PROTOCOL.
カッ
STAP

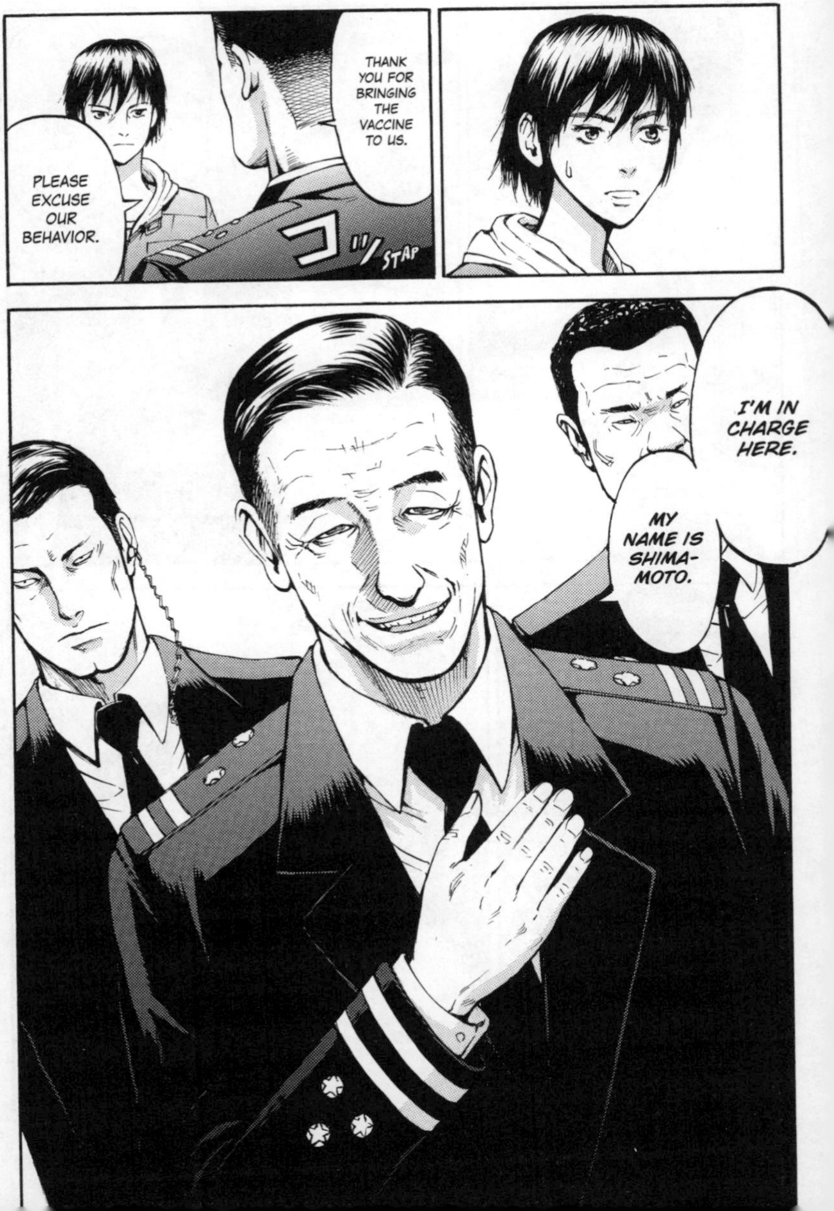
THANK YOU FOR BRINGING THE VACCINE TO US.
PLEASE EXCUSE OUR BEHAVIOR.
コツ
STAP
I'M IN CHARGE HERE.
MY NAME IS SHIMA-MOTO.

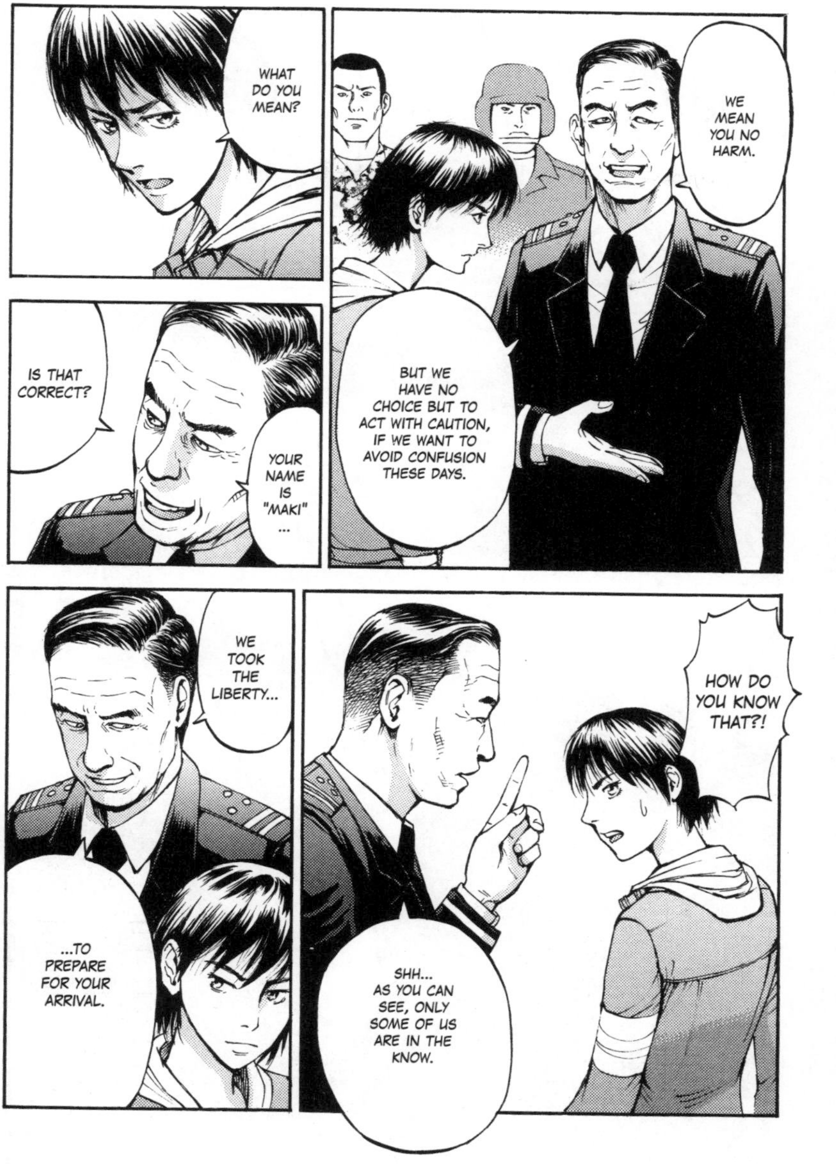
WE MEAN YOU NO HARM.
BUT WE HAVE NO CHOICE BUT TO ACT WITH CAUTION, IF WE WANT TO AVOID CONFUSION THESE DAYS.
WHAT DO YOU MEAN?
YOUR NAME IS "MAKI" ...
IS THAT CORRECT?
HOW DO YOU KNOW THAT?!
SHH... AS YOU CAN SEE, ONLY SOME OF US ARE IN THE KNOW.
WE TOOK THE LIBERTY...
...TO PREPARE FOR YOUR ARRIVAL.

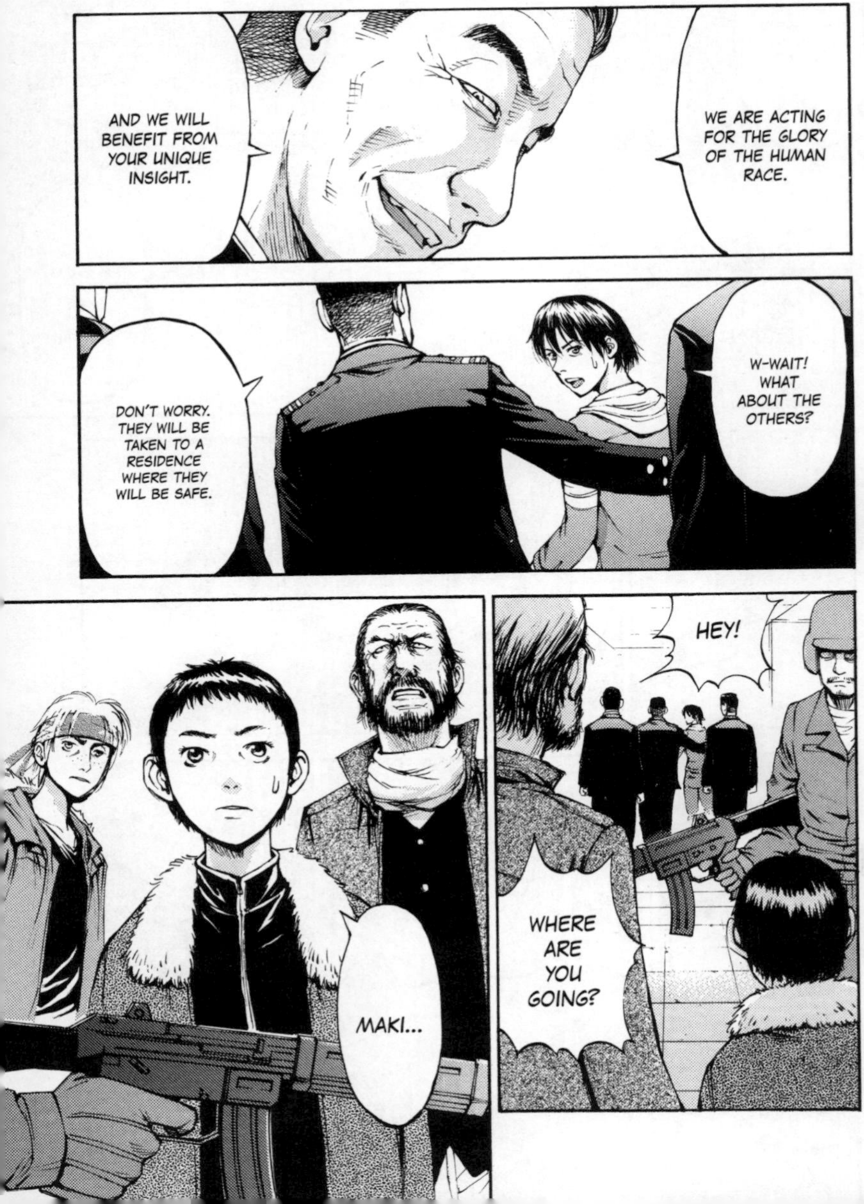
WE ARE ACTING FOR THE GLORY OF THE HUMAN RACE.
AND WE WILL BENEFIT FROM YOUR UNIQUE INSIGHT.
W-WAIT! WHAT ABOUT THE OTHERS?
DON'T WORRY. THEY WILL BE TAKEN TO A RESIDENCE WHERE THEY WILL BE SAFE.
HEY!
WHERE ARE YOU GOING?
MAKI...

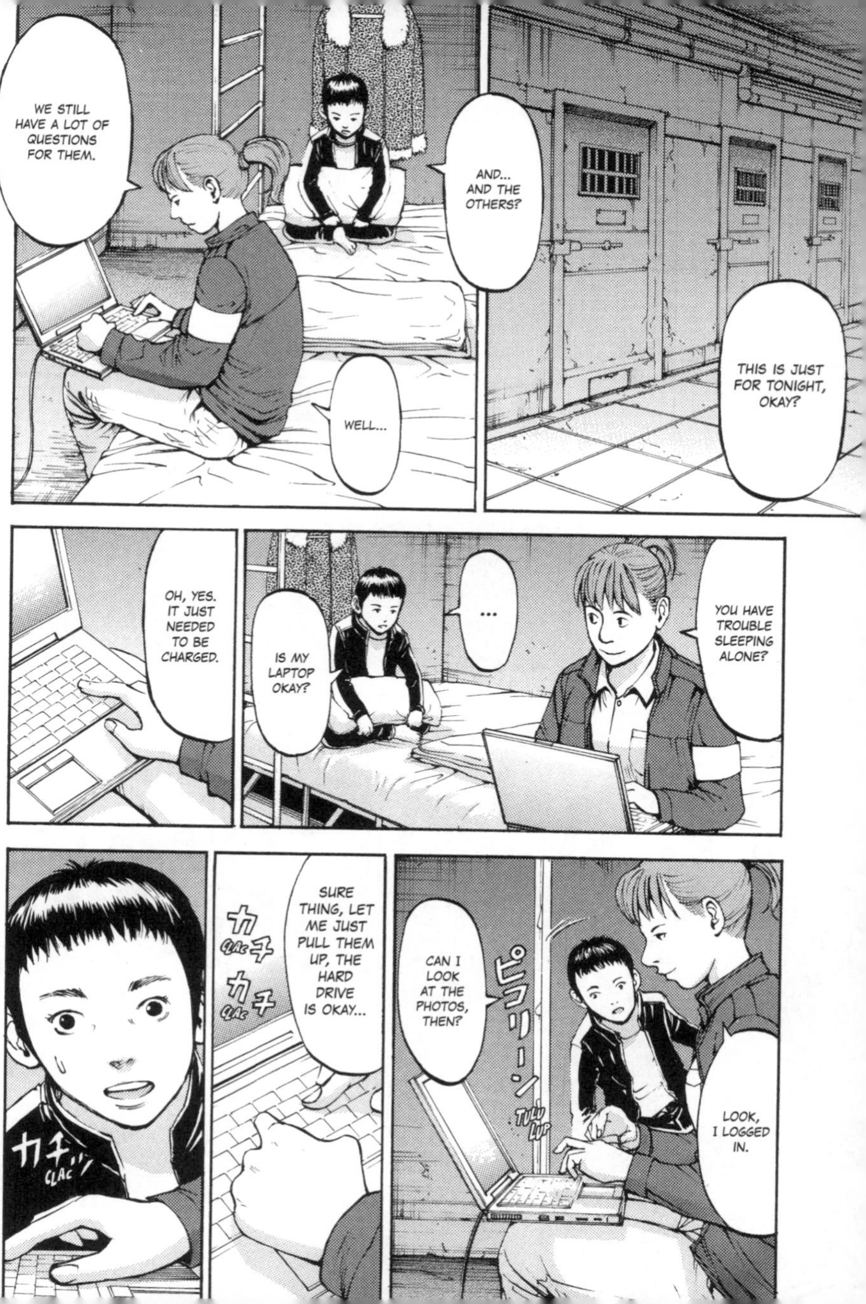
THIS IS JUST FOR TONIGHT, OKAY?
AND... AND THE OTHERS?
WELL...
WE STILL HAVE A LOT OF QUESTIONS FOR THEM.
YOU HAVE TROUBLE SLEEPING ALONE?
...
IS MY LAPTOP OKAY?
OH, YES. IT JUST NEEDED TO BE CHARGED.
ピラリーン
TULU LUP
LOOK, I LOGGED IN.
CAN I LOOK AT THE PHOTOS, THEN?
SURE THING, LET ME JUST PULL THEM UP, THE HARD DRIVE IS OKAY...
カチ
CLAC
カチ
CLAC
カチッ
CLAC

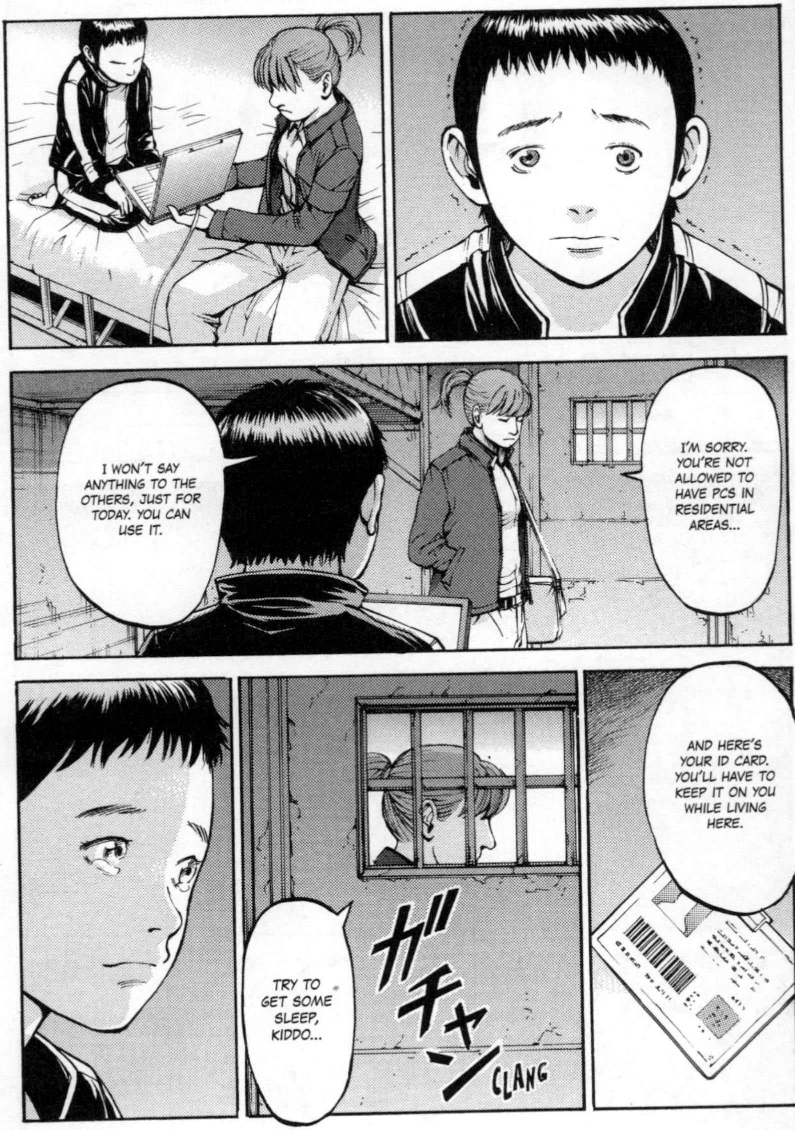
I'M SORRY. YOU'RE NOT ALLOWED TO HAVE PCS IN RESIDENTIAL AREAS...
I WON'T SAY ANYTHING TO THE OTHERS, JUST FOR TODAY. YOU CAN USE IT.
AND HERE'S YOUR ID CARD. YOU'LL HAVE TO KEEP IT ON YOU WHILE LIVING HERE.
ガチャン
CLANG
TRY TO GET SOME SLEEP, KIDDO...

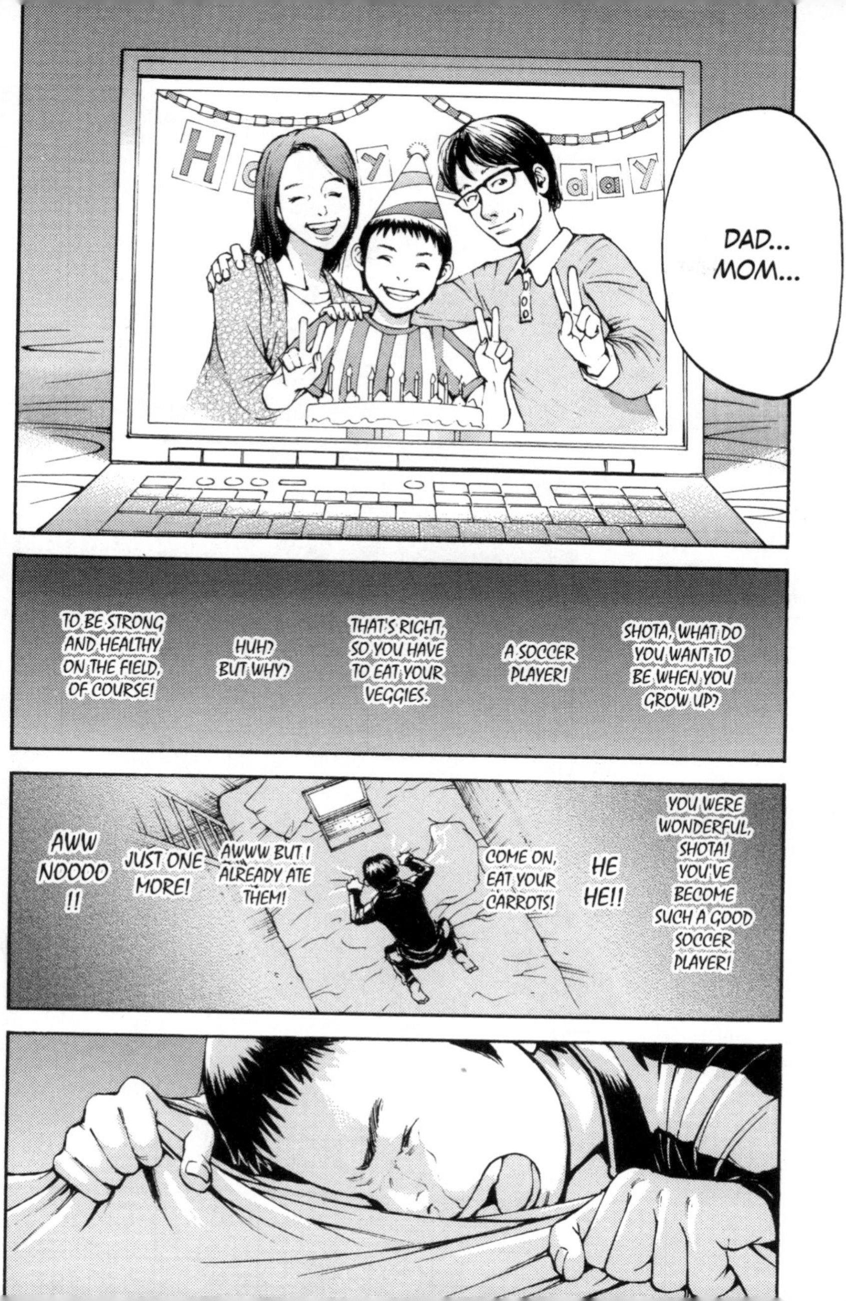
DAD... MOM...
SHOTA, WHAT DO YOU WANT TO BE WHEN YOU GROW UP?
A SOCCER PLAYER!
THAT'S RIGHT, SO YOU HAVE TO EAT YOUR VEGGIES.
HUH? BUT WHY?
TO BE STRONG AND HEALTHY ON THE FIELD, OF COURSE!
YOU WERE WONDERFUL, SHOTA! YOU'VE BECOME SUCH A GOOD SOCCER PLAYER!
HE HE!!
COME ON, EAT YOUR CARROTS!
AWWW BUT I ALREADY ATE THEM!
JUST ONE MORE!
AWW NOOOO !!

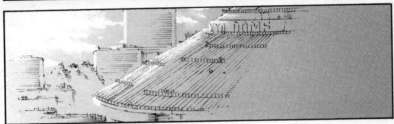

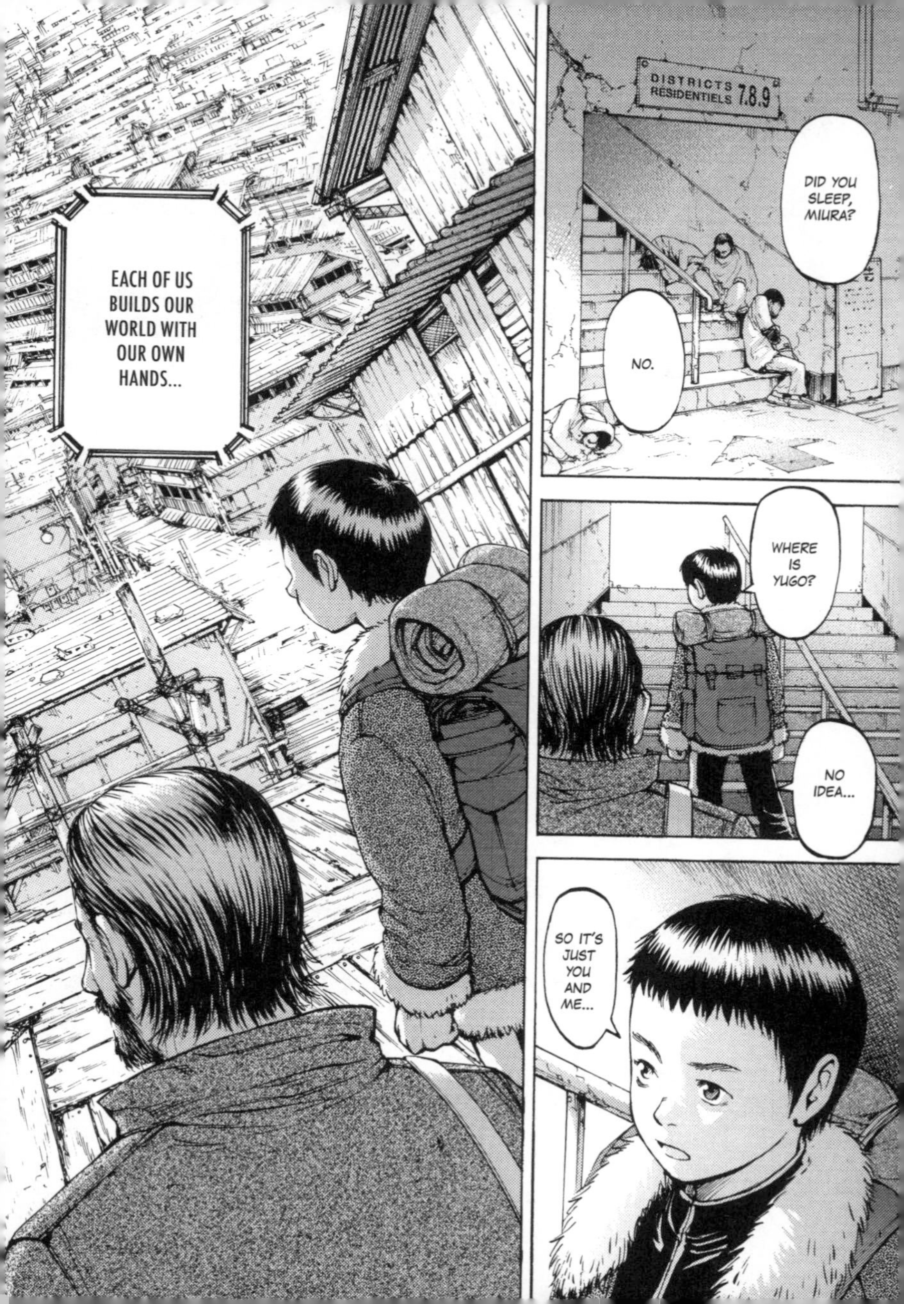
DISTRICTS RESIDENTIELS 7.8.9
DID YOU SLEEP, MIURA?
NO.
WHERE IS YUGO?
NO IDEA...
SO IT'S JUST YOU AND ME...
EACH OF US BUILDS OUR WORLD WITH OUR OWN HANDS...

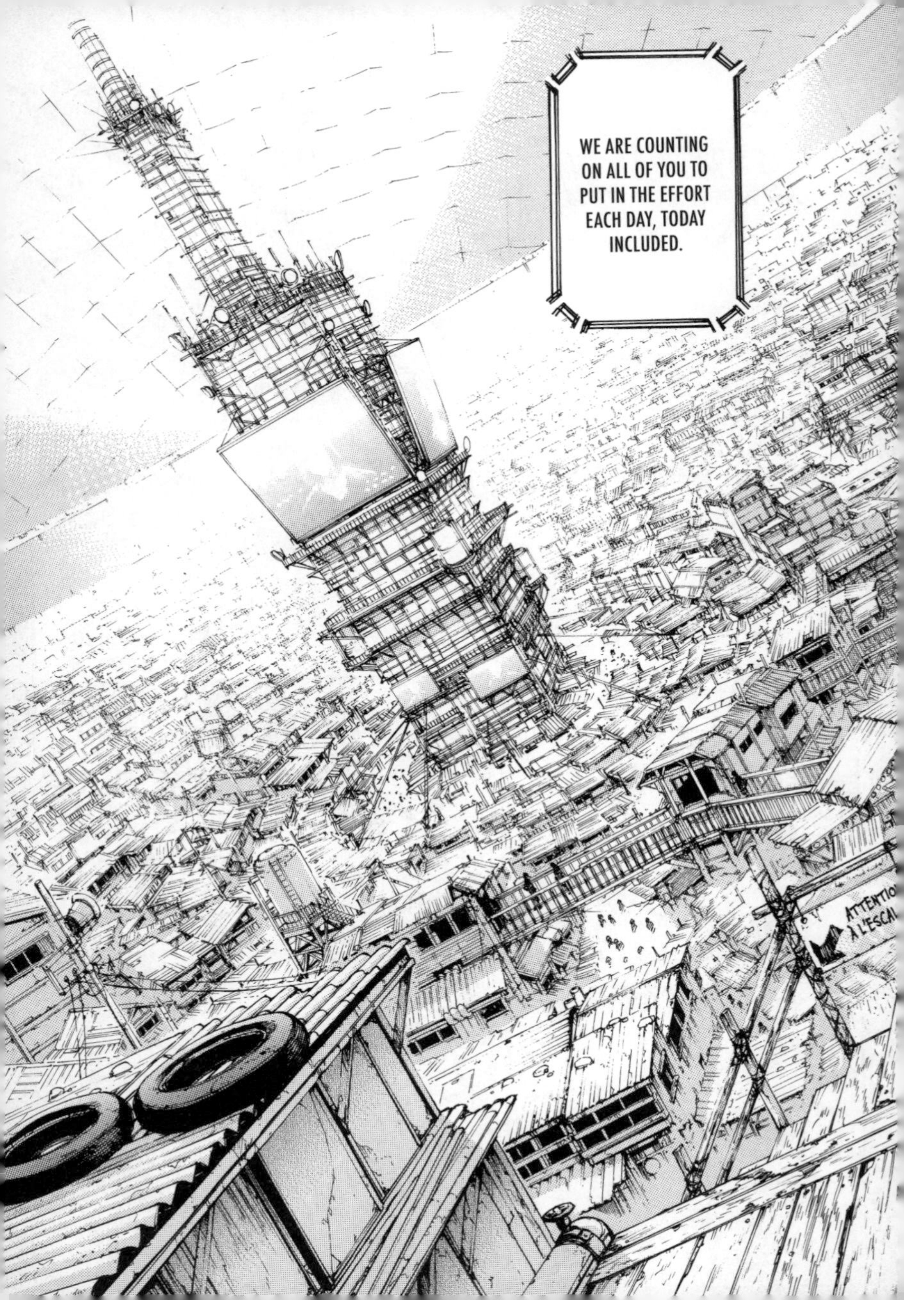
WE ARE COUNTING ON ALL OF YOU TO PUT IN THE EFFORT EACH DAY, TODAY INCLUDED.
ATTENTIO
À L'ESCAL

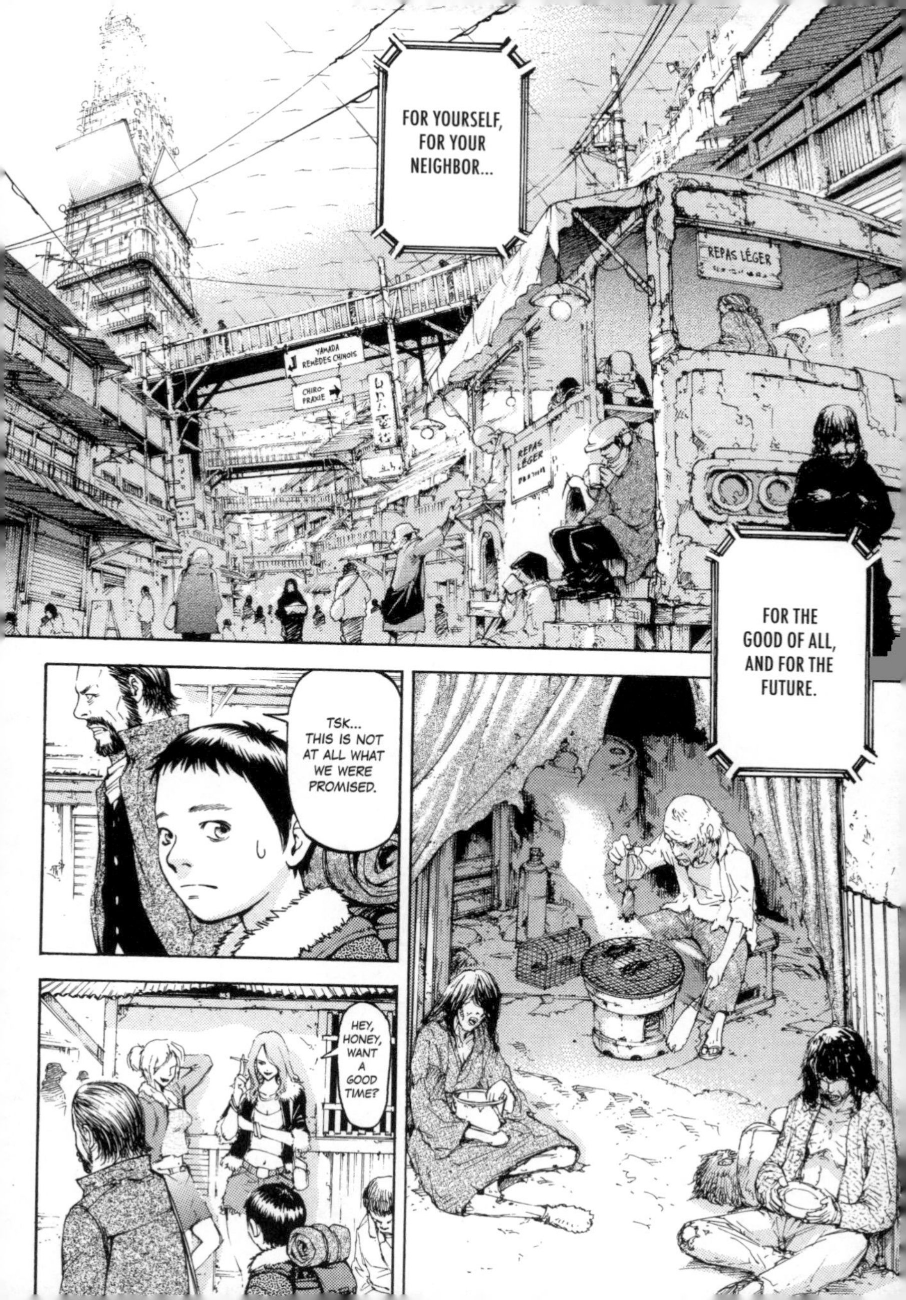
FOR YOURSELF, FOR YOUR NEIGHBOR...
REPAS LÉGER
YAMADA REMÈDES CHINOIS
CHIRO-PRAXIE
REPAS LÉGER
FOR THE GOOD OF ALL, AND FOR THE FUTURE.
TSK... THIS IS NOT AT ALL WHAT WE WERE PROMISED.
HEY, HONEY, WANT A GOOD TIME?

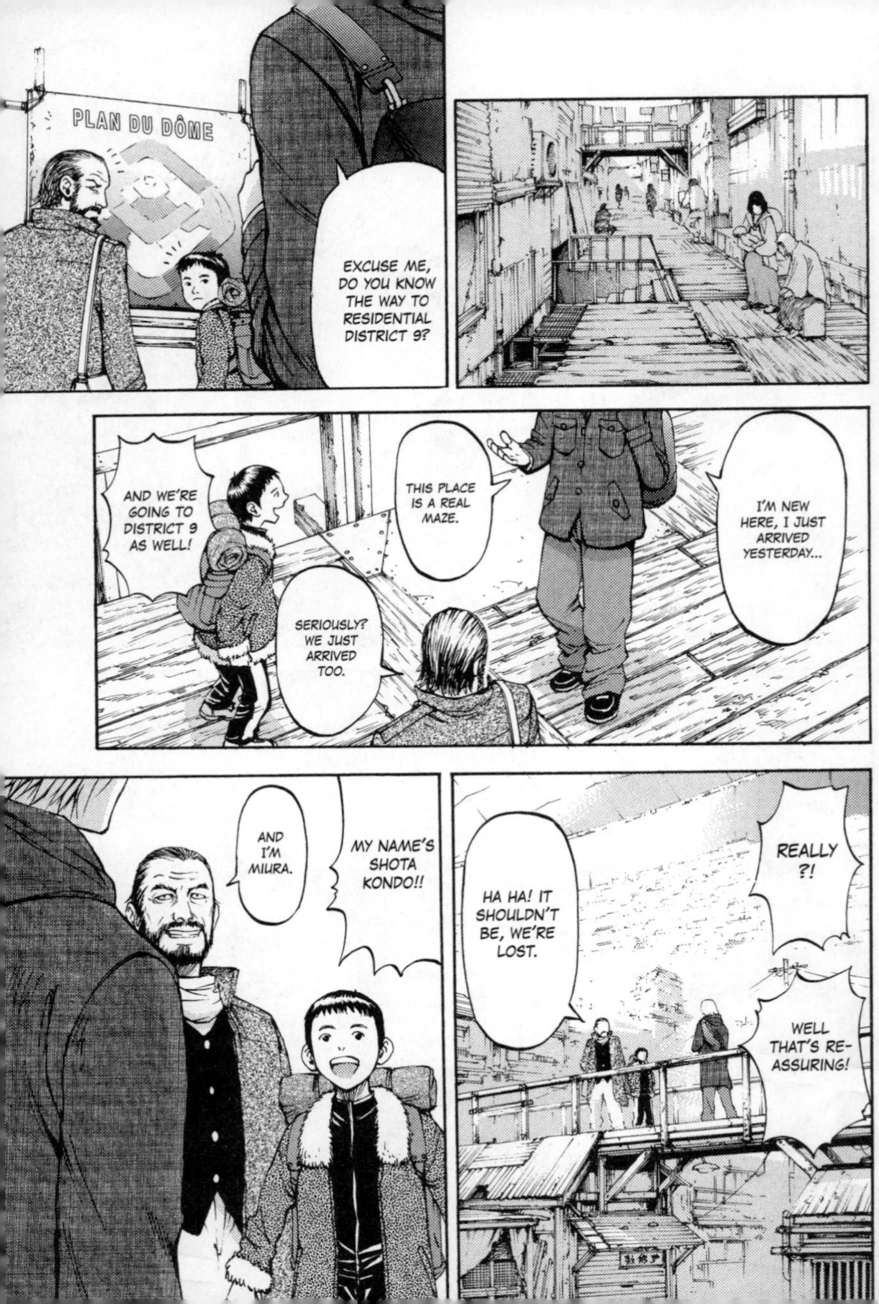
EXCUSE ME, DO YOU KNOW THE WAY TO RESIDENTIAL DISTRICT 9?
PLAN DU DÔME
I'M NEW HERE, I JUST ARRIVED YESTERDAY...
THIS PLACE IS A REAL MAZE.
SERIOUSLY? WE JUST ARRIVED TOO.
AND WE'RE GOING TO DISTRICT 9 AS WELL!
REALLY ?!
HA HA! IT SHOULDN'T BE, WE'RE LOST.
WELL THAT'S RE-ASSURING!
MY NAME'S SHOTA KONDO!!
AND I'M MIURA.

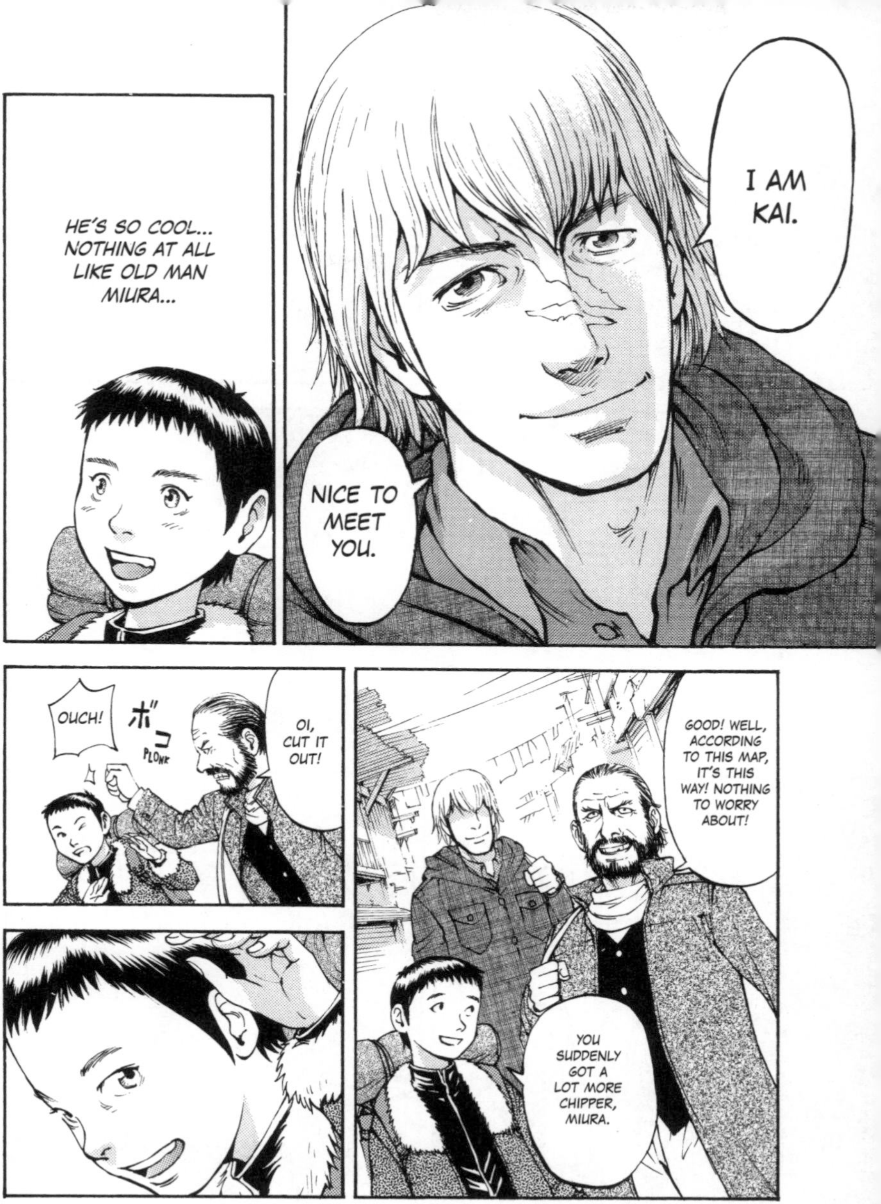
I AM KAI.
NICE TO MEET YOU.
HE'S SO COOL... NOTHING AT ALL LIKE OLD MAN MIURA...
GOOD! WELL, ACCORDING TO THIS MAP, IT'S THIS WAY! NOTHING TO WORRY ABOUT!
YOU SUDDENLY GOT A LOT MORE CHIPPER, MIURA.
OI, CUT IT OUT!
ボコ
PLONK
OUCH!

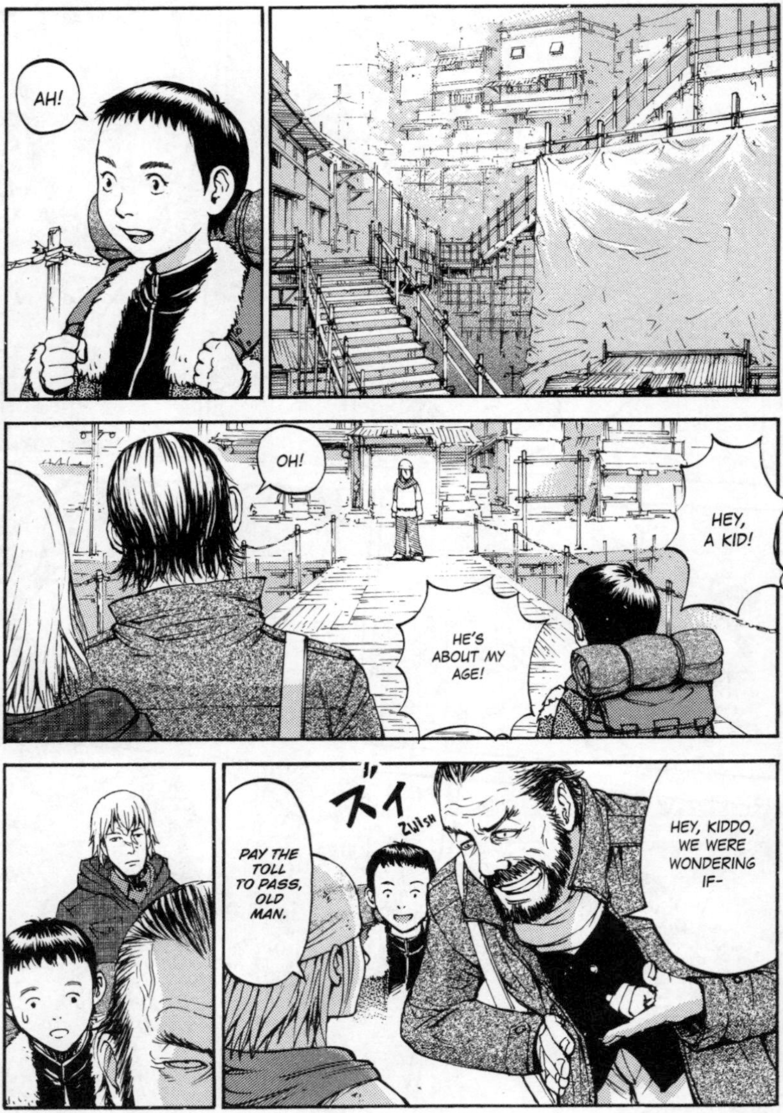
AH!
HEY, A KID!
OH!
HE'S ABOUT MY AGE!
HEY, KIDDO, WE WERE WONDERING IF-
ズイ
ZWISH
PAY THE TOLL TO PASS, OLD MAN.

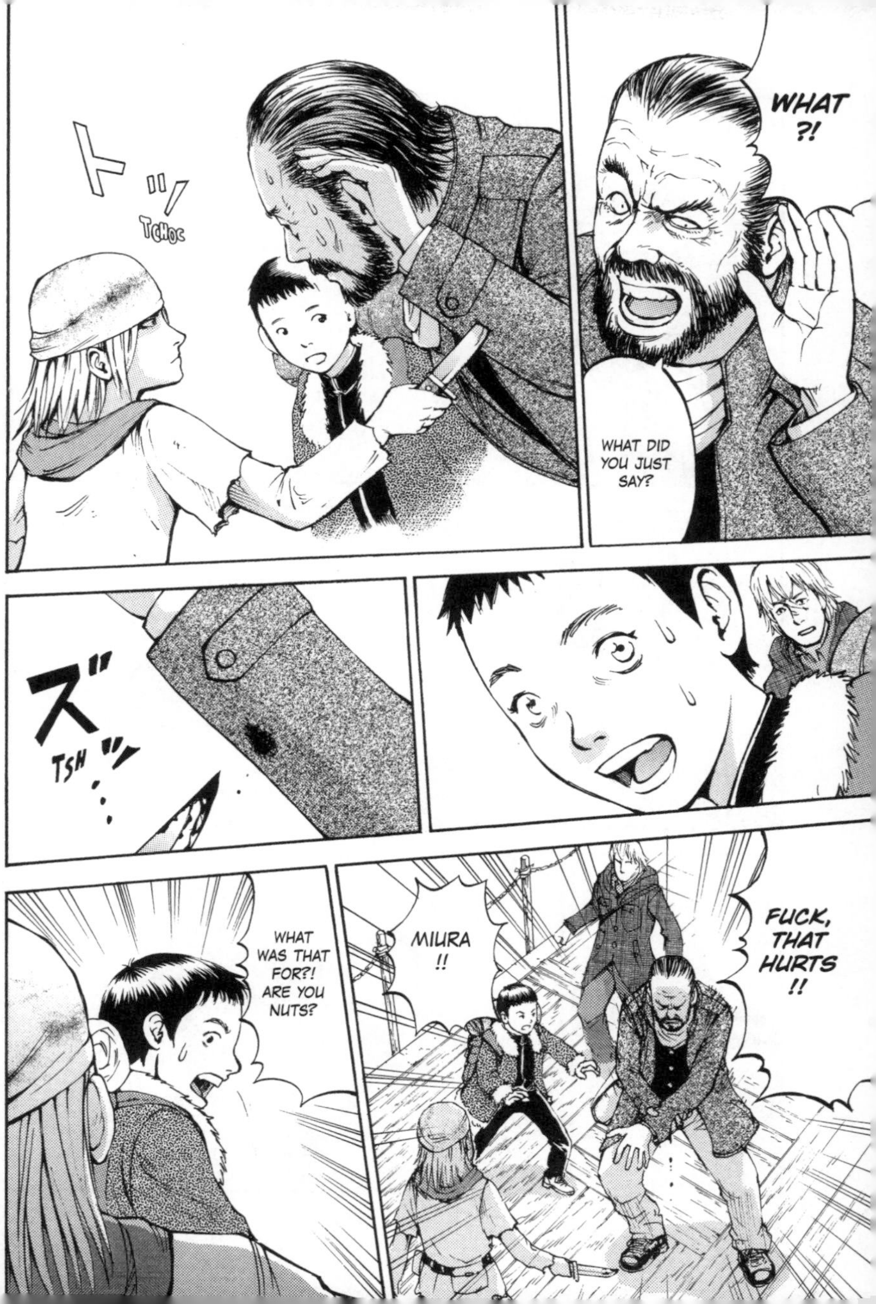
WHAT ?!
WHAT DID YOU JUST SAY?
トッ
TCHOC
ズッ
TSH
...
FUCK, THAT HURTS !!
MIURA !!
WHAT WAS THAT FOR?! ARE YOU NUTS?

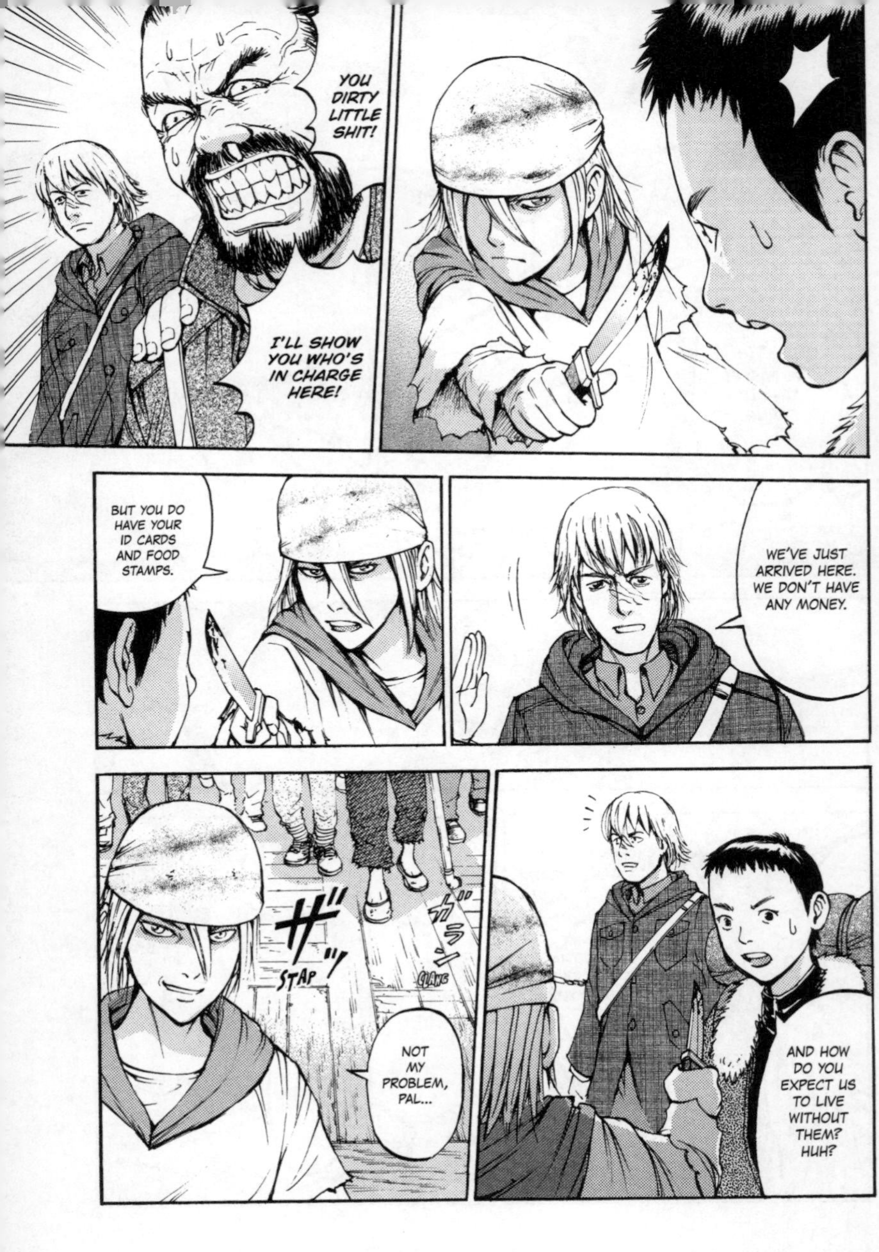
YOU DIRTY LITTLE SHIT!
I'LL SHOW YOU WHO'S IN CHARGE HERE!
WE'VE JUST ARRIVED HERE. WE DON'T HAVE ANY MONEY.
BUT YOU DO HAVE YOUR ID CARDS AND FOOD STAMPS.
AND HOW DO YOU EXPECT US TO LIVE WITHOUT THEM? HUH?
CLANG
STAP
NOT MY PROBLEM, PAL...

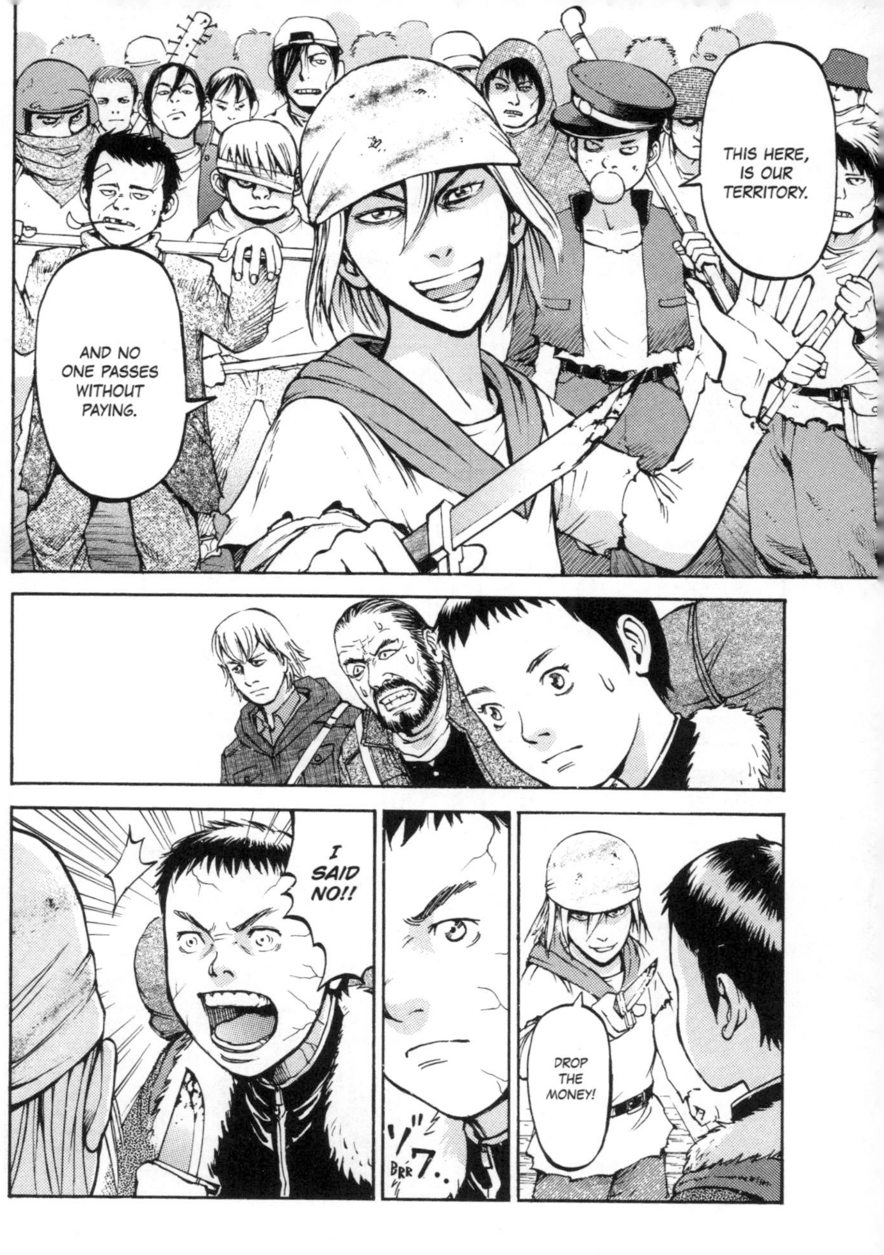
THIS HERE, IS OUR TERRITORY.
AND NO ONE PASSES WITHOUT PAYING.
DROP THE MONEY!
BRR
I SAID NO!!

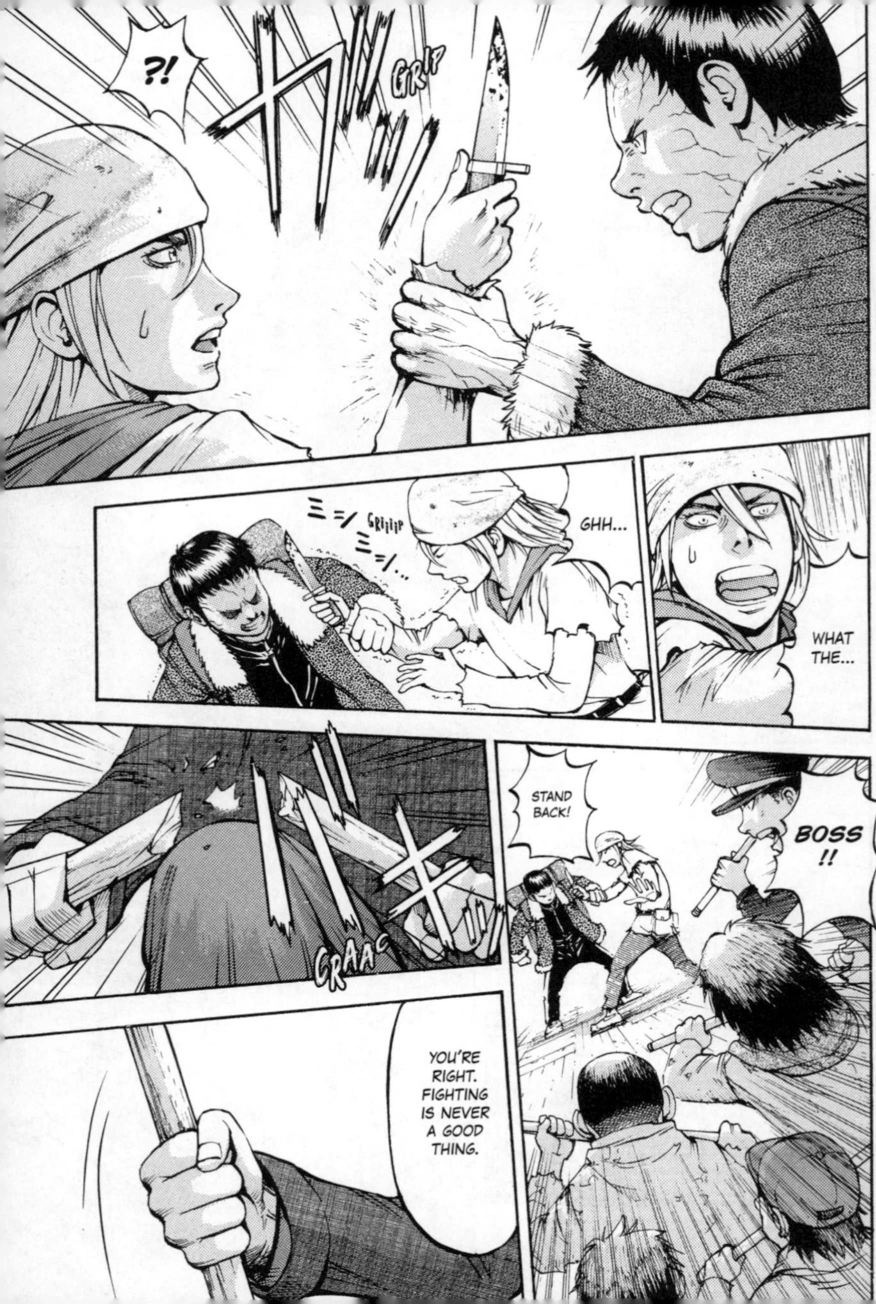
GRIP
?!
WHAT THE...
GHH...
GRIIIP
BOSS !!
STAND BACK!
CRAAG
YOU'RE RIGHT. FIGHTING IS NEVER A GOOD THING.

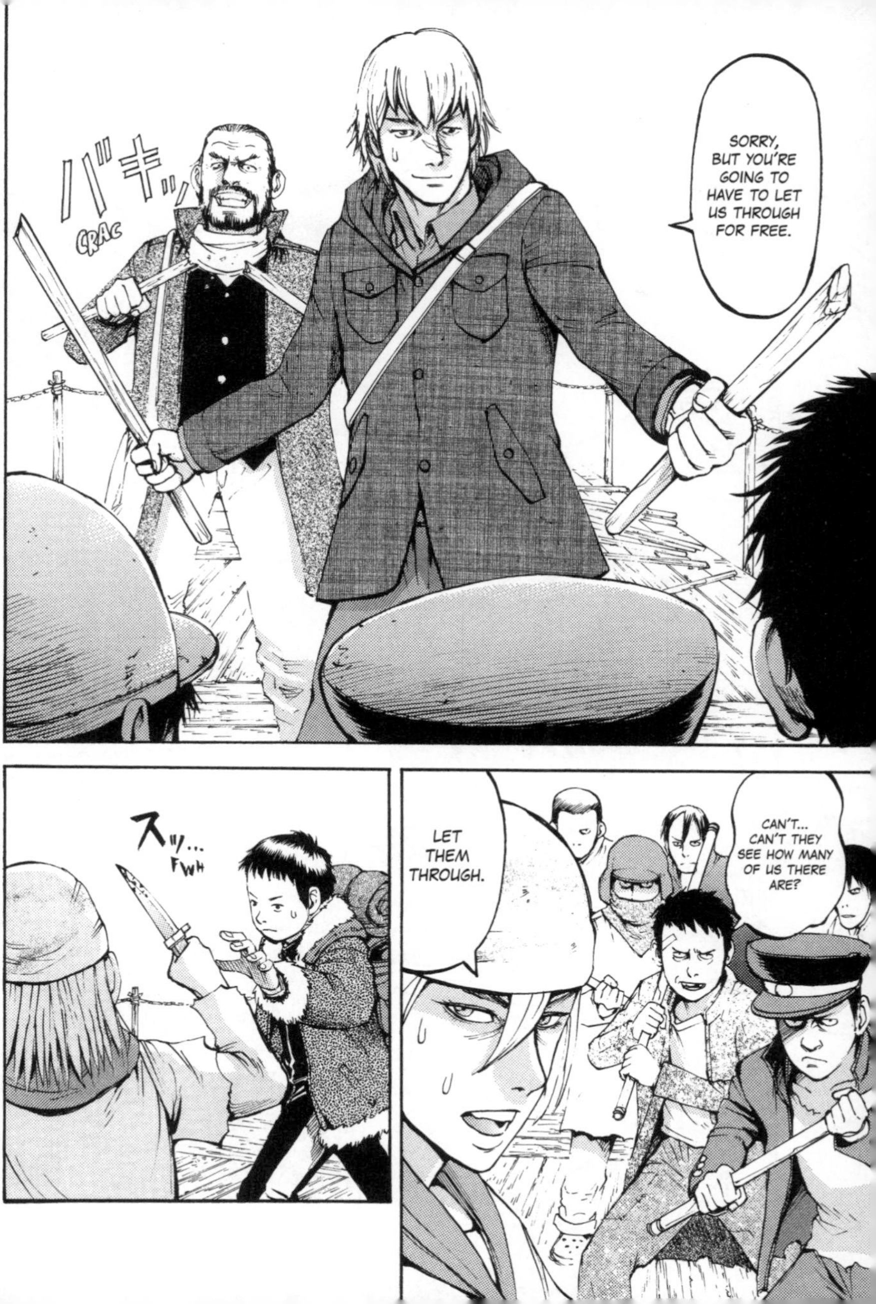
SORRY, BUT YOU'RE GOING TO HAVE TO LET US THROUGH FOR FREE.
バキッ
CRAC
CAN'T... CAN'T THEY SEE HOW MANY OF US THERE ARE?
LET THEM THROUGH.
スッ...
FWH

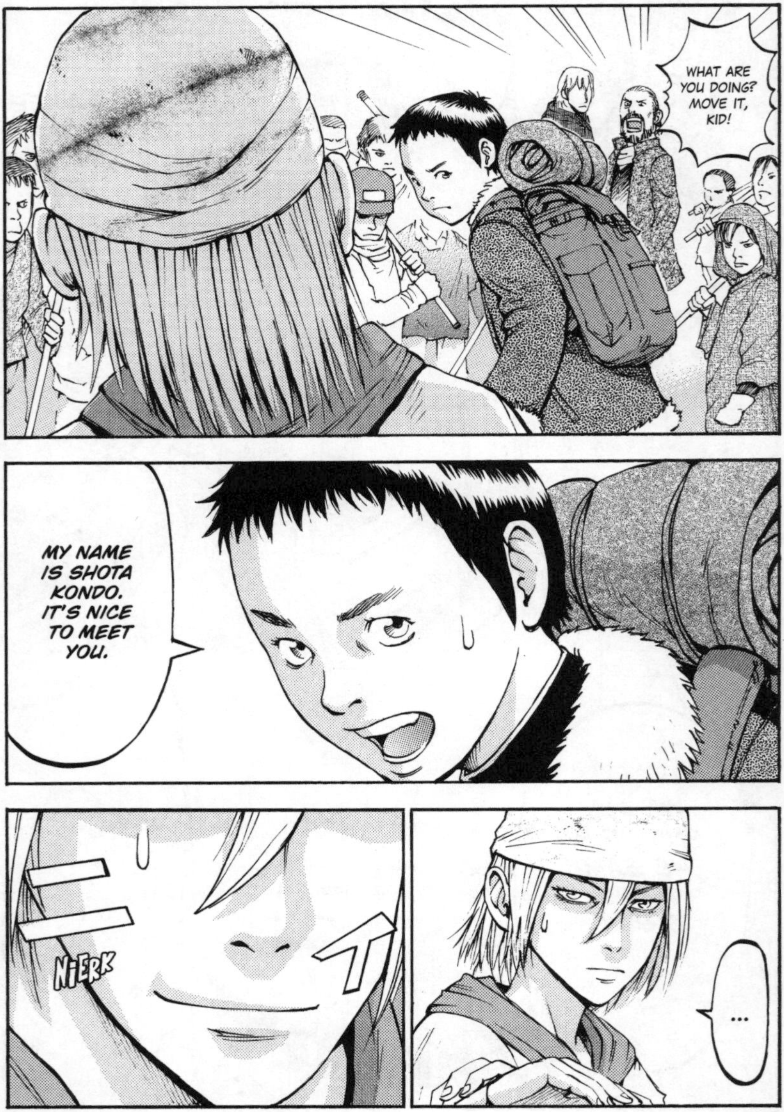
WHAT ARE YOU DOING? MOVE IT, KID!
MY NAME IS SHOTA KONDO. IT'S NICE TO MEET YOU.
...
NIERK

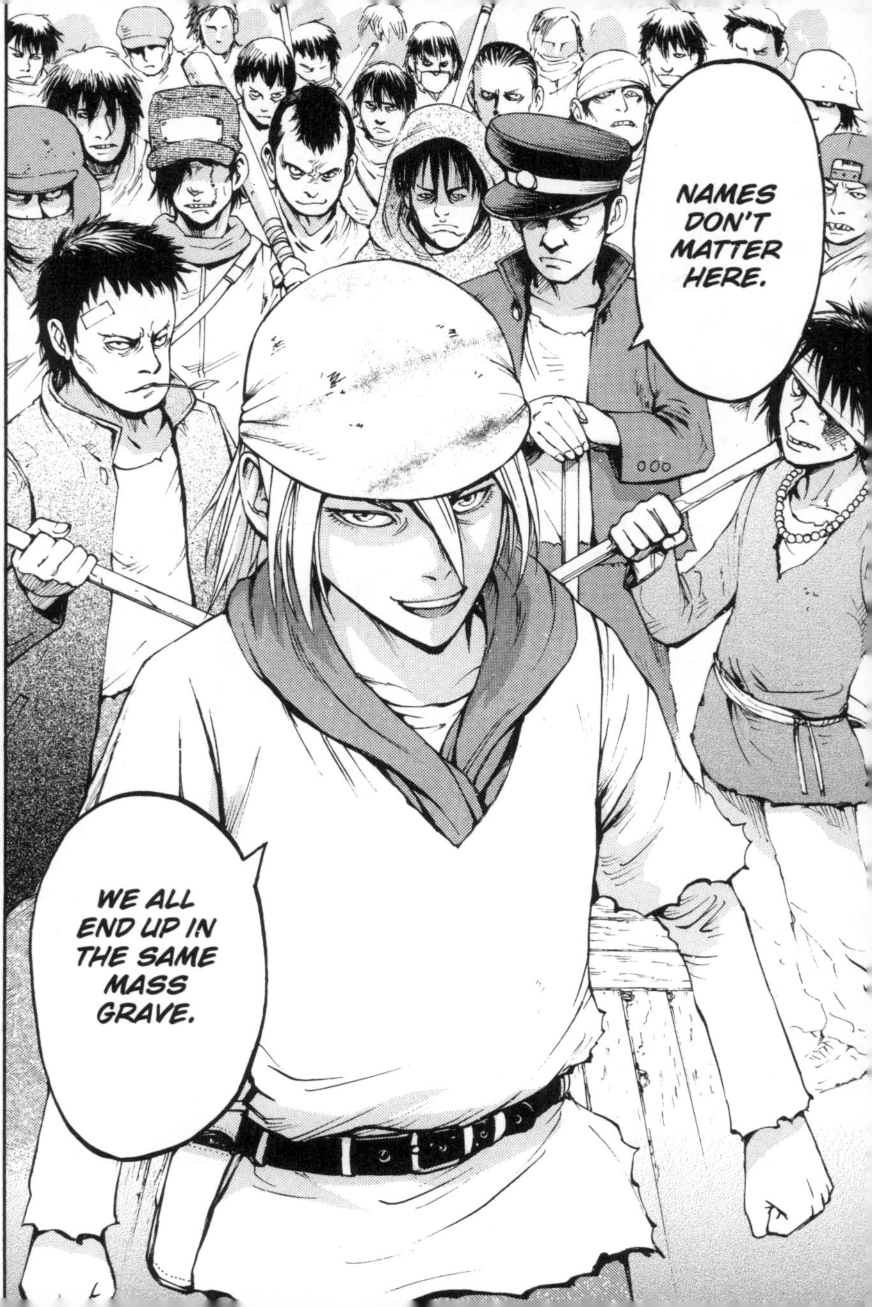
NAMES DON'T MATTER HERE.
WE ALL END UP IN THE SAME MASS GRAVE.

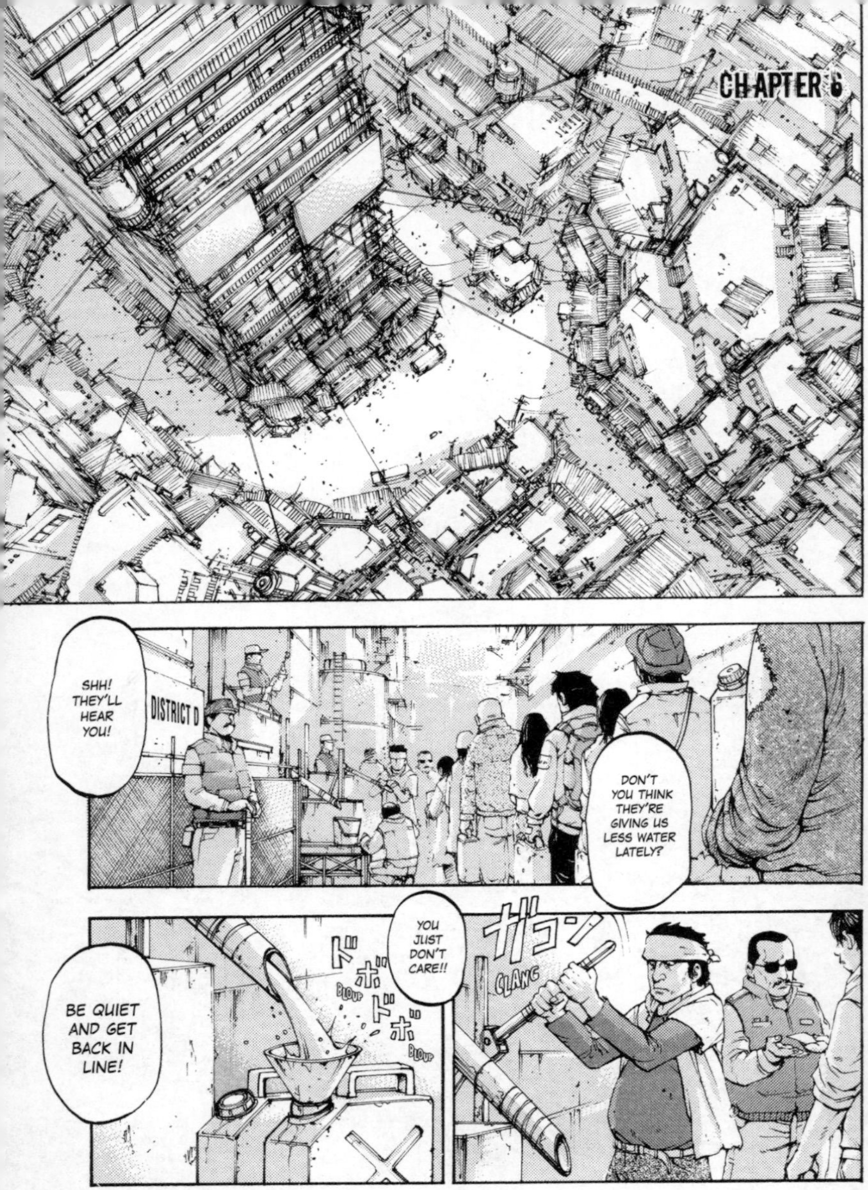
CHAPTER 6
DON'T YOU THINK THEY'RE GIVING US LESS WATER LATELY?
SHH! THEY'LL HEAR YOU!
DISTRICT D
ガコン
CLANG
YOU JUST DON'T CARE!!
ドボドボ
BLOUP
BLOUP
BE QUIET AND GET BACK IN LINE!

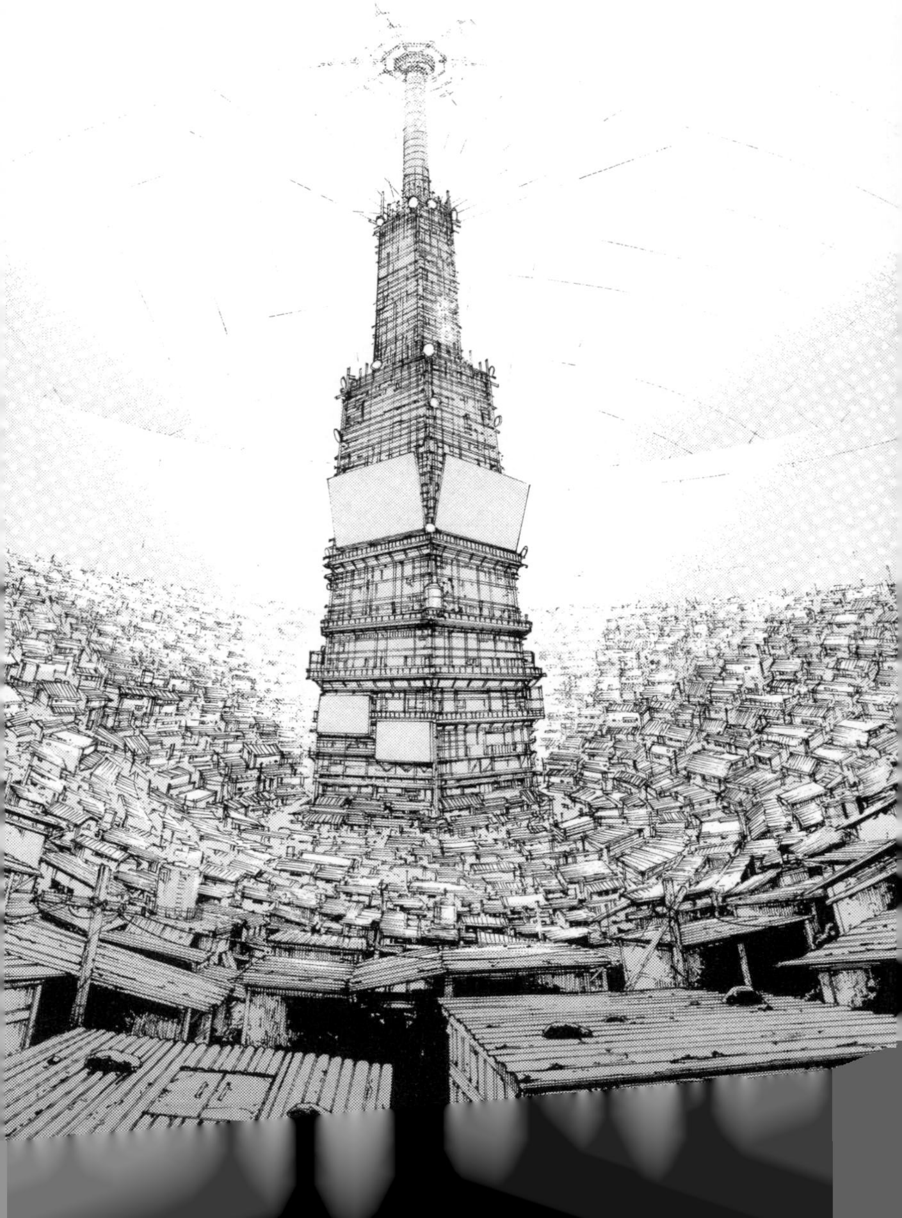

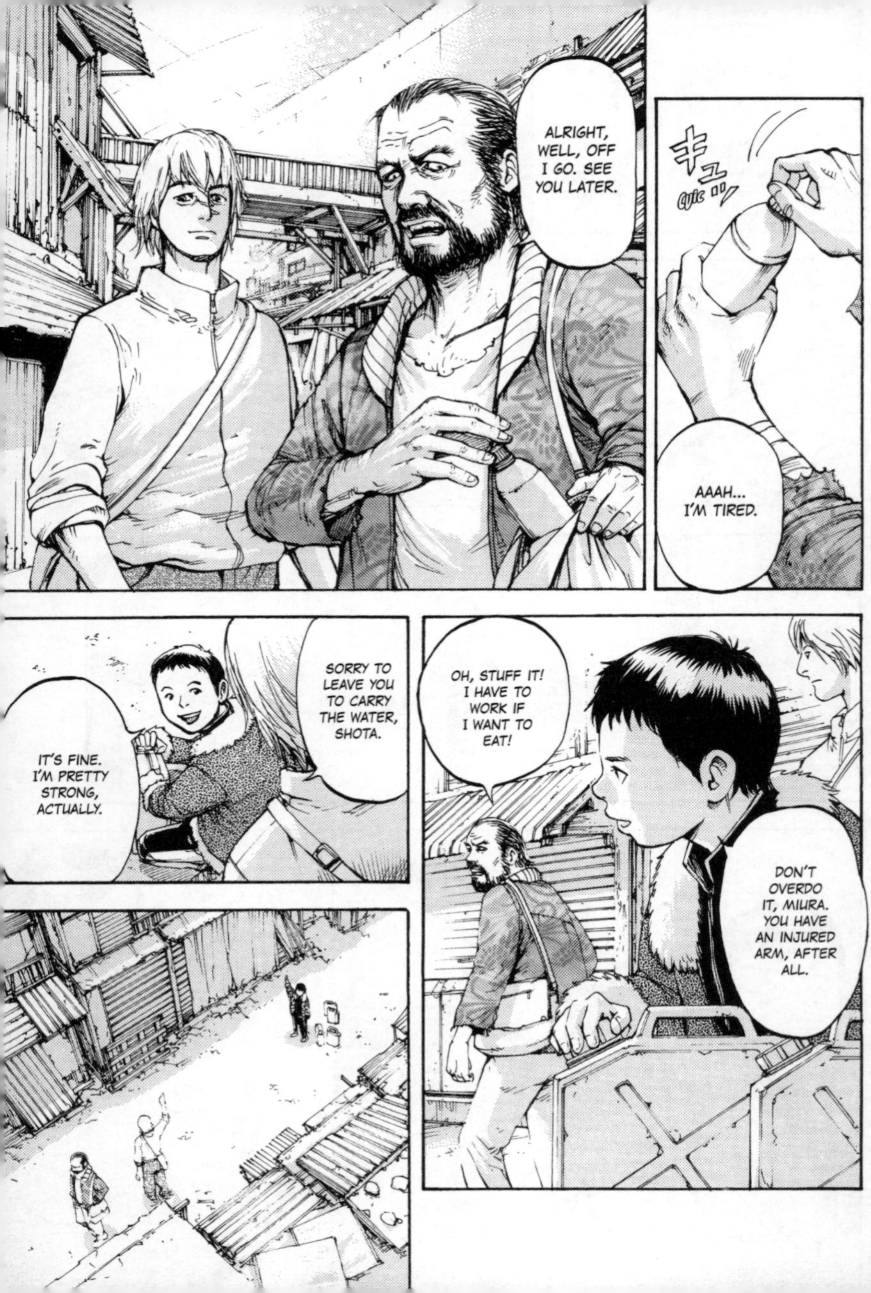
キュッ
Cyuic
AAAH... I'M TIRED.
ALRIGHT, WELL, OFF I GO. SEE YOU LATER.
DON'T OVERDO IT, MIURA. YOU HAVE AN INJURED ARM, AFTER ALL.
OH, STUFF IT! I HAVE TO WORK IF I WANT TO EAT!
SORRY TO LEAVE YOU TO CARRY THE WATER, SHOTA.
IT'S FINE. I'M PRETTY STRONG, ACTUALLY.

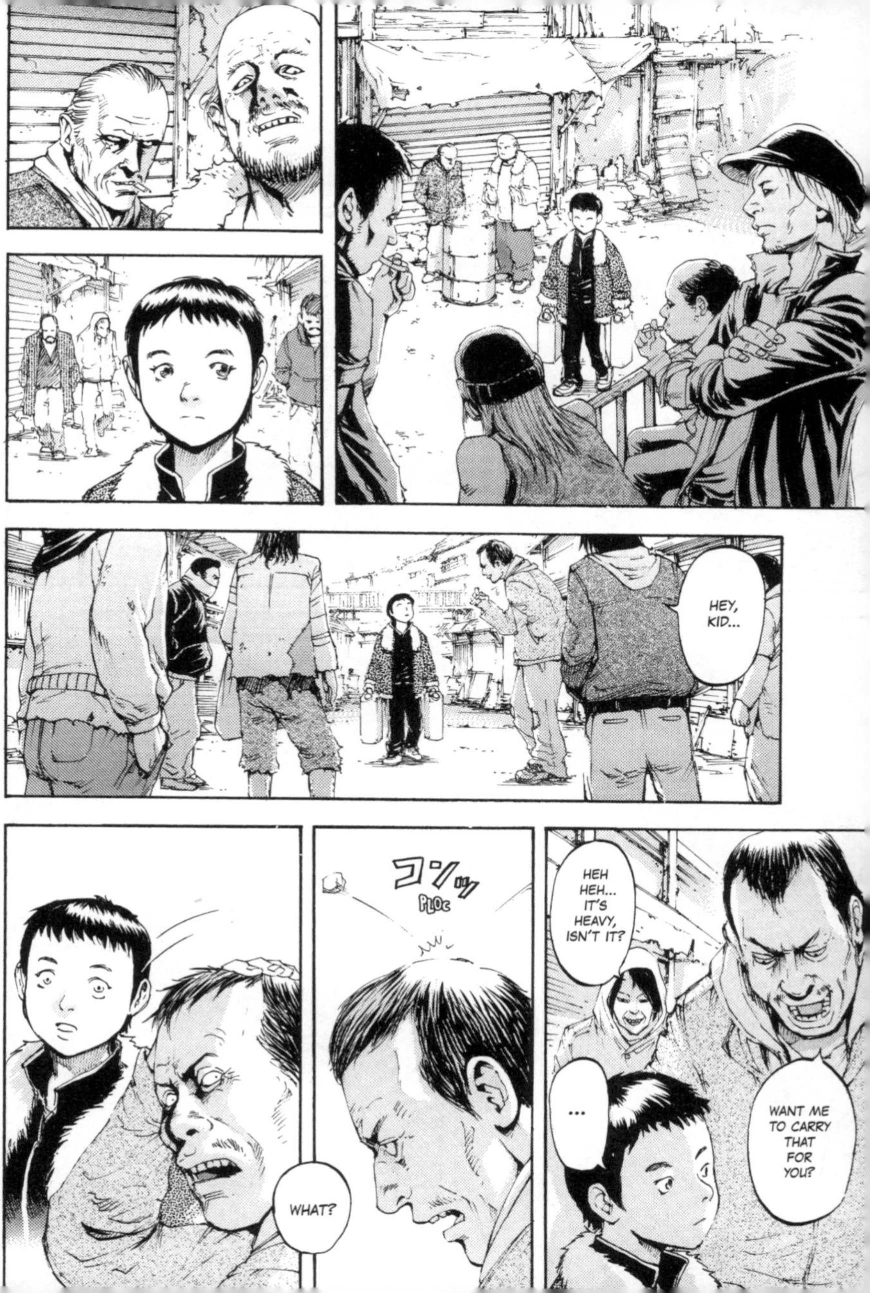
HEY, KID...
HEH HEH... IT'S HEAVY, ISN'T IT?
WANT ME TO CARRY THAT FOR YOU?
...
コンッ
PLOC
WHAT?

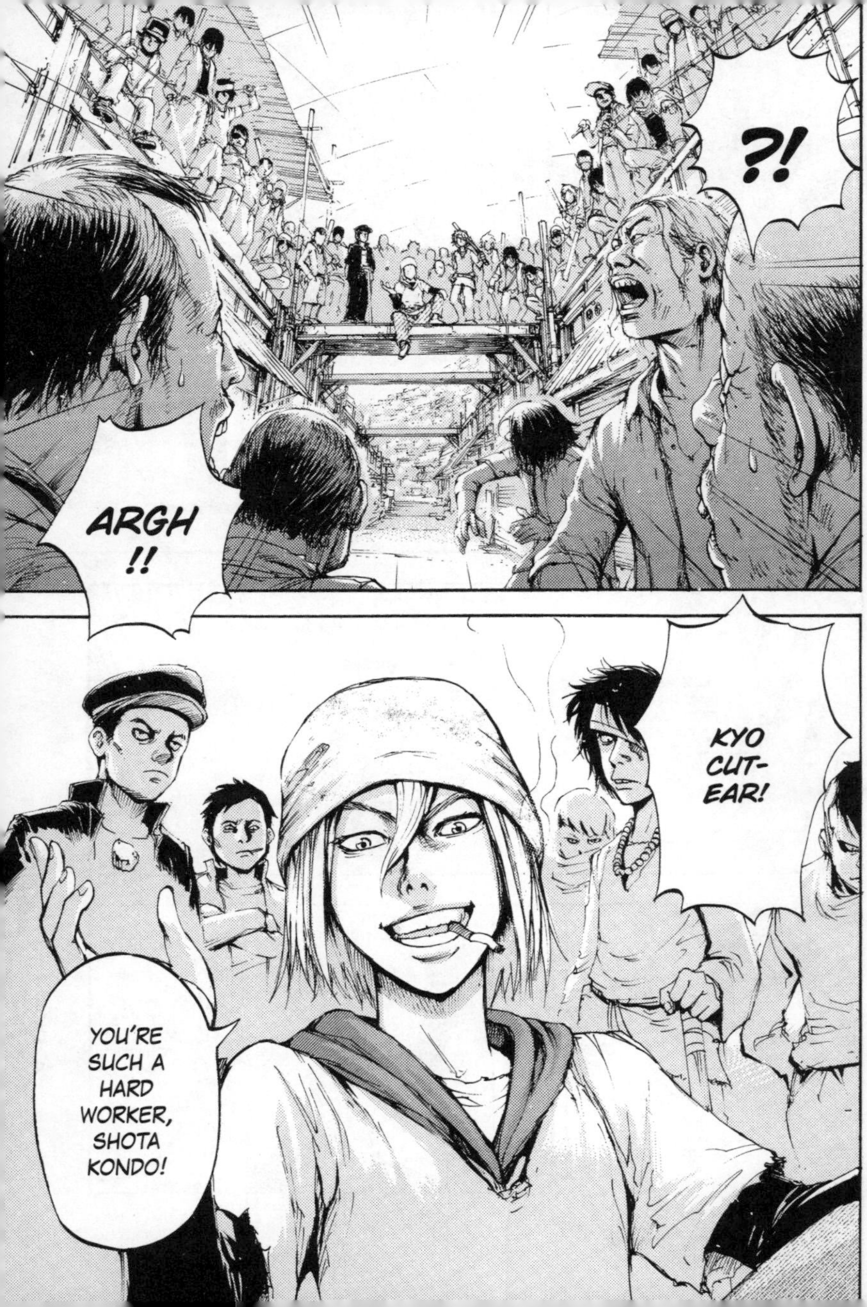
?!
ARGH !!
KYO CUT-EAR!
YOU'RE SUCH A HARD WORKER, SHOTA KONDO!

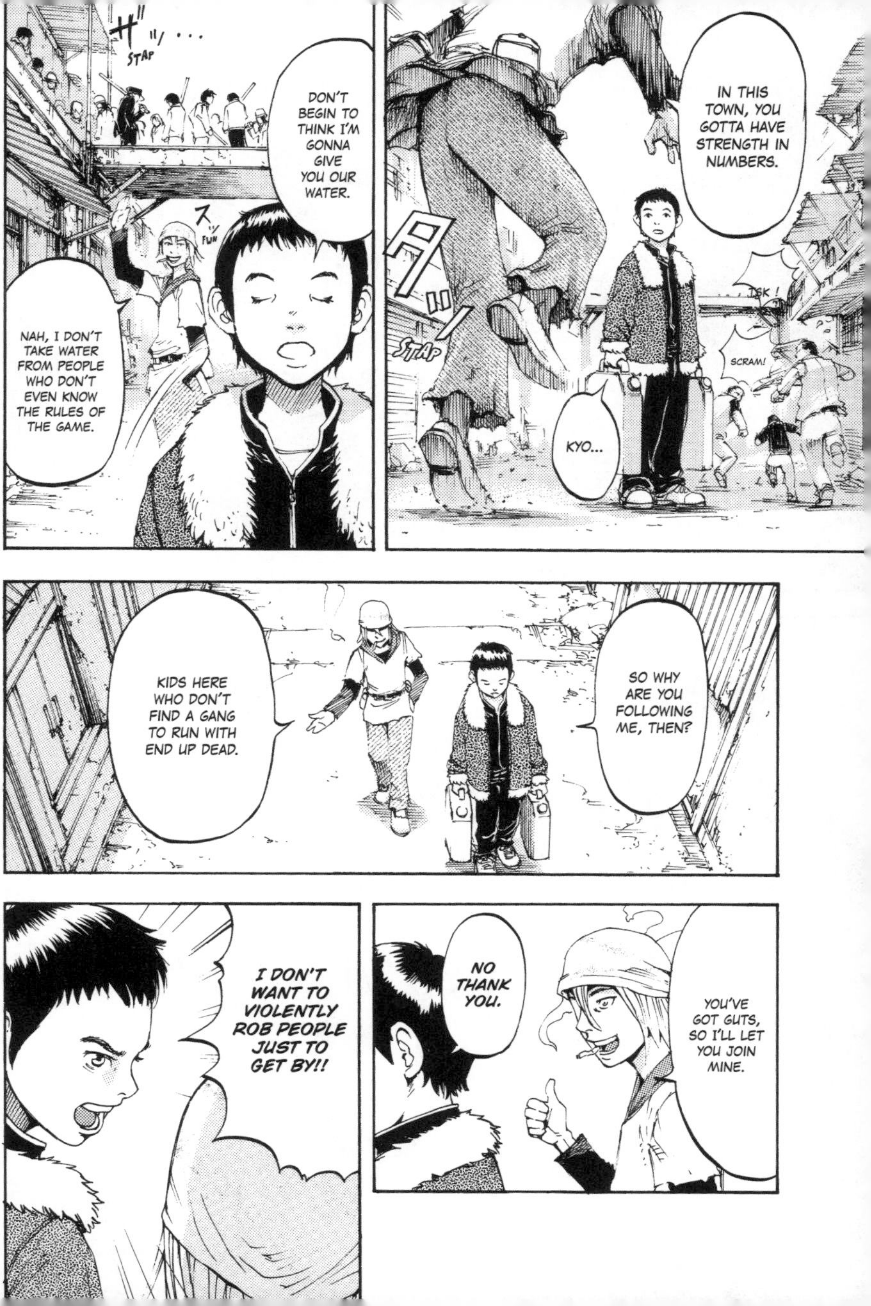
ザ
STAP
DON'T BEGIN TO THINK I'M GONNA GIVE YOU OUR WATER.
ス
FWN
NAH, I DON'T TAKE WATER FROM PEOPLE WHO DON'T EVEN KNOW THE RULES OF THE GAME.
IN THIS TOWN, YOU GOTTA HAVE STRENGTH IN NUMBERS.
STAP
TSK!
SCRAM!
KYO...
KIDS HERE WHO DON'T FIND A GANG TO RUN WITH END UP DEAD.
SO WHY ARE YOU FOLLOWING ME, THEN?
I DON'T WANT TO VIOLENTLY ROB PEOPLE JUST TO GET BY!!
YOU'VE GOT GUTS, SO I'LL LET YOU JOIN MINE.
NO THANK YOU.

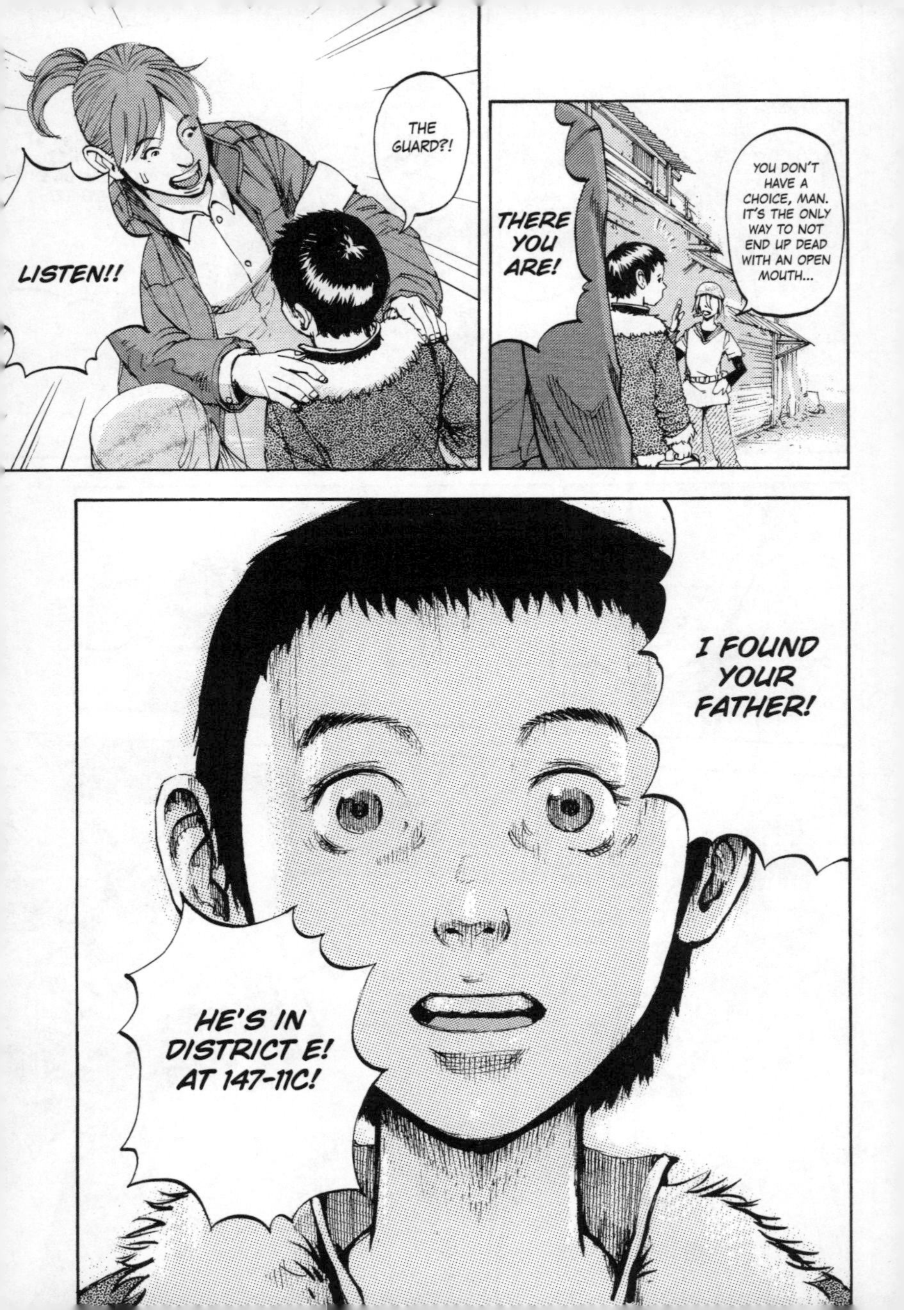
YOU DON'T HAVE A CHOICE, MAN. IT'S THE ONLY WAY TO NOT END UP DEAD WITH AN OPEN MOUTH...
THERE YOU ARE!
THE GUARD?!
LISTEN!!
I FOUND YOUR FATHER!
HE'S IN DISTRICT E! AT 147-11C!

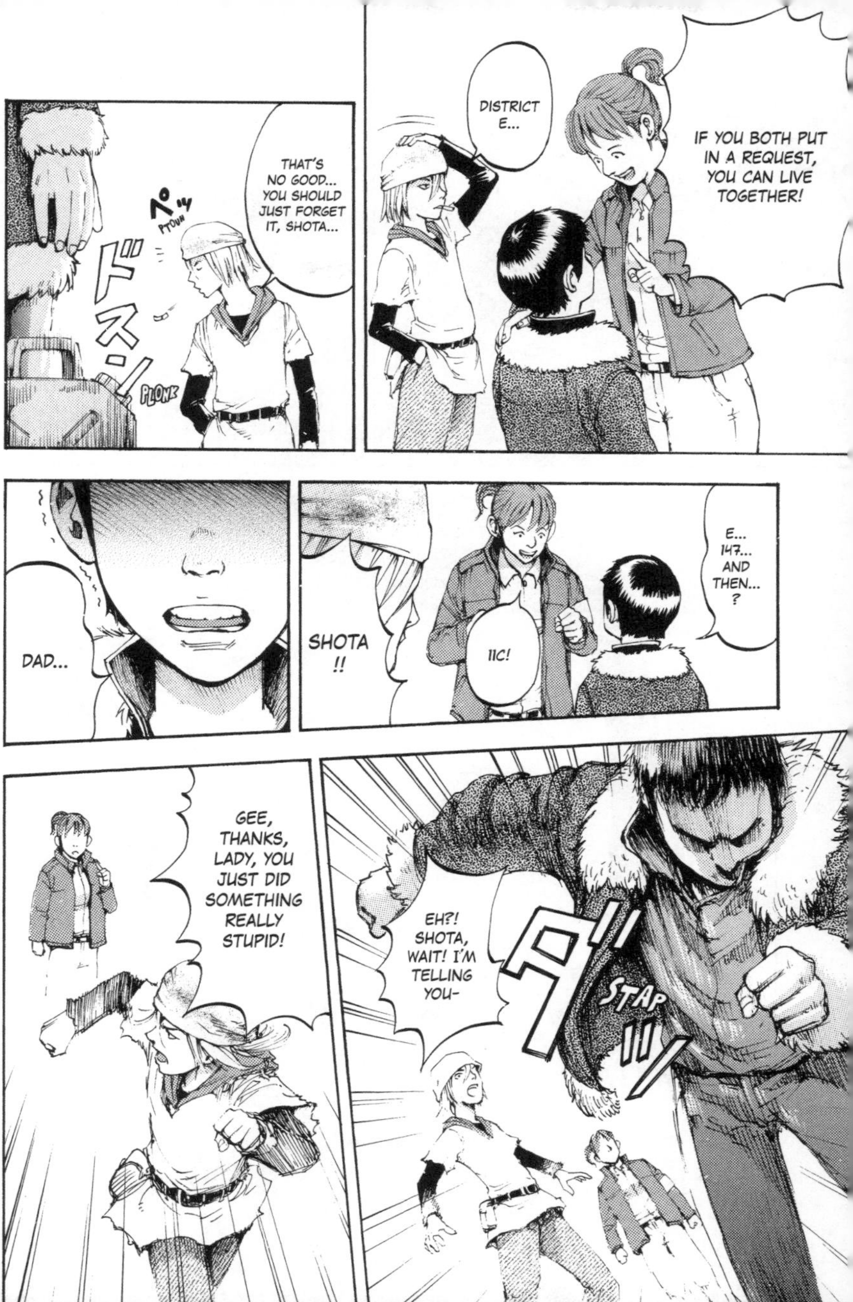
IF YOU BOTH PUT IN A REQUEST, YOU CAN LIVE TOGETHER!
DISTRICT E...
ペッ
PTOUH
THAT'S NO GOOD... YOU SHOULD JUST FORGET IT, SHOTA...
ドスン
PLONK
E... 147... AND THEN... ?
IIC!
SHOTA !!
DAD...
ダッ
STAP
EH?! SHOTA, WAIT! I'M TELLING YOU-
GEE, THANKS, LADY, YOU JUST DID SOMETHING REALLY STUPID!

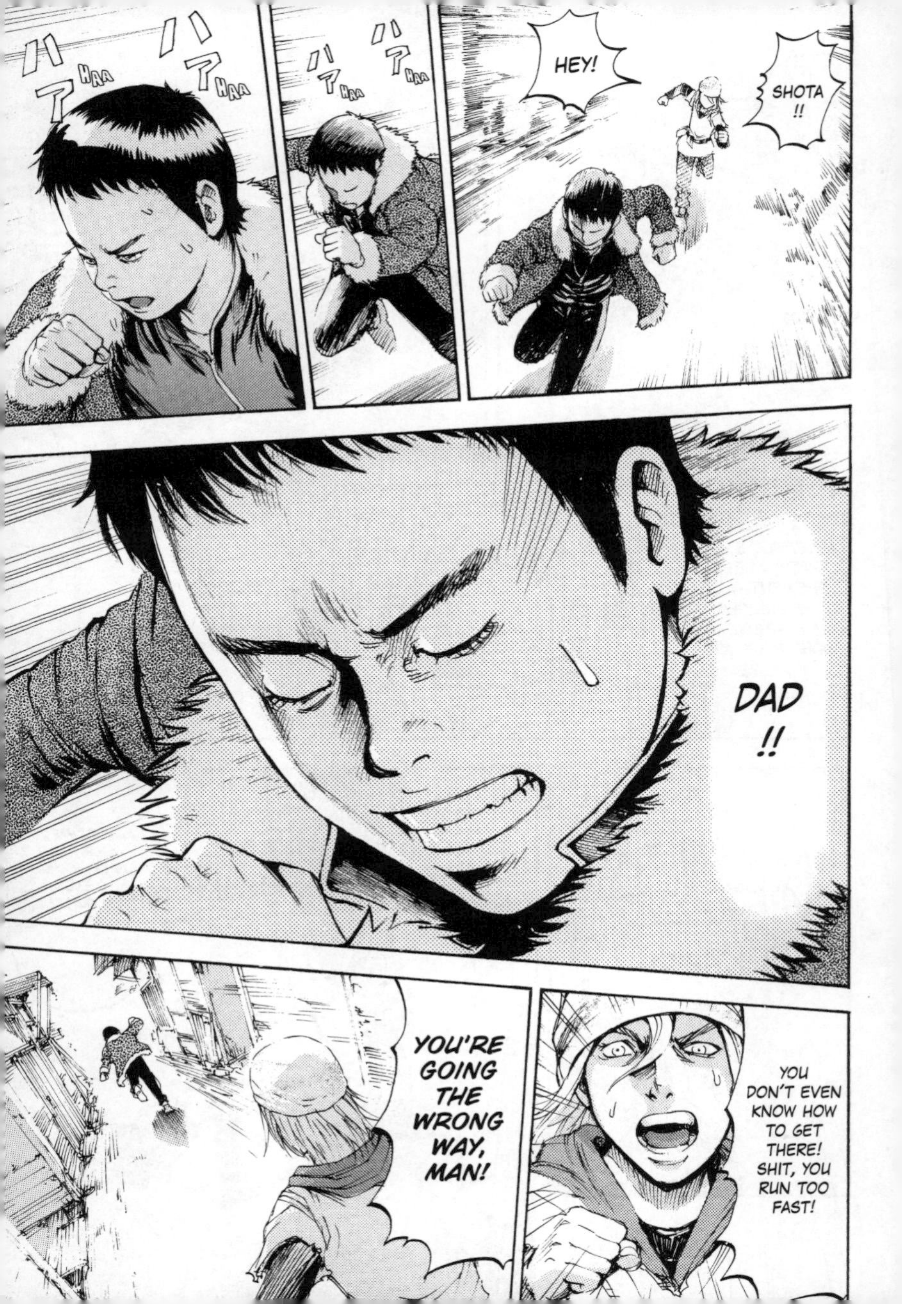
HEY!
SHOTA !!
ハア HAA
ハア HAA
ハア HAA
ハア HAA
DAD !!
YOU DON'T EVEN KNOW HOW TO GET THERE! SHIT, YOU RUN TOO FAST!
YOU'RE GOING THE WRONG WAY, MAN!

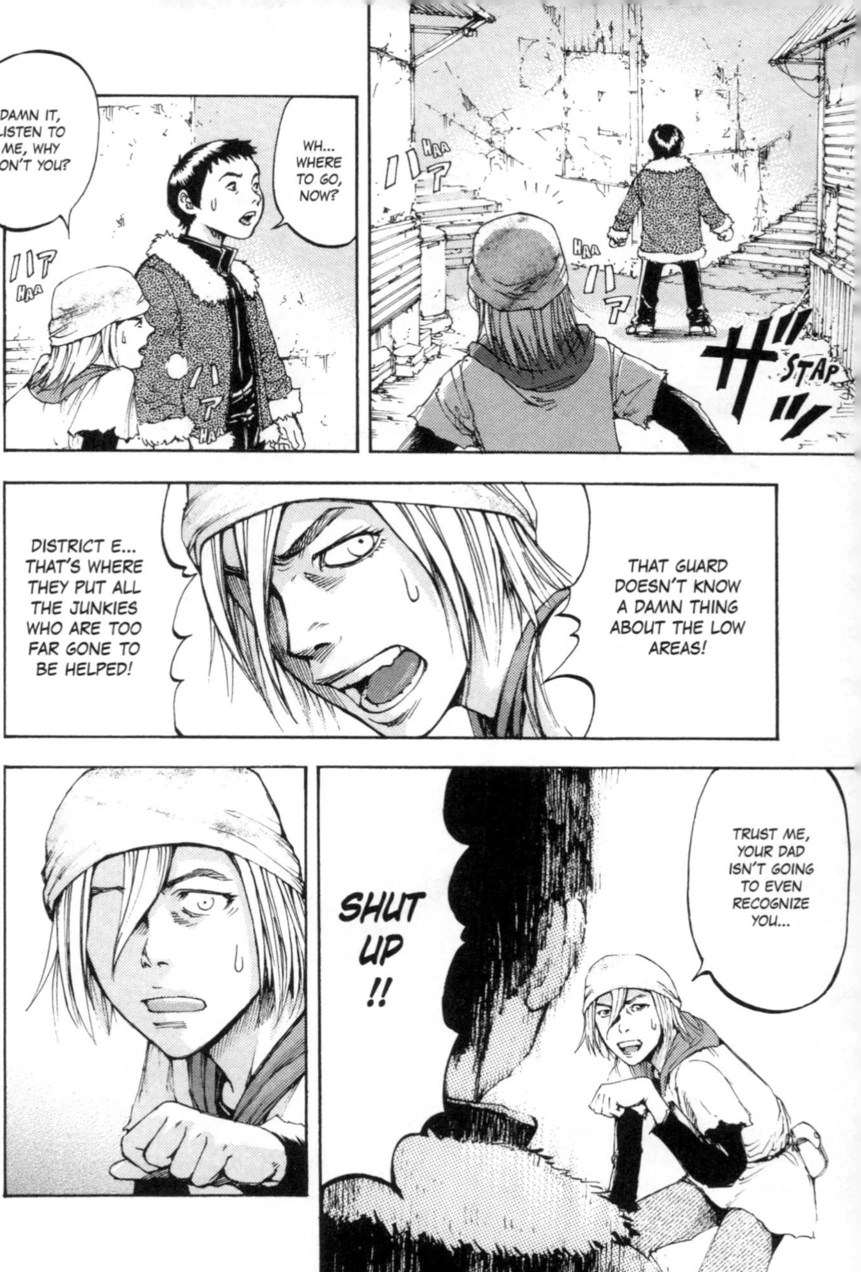
HAA
HAA
STAP
WH... WHERE TO GO, NOW?
DAMN IT, LISTEN TO ME, WHY DON'T YOU?
HAA
HAA
THAT GUARD DOESN'T KNOW A DAMN THING ABOUT THE LOW AREAS!
DISTRICT E... THAT'S WHERE THEY PUT ALL THE JUNKIES WHO ARE TOO FAR GONE TO BE HELPED!
TRUST ME, YOUR DAD ISN'T GOING TO EVEN RECOGNIZE YOU...
SHUT UP !!

...

GRR

I DIDN'T EVEN KNOW HE WAS STILL ALIVE...

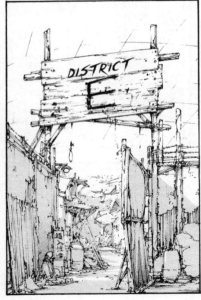

DISTRICT E

THIS WAY.

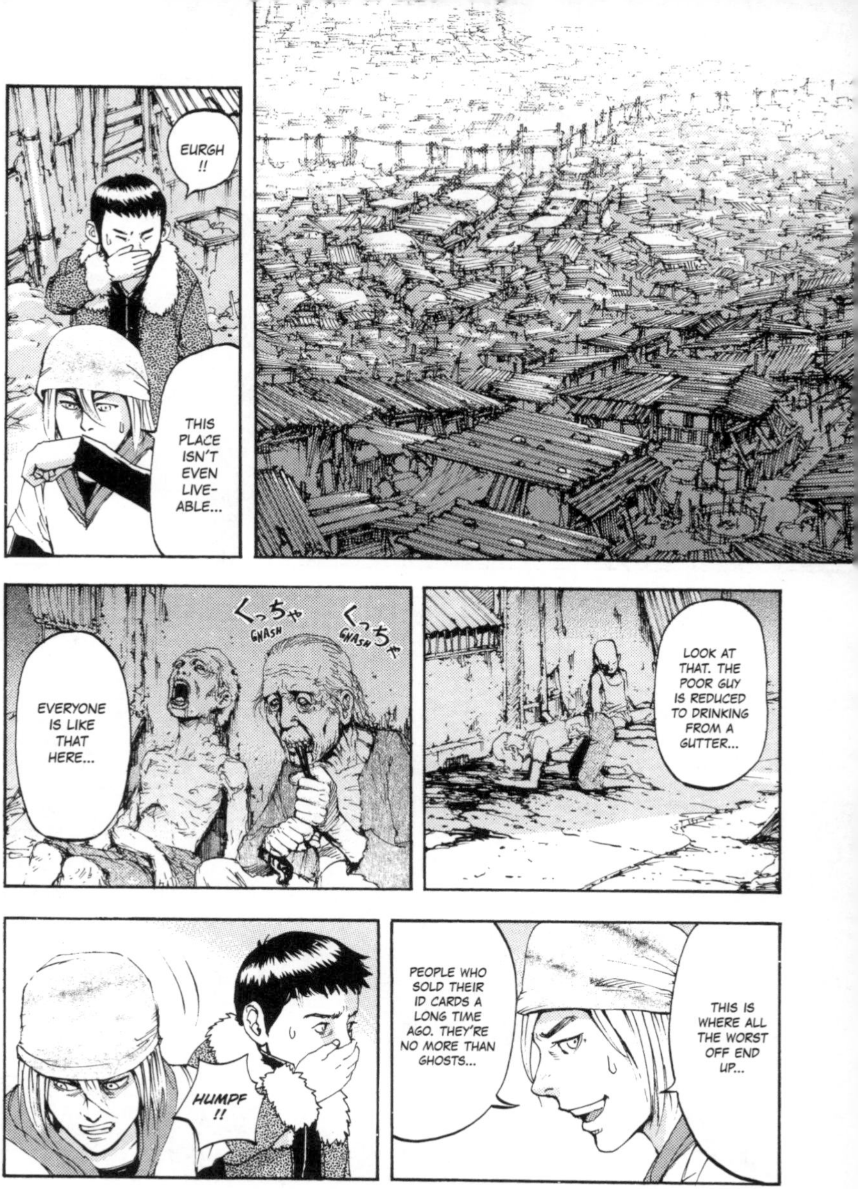
EURGH !!
THIS PLACE ISN'T EVEN LIVE-ABLE...
LOOK AT THAT. THE POOR GUY IS REDUCED TO DRINKING FROM A GUTTER...
くっちゃ
GNASH
くっちゃ
GNASH
EVERYONE IS LIKE THAT HERE...
THIS IS WHERE ALL THE WORST OFF END UP...
PEOPLE WHO SOLD THEIR ID CARDS A LONG TIME AGO. THEY'RE NO MORE THAN GHOSTS...
HUMPF !!

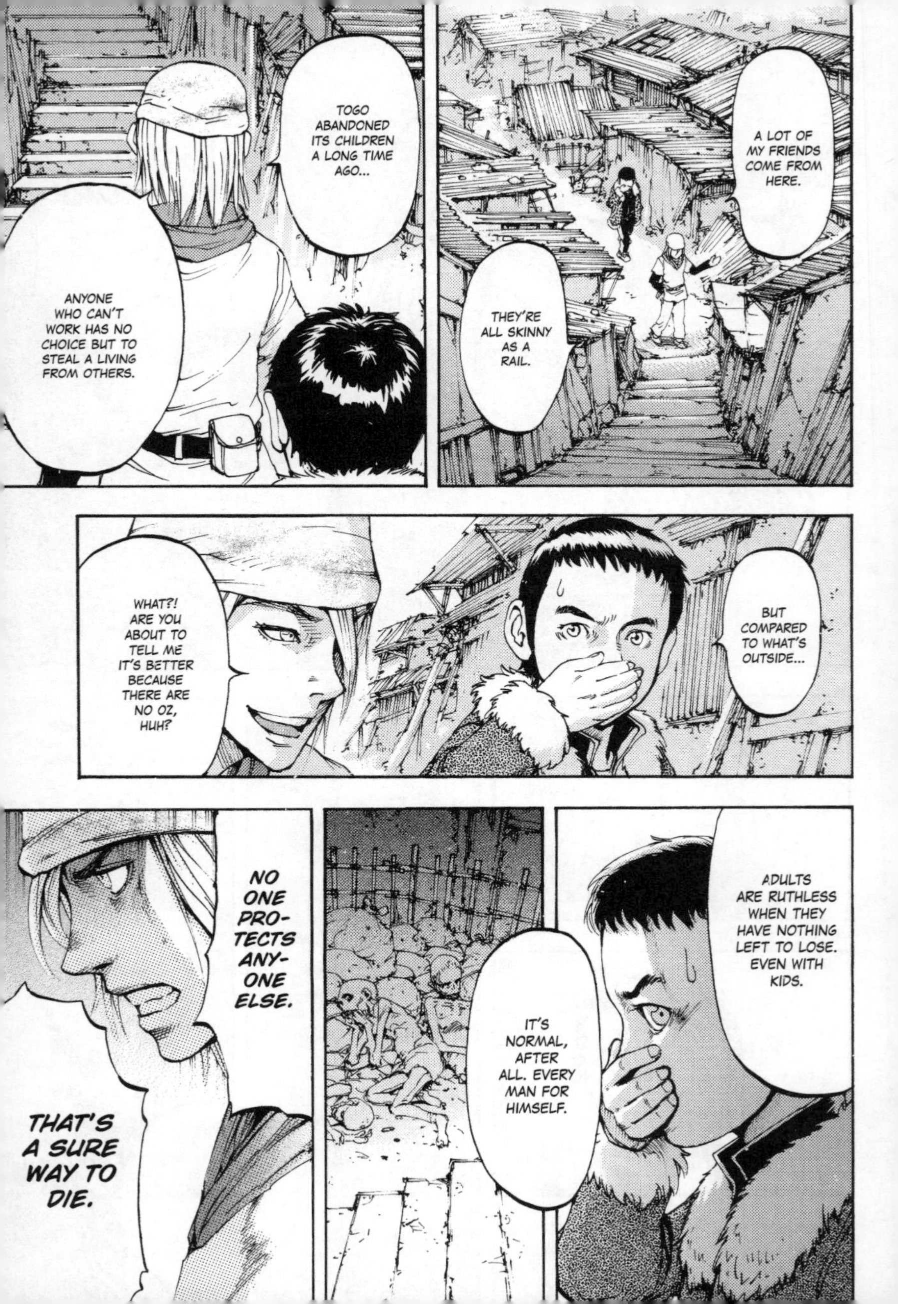
A LOT OF MY FRIENDS COME FROM HERE.
THEY'RE ALL SKINNY AS A RAIL.
TOGO ABANDONED ITS CHILDREN A LONG TIME AGO...
ANYONE WHO CAN'T WORK HAS NO CHOICE BUT TO STEAL A LIVING FROM OTHERS.
BUT COMPARED TO WHAT'S OUTSIDE...
WHAT?! ARE YOU ABOUT TO TELL ME IT'S BETTER BECAUSE THERE ARE NO OZ, HUH?
ADULTS ARE RUTHLESS WHEN THEY HAVE NOTHING LEFT TO LOSE. EVEN WITH KIDS.
IT'S NORMAL, AFTER ALL. EVERY MAN FOR HIMSELF.
NO ONE PROTECTS ANYONE ELSE.
THAT'S A SURE WAY TO DIE.

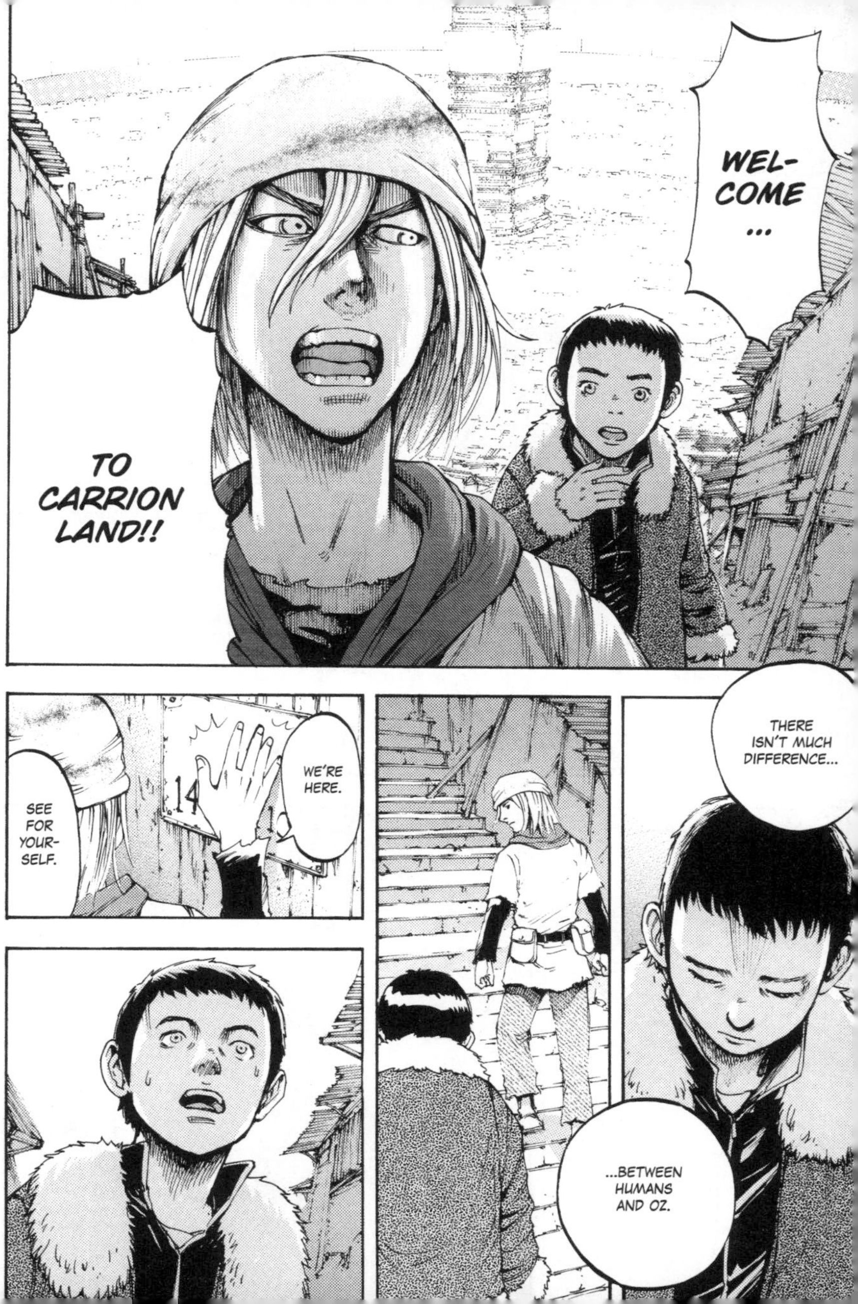
WEL-
COME
...
TO
CARRION
LAND!!
THERE
ISN'T MUCH
DIFFERENCE...
...BETWEEN
HUMANS
AND OZ.
WE'RE
HERE.
14
SEE
FOR
YOUR-
SELF.

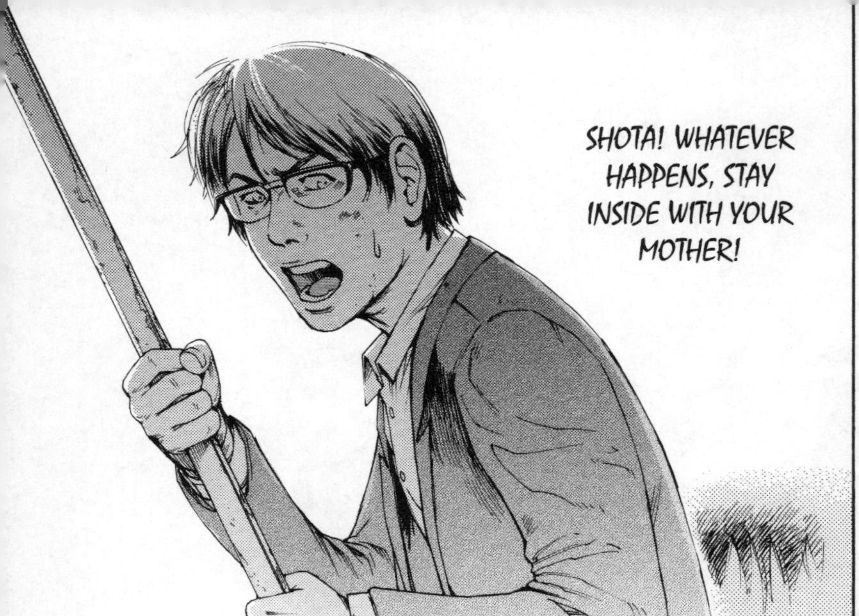
SHOTA! WHATEVER HAPPENS, STAY INSIDE WITH YOUR MOTHER!
DAD...
THIS INJURY IS NOTHING!
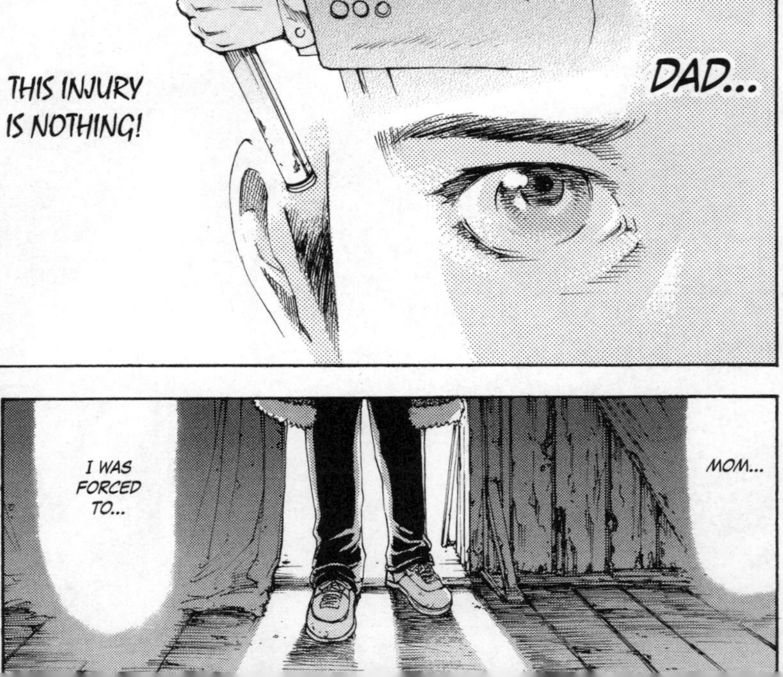
MOM...
I WAS FORCED TO...

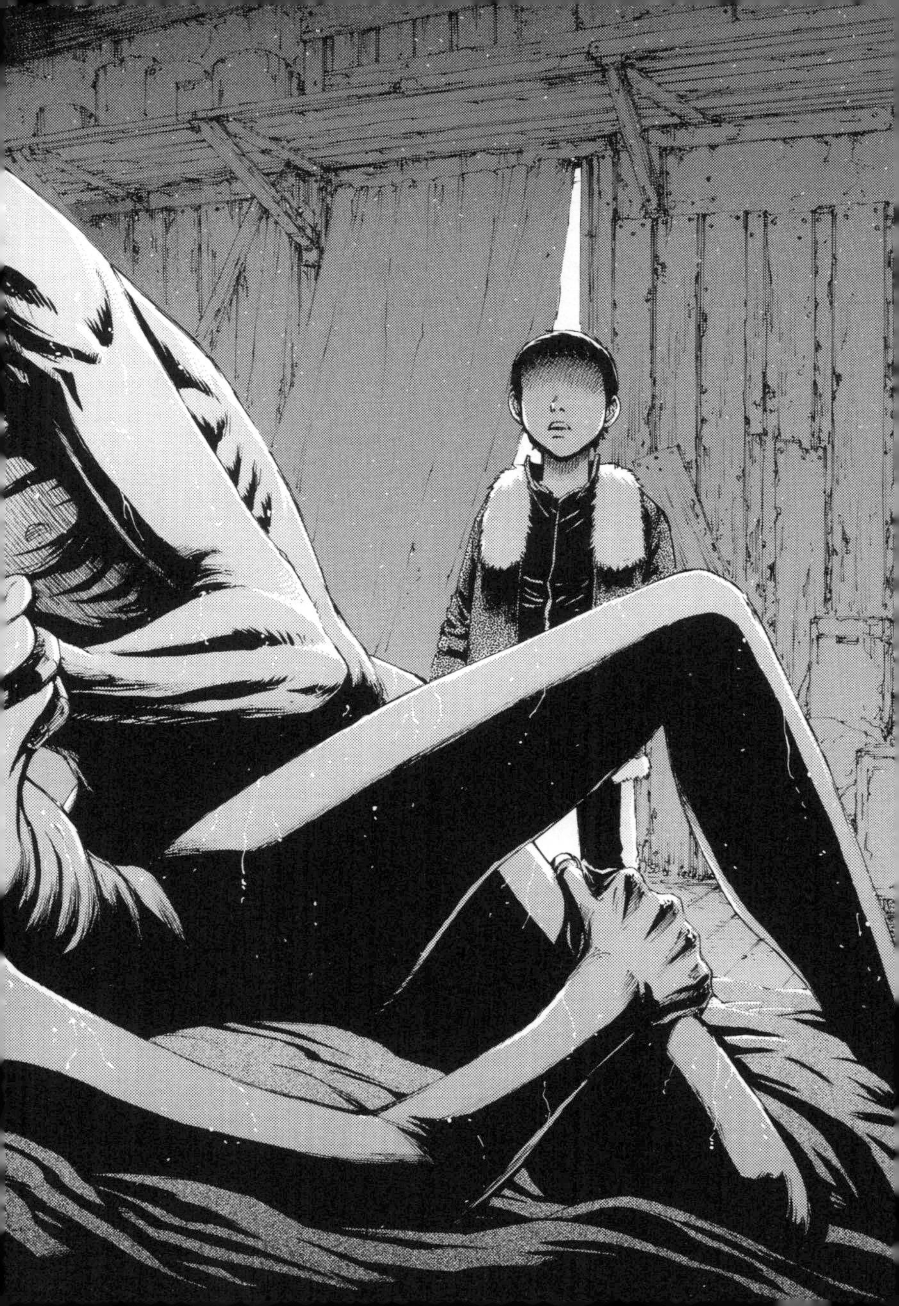

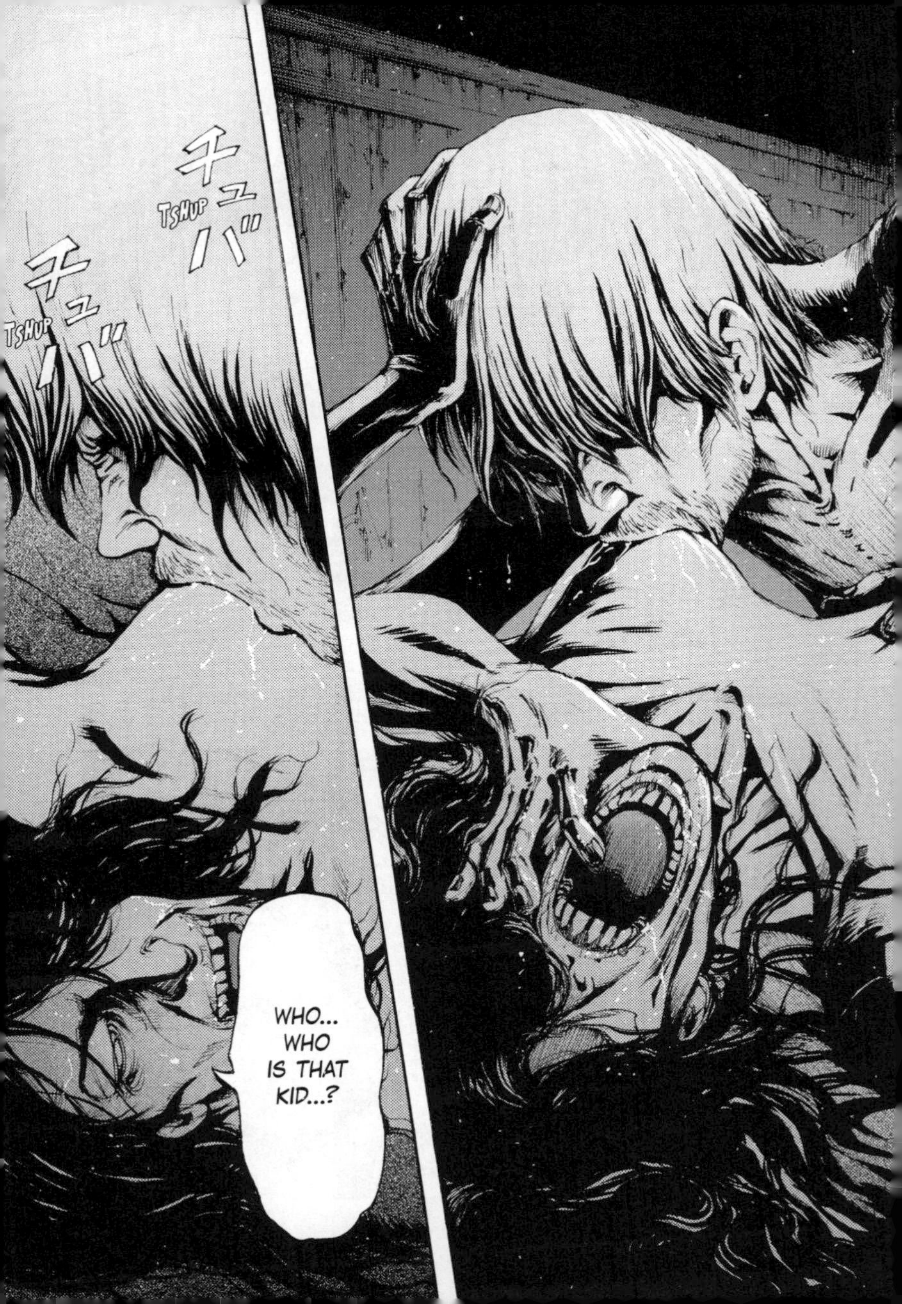
チュバ
TSHUP
チュバ
TSHUP
WHO... WHO IS THAT KID...?

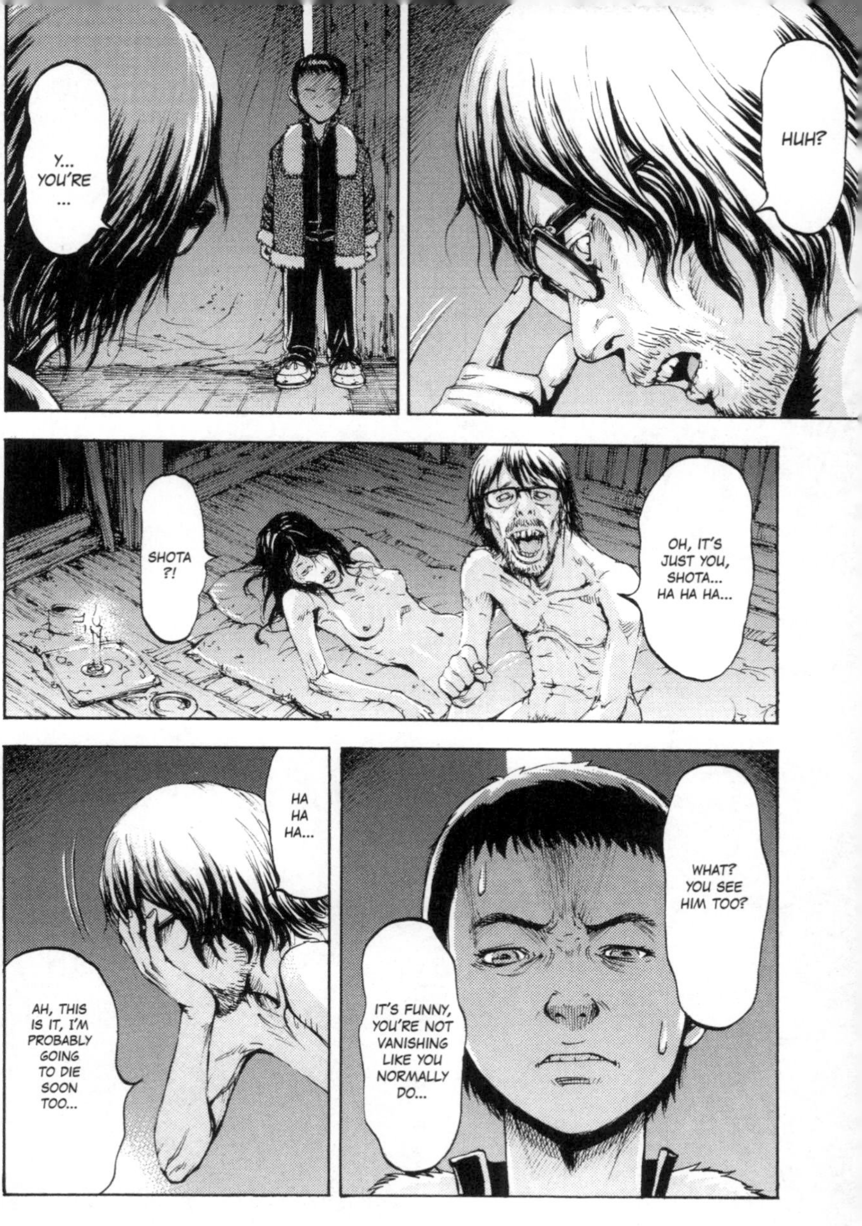
HUH?
Y... YOU'RE ...
OH, IT'S JUST YOU, SHOTA... HA HA HA...
SHOTA ?!
WHAT? YOU SEE HIM TOO?
IT'S FUNNY, YOU'RE NOT VANISHING LIKE YOU NORMALLY DO...
HA HA HA...
AH, THIS IS IT, I'M PROBABLY GOING TO DIE SOON TOO...

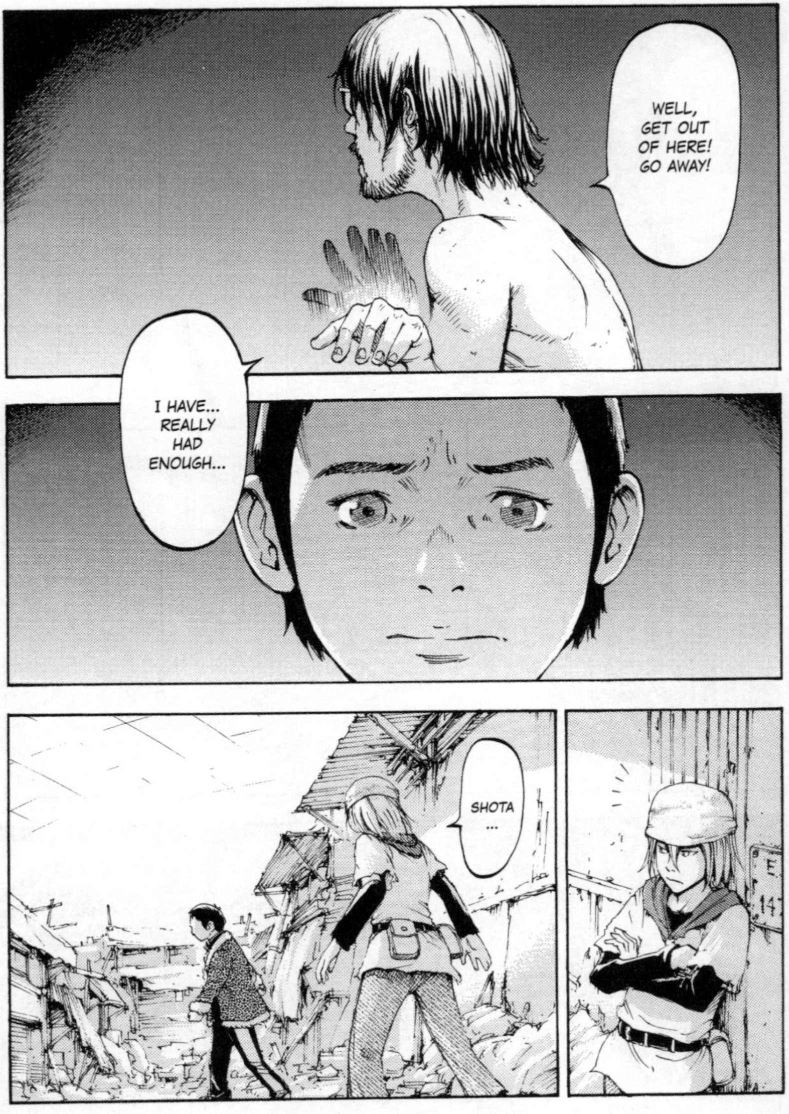
WELL, GET OUT OF HERE! GO AWAY!
I HAVE... REALLY HAD ENOUGH...
SHOTA ...

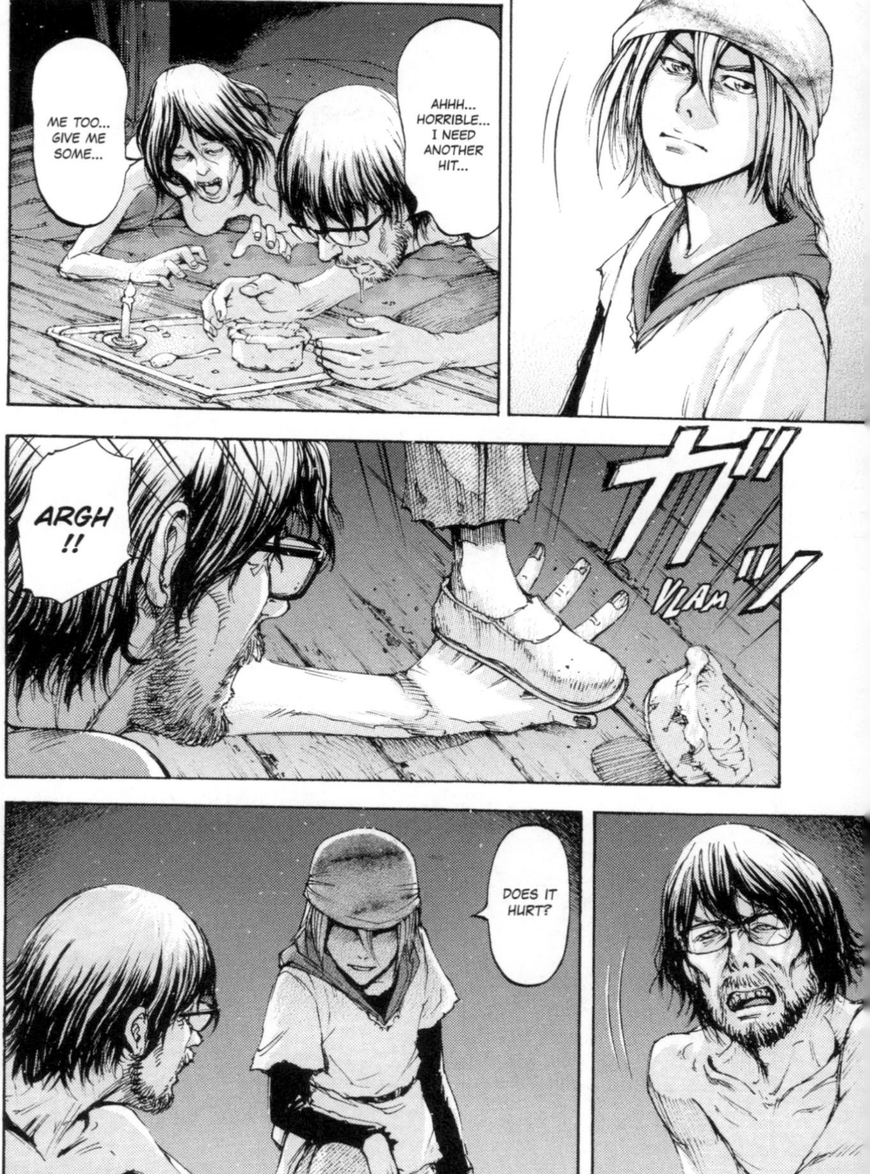
AHHH... HORRIBLE... I NEED ANOTHER HIT...
ME TOO... GIVE ME SOME...
ガッ
VLAM
ARGH!!
DOES IT HURT?

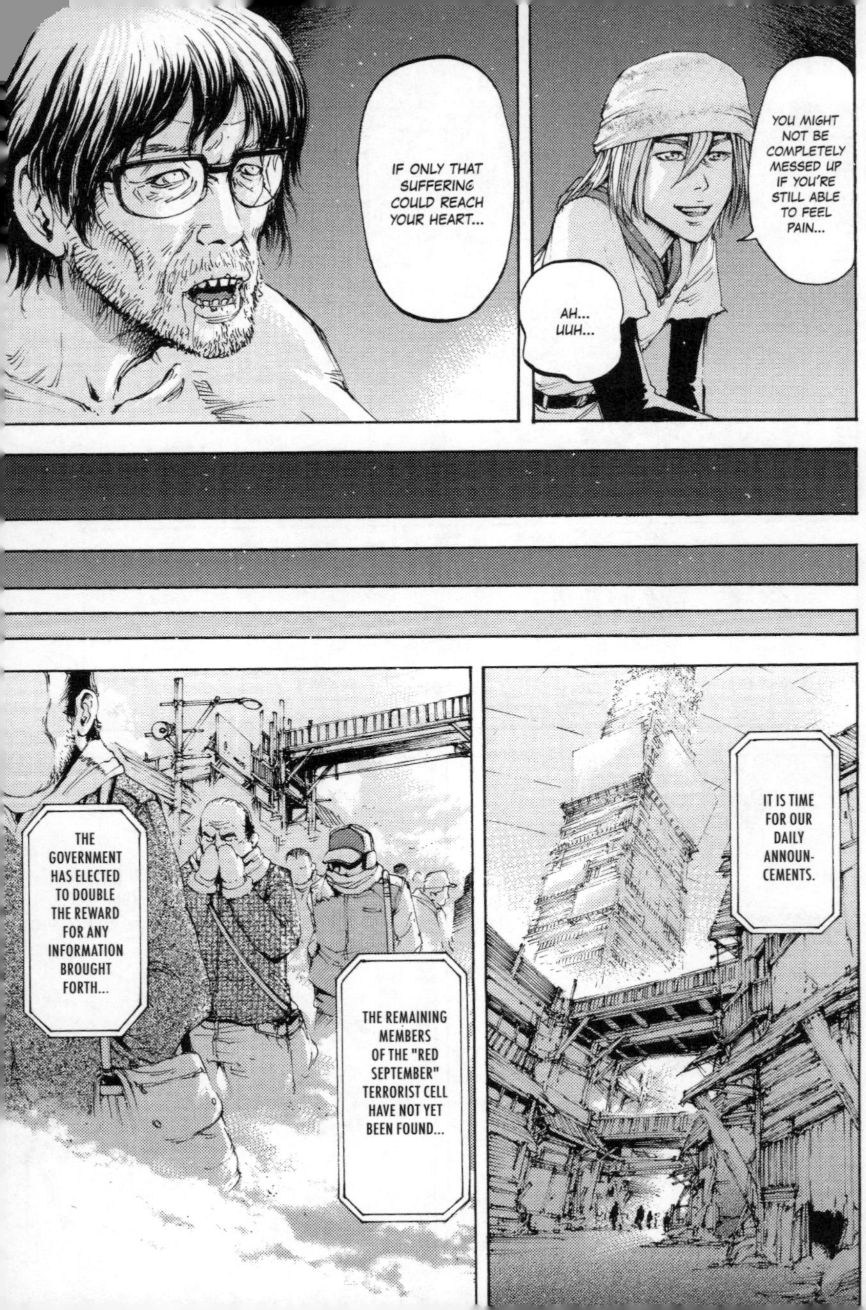
YOU MIGHT NOT BE COMPLETELY MESSED UP IF YOU'RE STILL ABLE TO FEEL PAIN...
AH... UUH...
IF ONLY THAT SUFFERING COULD REACH YOUR HEART...
IT IS TIME FOR OUR DAILY ANNOUN-CEMENTS.
THE REMAINING MEMBERS OF THE "RED SEPTEMBER" TERRORIST CELL HAVE NOT YET BEEN FOUND...
THE GOVERNMENT HAS ELECTED TO DOUBLE THE REWARD FOR ANY INFORMATION BROUGHT FORTH...

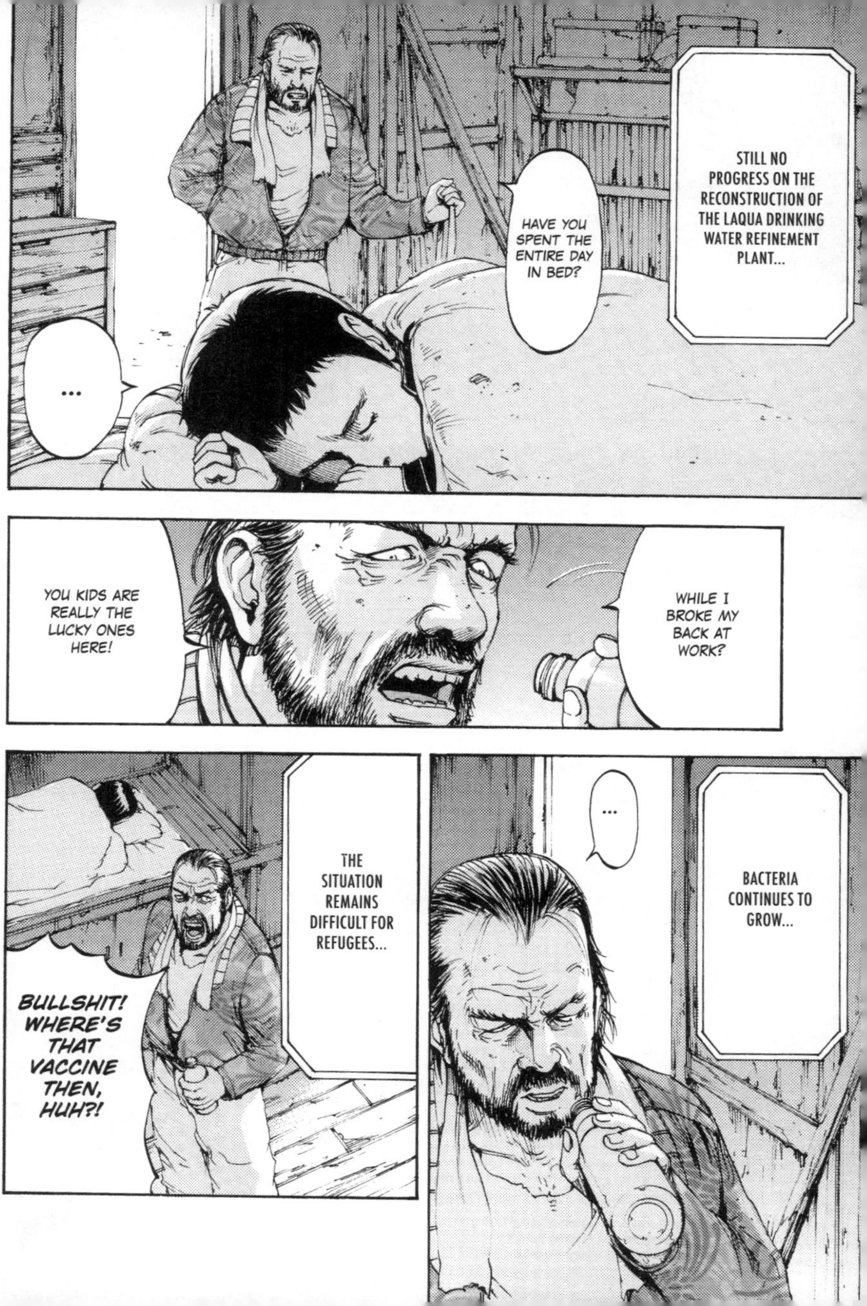
STILL NO PROGRESS ON THE RECONSTRUCTION OF THE LAQUA DRINKING WATER REFINEMENT PLANT...
HAVE YOU SPENT THE ENTIRE DAY IN BED?
...
WHILE I BROKE MY BACK AT WORK?
YOU KIDS ARE REALLY THE LUCKY ONES HERE!
BACTERIA CONTINUES TO GROW...
...
THE SITUATION REMAINS DIFFICULT FOR REFUGEES...
BULLSHIT! WHERE'S THAT VACCINE THEN, HUH?!

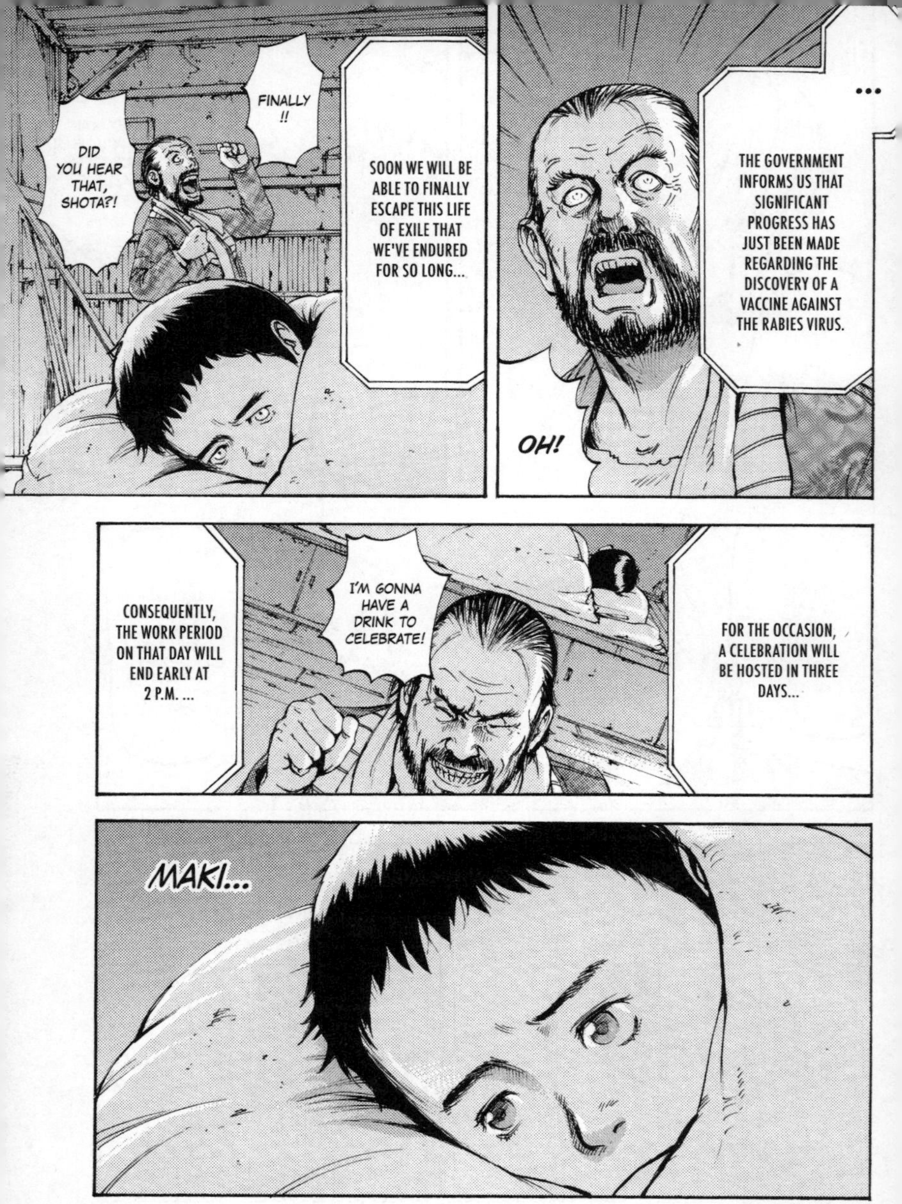
...
THE GOVERNMENT INFORMS US THAT SIGNIFICANT PROGRESS HAS JUST BEEN MADE REGARDING THE DISCOVERY OF A VACCINE AGAINST THE RABIES VIRUS.
OH!
SOON WE WILL BE ABLE TO FINALLY ESCAPE THIS LIFE OF EXILE THAT WE'VE ENDURED FOR SO LONG...
FINALLY !!
DID YOU HEAR THAT, SHOTA?!
FOR THE OCCASION, A CELEBRATION WILL BE HOSTED IN THREE DAYS...
I'M GONNA HAVE A DRINK TO CELEBRATE!
CONSEQUENTLY, THE WORK PERIOD ON THAT DAY WILL END EARLY AT 2 P.M. ...
MAKI...

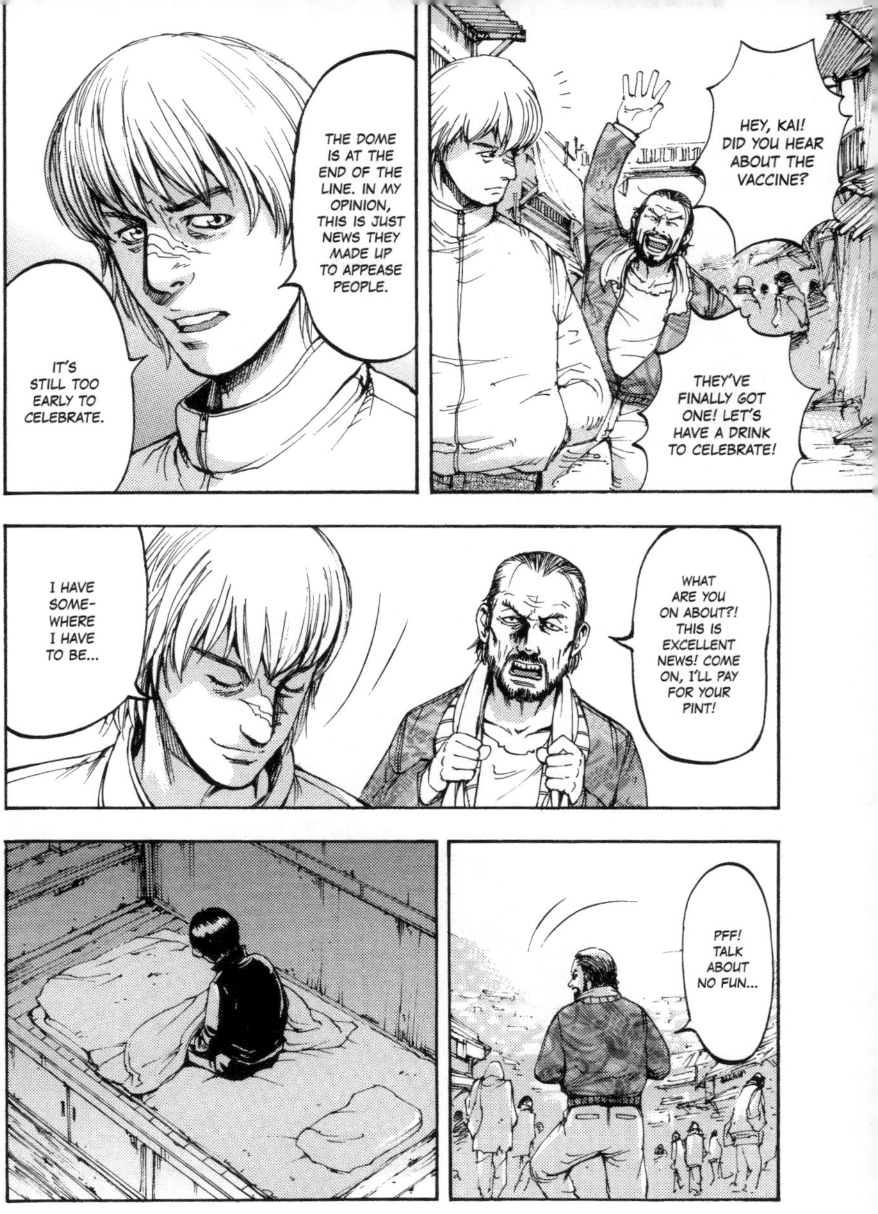
HEY, KAI! DID YOU HEAR ABOUT THE VACCINE?
THEY'VE FINALLY GOT ONE! LET'S HAVE A DRINK TO CELEBRATE!
THE DOME IS AT THE END OF THE LINE. IN MY OPINION, THIS IS JUST NEWS THEY MADE UP TO APPEASE PEOPLE.
IT'S STILL TOO EARLY TO CELEBRATE.
WHAT ARE YOU ON ABOUT?! THIS IS EXCELLENT NEWS! COME ON, I'LL PAY FOR YOUR PINT!
I HAVE SOME-WHERE I HAVE TO BE...
PFF! TALK ABOUT NO FUN...

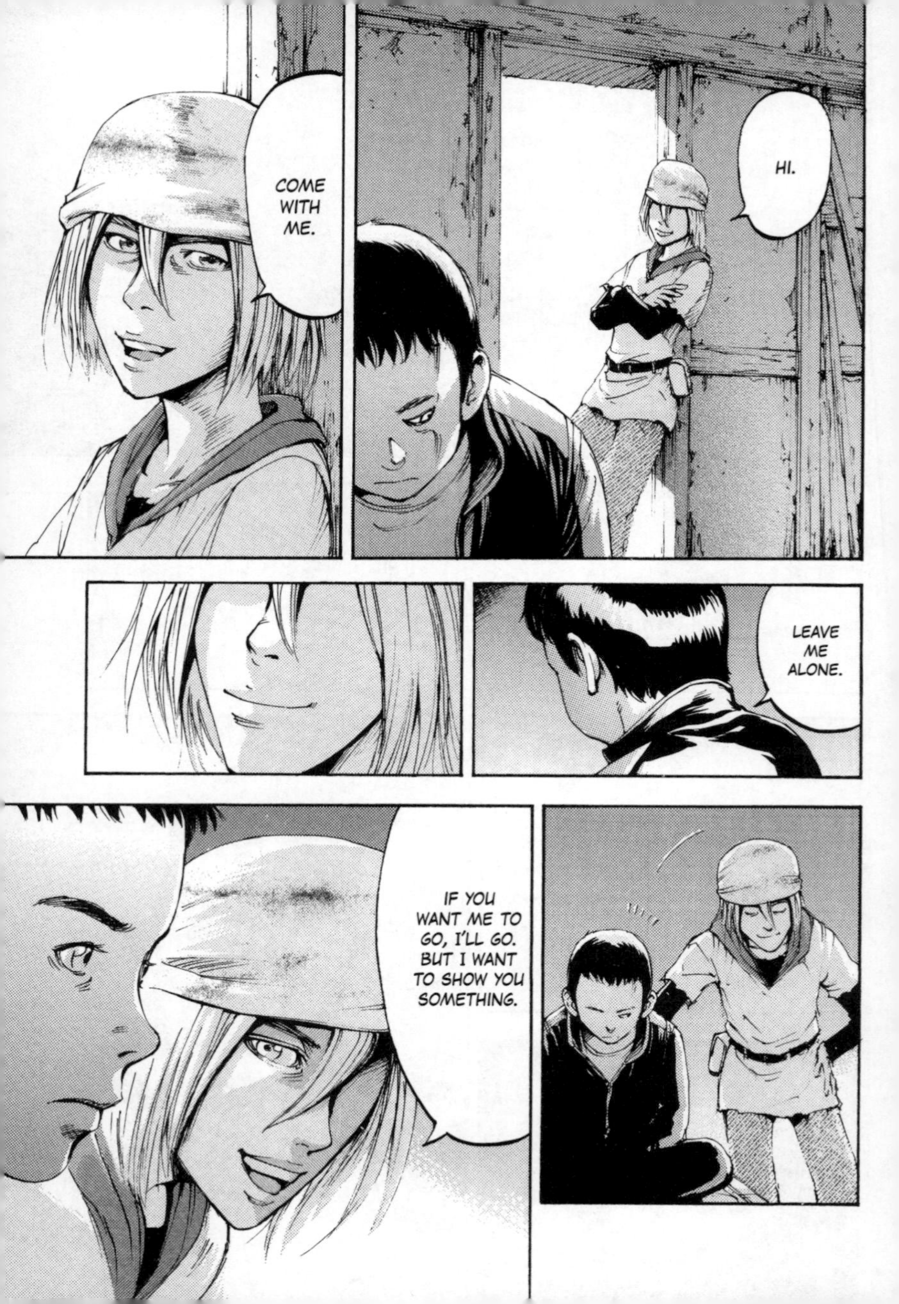
HI.
COME WITH ME.
LEAVE ME ALONE.
IF YOU WANT ME TO GO, I'LL GO. BUT I WANT TO SHOW YOU SOMETHING.

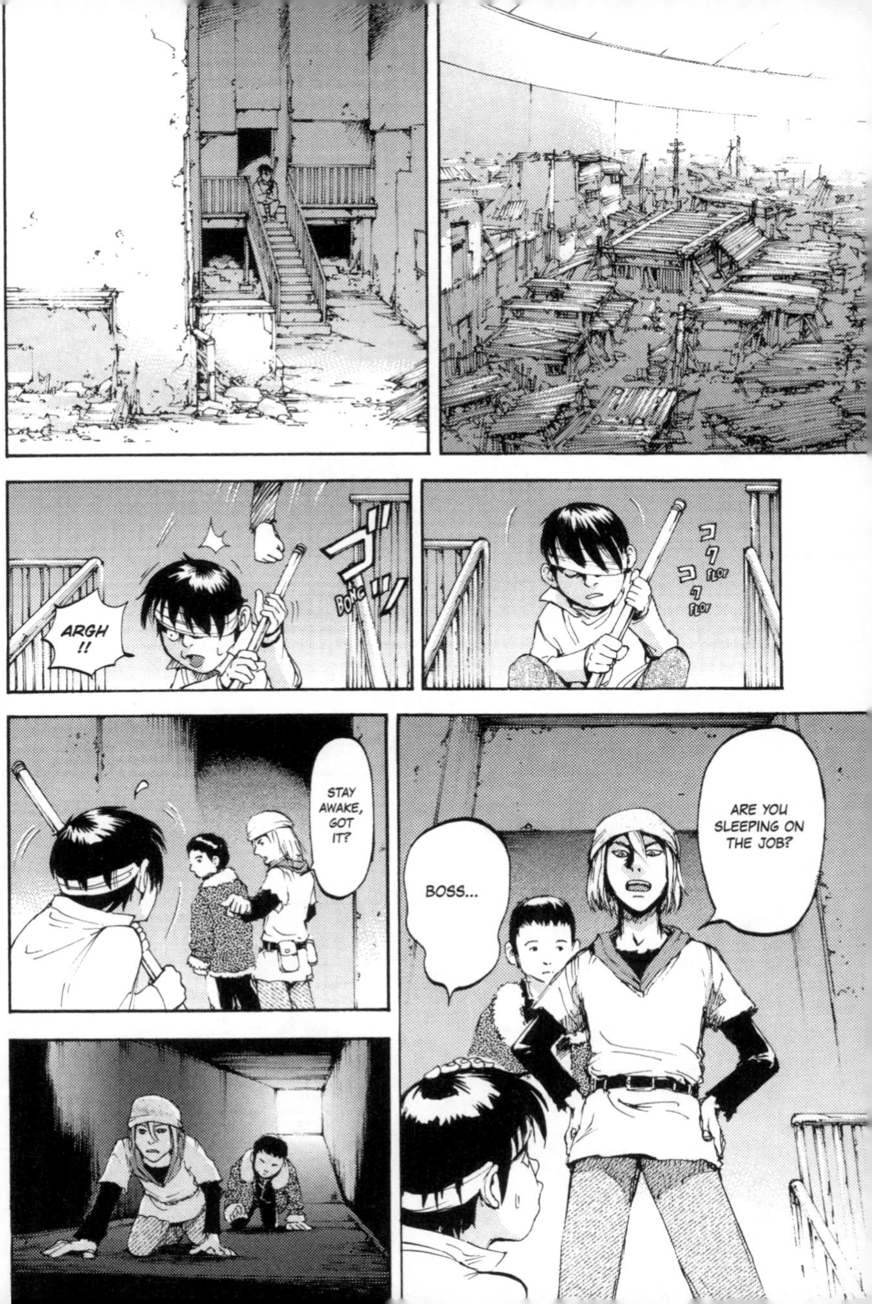

コク
FLOP
コク
FLOP
ゴッ
BONG
ARGH!!
ARE YOU SLEEPING ON THE JOB?
BOSS...
STAY AWAKE, GOT IT?

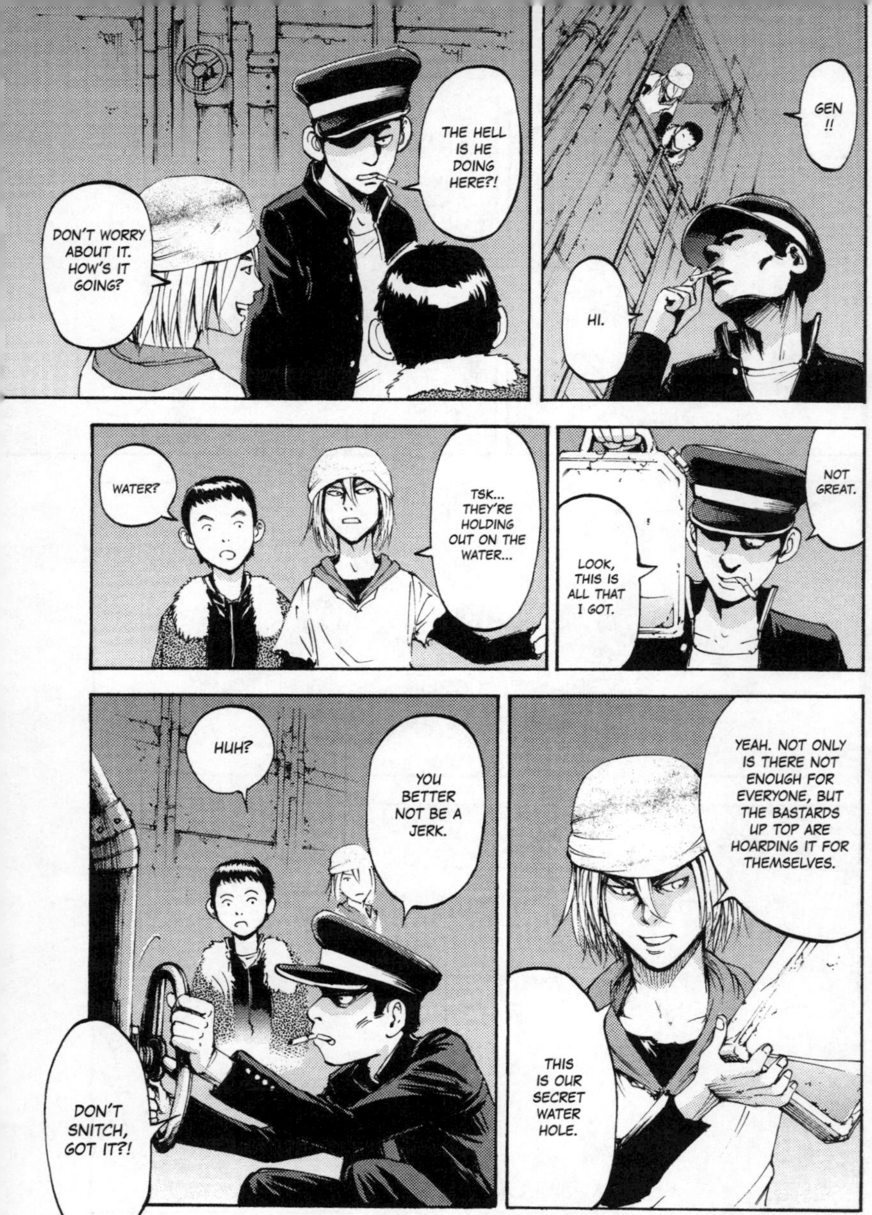
GEN !!
HI.
THE HELL IS HE DOING HERE?!
DON'T WORRY ABOUT IT. HOW'S IT GOING?
NOT GREAT.
LOOK, THIS IS ALL THAT I GOT.
TSK... THEY'RE HOLDING OUT ON THE WATER...
WATER?
YEAH. NOT ONLY IS THERE NOT ENOUGH FOR EVERYONE, BUT THE BASTARDS UP TOP ARE HOARDING IT FOR THEMSELVES.
THIS IS OUR SECRET WATER HOLE.
YOU BETTER NOT BE A JERK.
HUH?
DON'T SNITCH, GOT IT?!

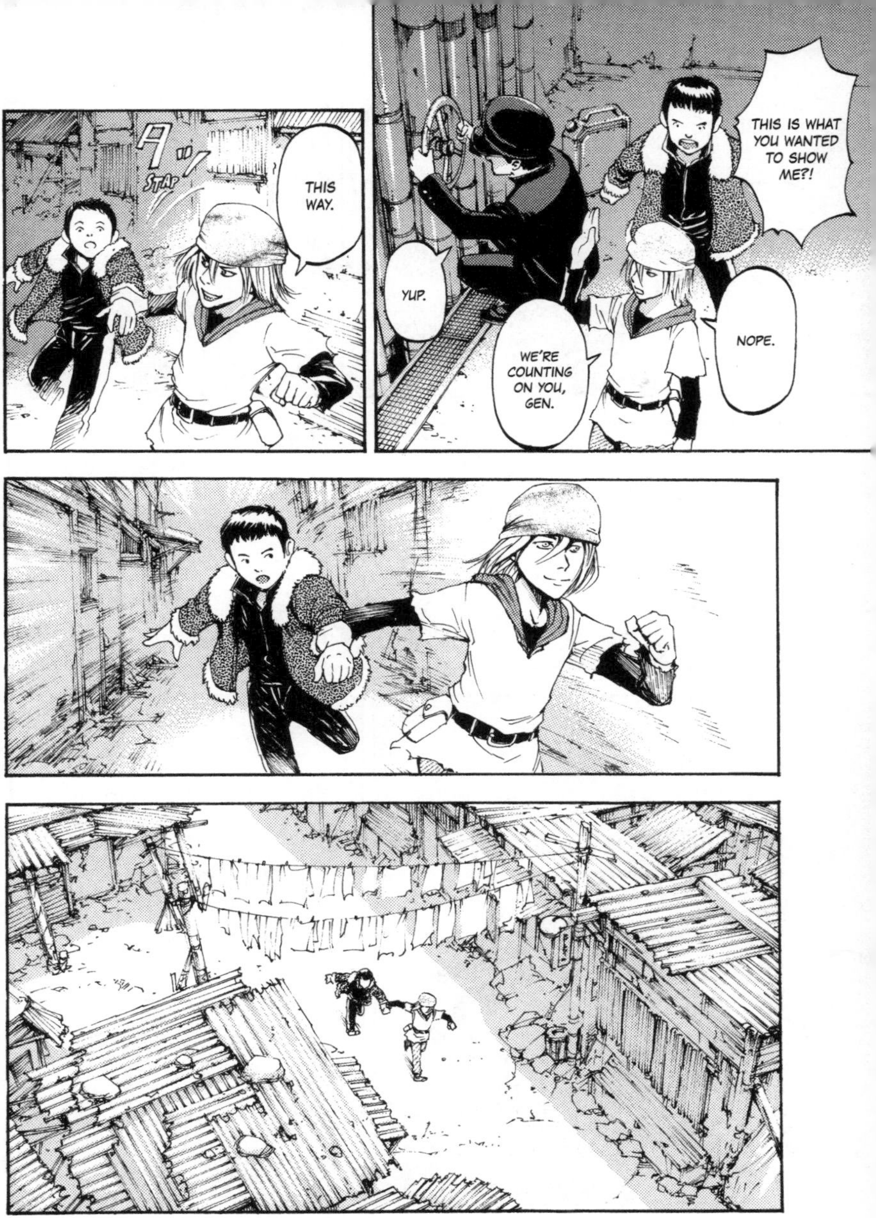
THIS IS WHAT YOU WANTED TO SHOW ME?!
NOPE.
WE'RE COUNTING ON YOU, GEN.
YUP.
STAP
THIS WAY.

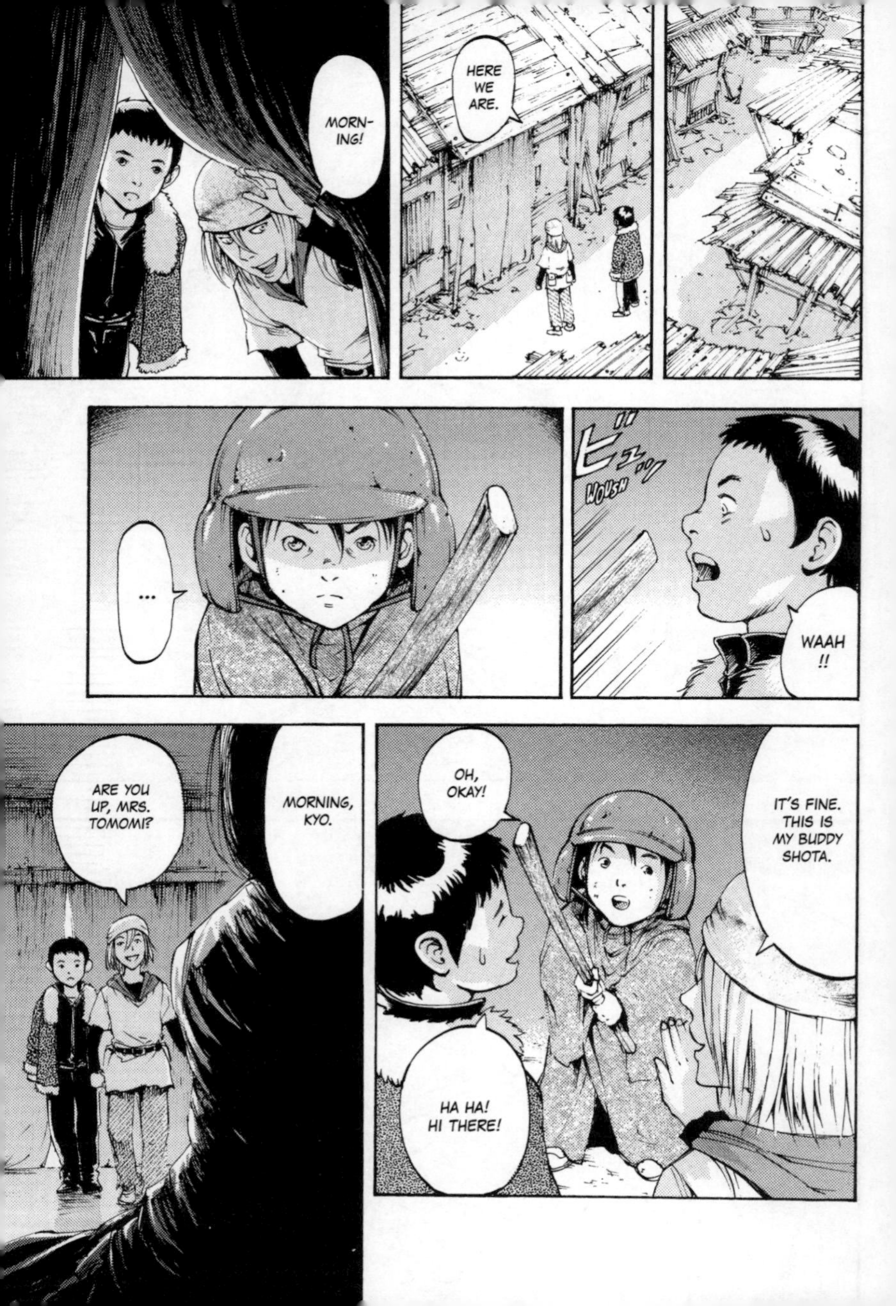
HERE WE ARE.
MORN-ING!
WOOSH
WAAH !!
...
IT'S FINE. THIS IS MY BUDDY SHOTA.
OH, OKAY!
HA HA! HI THERE!
MORNING, KYO.
ARE YOU UP, MRS. TOMOMI?

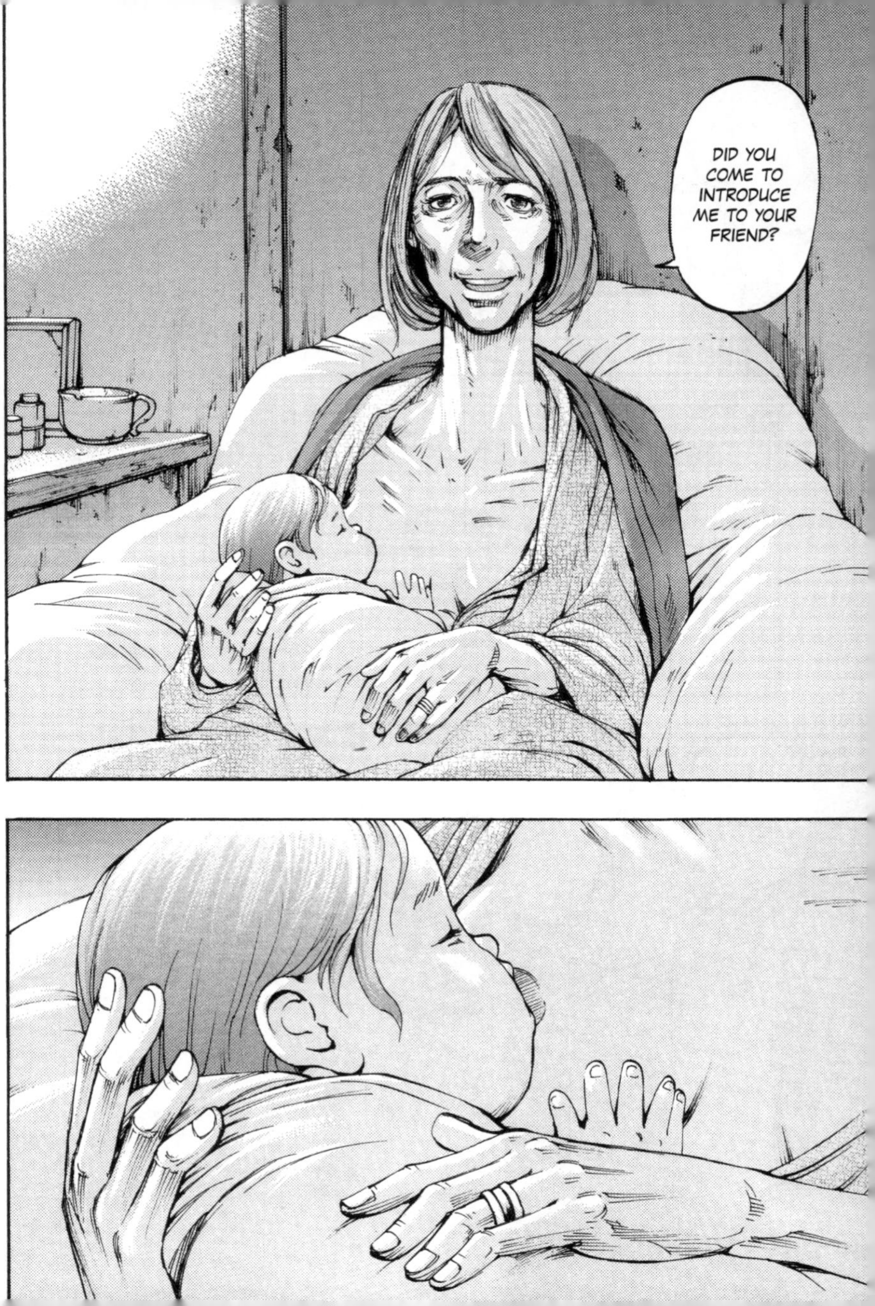
DID YOU COME TO INTRODUCE ME TO YOUR FRIEND?

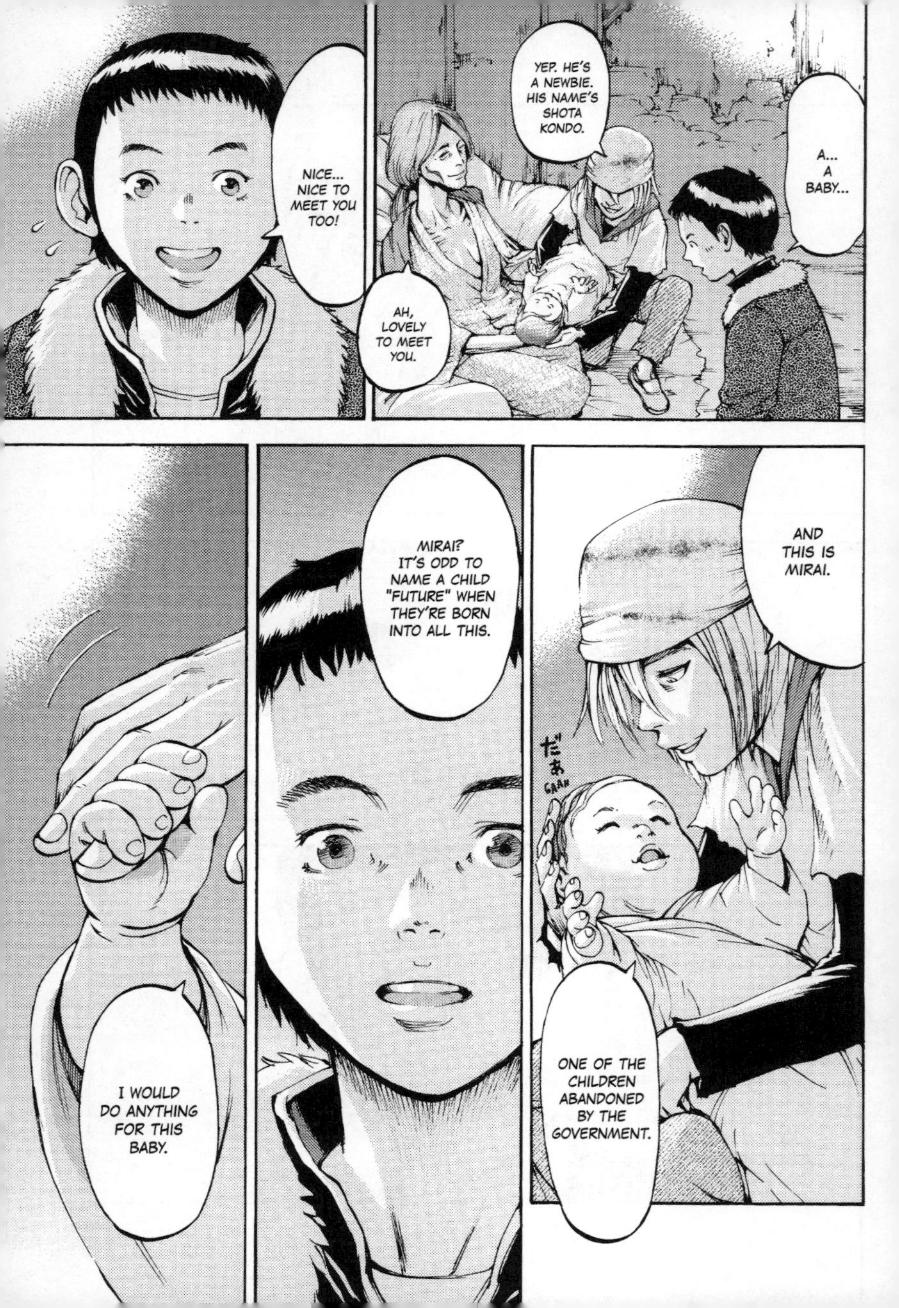
A... A BABY...
YEP. HE'S A NEWBIE. HIS NAME'S SHOTA KONDO.
AH, LOVELY TO MEET YOU.
NICE... NICE TO MEET YOU TOO!
AND THIS IS MIRAI.
だあ
GAAH
ONE OF THE CHILDREN ABANDONED BY THE GOVERNMENT.
MIRAI? IT'S ODD TO NAME A CHILD "FUTURE" WHEN THEY'RE BORN INTO ALL THIS.
I WOULD DO ANYTHING FOR THIS BABY.

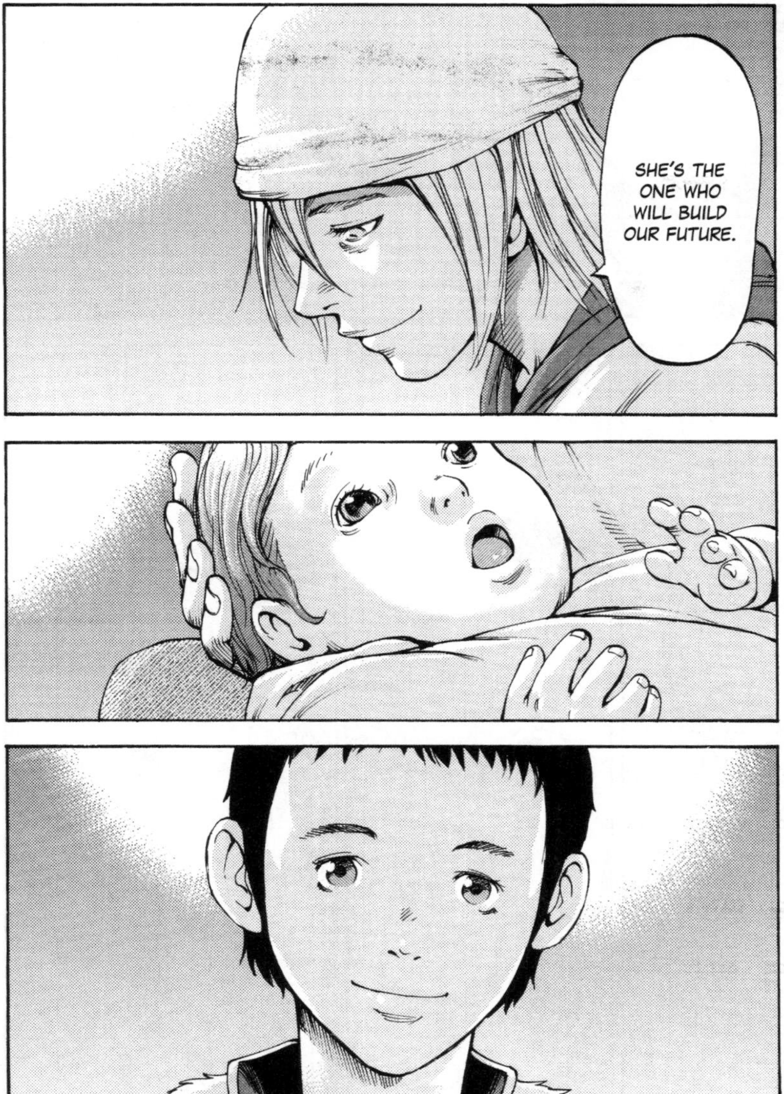
SHE'S THE ONE WHO WILL BUILD OUR FUTURE.

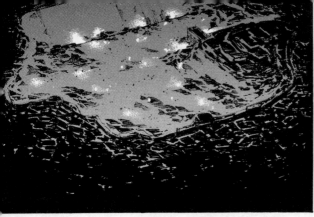

NUMBER 701! YOU HAVE A VISITOR!

YOU GOT THREE MINUTES, NO MORE.

...

701

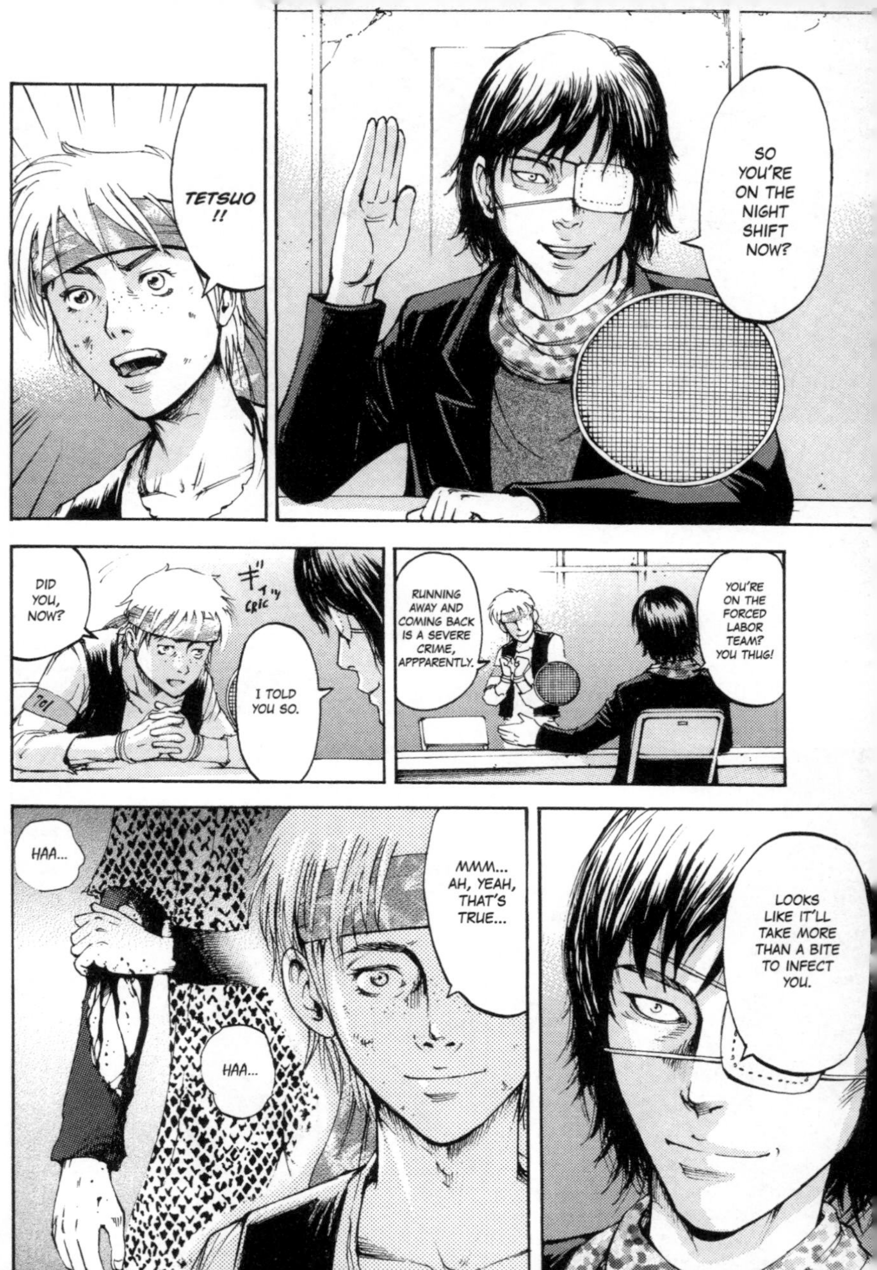
SO YOU'RE ON THE NIGHT SHIFT NOW?
TETSUO !!
YOU'RE ON THE FORCED LABOR TEAM? YOU THUG!
RUNNING AWAY AND COMING BACK IS A SEVERE CRIME, APPPARENTLY.
CRIC
I TOLD YOU SO.
DID YOU, NOW?
LOOKS LIKE IT'LL TAKE MORE THAN A BITE TO INFECT YOU.
MMM... AH, YEAH, THAT'S TRUE...
HAA...
HAA...

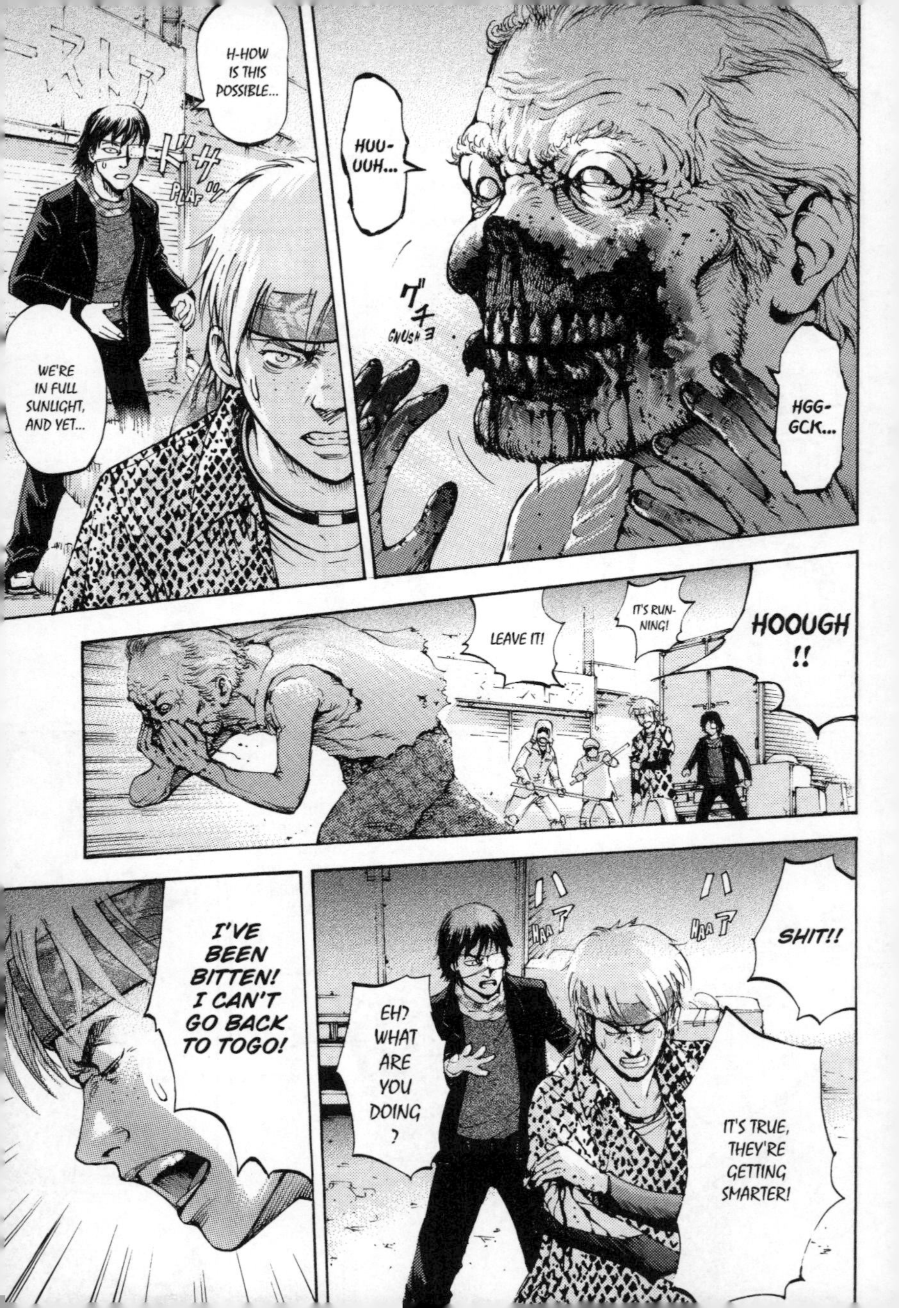
HUU-UUH...
GNUSH
HGG-GCK...
H-HOW IS THIS POSSIBLE...
PLAF
WE'RE IN FULL SUNLIGHT, AND YET...
HOOUGH!!
IT'S RUN-NING!
LEAVE IT!
SHIT!!
HAA
HAA
EH? WHAT ARE YOU DOING?
IT'S TRUE, THEY'RE GETTING SMARTER!
I'VE BEEN BITTEN! I CAN'T GO BACK TO TOGO!

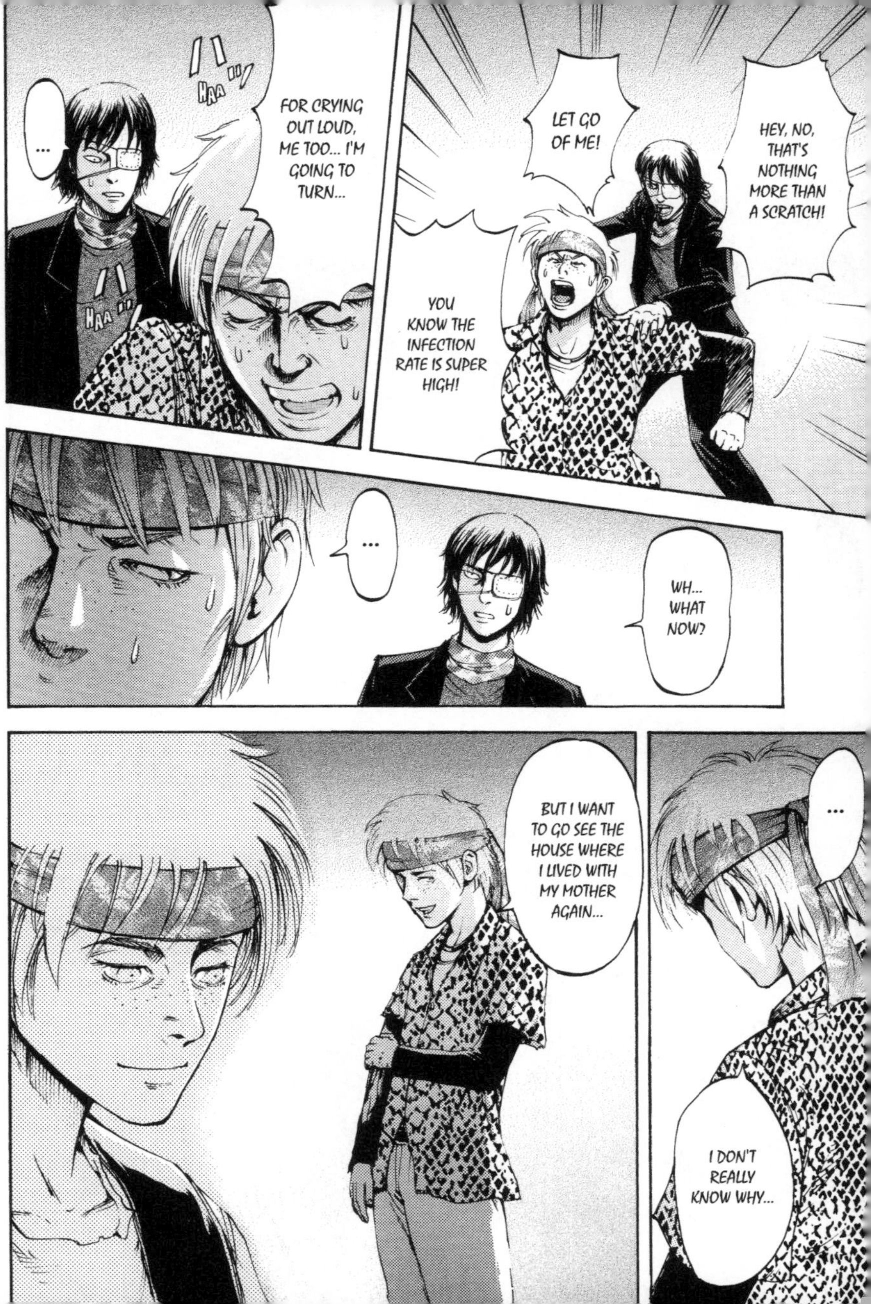
HEY, NO, THAT'S NOTHING MORE THAN A SCRATCH!
LET GO OF ME!
YOU KNOW THE INFECTION RATE IS SUPER HIGH!
HAA
FOR CRYING OUT LOUD, ME TOO... I'M GOING TO TURN...
...
HAA
WH... WHAT NOW?
...
...
I DON'T REALLY KNOW WHY...
BUT I WANT TO GO SEE THE HOUSE WHERE I LIVED WITH MY MOTHER AGAIN...

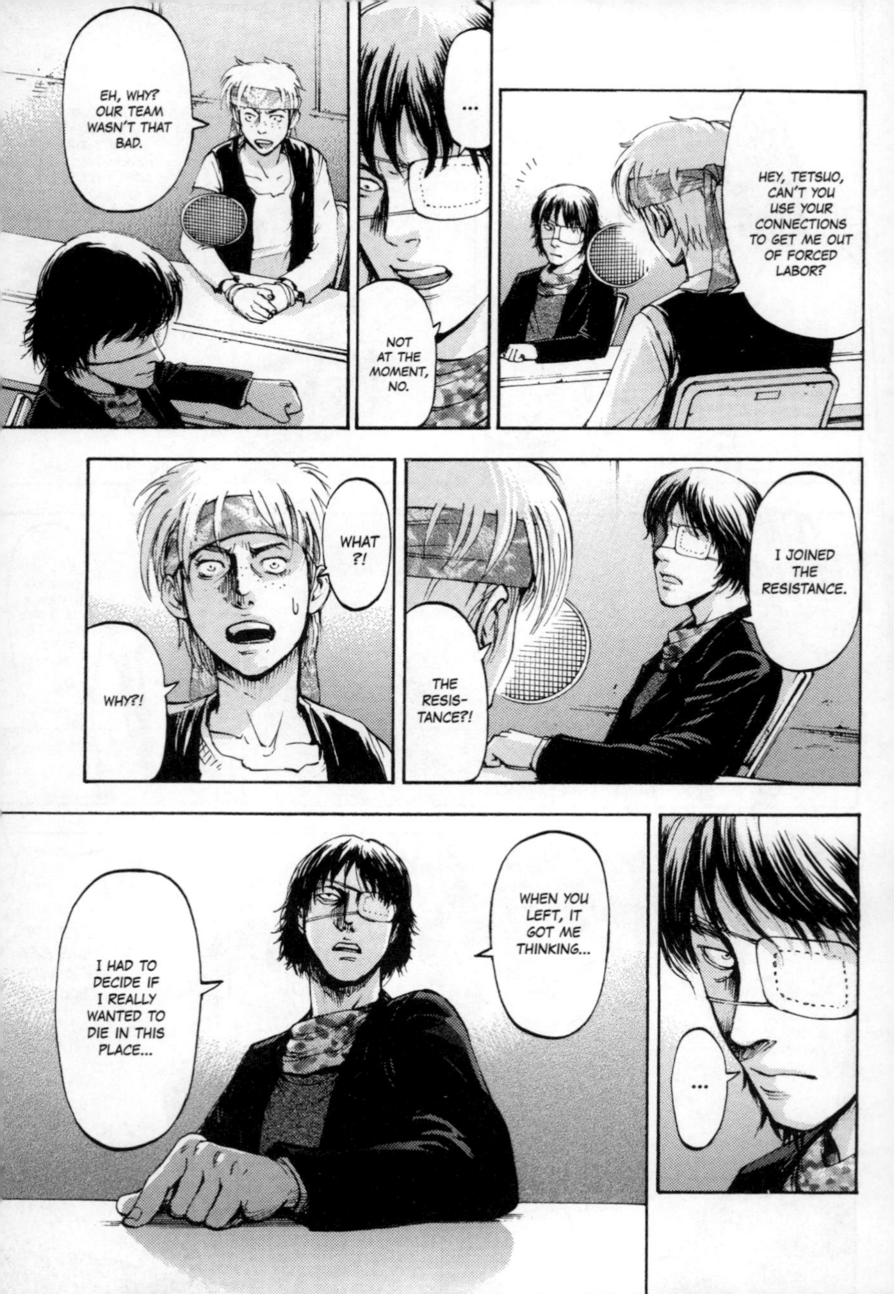
HEY, TETSUO, CAN'T YOU USE YOUR CONNECTIONS TO GET ME OUT OF FORCED LABOR?
...
NOT AT THE MOMENT, NO.
EH, WHY? OUR TEAM WASN'T THAT BAD.
I JOINED THE RESISTANCE.
THE RESIS-TANCE?!
WHAT?!
WHY?!
...
WHEN YOU LEFT, IT GOT ME THINKING...
I HAD TO DECIDE IF I REALLY WANTED TO DIE IN THIS PLACE...

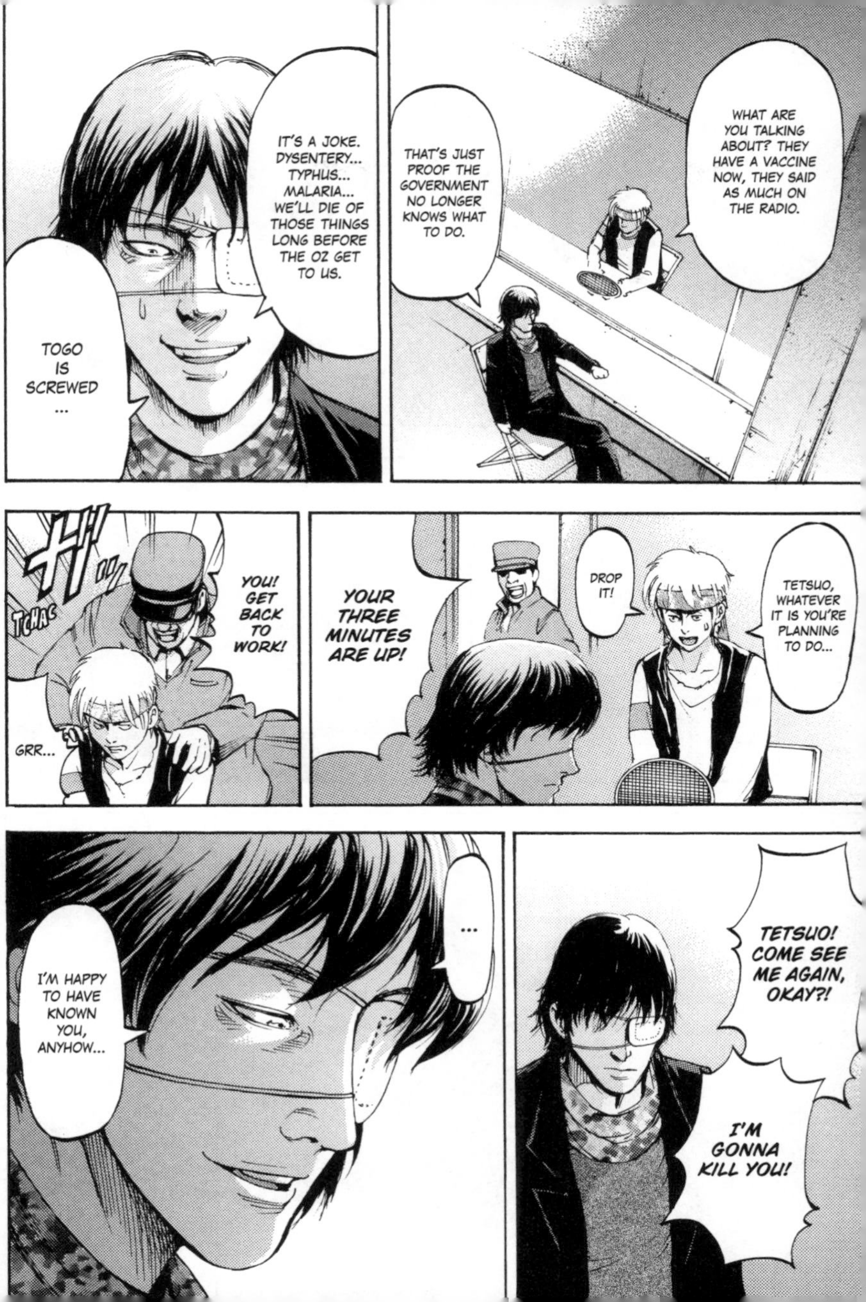
WHAT ARE YOU TALKING ABOUT? THEY HAVE A VACCINE NOW, THEY SAID AS MUCH ON THE RADIO.
THAT'S JUST PROOF THE GOVERNMENT NO LONGER KNOWS WHAT TO DO.
IT'S A JOKE. DYSENTERY... TYPHUS... MALARIA... WE'LL DIE OF THOSE THINGS LONG BEFORE THE OZ GET TO US.
TOGO IS SCREWED ...
TETSUO, WHATEVER IT IS YOU'RE PLANNING TO DO...
DROP IT!
YOUR THREE MINUTES ARE UP!
YOU! GET BACK TO WORK!
TCHAC
GRR...
TETSUO! COME SEE ME AGAIN, OKAY?!
I'M GONNA KILL YOU!
...
I'M HAPPY TO HAVE KNOWN YOU, ANYHOW...

YEAH, I'M ABLE TO DO IT, THANKS TO THE GAS MASK...
SO MUCH BETTER ...
I WAS WORRIED ABOUT YOU, YOU LEFT TOGO IN A BAD STATE...
LISTEN UP, EVERY-ONE.
I HAVE RECEIVED WORD FROM A FORMER COMRADE...

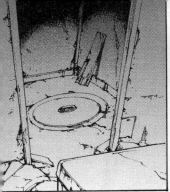

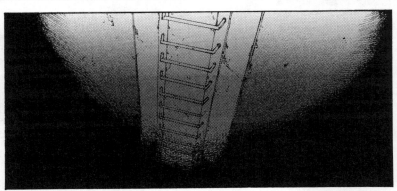

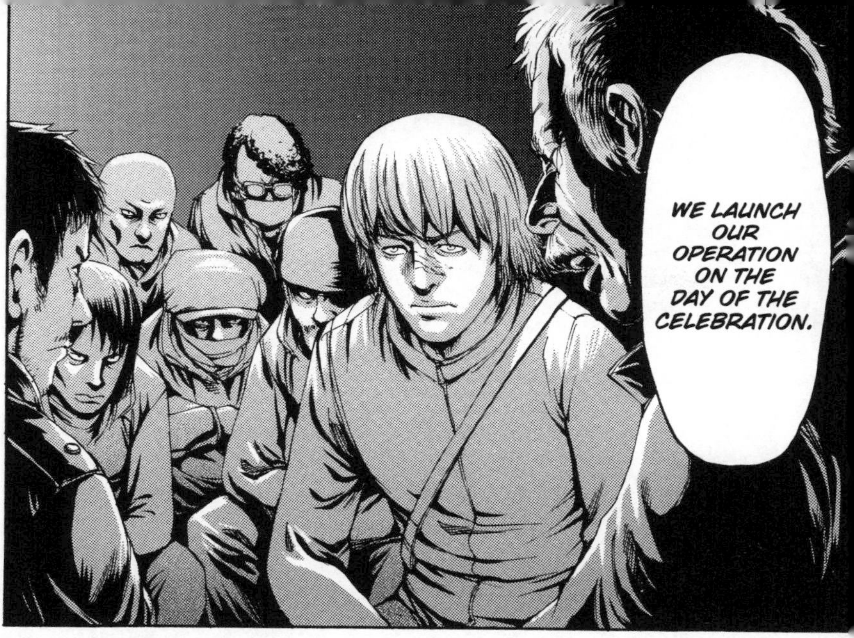
WE LAUNCH OUR OPERATION ON THE DAY OF THE CELEBRATION.
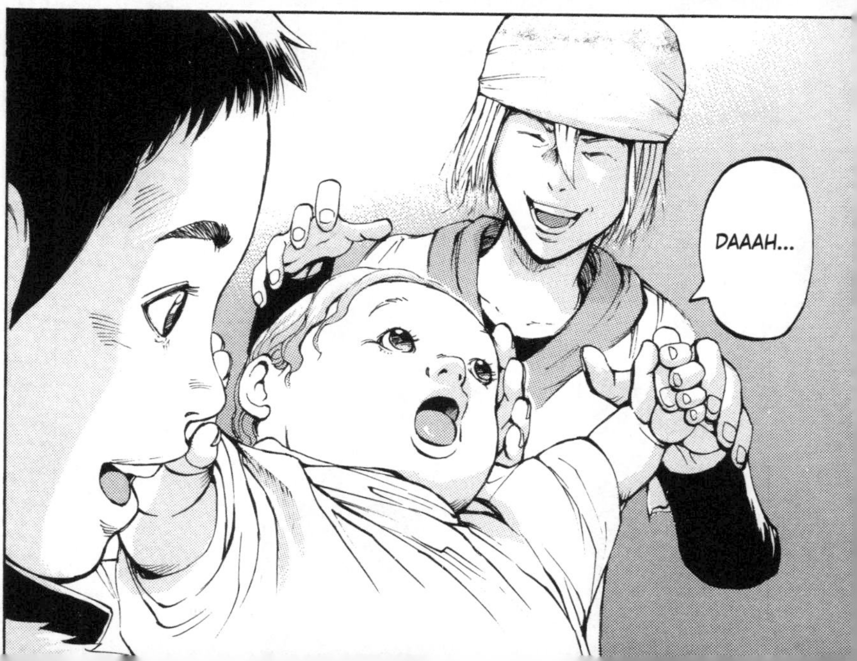
DAAAH...

CHAPTER 7

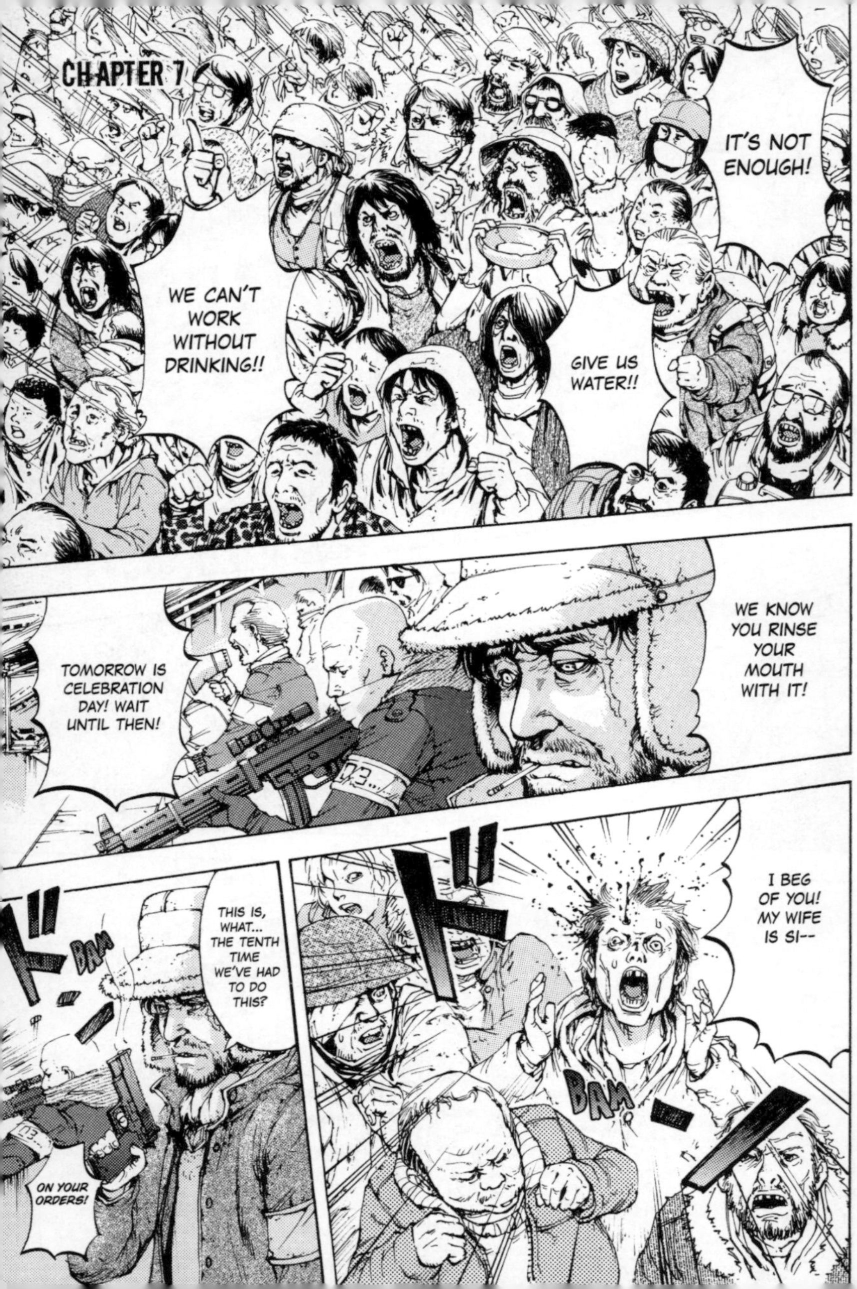
IT'S NOT ENOUGH!
GIVE US WATER!!
WE CAN'T WORK WITHOUT DRINKING!!
WE KNOW YOU RINSE YOUR MOUTH WITH IT!
TOMORROW IS CELEBRATION DAY! WAIT UNTIL THEN!
I BEG OF YOU! MY WIFE IS SI--
BAM--
THIS IS, WHAT... THE TENTH TIME WE'VE HAD TO DO THIS?
BAM
ON YOUR ORDERS!

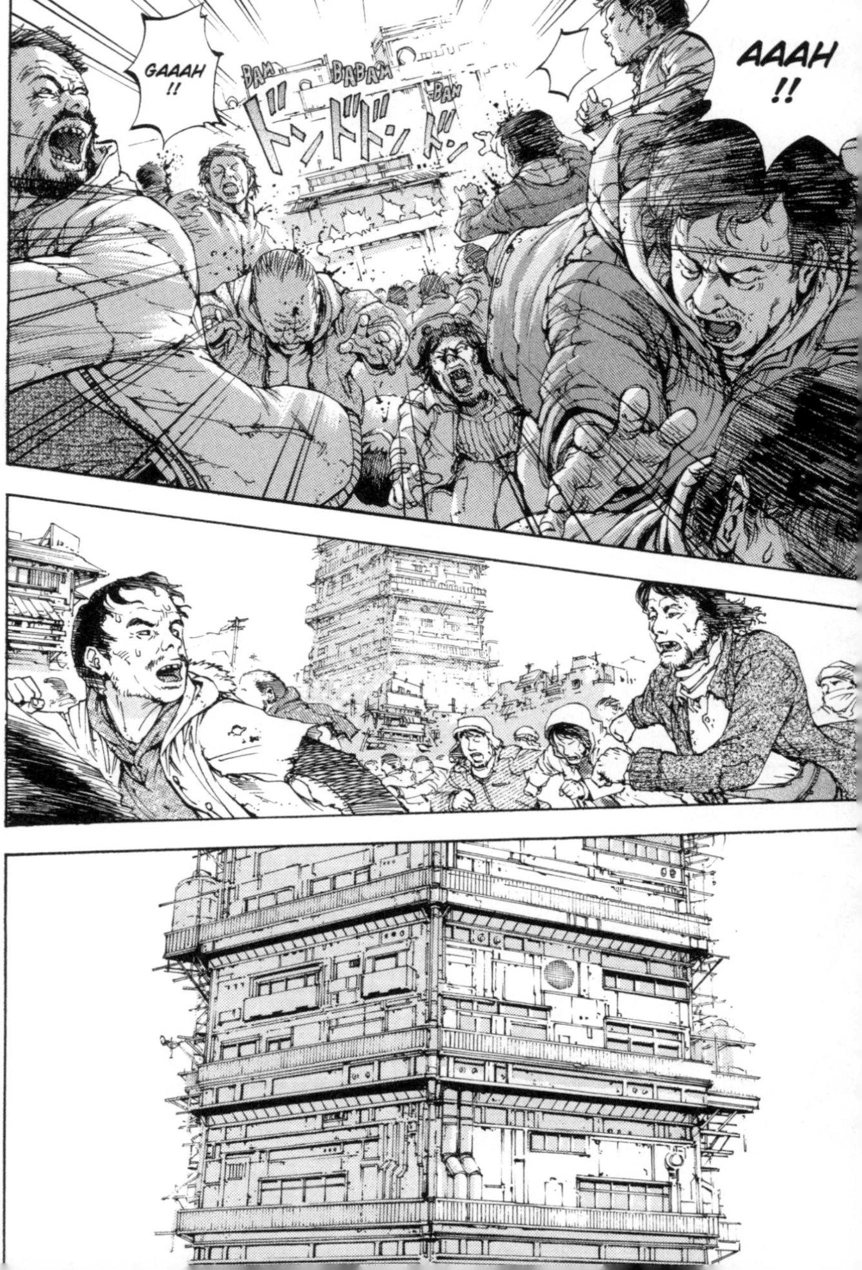
AAAH !!
BAM
BABAM
BAM
GAAAH !!

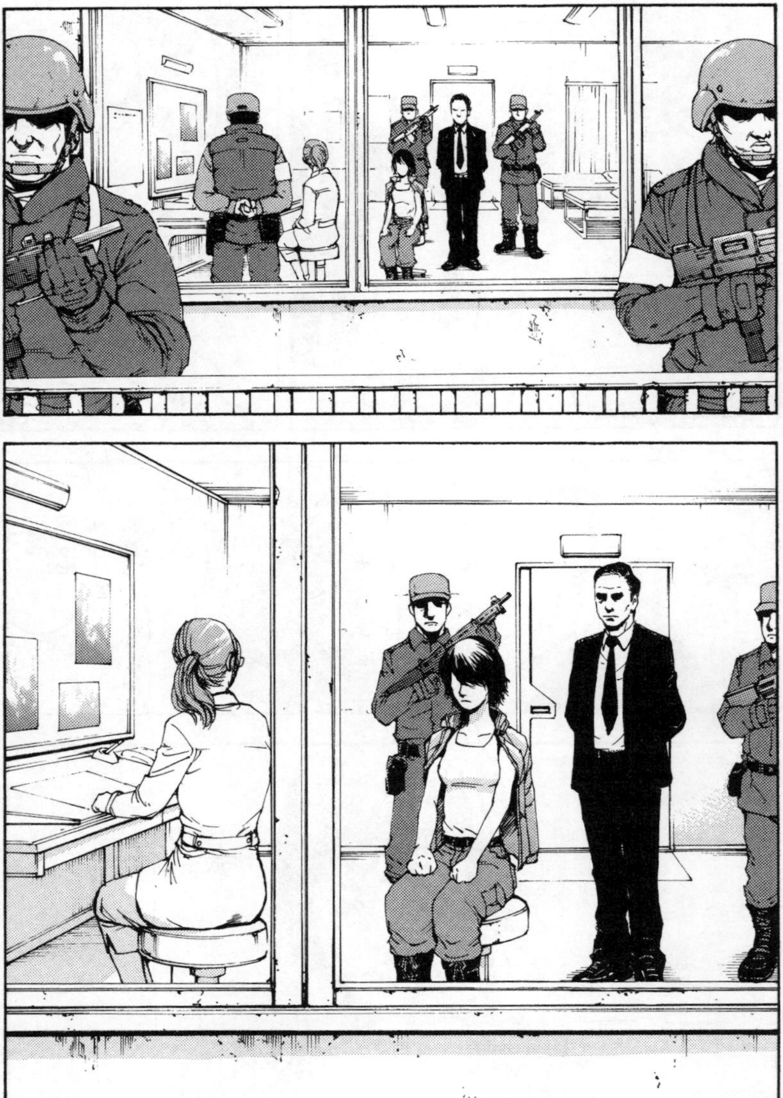

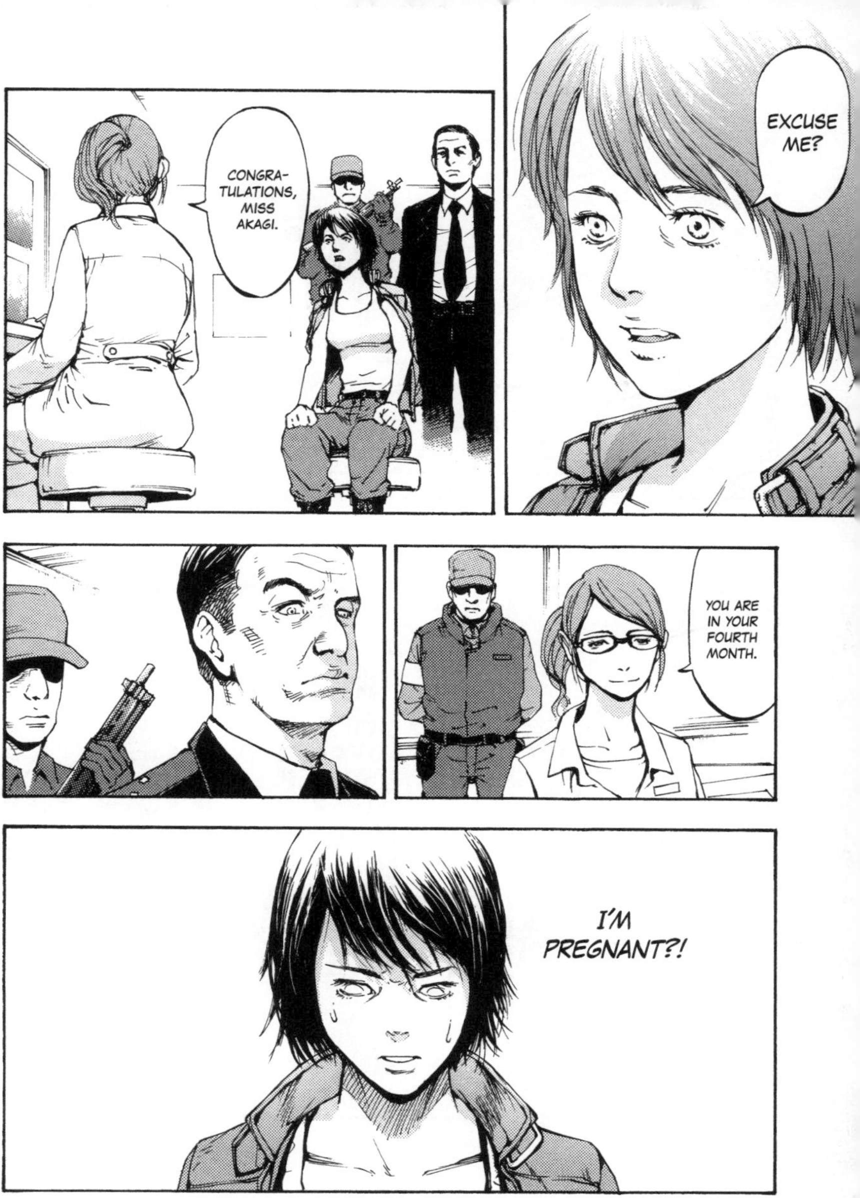
CONGRATULATIONS, MISS AKAGI.
EXCUSE ME?
YOU ARE IN YOUR FOURTH MONTH.
I'M PREGNANT?!

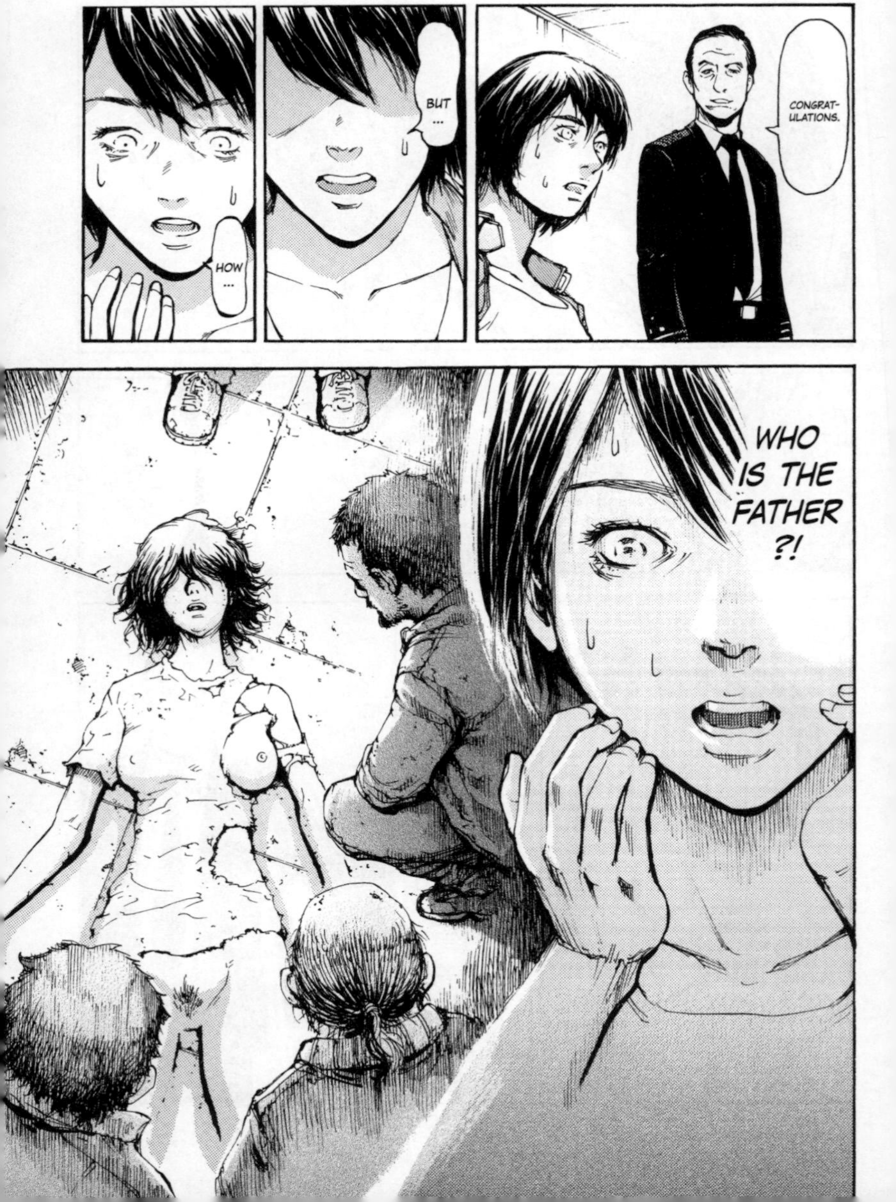
CONGRAT-ULATIONS.
BUT ...
HOW ...
WHO IS THE FATHER ?!

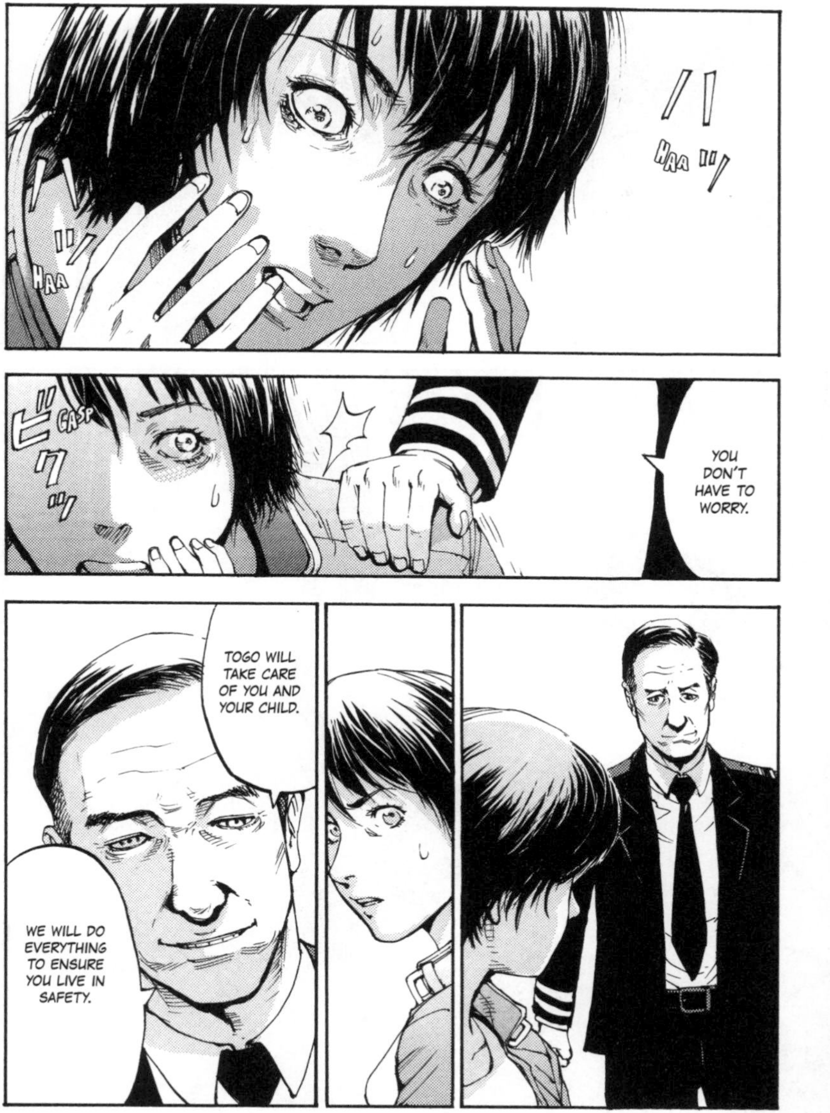
HAA
HAA
YOU DON'T HAVE TO WORRY.
GASP
TOGO WILL TAKE CARE OF YOU AND YOUR CHILD.
WE WILL DO EVERYTHING TO ENSURE YOU LIVE IN SAFETY.

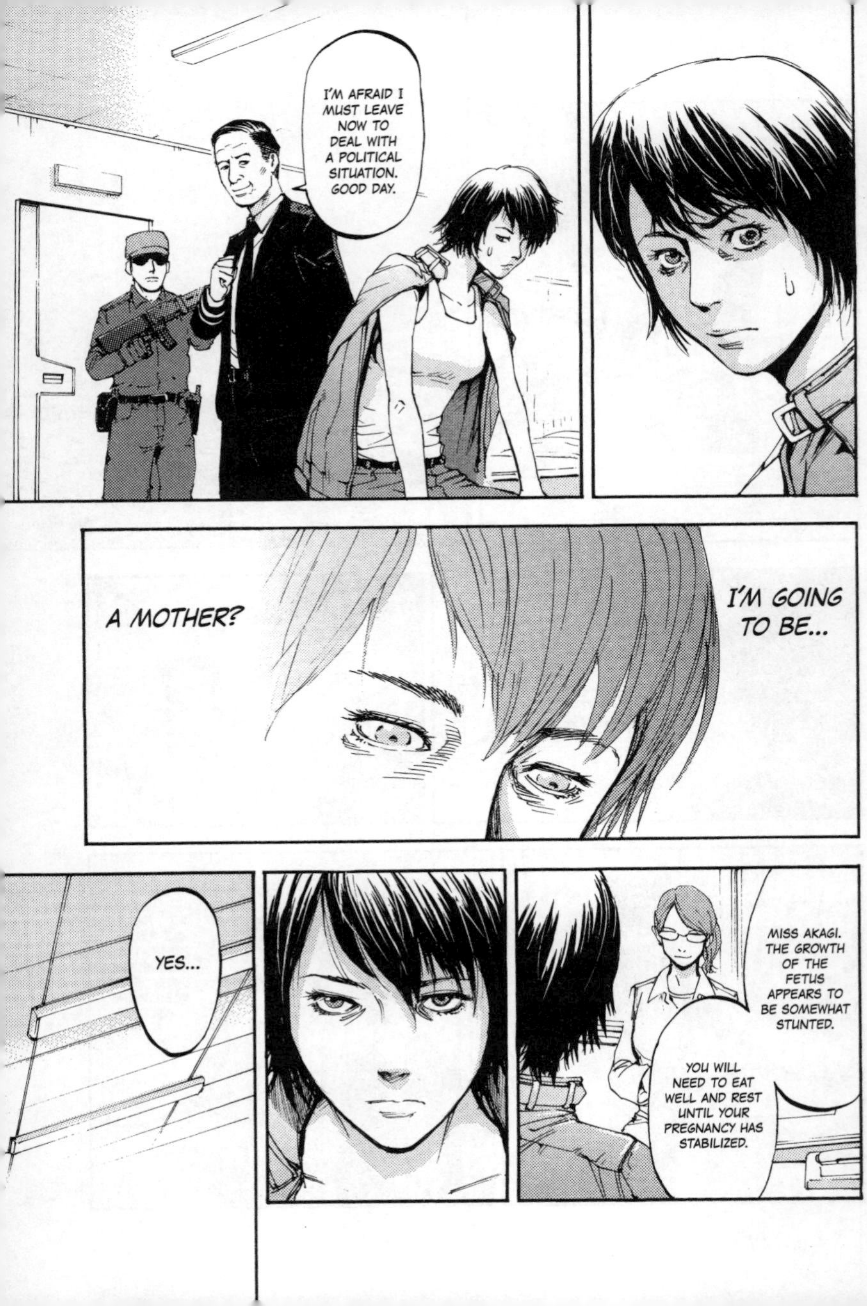
I'M AFRAID I MUST LEAVE NOW TO DEAL WITH A POLITICAL SITUATION. GOOD DAY.
I'M GOING TO BE...
A MOTHER?
MISS AKAGI. THE GROWTH OF THE FETUS APPEARS TO BE SOMEWHAT STUNTED.
YOU WILL NEED TO EAT WELL AND REST UNTIL YOUR PREGNANCY HAS STABILIZED.
YES...

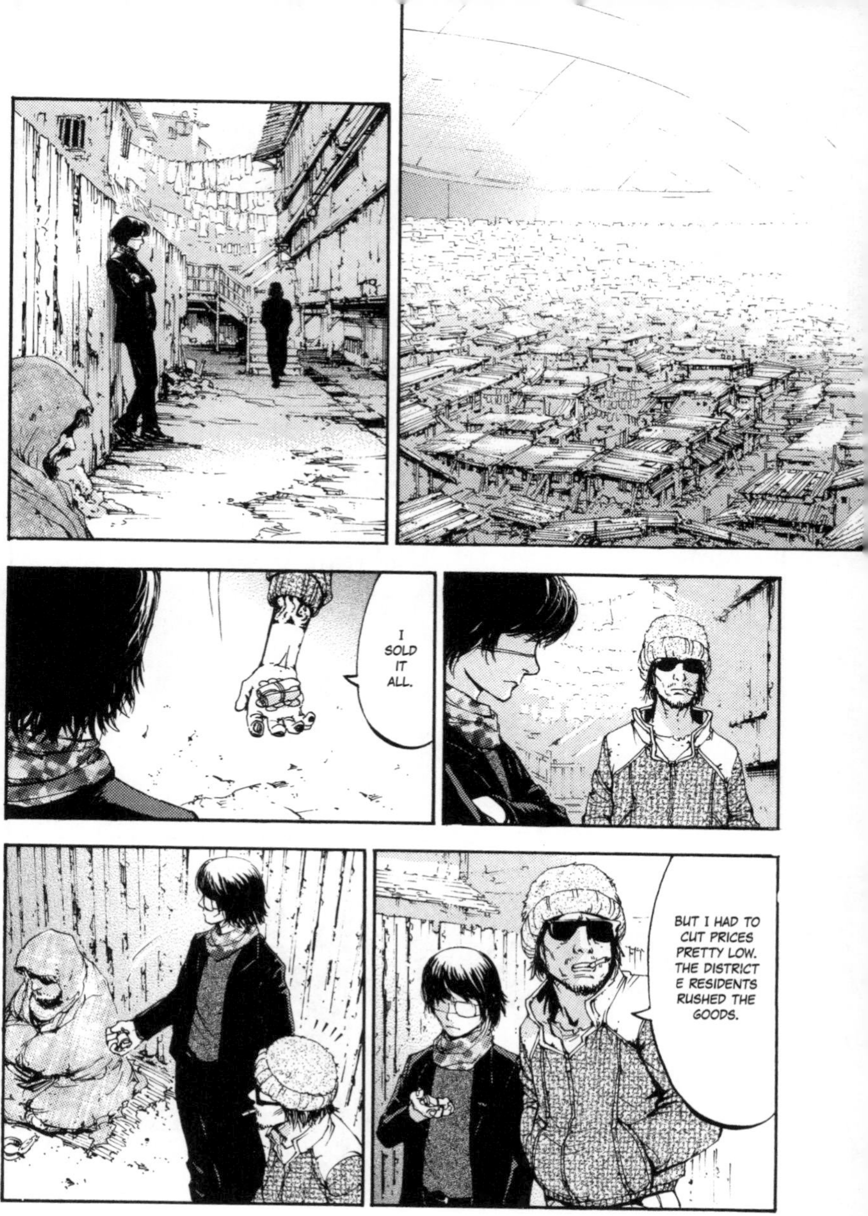
I SOLD IT ALL.
BUT I HAD TO CUT PRICES PRETTY LOW. THE DISTRICT E RESIDENTS RUSHED THE GOODS.

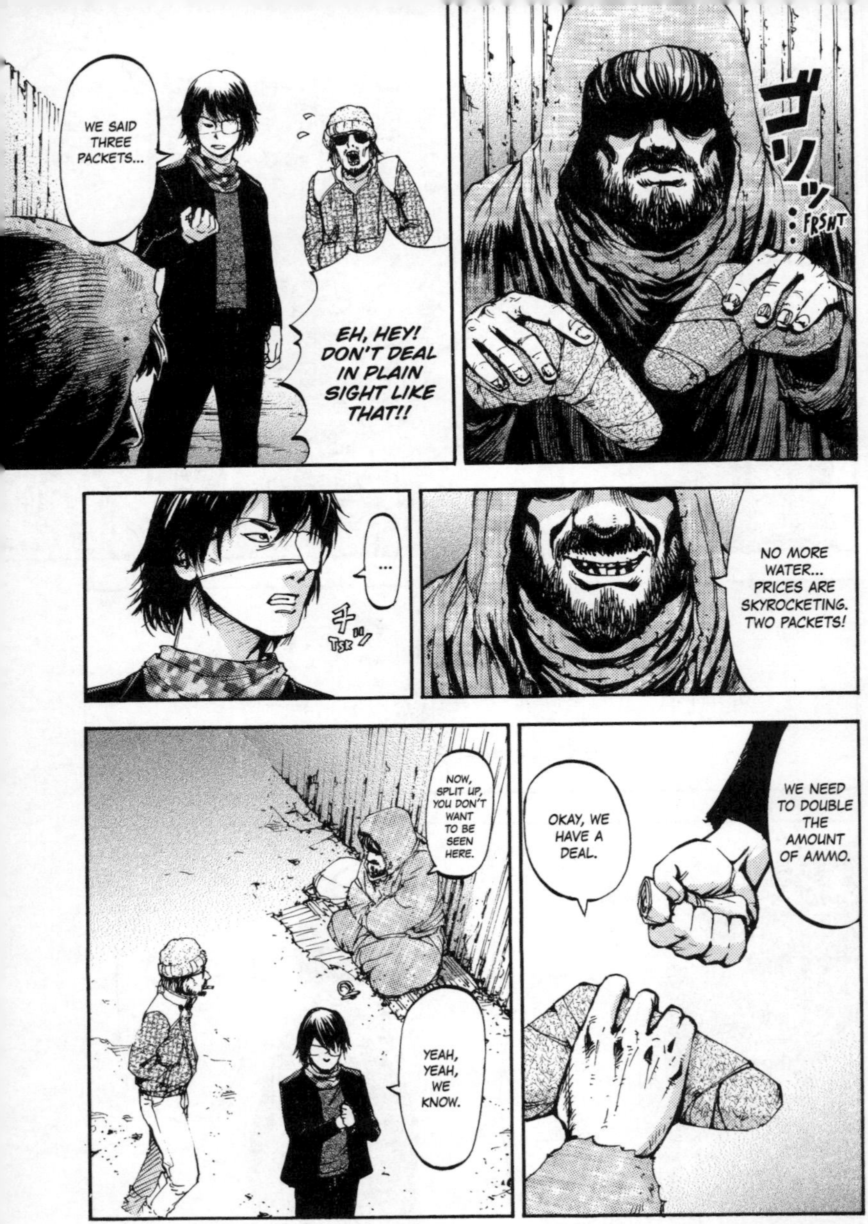
ゴソッ
FRSHT
WE SAID THREE PACKETS...
EH, HEY! DON'T DEAL IN PLAIN SIGHT LIKE THAT!!
NO MORE WATER... PRICES ARE SKYROCKETING. TWO PACKETS!
...
チッ
TSK
WE NEED TO DOUBLE THE AMOUNT OF AMMO.
OKAY, WE HAVE A DEAL.
NOW, SPLIT UP, YOU DON'T WANT TO BE SEEN HERE.
YEAH, YEAH, WE KNOW.

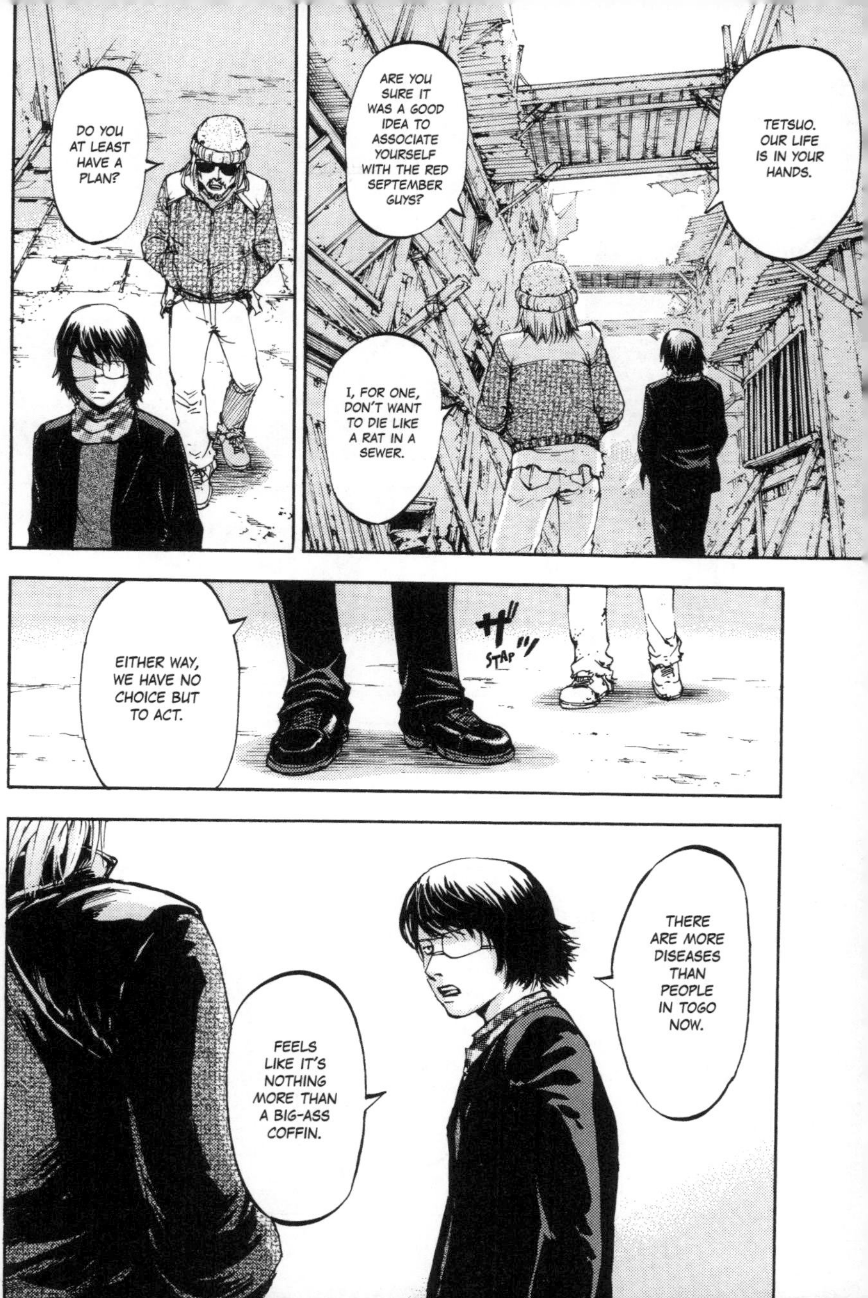
TETSUO. OUR LIFE IS IN YOUR HANDS.
ARE YOU SURE IT WAS A GOOD IDEA TO ASSOCIATE YOURSELF WITH THE RED SEPTEMBER GUYS?
I, FOR ONE, DON'T WANT TO DIE LIKE A RAT IN A SEWER.
DO YOU AT LEAST HAVE A PLAN?
STAP
EITHER WAY, WE HAVE NO CHOICE BUT TO ACT.
THERE ARE MORE DISEASES THAN PEOPLE IN TOGO NOW.
FEELS LIKE IT'S NOTHING MORE THAN A BIG-ASS COFFIN.

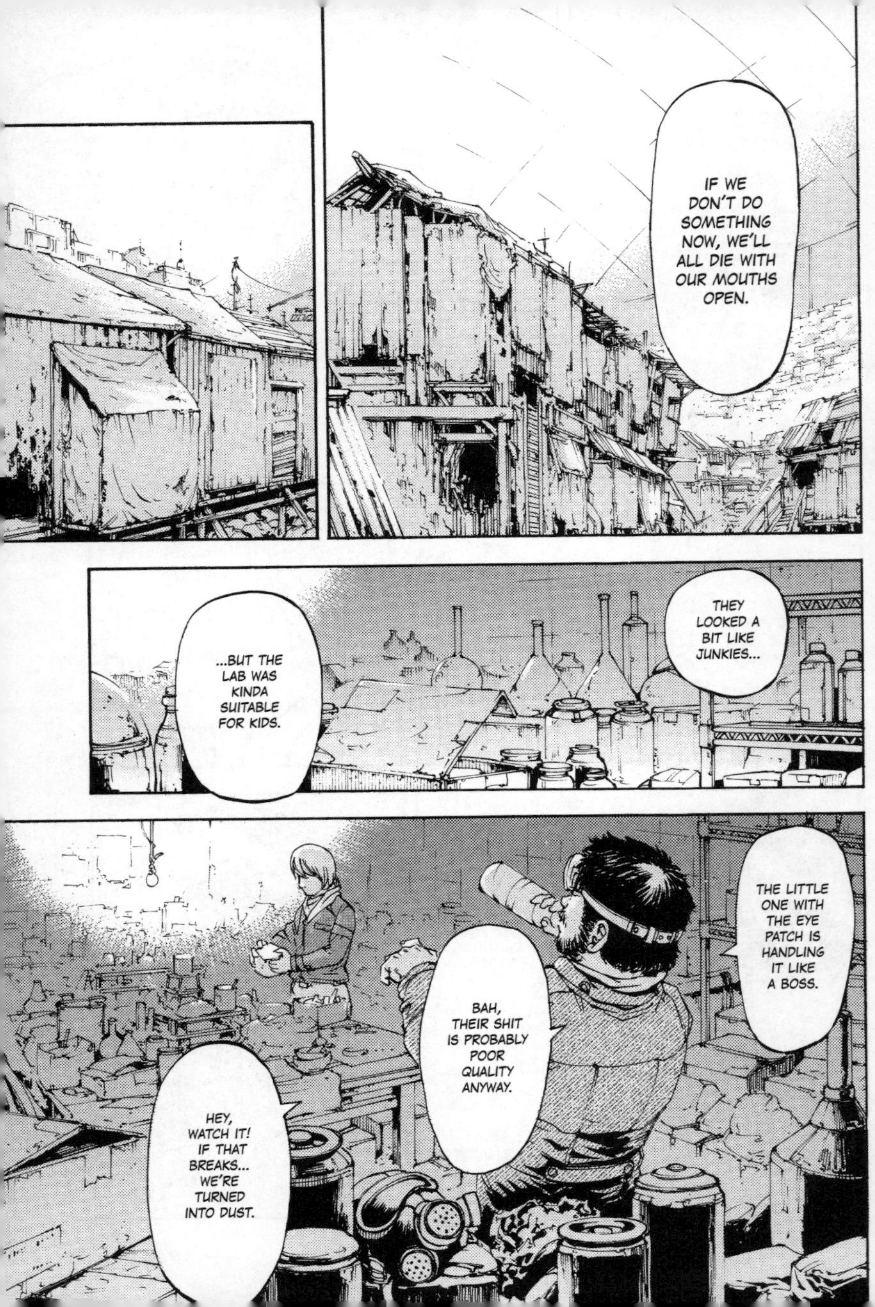
IF WE DON'T DO SOMETHING NOW, WE'LL ALL DIE WITH OUR MOUTHS OPEN.
THEY LOOKED A BIT LIKE JUNKIES...
...BUT THE LAB WAS KINDA SUITABLE FOR KIDS.
THE LITTLE ONE WITH THE EYE PATCH IS HANDLING IT LIKE A BOSS.
BAH, THEIR SHIT IS PROBABLY POOR QUALITY ANYWAY.
HEY, WATCH IT! IF THAT BREAKS... WE'RE TURNED INTO DUST.

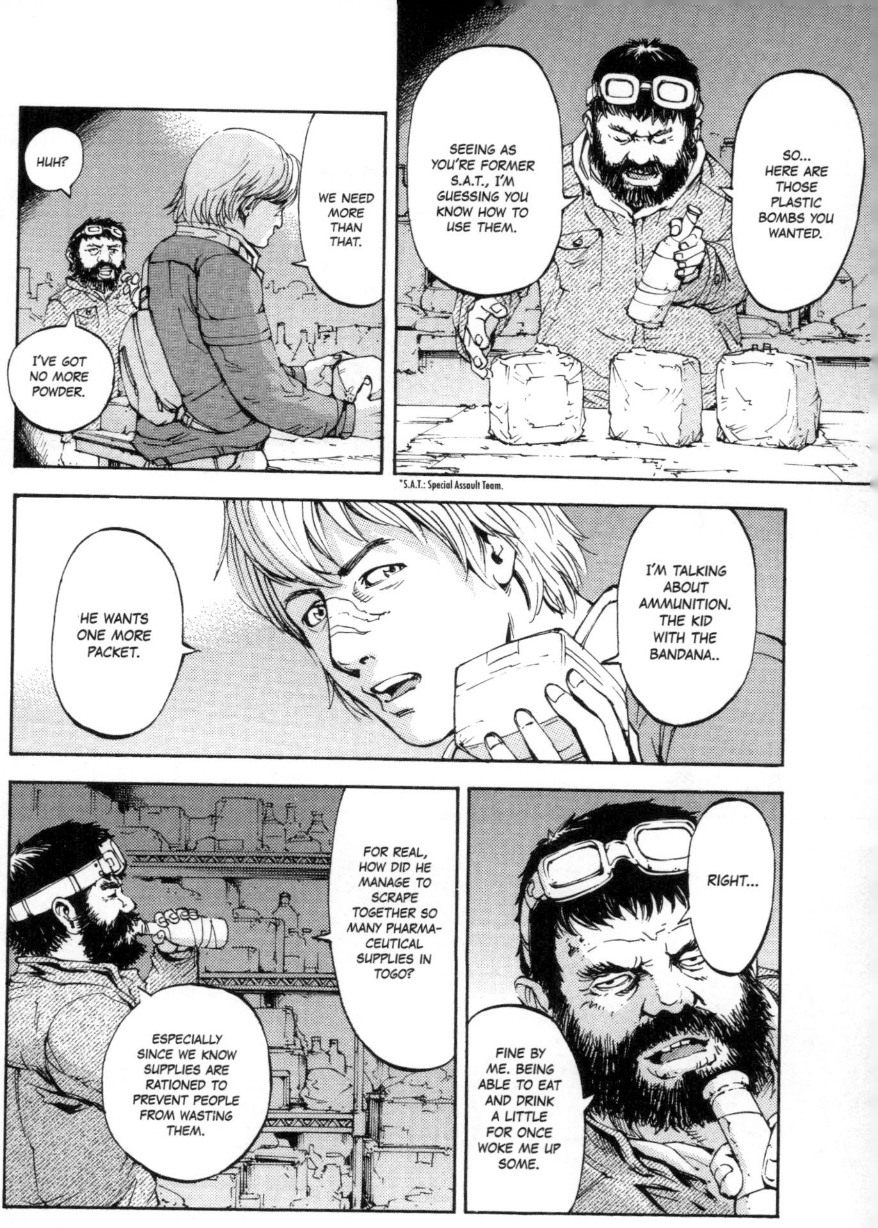
SO... HERE ARE THOSE PLASTIC BOMBS YOU WANTED.
SEEING AS YOU'RE FORMER S.A.T., I'M GUESSING YOU KNOW HOW TO USE THEM.
WE NEED MORE THAN THAT.
HUH?
I'VE GOT NO MORE POWDER.
I'M TALKING ABOUT AMMUNITION. THE KID WITH THE BANDANA..
HE WANTS ONE MORE PACKET.
RIGHT...
FINE BY ME. BEING ABLE TO EAT AND DRINK A LITTLE FOR ONCE WOKE ME UP SOME.
FOR REAL, HOW DID HE MANAGE TO SCRAPE TOGETHER SO MANY PHARMA-CEUTICAL SUPPLIES IN TOGO?
ESPECIALLY SINCE WE KNOW SUPPLIES ARE RATIONED TO PREVENT PEOPLE FROM WASTING THEM.

*S.A.T.: Special Assault Team.

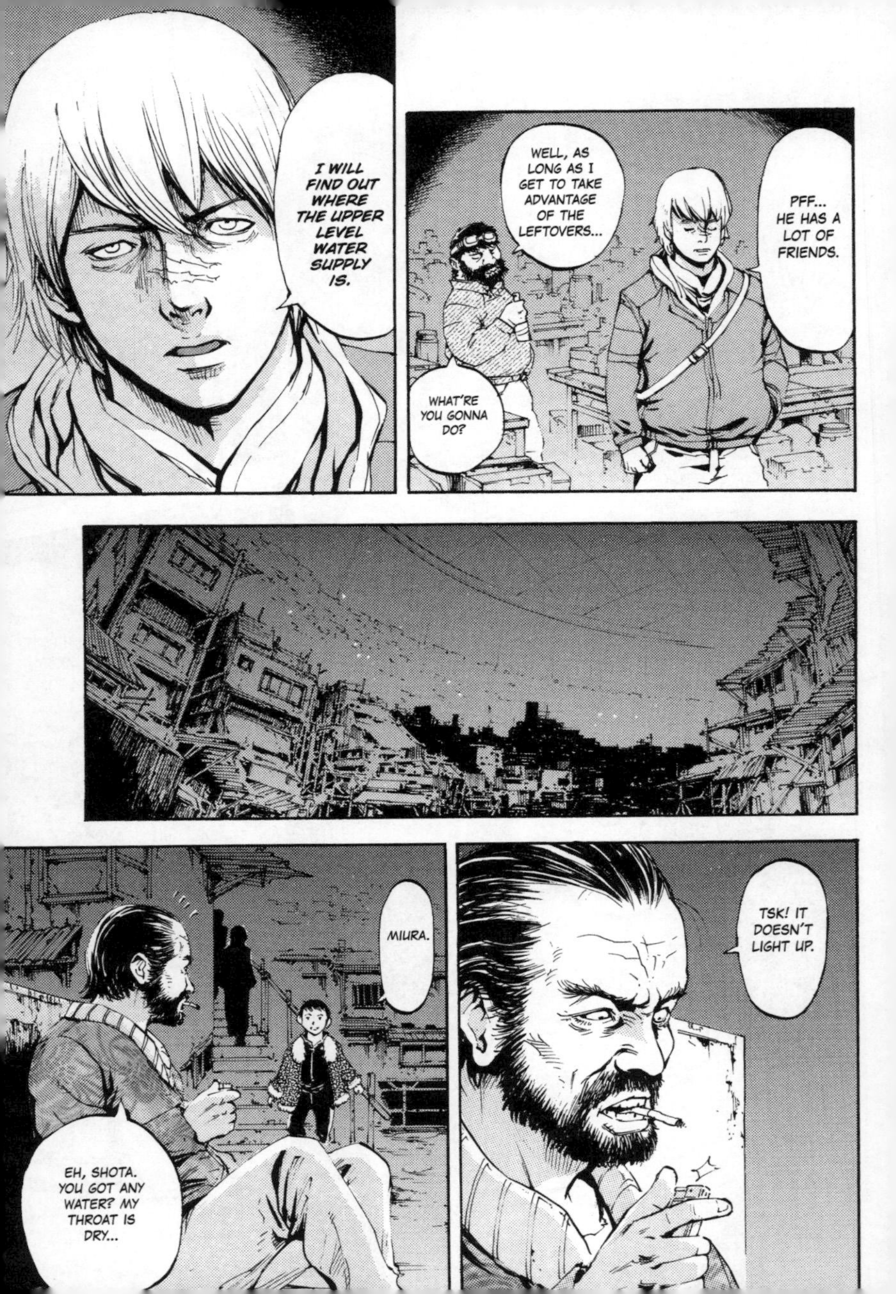
PFF... HE HAS A LOT OF FRIENDS.
WELL, AS LONG AS I GET TO TAKE ADVANTAGE OF THE LEFTOVERS...
WHAT'RE YOU GONNA DO?
I WILL FIND OUT WHERE THE UPPER LEVEL WATER SUPPLY IS.
TSK! IT DOESN'T LIGHT UP.
MIURA.
EH, SHOTA. YOU GOT ANY WATER? MY THROAT IS DRY...

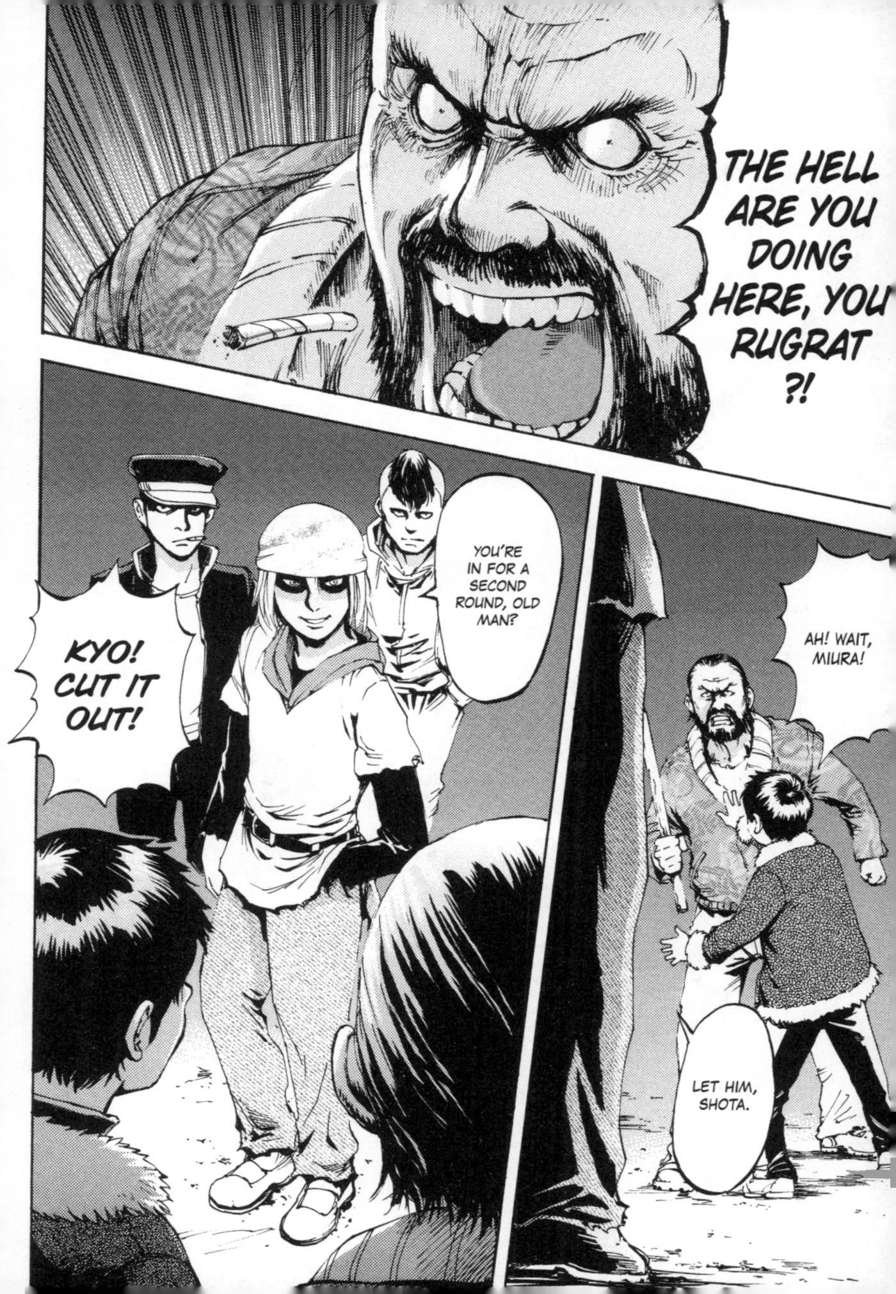
THE HELL ARE YOU DOING HERE, YOU RUGRAT ?!
AH! WAIT, MIURA!
LET HIM, SHOTA.
YOU'RE IN FOR A SECOND ROUND, OLD MAN?
KYO! CUT IT OUT!

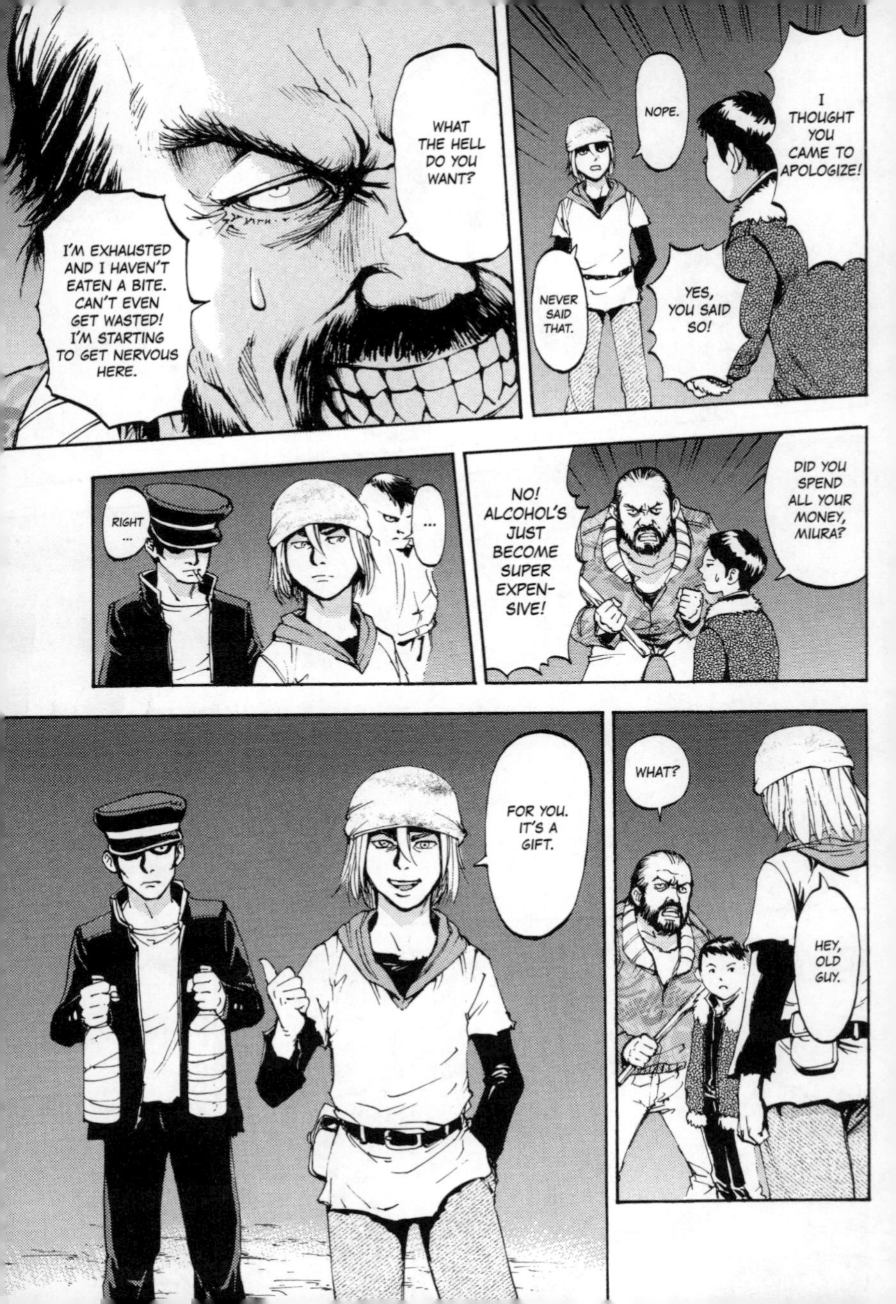
I THOUGHT YOU CAME TO APOLOGIZE!
NOPE.
YES, YOU SAID SO!
NEVER SAID THAT.
WHAT THE HELL DO YOU WANT?
I'M EXHAUSTED AND I HAVEN'T EATEN A BITE. CAN'T EVEN GET WASTED! I'M STARTING TO GET NERVOUS HERE.
DID YOU SPEND ALL YOUR MONEY, MIURA?
NO! ALCOHOL'S JUST BECOME SUPER EXPEN-SIVE!
...
RIGHT ...
HEY, OLD GUY.
WHAT?
FOR YOU. IT'S A GIFT.

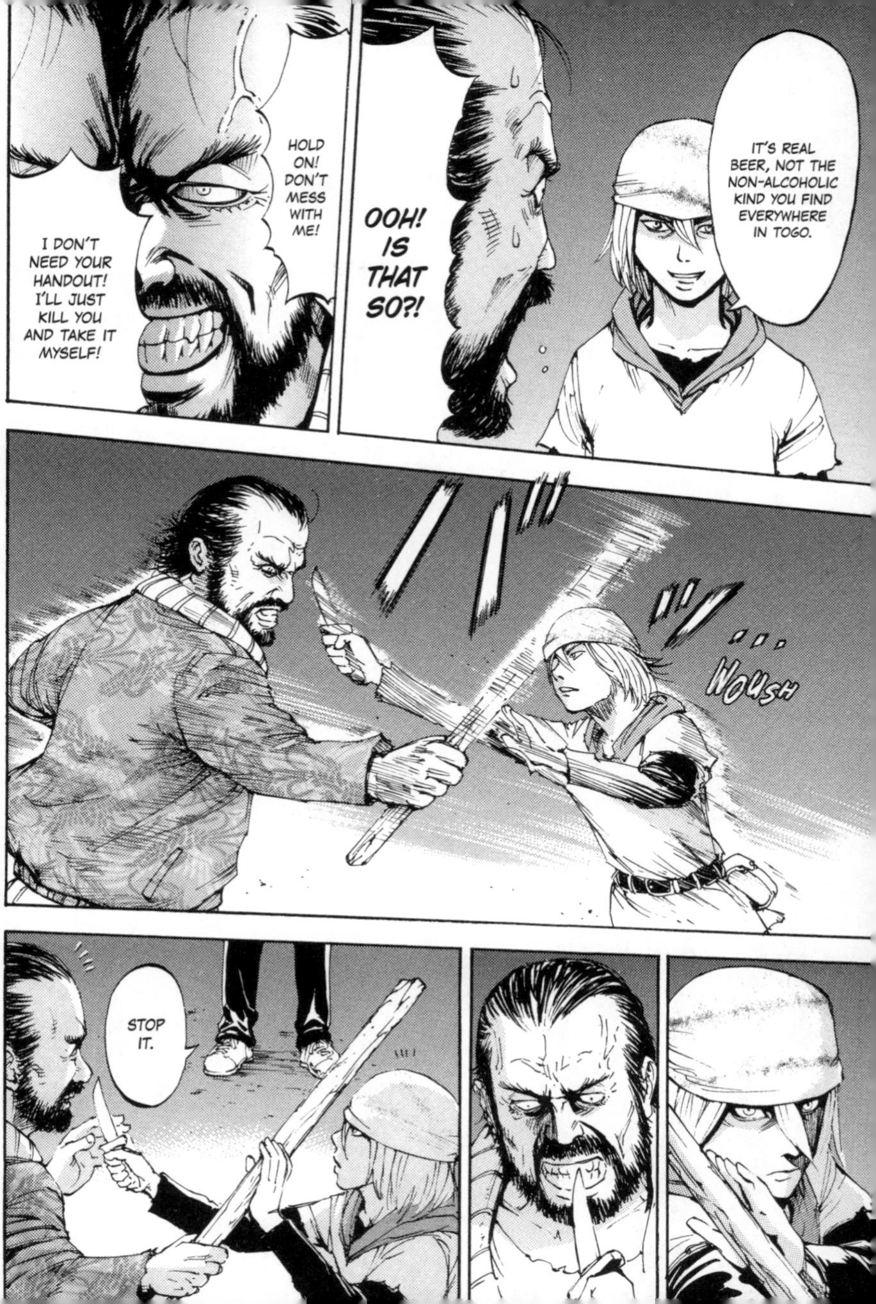
IT'S REAL BEER, NOT THE NON-ALCOHOLIC KIND YOU FIND EVERYWHERE IN TOGO.
OOH! IS THAT SO?!
HOLD ON! DON'T MESS WITH ME!
I DON'T NEED YOUR HANDOUT! I'LL JUST KILL YOU AND TAKE IT MYSELF!
WOUSH
STOP IT.

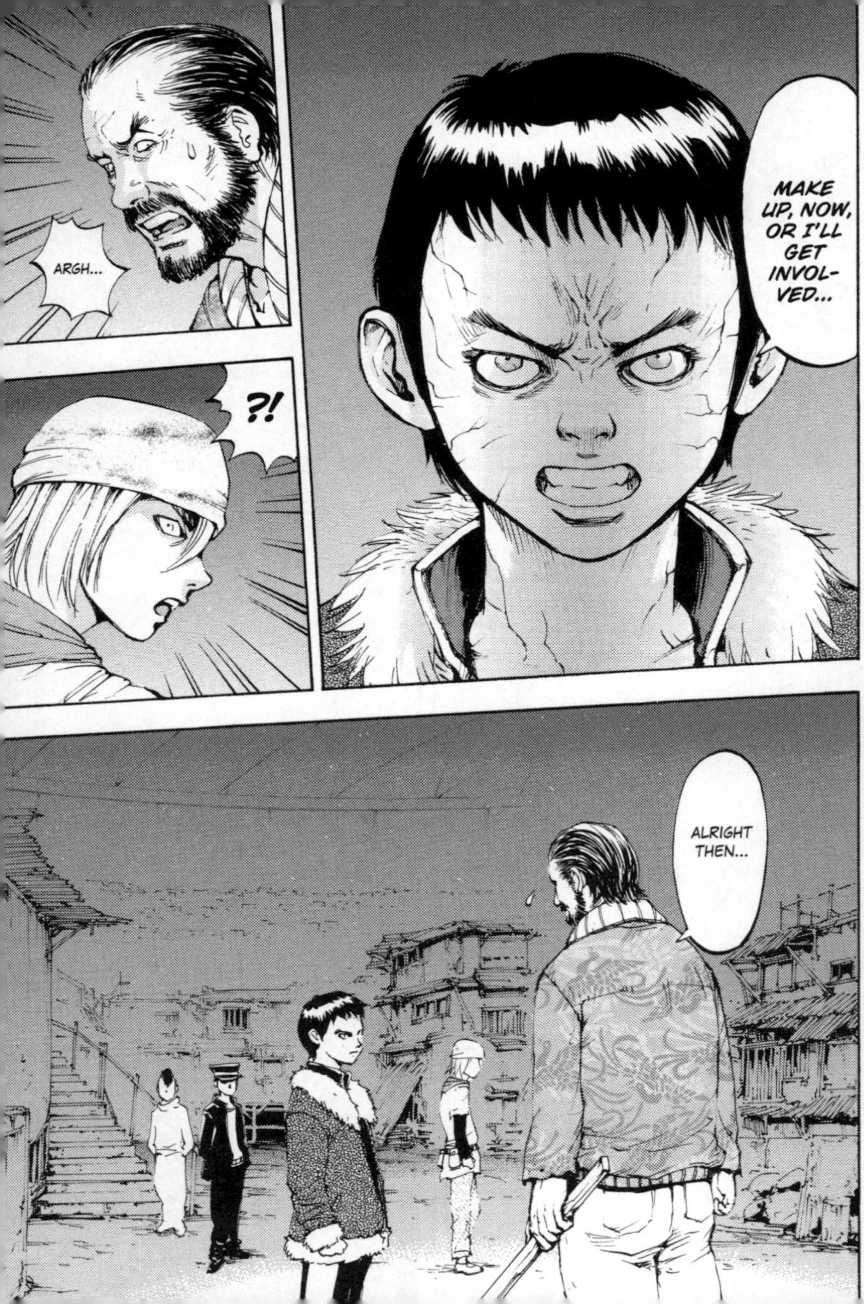
MAKE UP, NOW, OR I'LL GET INVOLVED...
ARGH...
?!
ALRIGHT THEN...

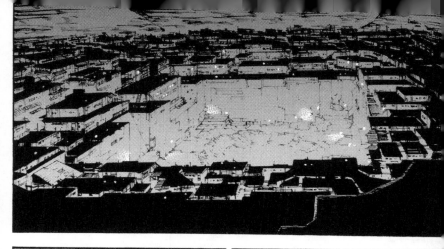

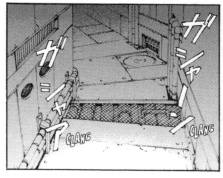

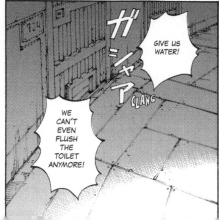

ガシャーン
CLANG
ガシャア
CLANG
ガシャア
GIVE US WATER!
CLANG
WE CAN'T EVEN FLUSH THE TOILET ANYMORE!

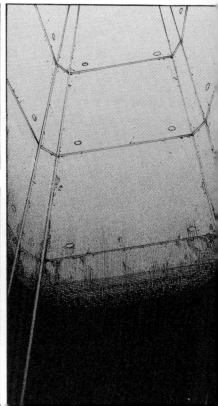

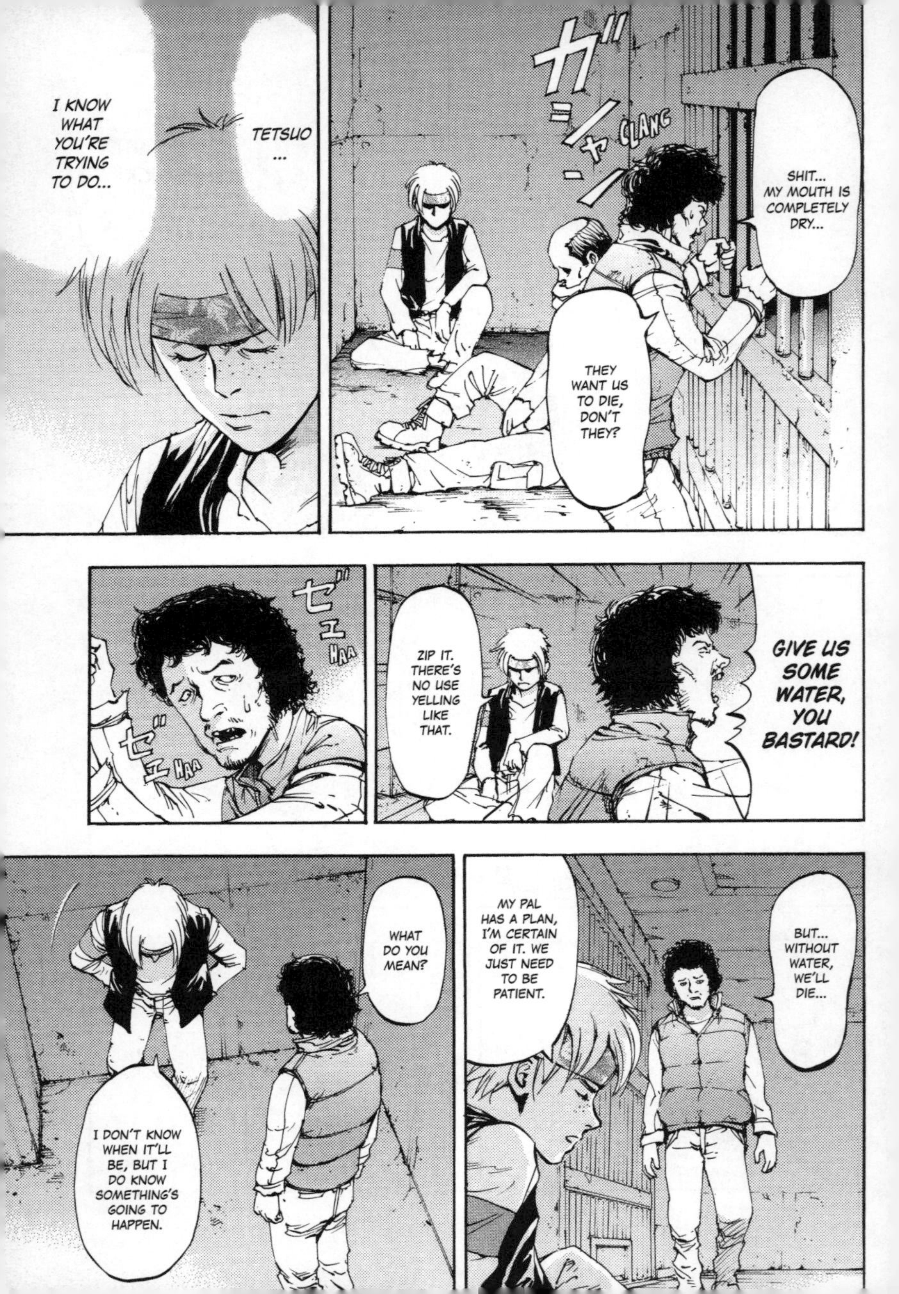
CLANG
SHIT... MY MOUTH IS COMPLETELY DRY...
THEY WANT US TO DIE, DON'T THEY?
TETSUO ...
I KNOW WHAT YOU'RE TRYING TO DO...
GIVE US SOME WATER, YOU BASTARD!
ZIP IT. THERE'S NO USE YELLING LIKE THAT.
ゼェ HAA
ゼェ HAA
BUT... WITHOUT WATER, WE'LL DIE...
MY PAL HAS A PLAN, I'M CERTAIN OF IT. WE JUST NEED TO BE PATIENT.
WHAT DO YOU MEAN?
I DON'T KNOW WHEN IT'LL BE, BUT I DO KNOW SOMETHING'S GOING TO HAPPEN.

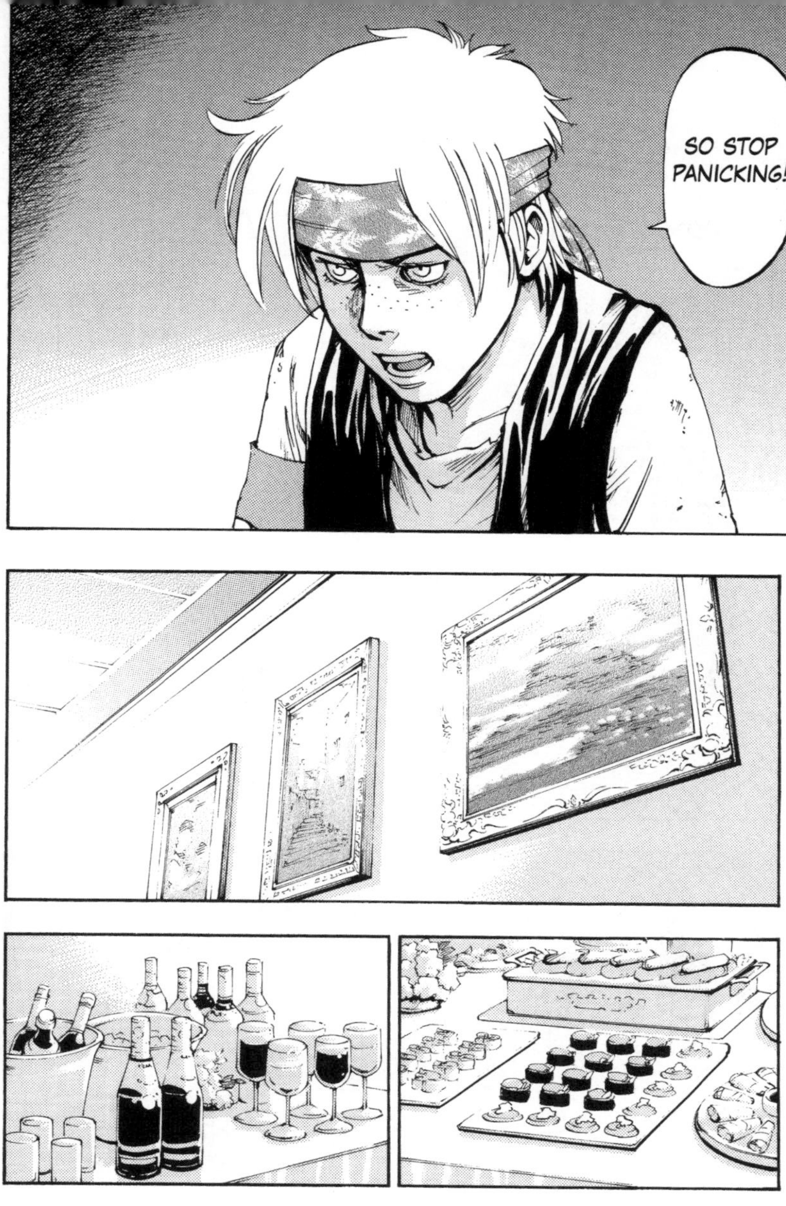
SO STOP PANICKING!

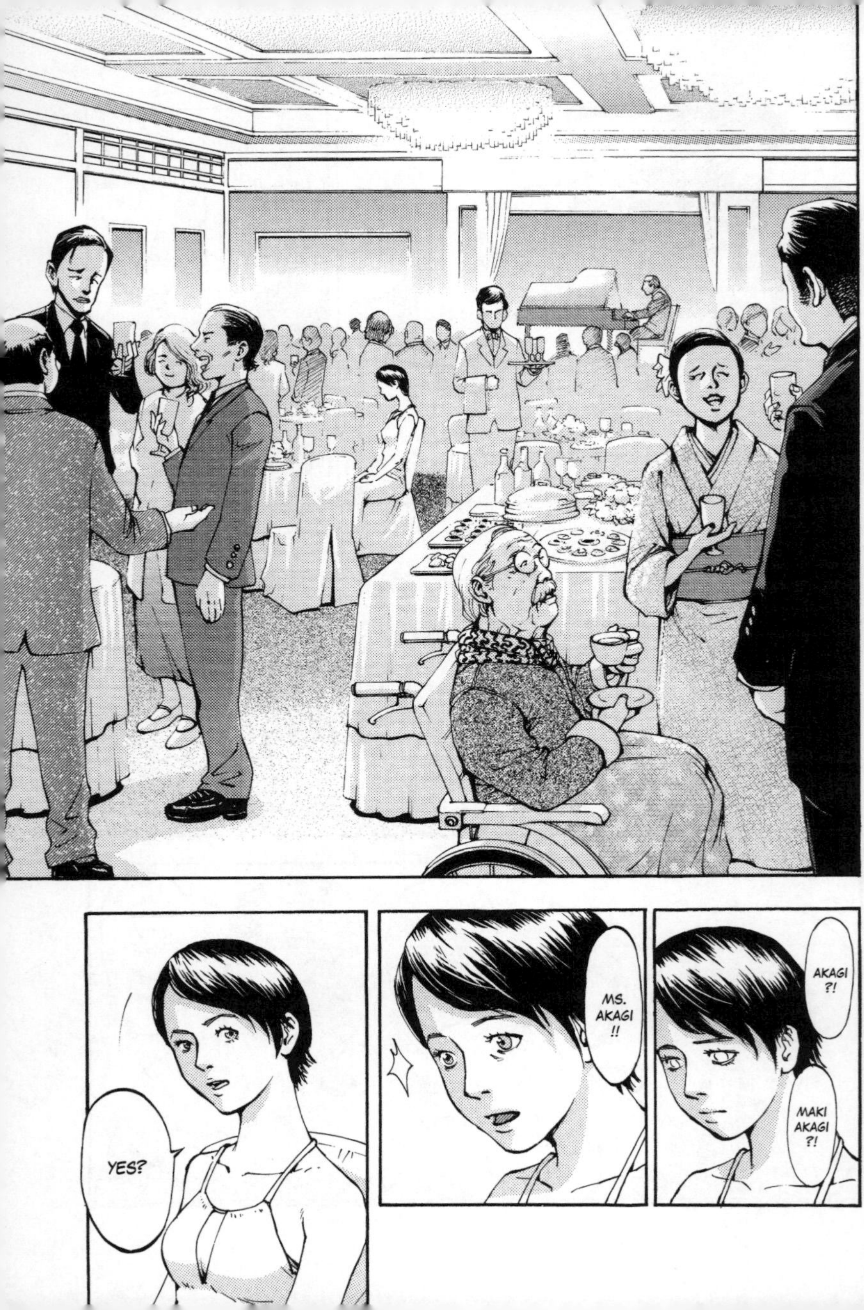
AKAGI ?!
MAKI AKAGI ?!
MS. AKAGI !!
YES?

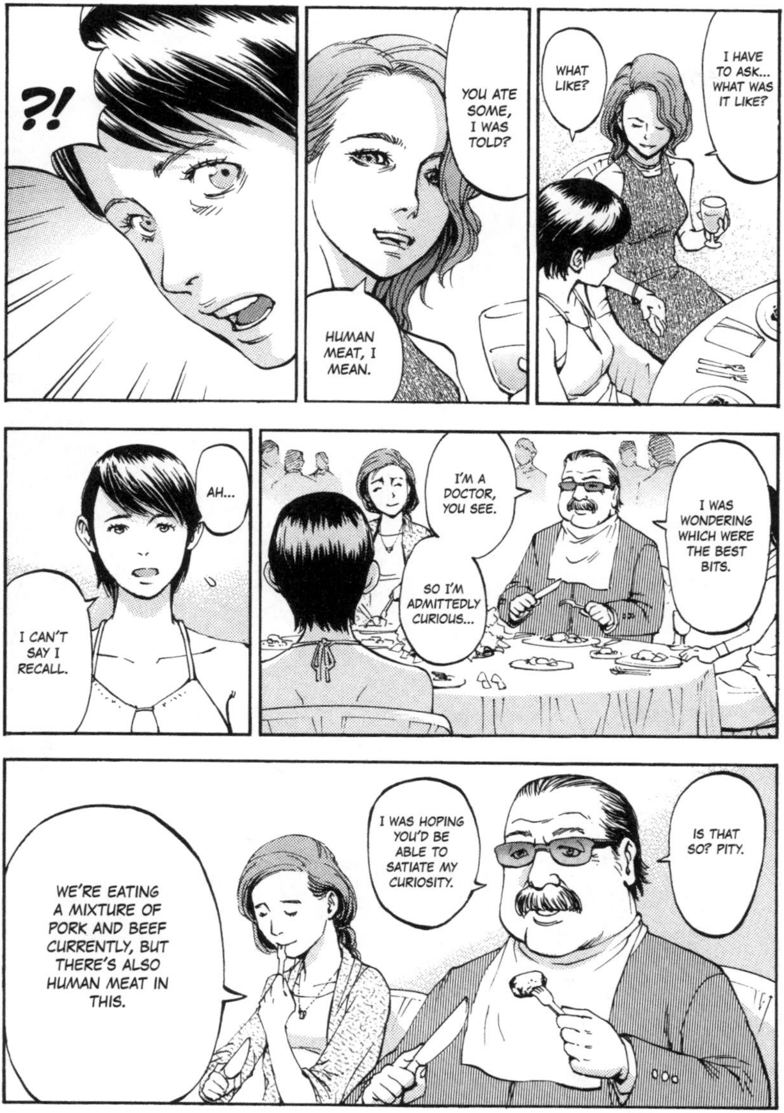
I HAVE TO ASK... WHAT WAS IT LIKE?
WHAT LIKE?
YOU ATE SOME, I WAS TOLD?
HUMAN MEAT, I MEAN.
?!
I WAS WONDERING WHICH WERE THE BEST BITS.
I'M A DOCTOR, YOU SEE.
SO I'M ADMITTEDLY CURIOUS...
AH...
I CAN'T SAY I RECALL.
IS THAT SO? PITY.
I WAS HOPING YOU'D BE ABLE TO SATIATE MY CURIOSITY.
WE'RE EATING A MIXTURE OF PORK AND BEEF CURRENTLY, BUT THERE'S ALSO HUMAN MEAT IN THIS.

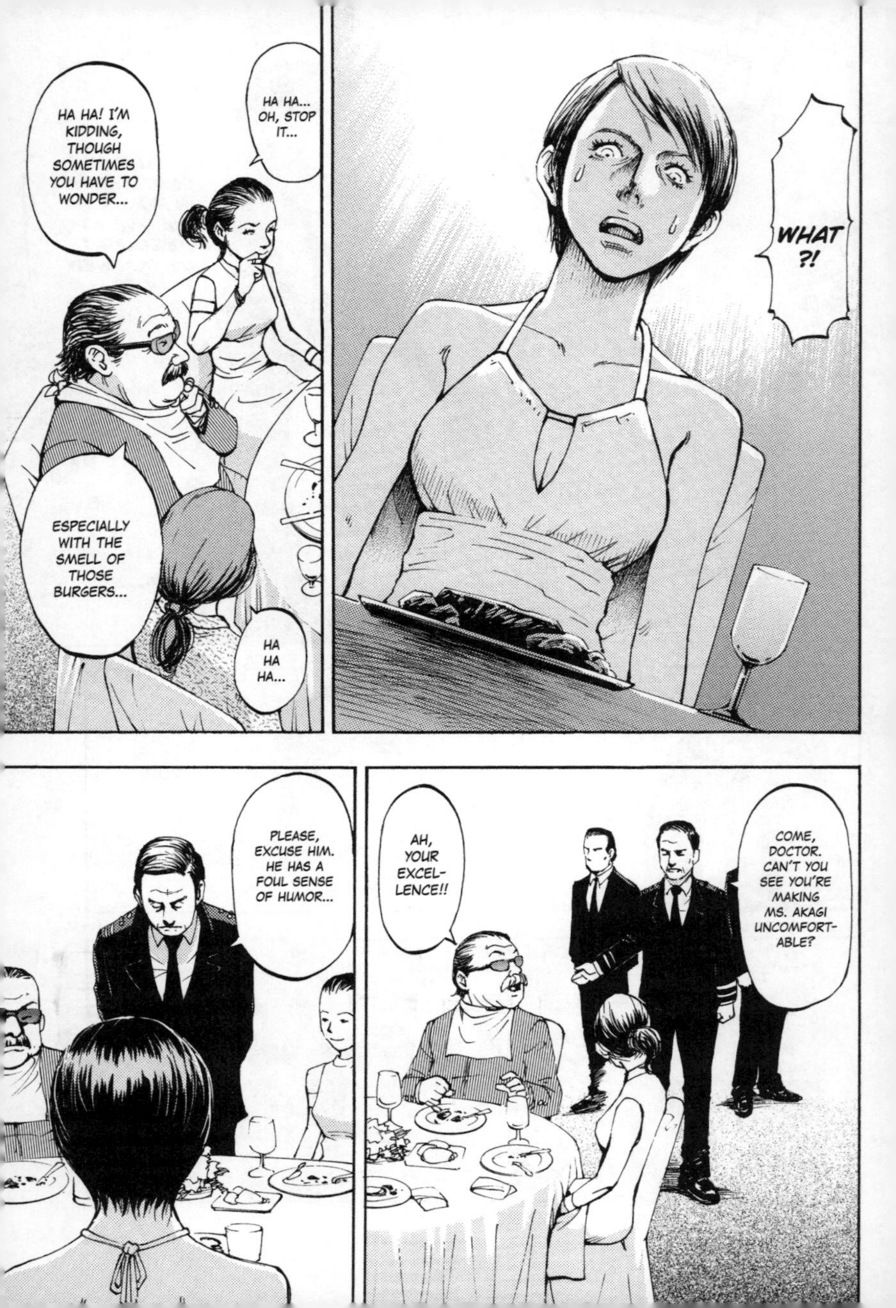
WHAT?!
HA HA... OH, STOP IT...
HA HA! I'M KIDDING, THOUGH SOMETIMES YOU HAVE TO WONDER...
ESPECIALLY WITH THE SMELL OF THOSE BURGERS...
HA HA HA...
COME, DOCTOR. CAN'T YOU SEE YOU'RE MAKING MS. AKAGI UNCOMFORTABLE?
AH, YOUR EXCELLENCE!!
PLEASE, EXCUSE HIM. HE HAS A FOUL SENSE OF HUMOR...

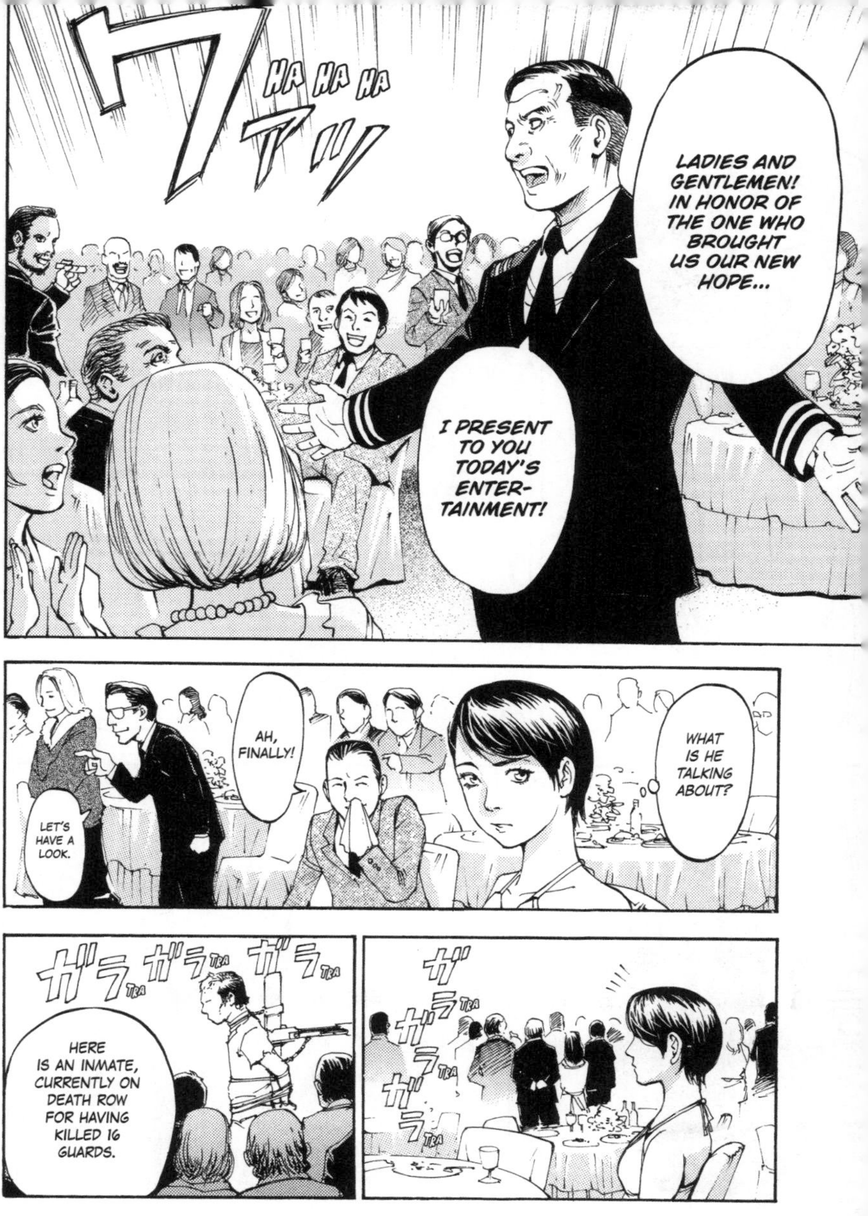
HA HA HA
LADIES AND GENTLEMEN! IN HONOR OF THE ONE WHO BROUGHT US OUR NEW HOPE...
I PRESENT TO YOU TODAY'S ENTER-TAINMENT!
WHAT IS HE TALKING ABOUT?
AH, FINALLY!
LET'S HAVE A LOOK.
TRA TRA TRA
TRA TRA TRA
HERE IS AN INMATE, CURRENTLY ON DEATH ROW FOR HAVING KILLED 16 GUARDS.

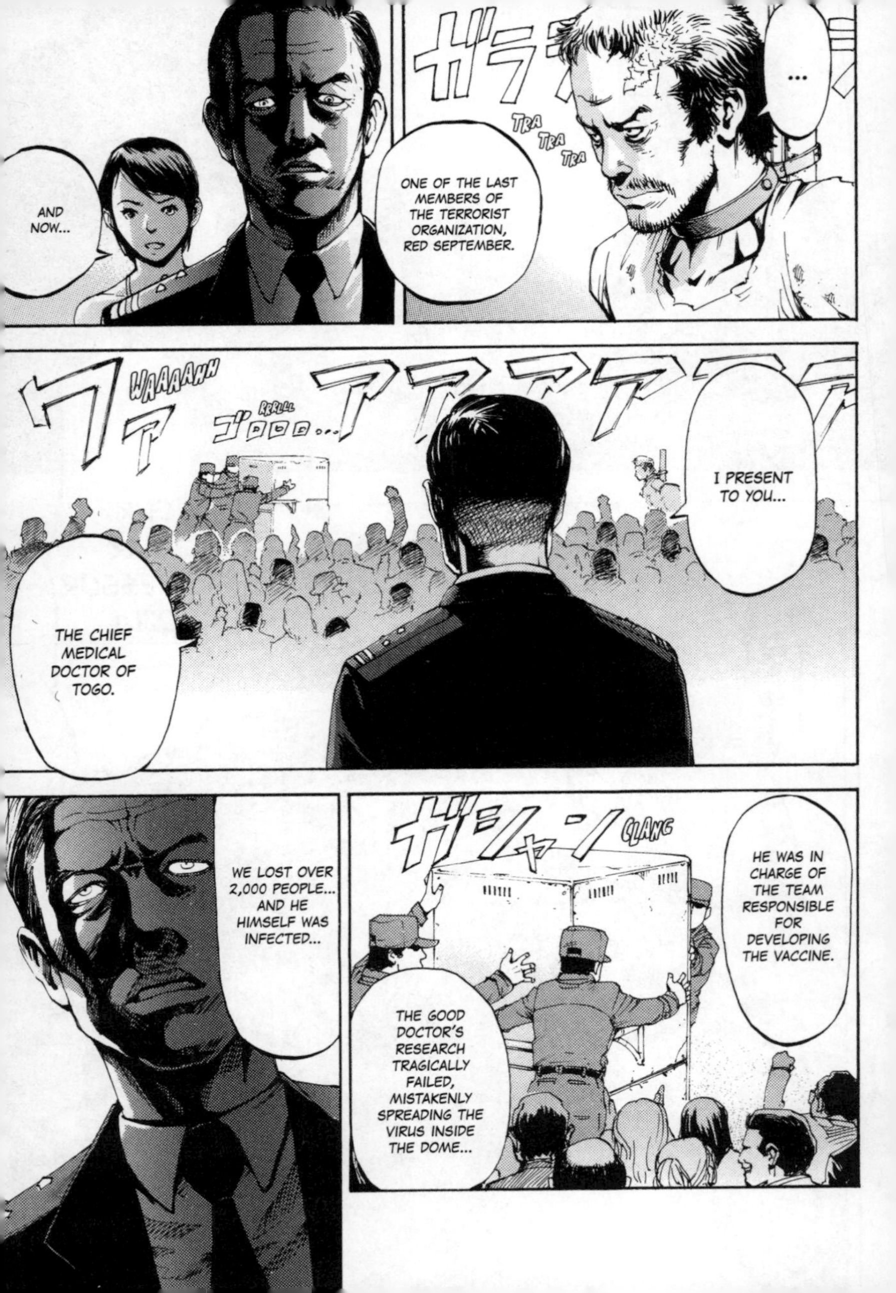
...
TRA TRA TRA
ONE OF THE LAST MEMBERS OF THE TERRORIST ORGANIZATION, RED SEPTEMBER.
AND NOW...
I PRESENT TO YOU...
WAAAAHH
RRRLLL
THE CHIEF MEDICAL DOCTOR OF TOGO.
HE WAS IN CHARGE OF THE TEAM RESPONSIBLE FOR DEVELOPING THE VACCINE.
CLANG
THE GOOD DOCTOR'S RESEARCH TRAGICALLY FAILED, MISTAKENLY SPREADING THE VIRUS INSIDE THE DOME...
WE LOST OVER 2,000 PEOPLE... AND HE HIMSELF WAS INFECTED...

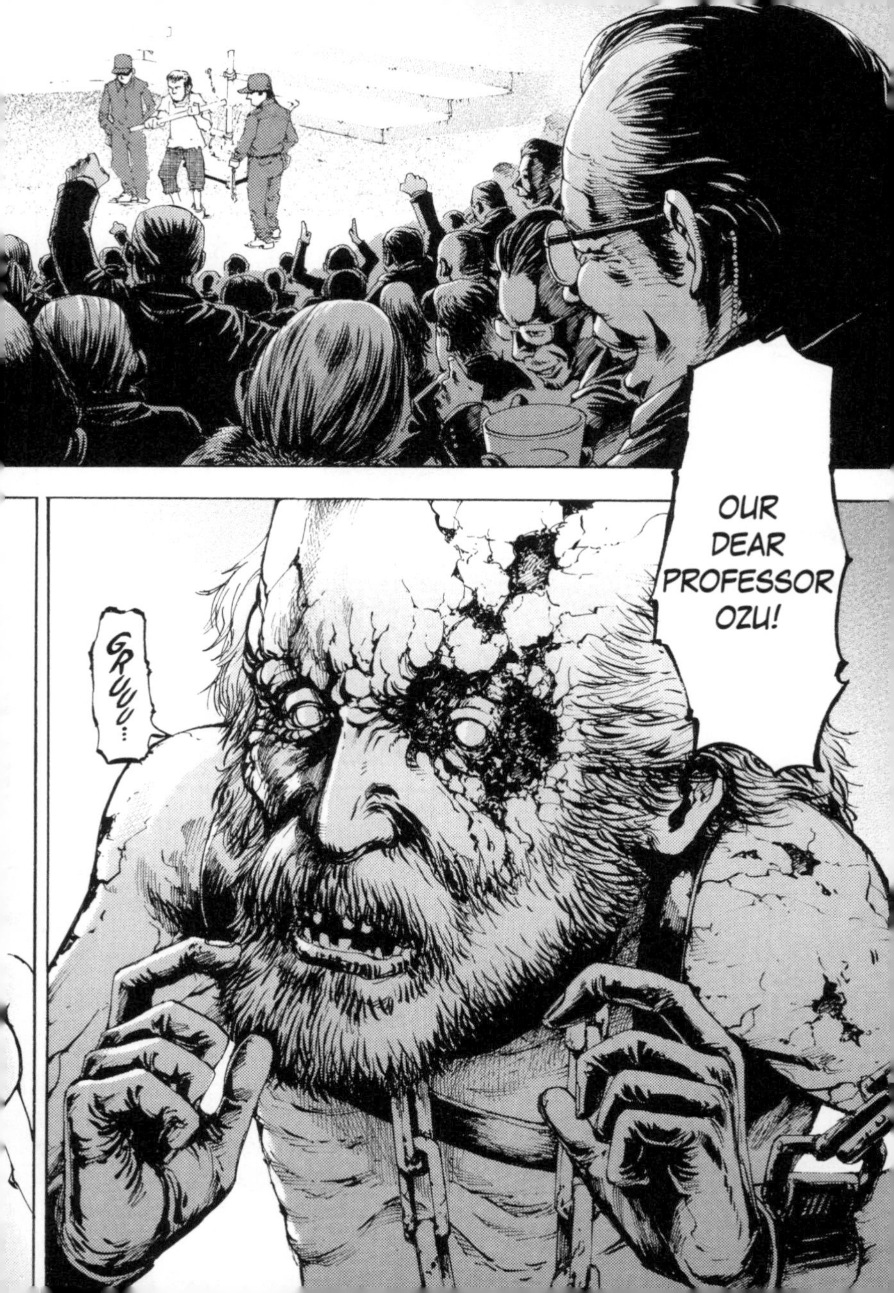
OUR DEAR PROFESSOR OZU!
GRUUU...

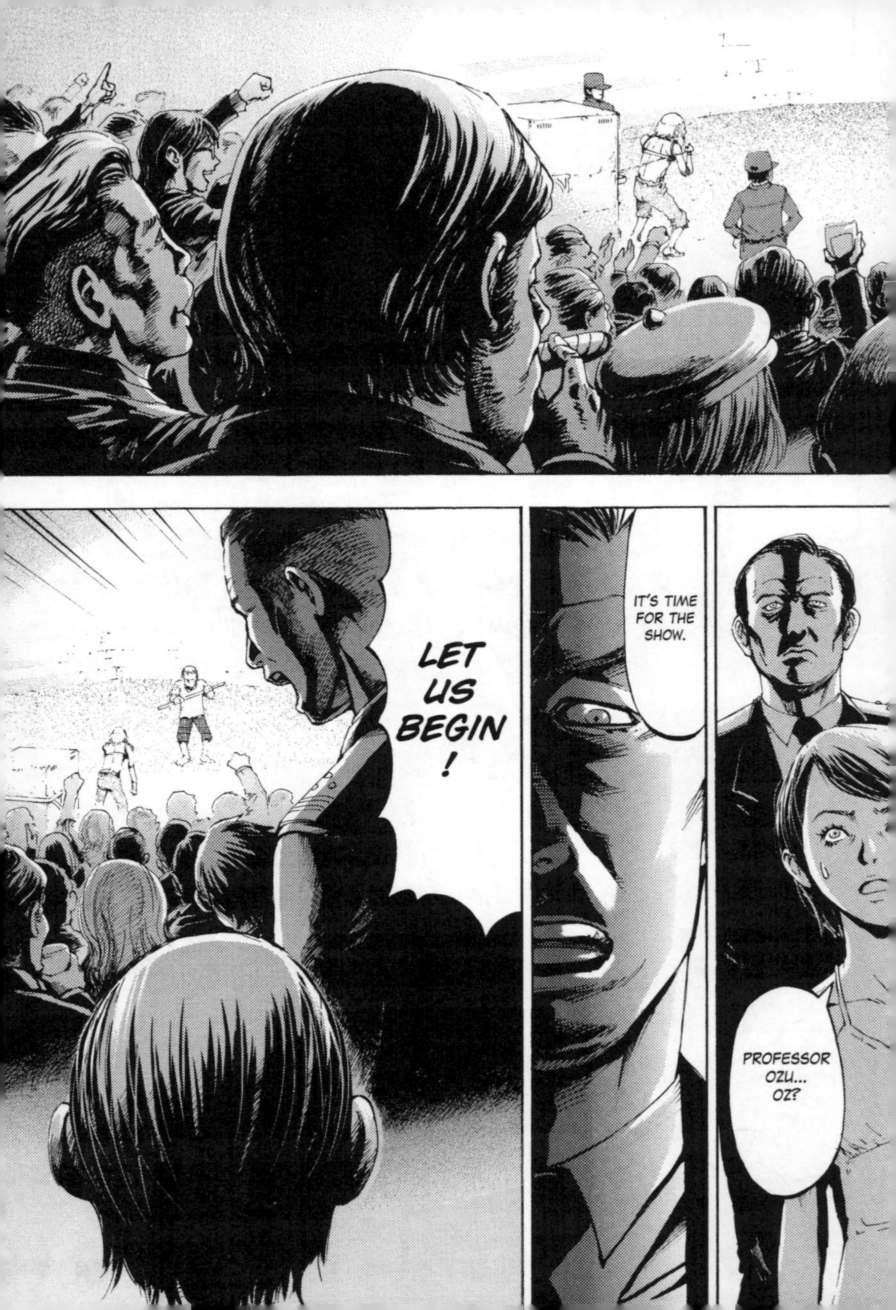
PROFESSOR OZU... OZ?
IT'S TIME FOR THE SHOW.
LET US BEGIN!

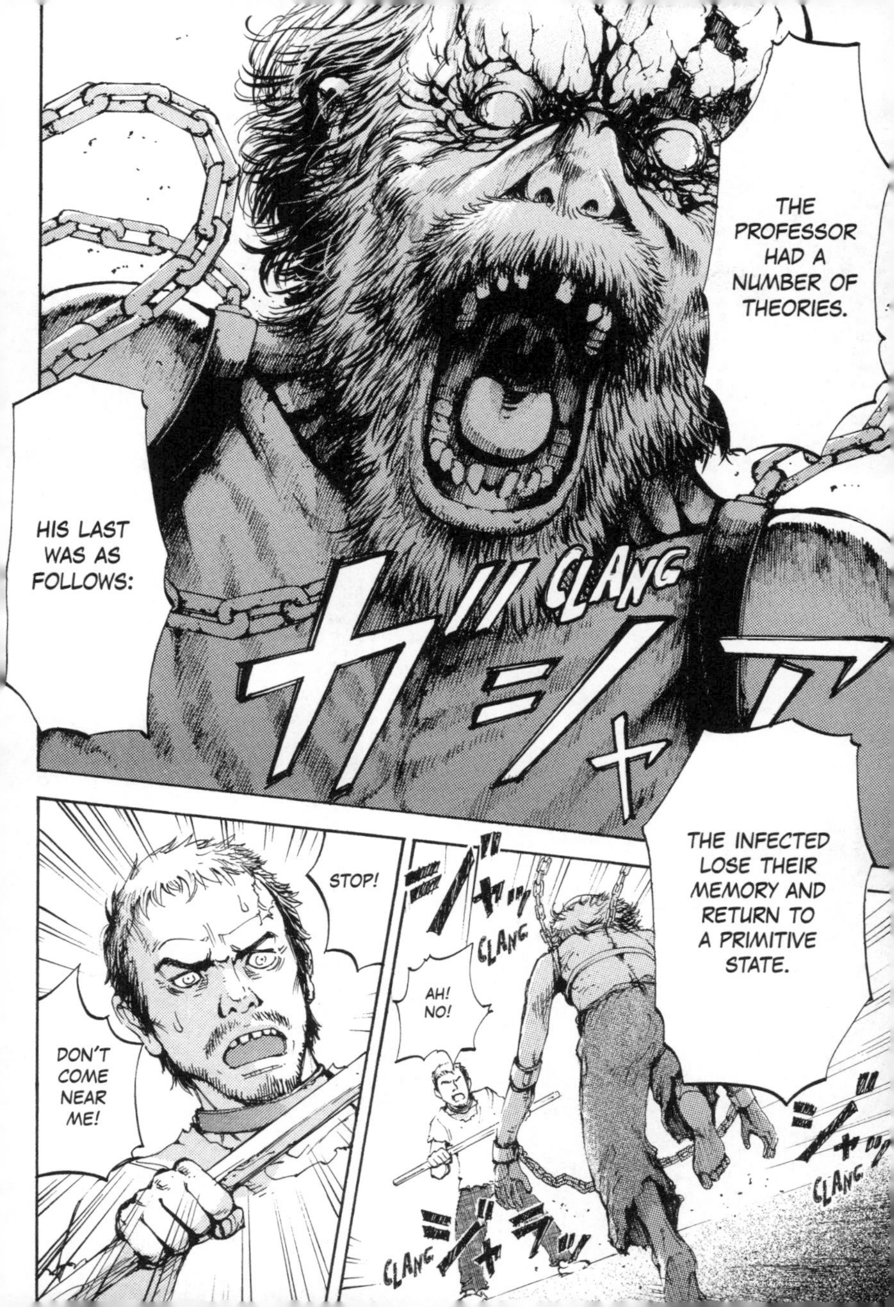
THE PROFESSOR HAD A NUMBER OF THEORIES.
HIS LAST WAS AS FOLLOWS:
CLANG
THE INFECTED LOSE THEIR MEMORY AND RETURN TO A PRIMITIVE STATE.
CLANG
AH! NO!
CLANG
CLANG
STOP!
DON'T COME NEAR ME!

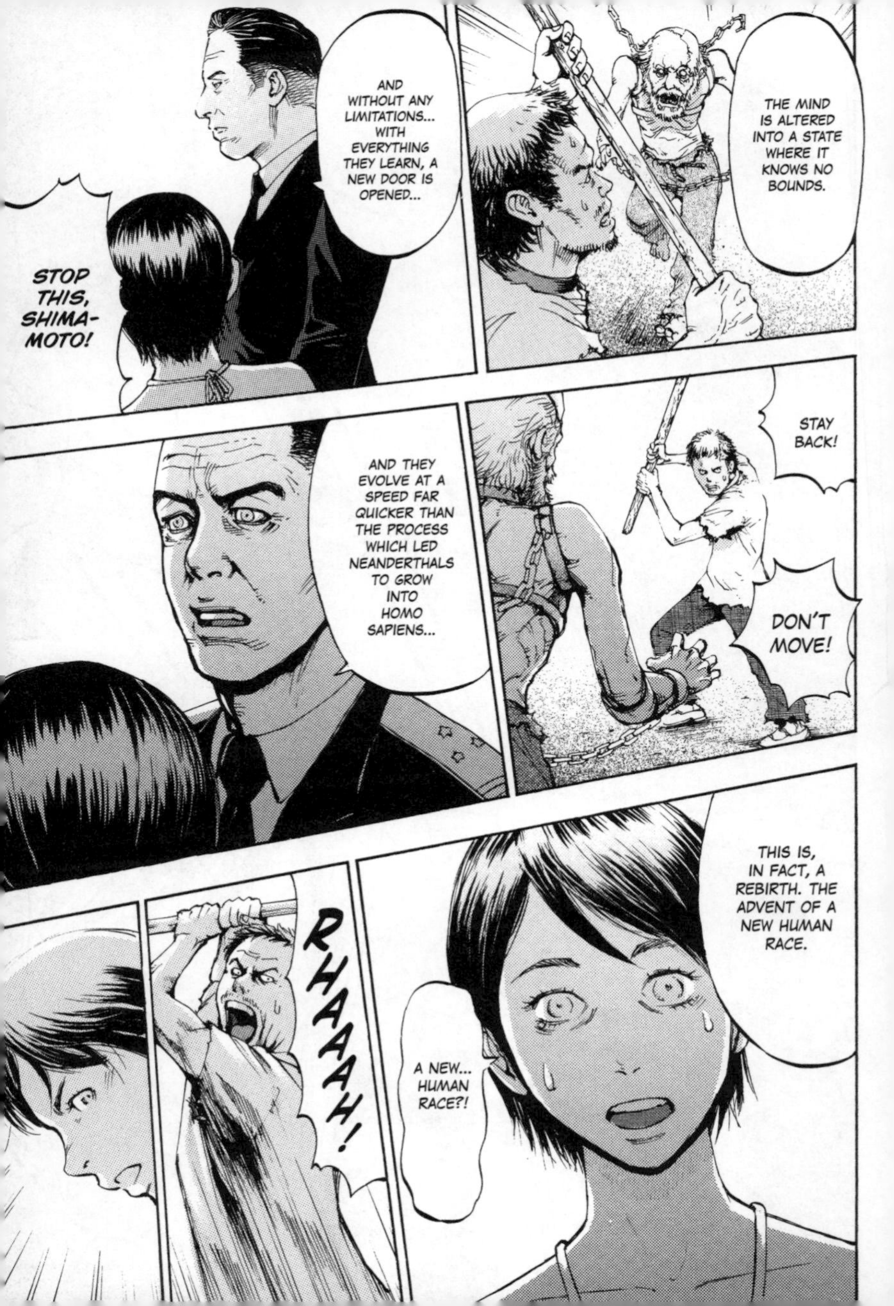
THE MIND IS ALTERED INTO A STATE WHERE IT KNOWS NO BOUNDS.
AND WITHOUT ANY LIMITATIONS... WITH EVERYTHING THEY LEARN, A NEW DOOR IS OPENED...
STOP THIS, SHIMAMOTO!
STAY BACK!
DON'T MOVE!
AND THEY EVOLVE AT A SPEED FAR QUICKER THAN THE PROCESS WHICH LED NEANDERTHALS TO GROW INTO HOMO SAPIENS...
THIS IS, IN FACT, A REBIRTH. THE ADVENT OF A NEW HUMAN RACE.
A NEW... HUMAN RACE?!
RHAAAAH!

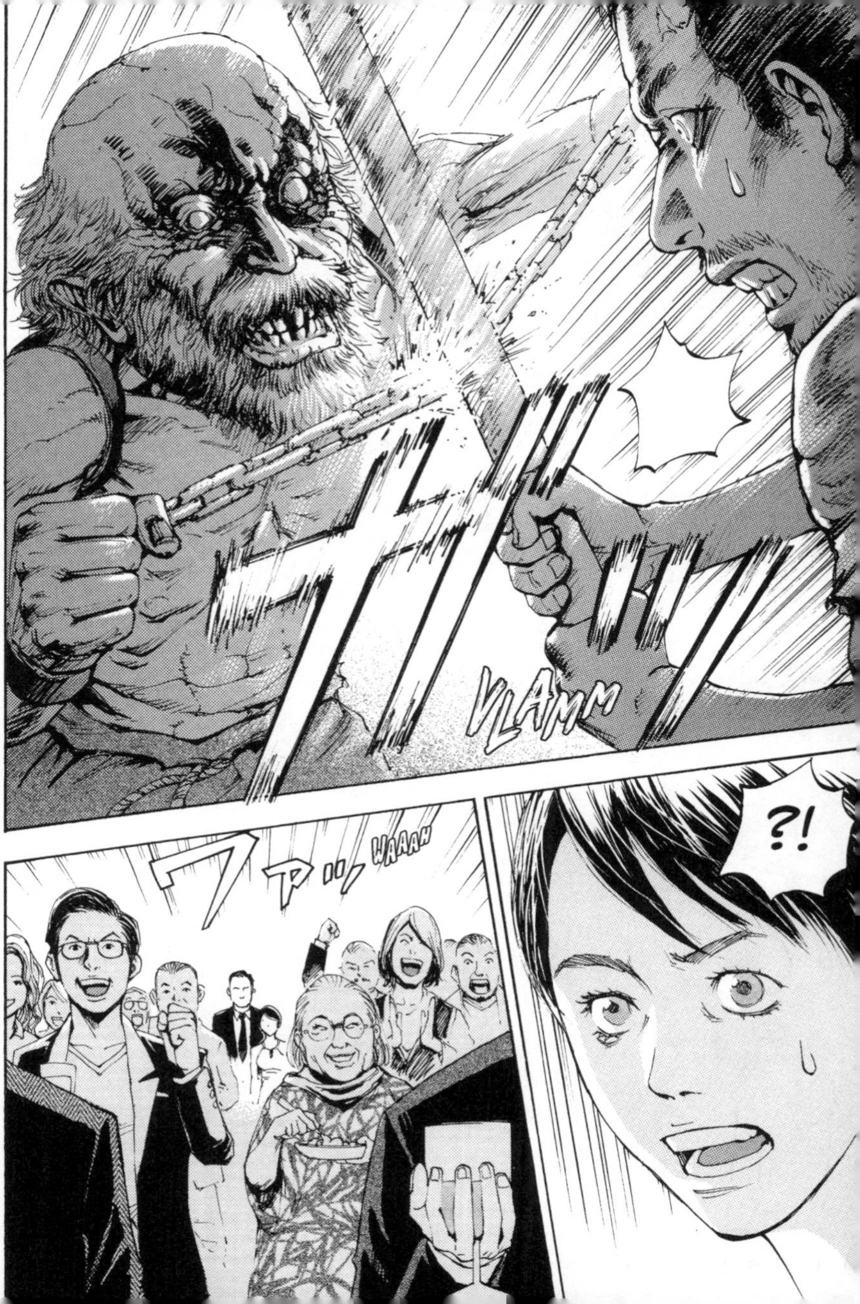
VLAMM
?!
WAAAH

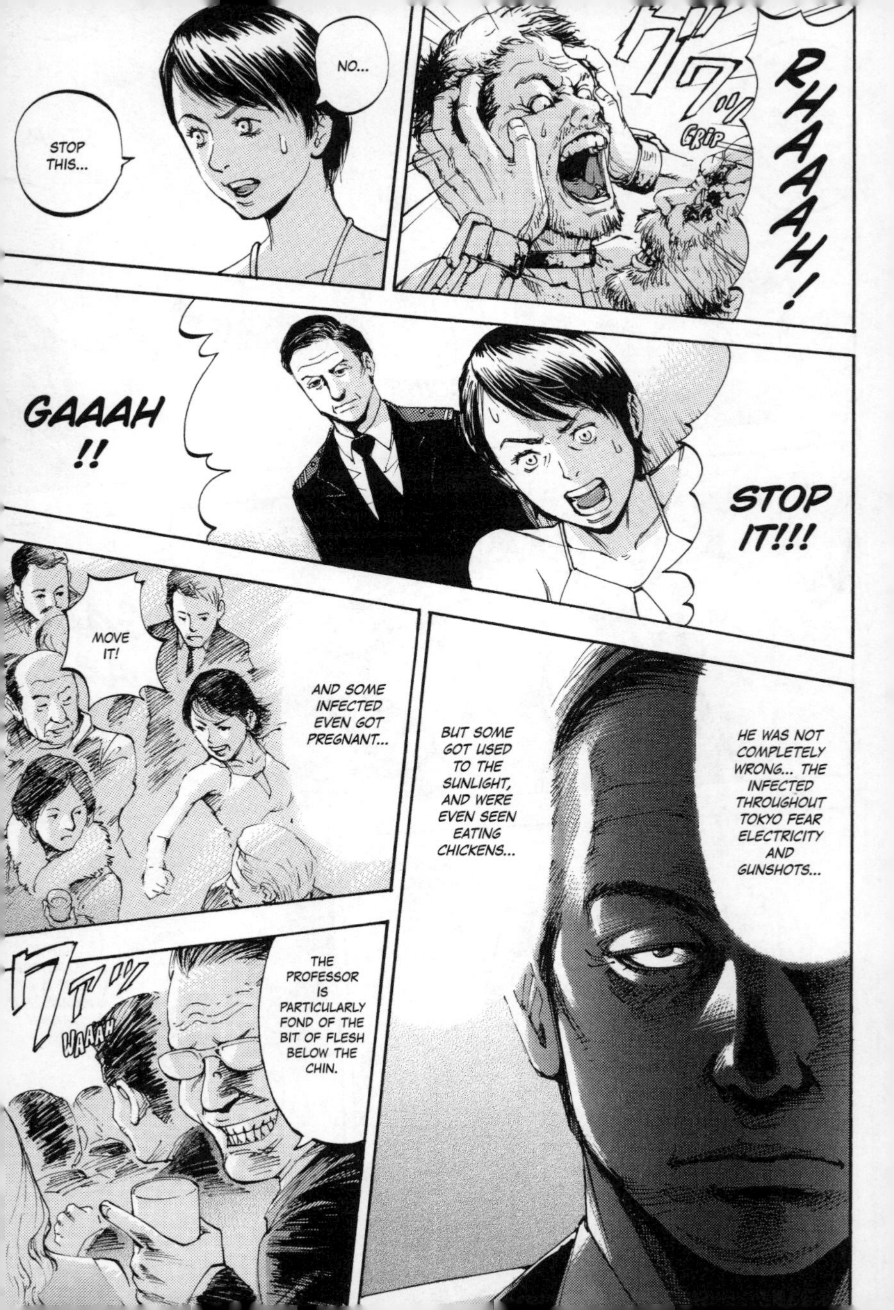
RHAAAAH!
GRIP
NO...
STOP THIS...
GAAAH!!
STOP IT!!!
HE WAS NOT COMPLETELY WRONG... THE INFECTED THROUGHOUT TOKYO FEAR ELECTRICITY AND GUNSHOTS...
BUT SOME GOT USED TO THE SUNLIGHT, AND WERE EVEN SEEN EATING CHICKENS...
AND SOME INFECTED EVEN GOT PREGNANT...
MOVE IT!
THE PROFESSOR IS PARTICULARLY FOND OF THE BIT OF FLESH BELOW THE CHIN.
WAAAAH

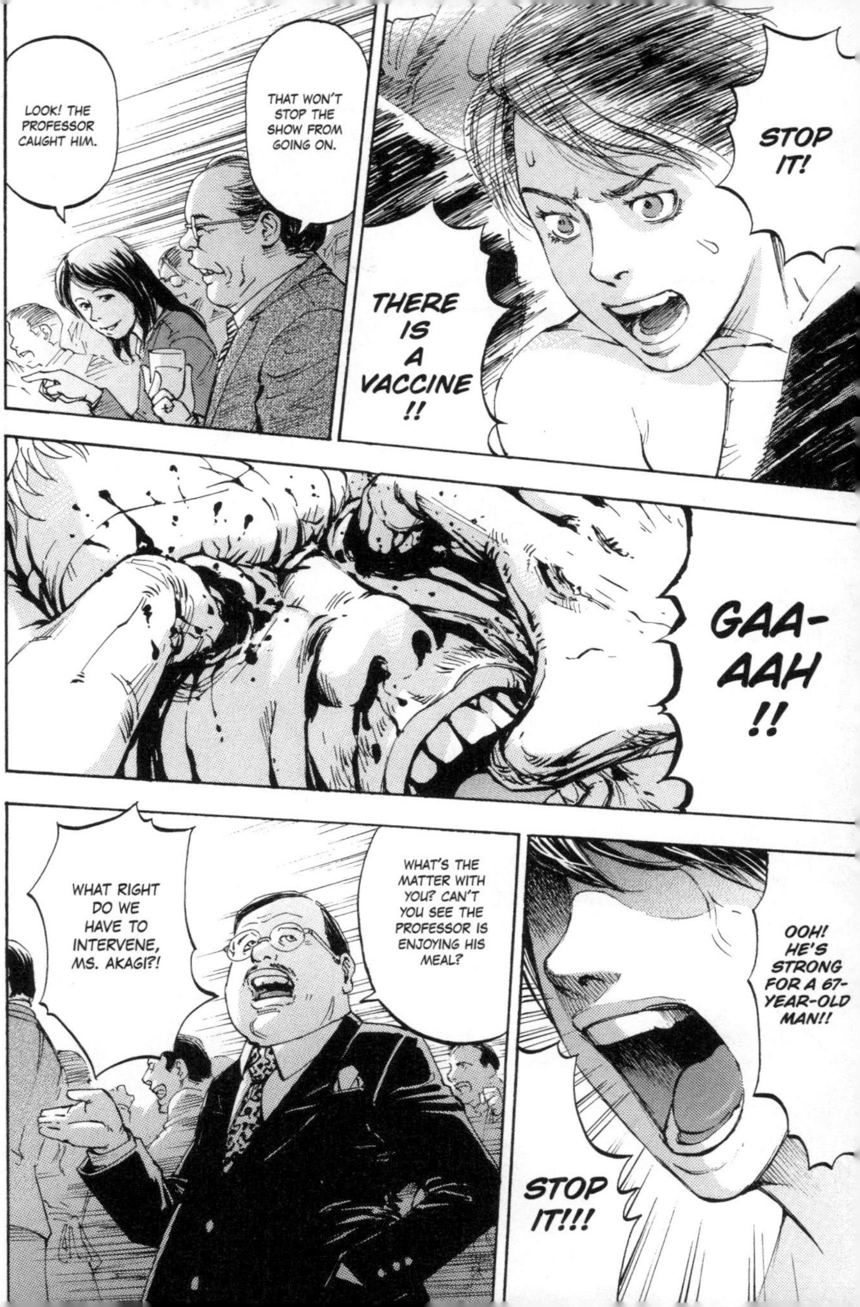
STOP IT!
THERE IS A VACCINE !!
THAT WON'T STOP THE SHOW FROM GOING ON.
LOOK! THE PROFESSOR CAUGHT HIM.
GAAA-AAH !!
OOH! HE'S STRONG FOR A 67-YEAR-OLD MAN!!
STOP IT!!!
WHAT'S THE MATTER WITH YOU? CAN'T YOU SEE THE PROFESSOR IS ENJOYING HIS MEAL?
WHAT RIGHT DO WE HAVE TO INTERVENE, MS. AKAGI?!

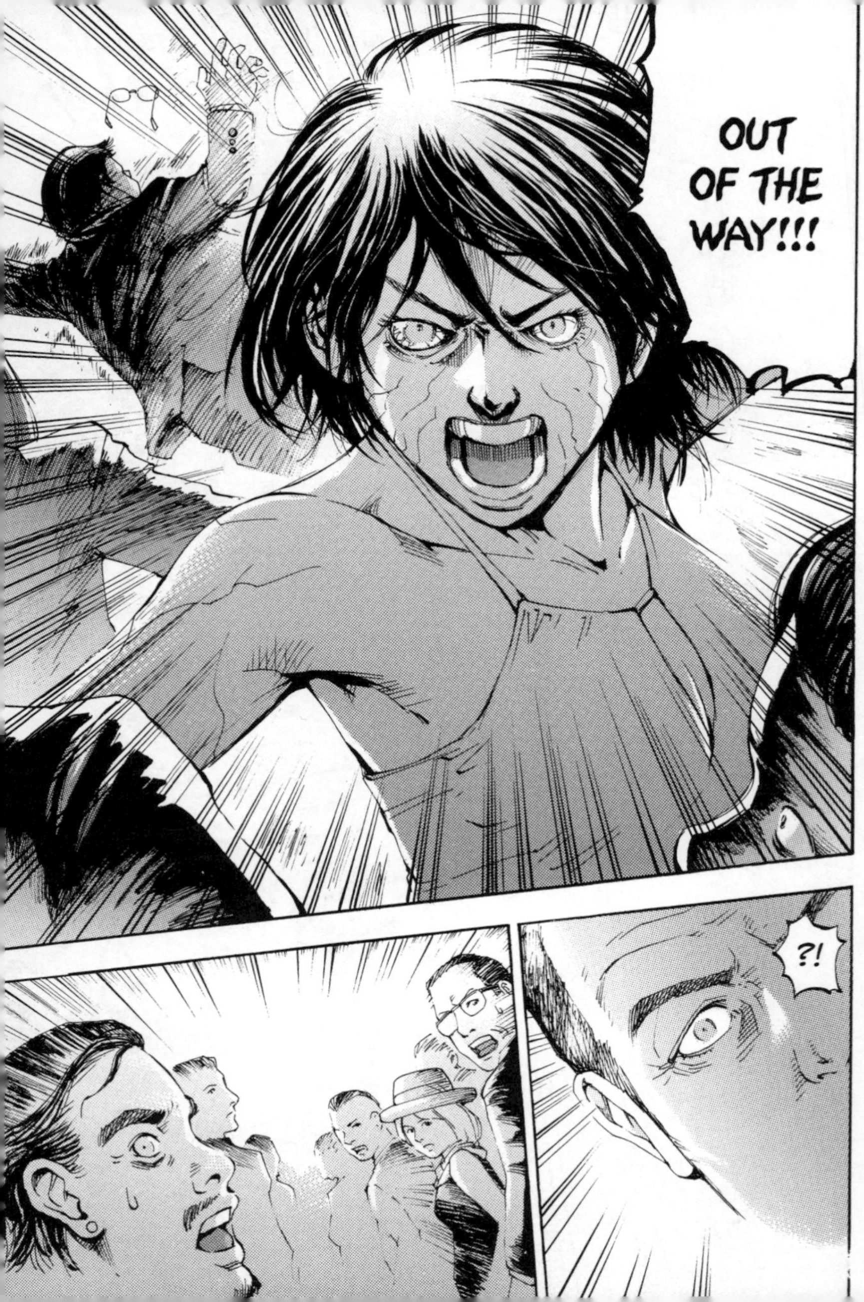
OUT OF THE WAY!!!
?!

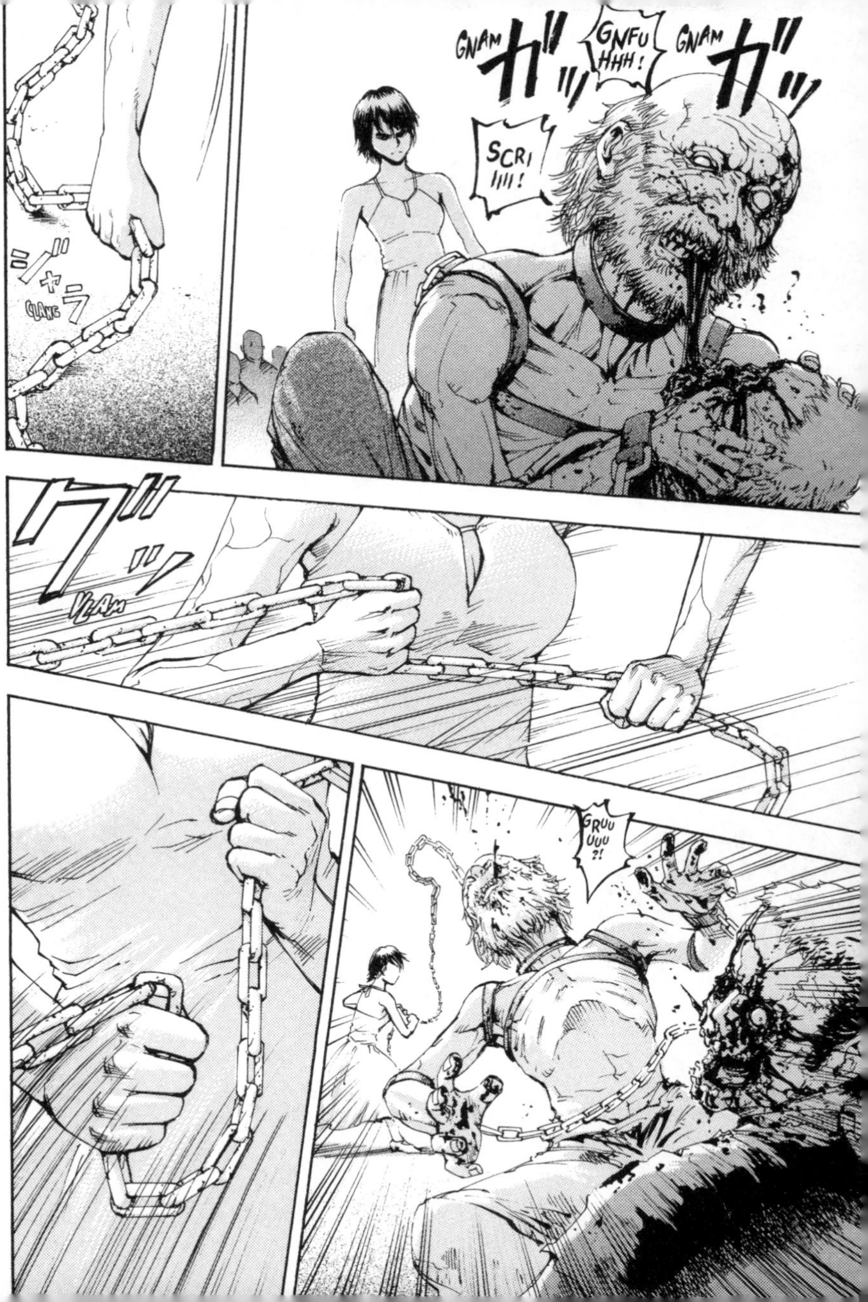
GNAM
ガッ
GNFU HHH!
GNAM
ガッ
SCRI IIII!
ジャラ
CLANG
グッ
VLAM
GRUU UUU?!

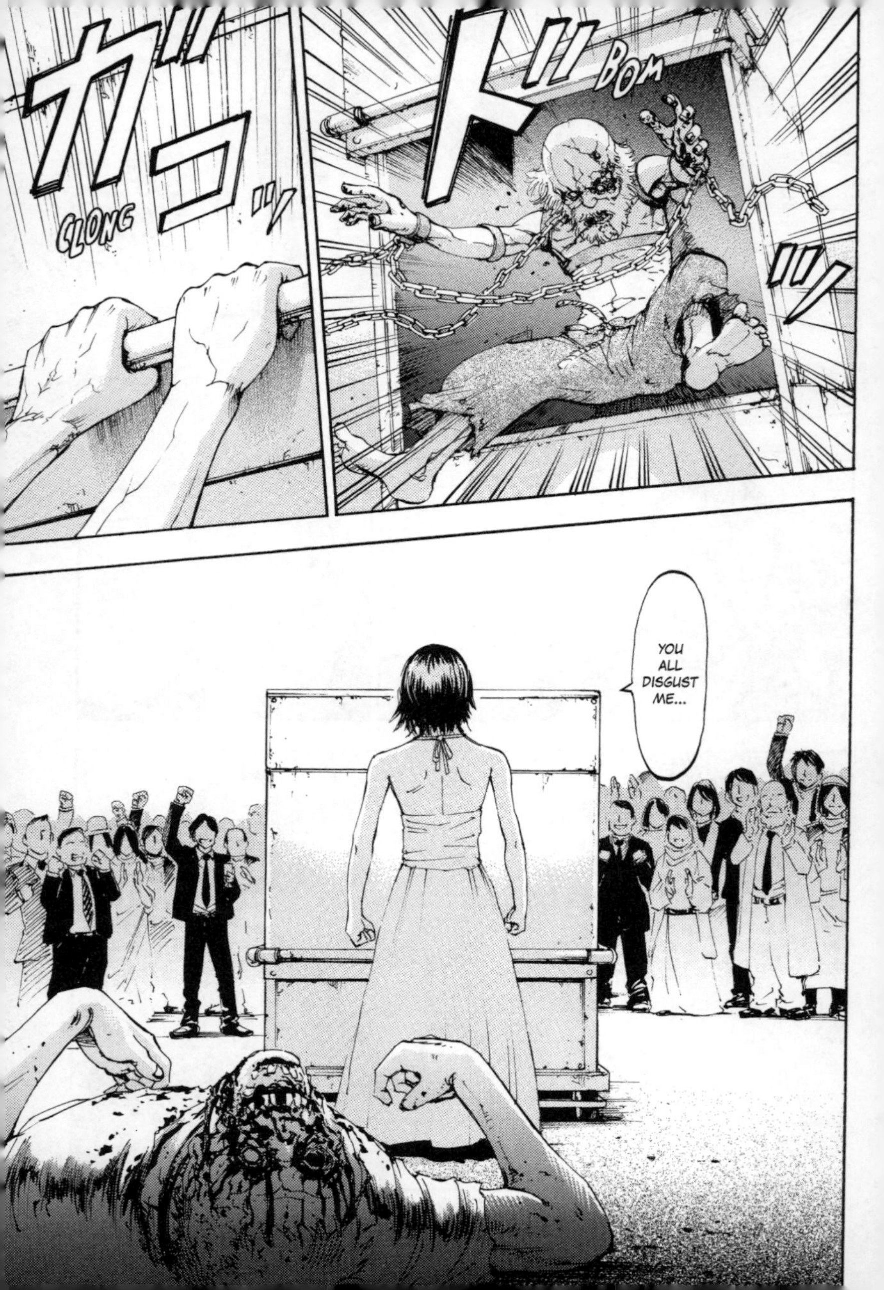
ドッ
BOM
ガゴッ
CLONG
YOU ALL DISGUST ME...

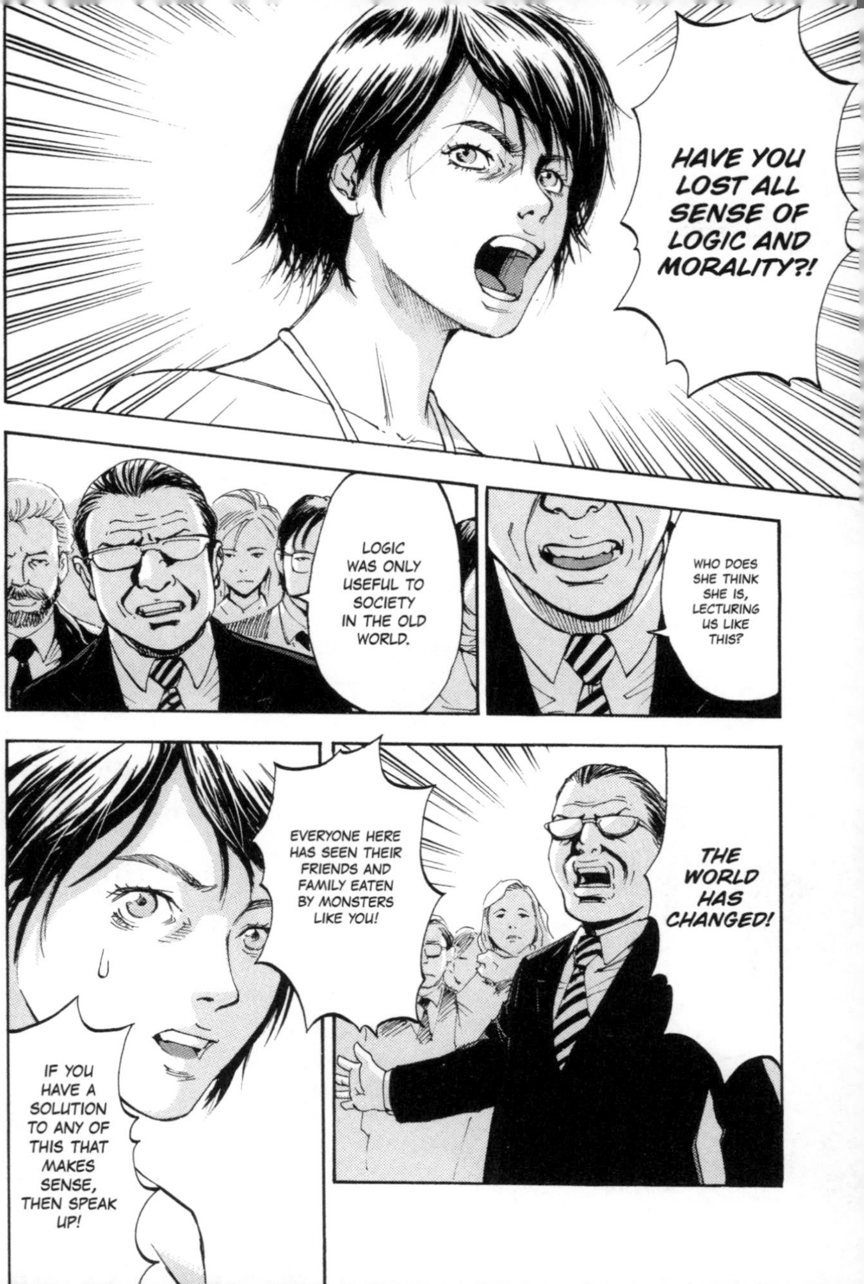
HAVE YOU LOST ALL SENSE OF LOGIC AND MORALITY?!
WHO DOES SHE THINK SHE IS, LECTURING US LIKE THIS?
LOGIC WAS ONLY USEFUL TO SOCIETY IN THE OLD WORLD.
THE WORLD HAS CHANGED!
EVERYONE HERE HAS SEEN THEIR FRIENDS AND FAMILY EATEN BY MONSTERS LIKE YOU!
IF YOU HAVE A SOLUTION TO ANY OF THIS THAT MAKES SENSE, THEN SPEAK UP!

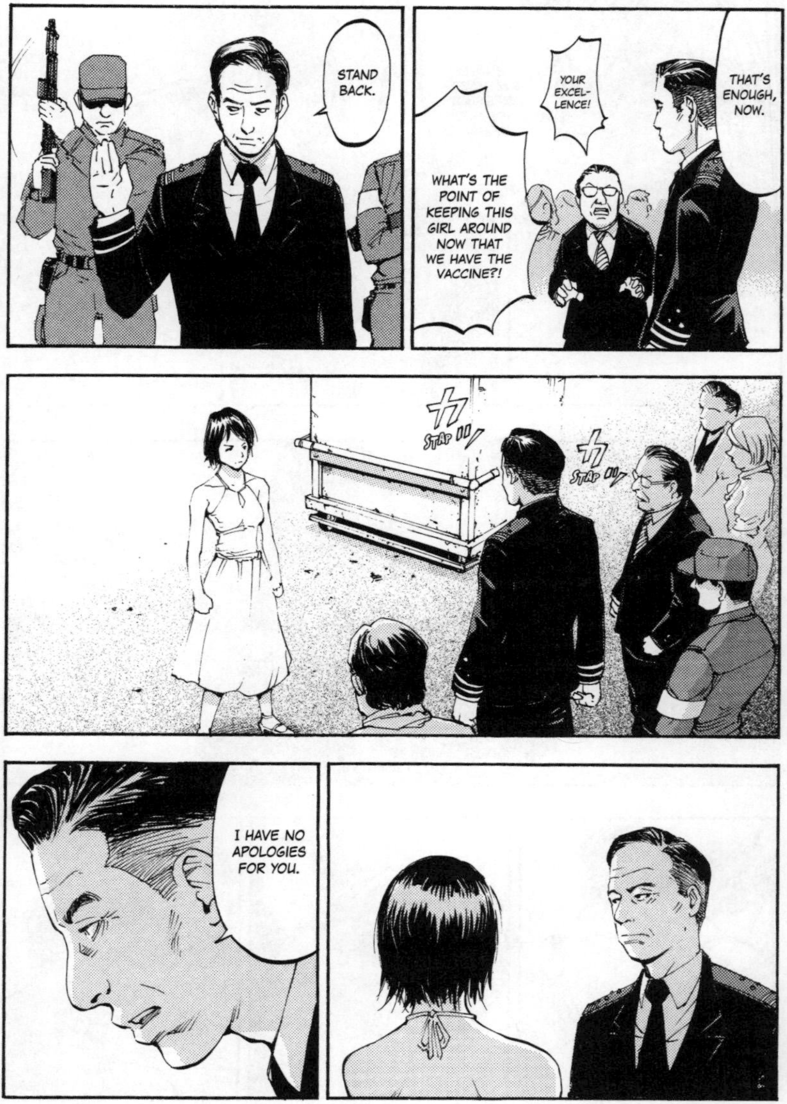
THAT'S ENOUGH, NOW.
YOUR EXCEL-LENCE!
WHAT'S THE POINT OF KEEPING THIS GIRL AROUND NOW THAT WE HAVE THE VACCINE?!
STAND BACK.
カ STAP
カ STAP
I HAVE NO APOLOGIES FOR YOU.

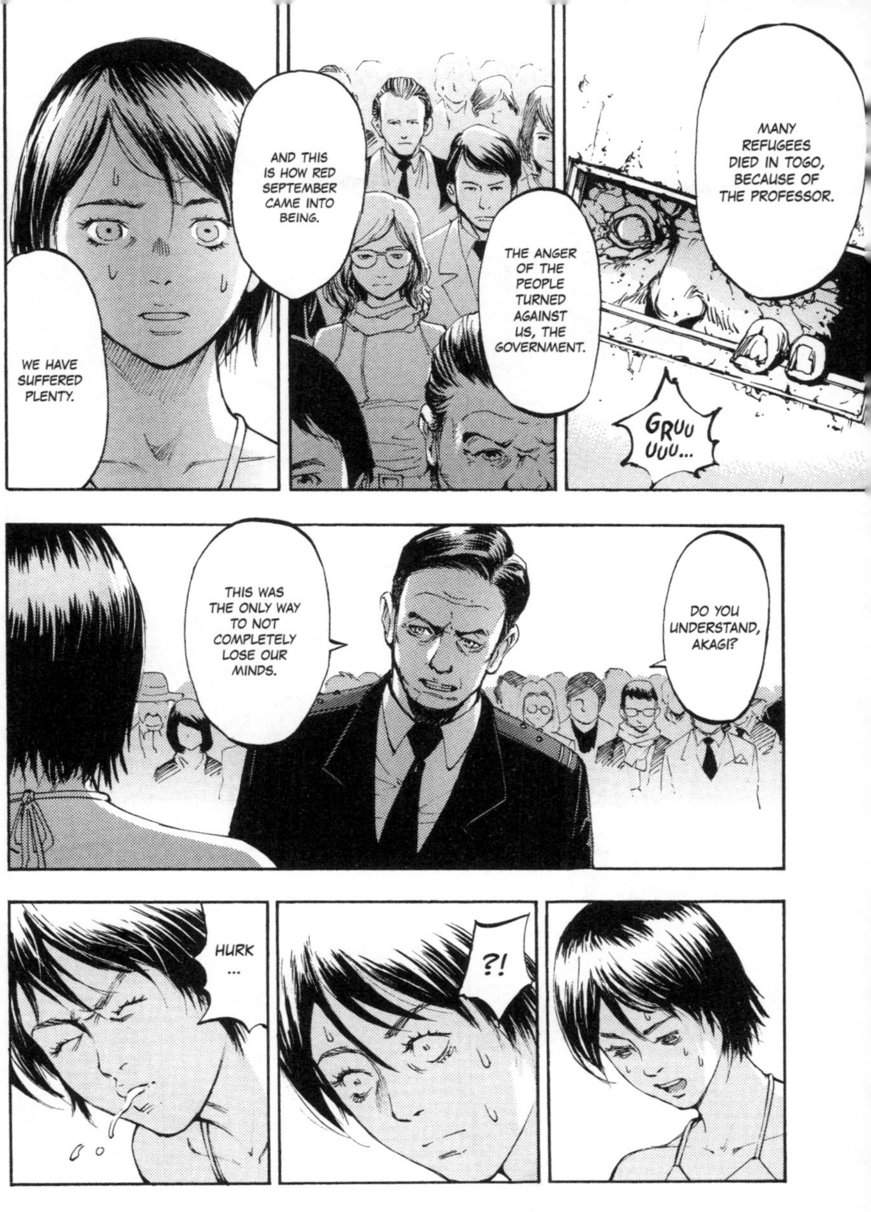
MANY REFUGEES DIED IN TOGO, BECAUSE OF THE PROFESSOR.
GRUU UUU...
THE ANGER OF THE PEOPLE TURNED AGAINST US, THE GOVERNMENT.
AND THIS IS HOW RED SEPTEMBER CAME INTO BEING.
WE HAVE SUFFERED PLENTY.
DO YOU UNDERSTAND, AKAGI?
THIS WAS THE ONLY WAY TO NOT COMPLETELY LOSE OUR MINDS.
?!
HURK ...

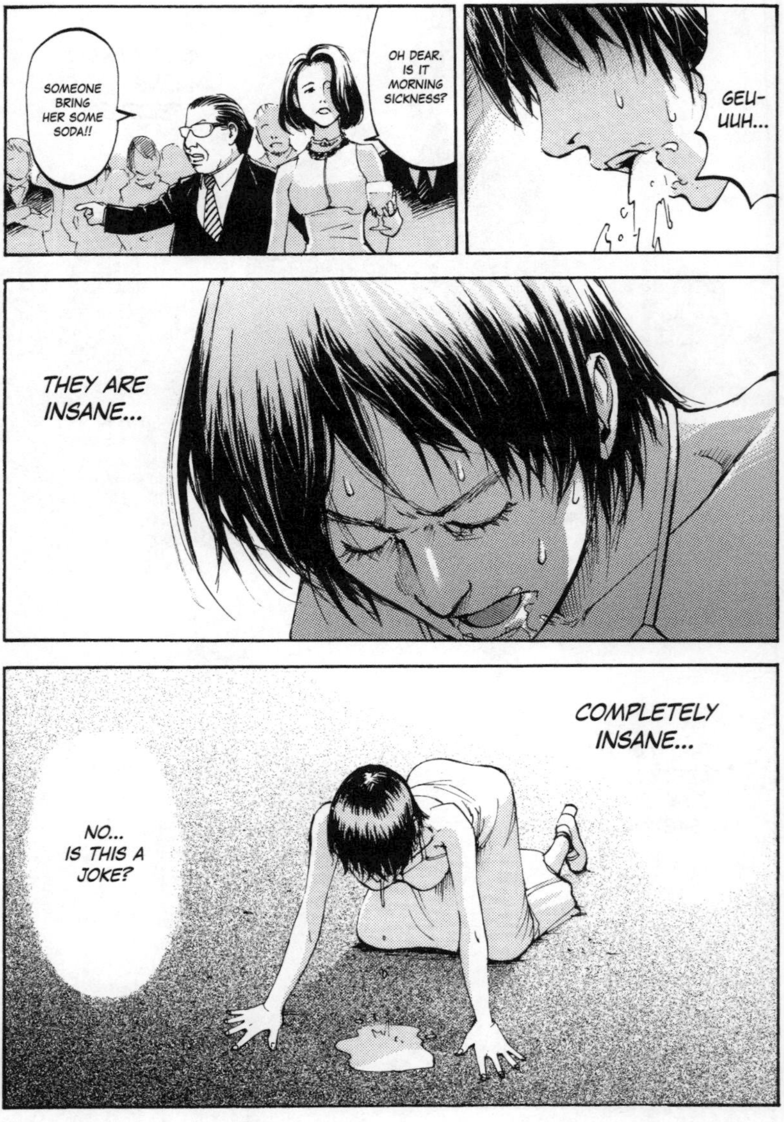
GEU-UUH...
OH DEAR. IS IT MORNING SICKNESS?
SOMEONE BRING HER SOME SODA!!
THEY ARE INSANE...
COMPLETELY INSANE...
NO... IS THIS A JOKE?

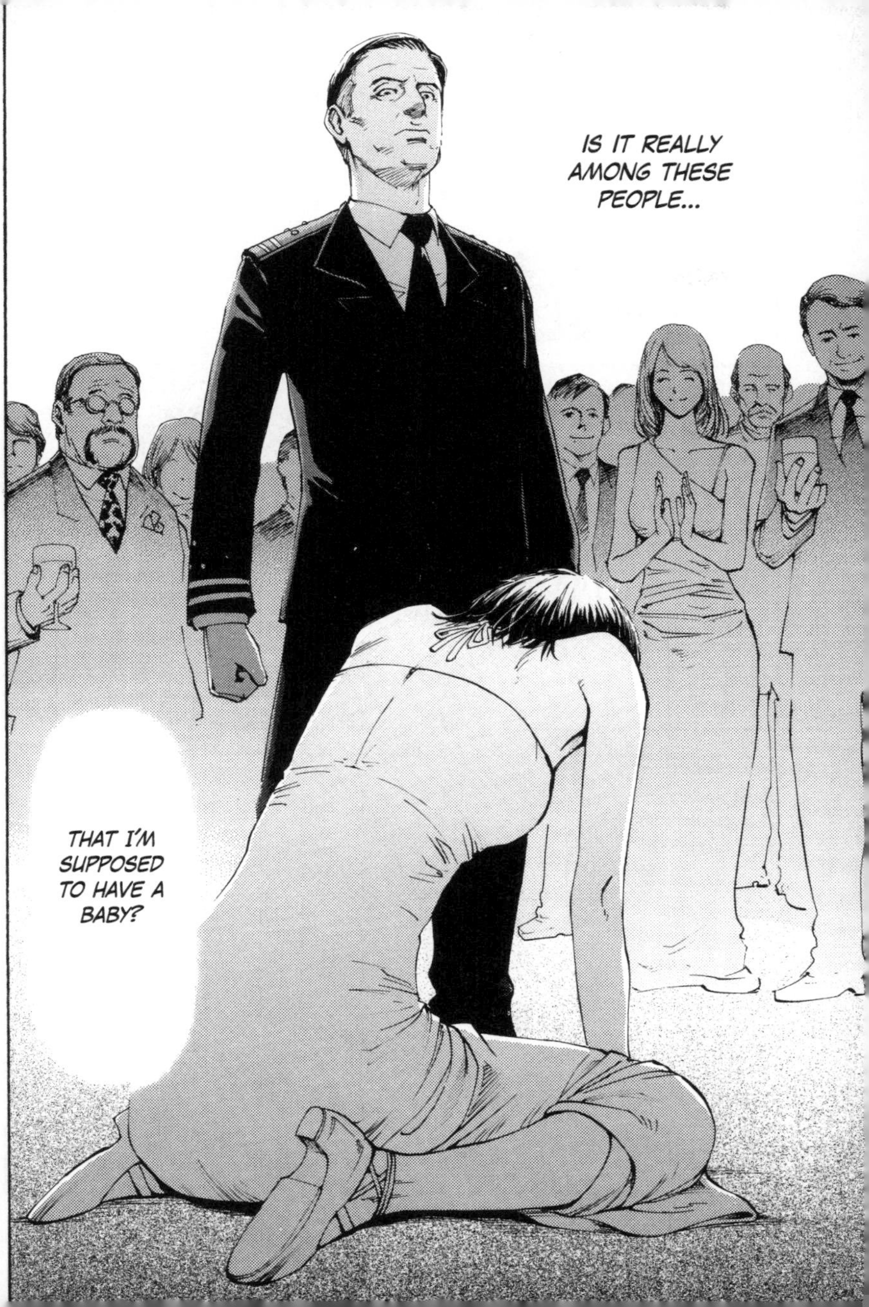
IS IT REALLY AMONG THESE PEOPLE...
THAT I'M SUPPOSED TO HAVE A BABY?

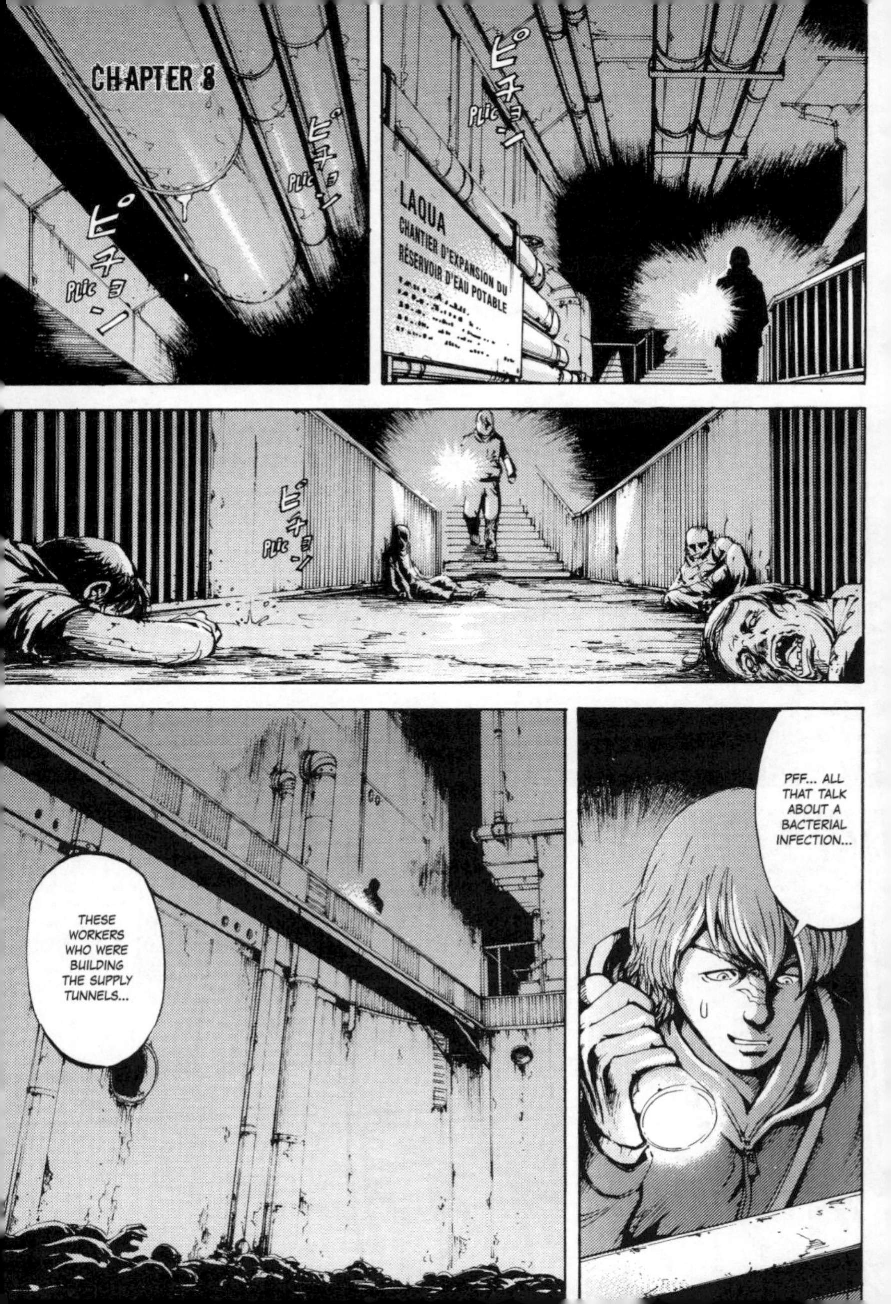
ピチョーン
PLIC
LAQUA
CHANTIER D'EXPANSION DU
RÉSERVOIR D'EAU POTABLE
CHAPTER 8
ピチョーン
PLIC
ピチョーン
PLIC
ピチョーン
PLIC
PFF... ALL THAT TALK ABOUT A BACTERIAL INFECTION...
THESE WORKERS WHO WERE BUILDING THE SUPPLY TUNNELS...

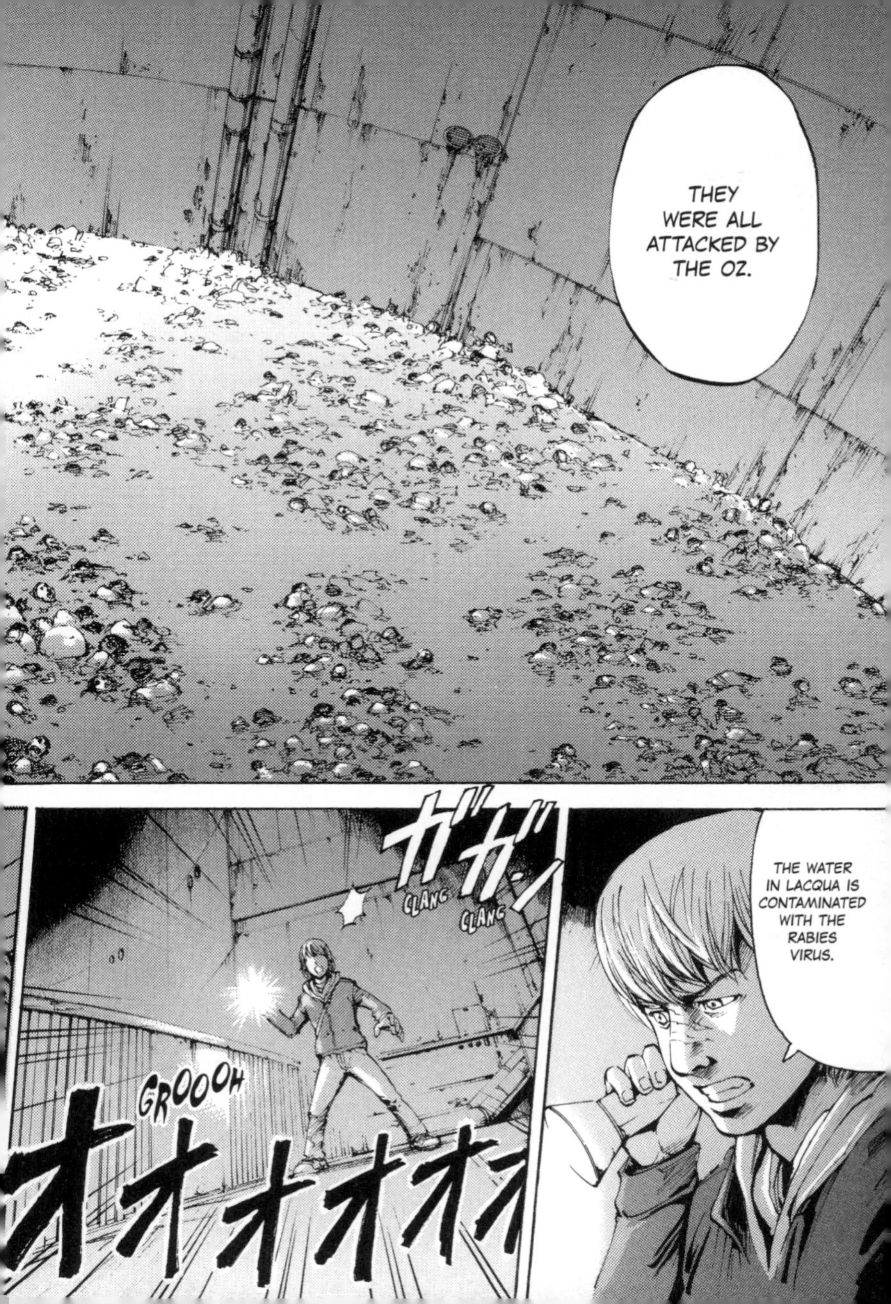
THEY WERE ALL ATTACKED BY THE OZ.
THE WATER IN LACQUA IS CONTAMINATED WITH THE RABIES VIRUS.
ガガン
CLANG
CLANG
オオオオ
GROOOH

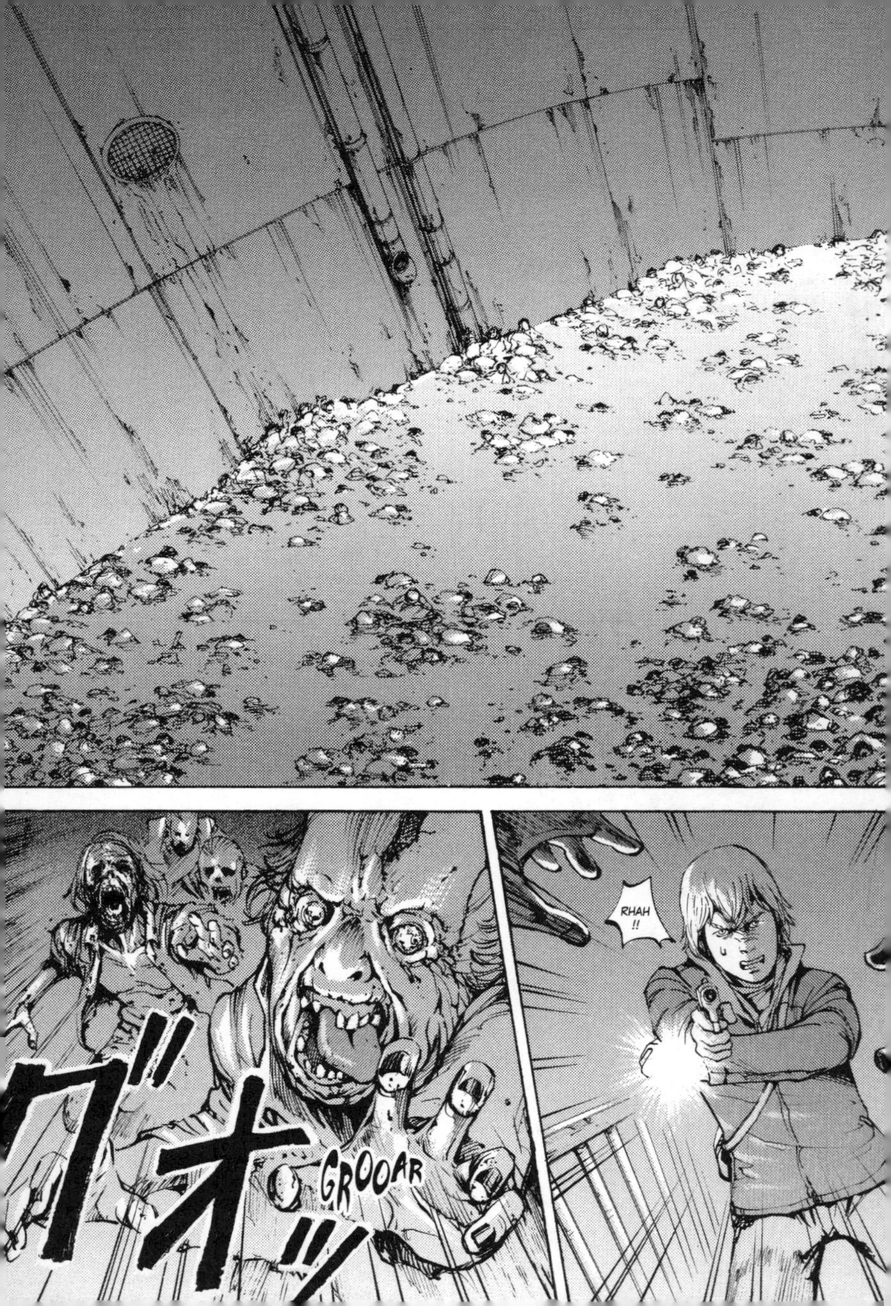
RHAH !!
グオッ!!
GROOAR

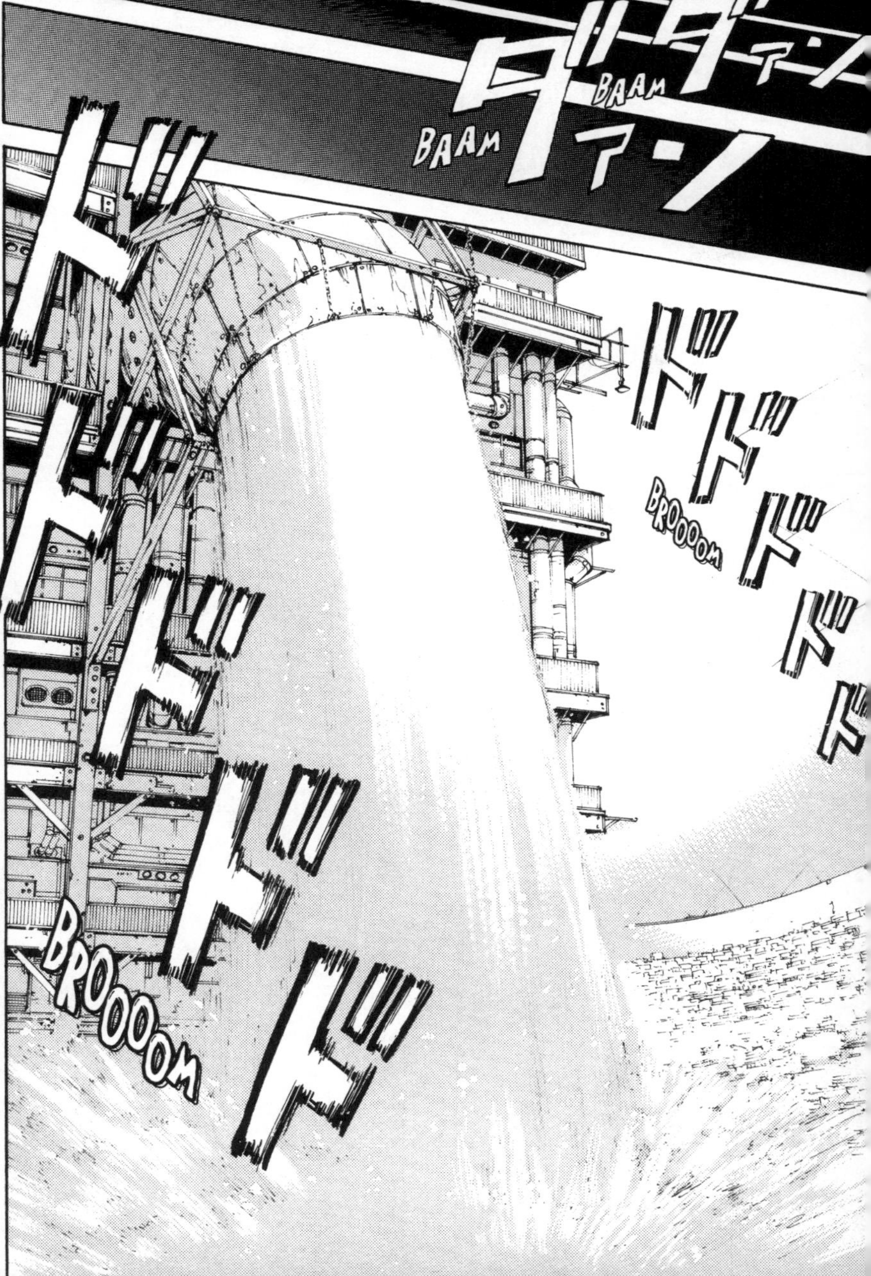

ダァーン
BAAM
ダァーン
BAAM
ドドドドド
BROOOOM
ドドドドド
BROOOOM

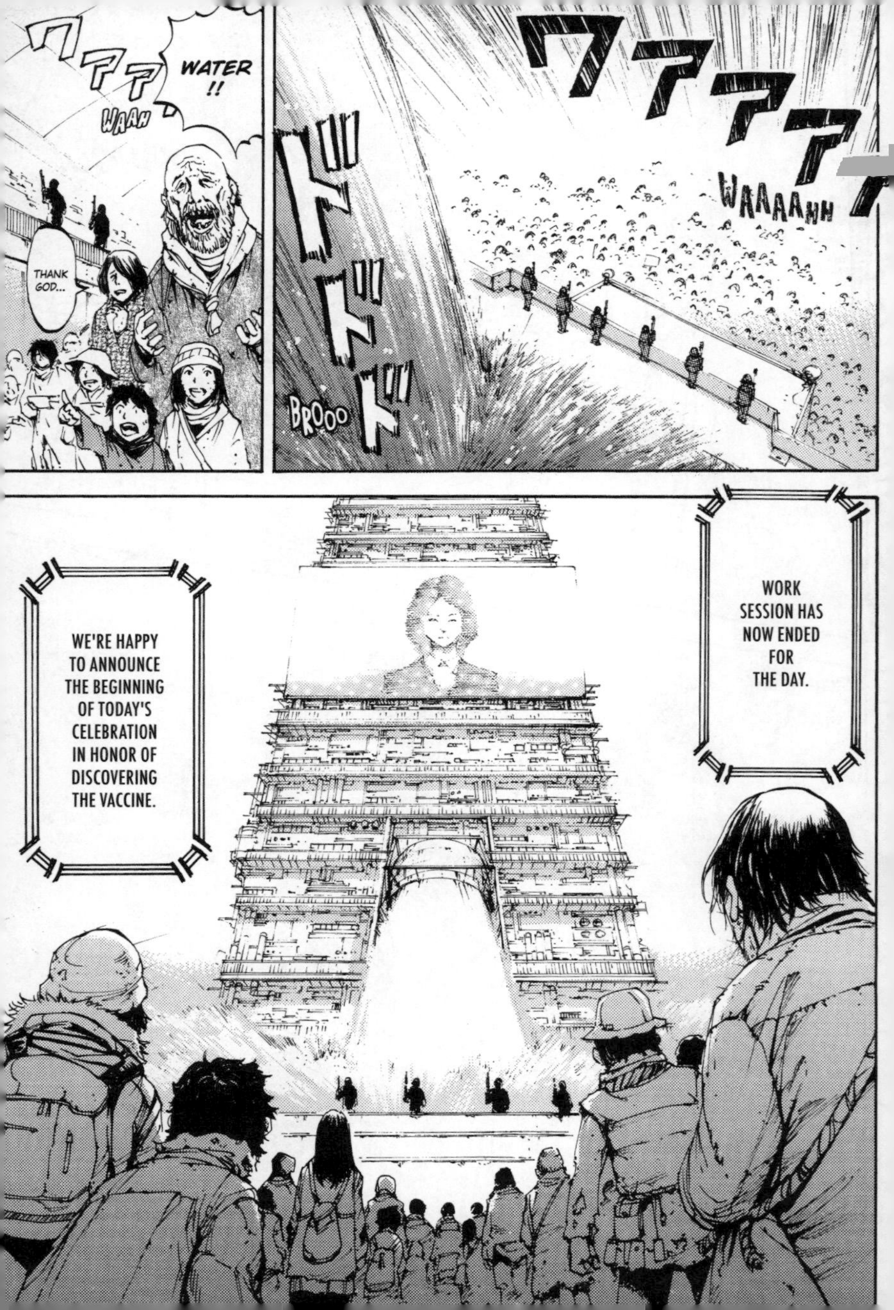
ワァァァ
WAAAANH
ドドド
BROOO
WATER !!
ワァァ
WAAH
THANK GOD...
WORK SESSION HAS NOW ENDED FOR THE DAY.
WE'RE HAPPY TO ANNOUNCE THE BEGINNING OF TODAY'S CELEBRATION IN HONOR OF DISCOVERING THE VACCINE.

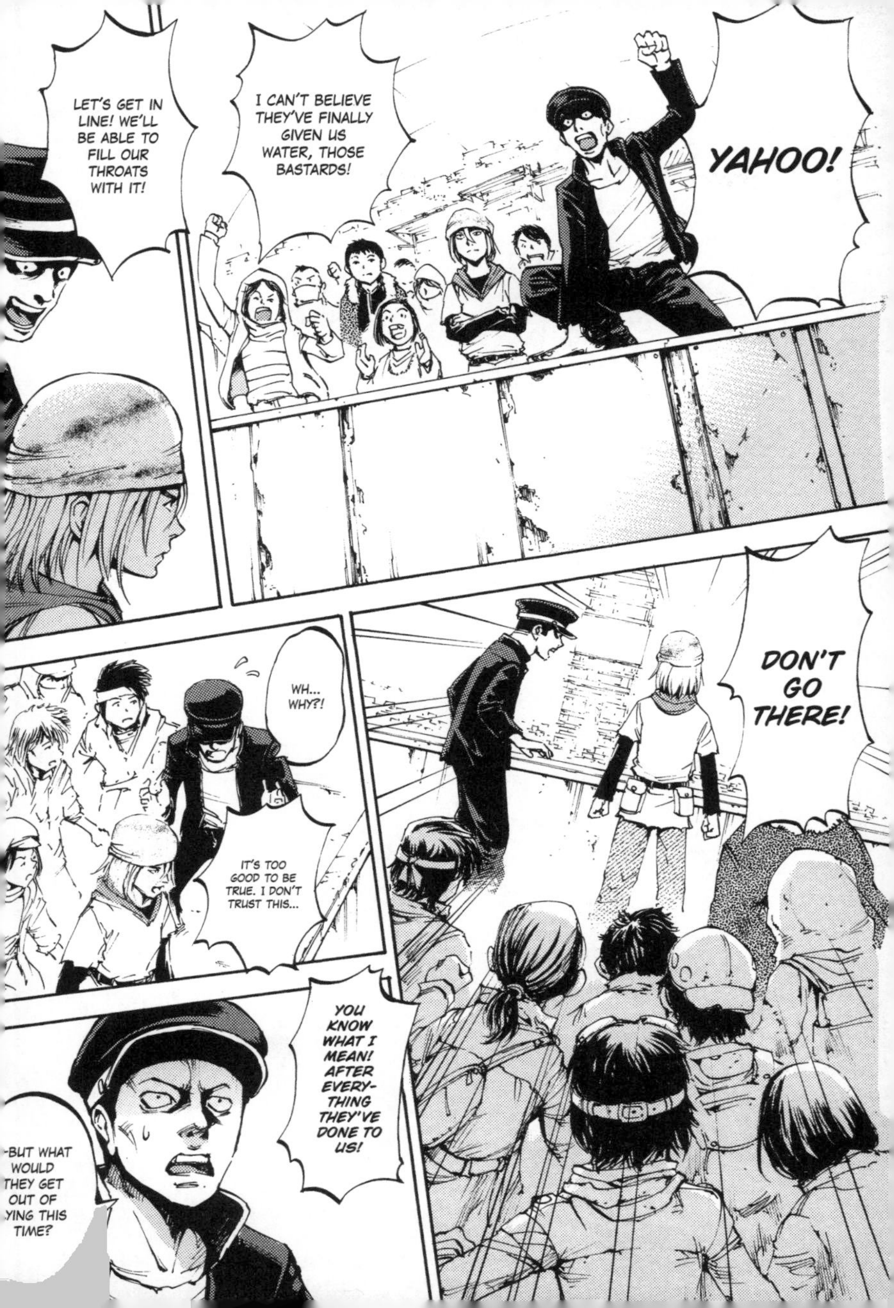

YAHOO!
I CAN'T BELIEVE THEY'VE FINALLY GIVEN US WATER, THOSE BASTARDS!
LET'S GET IN LINE! WE'LL BE ABLE TO FILL OUR THROATS WITH IT!
DON'T GO THERE!
WH... WHY?!
IT'S TOO GOOD TO BE TRUE. I DON'T TRUST THIS...
YOU KNOW WHAT I MEAN! AFTER EVERY-THING THEY'VE DONE TO US!
-BUT WHAT WOULD THEY GET OUT OF YING THIS TIME?

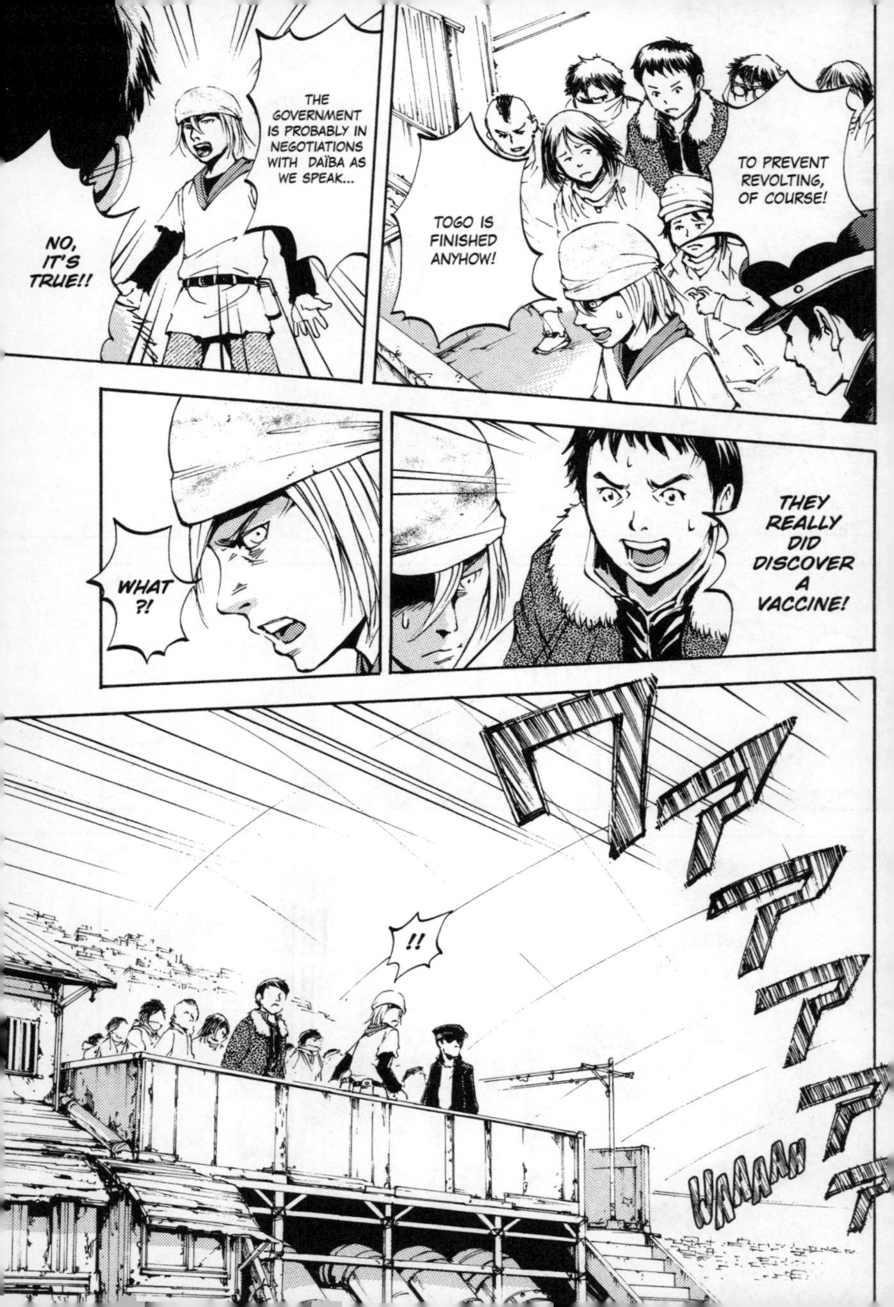
TO PREVENT REVOLTING, OF COURSE!
TOGO IS FINISHED ANYHOW!
THE GOVERNMENT IS PROBABLY IN NEGOTIATIONS WITH DAÏBA AS WE SPEAK...
NO, IT'S TRUE!!
THEY REALLY DID DISCOVER A VACCINE!
WHAT?!
!!
WAAAAH

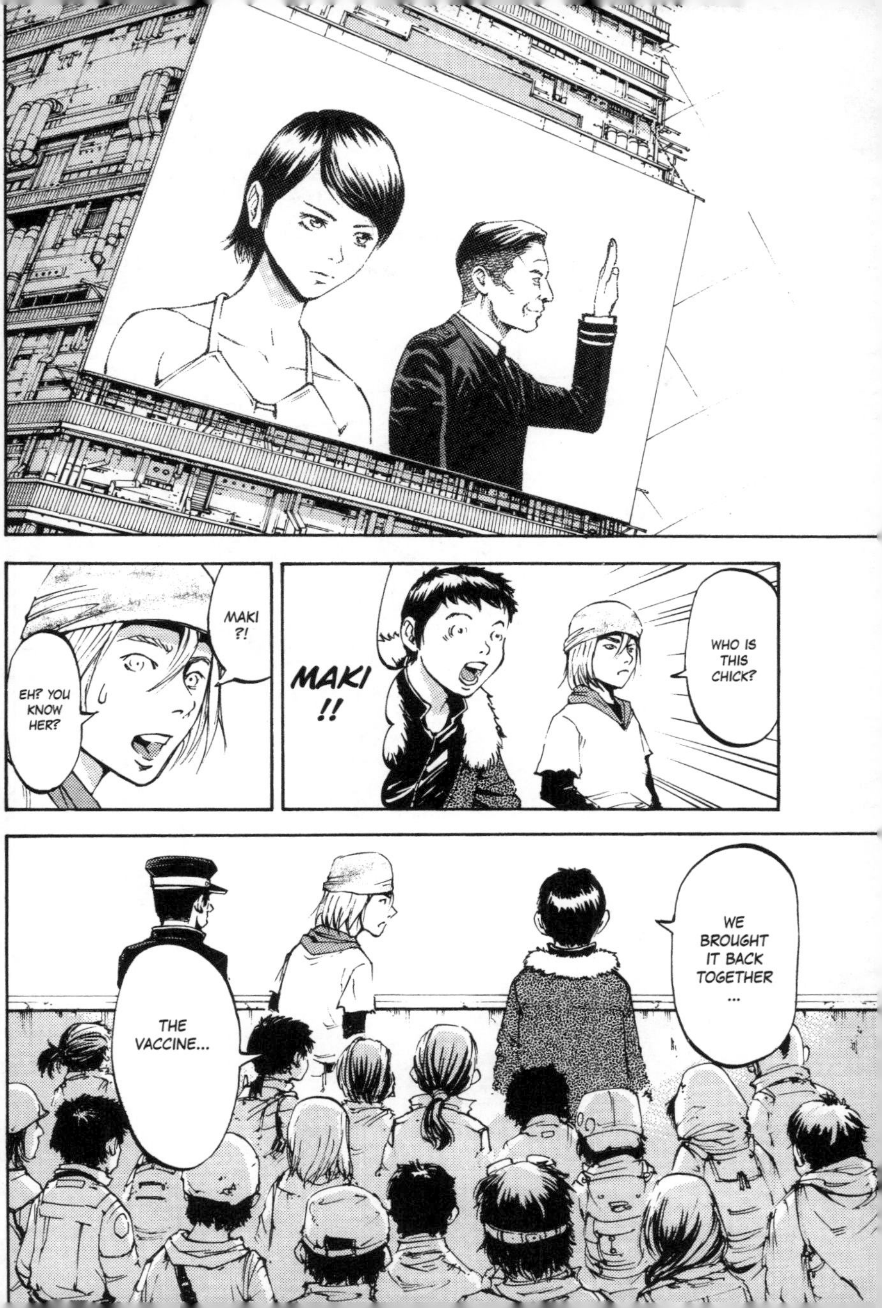
WHO IS THIS CHICK?
MAKI !!
MAKI ?!
EH? YOU KNOW HER?
WE BROUGHT IT BACK TOGETHER ...
THE VACCINE...

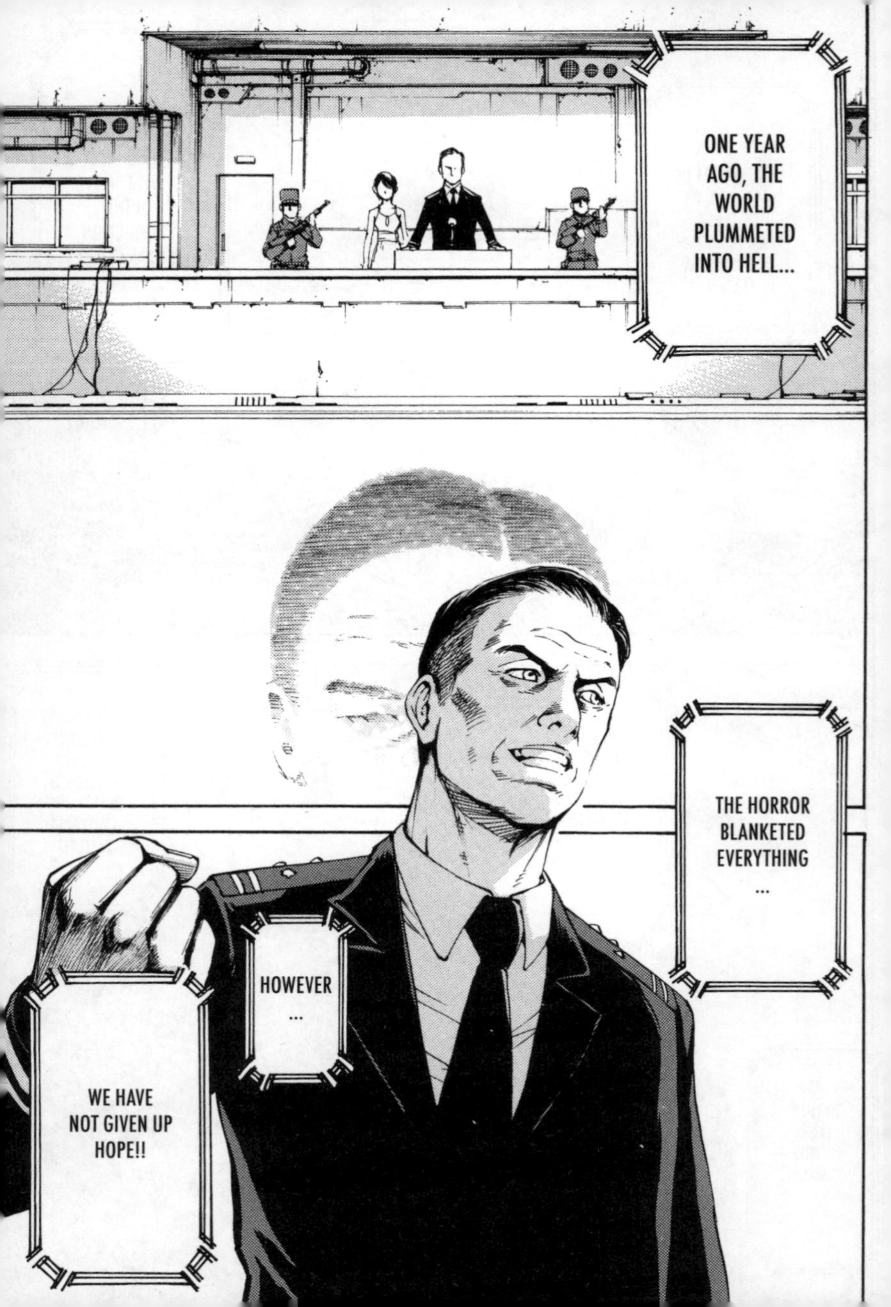
ONE YEAR AGO, THE WORLD PLUMMETED INTO HELL...
THE HORROR BLANKETED EVERYTHING ...
HOWEVER ...
WE HAVE NOT GIVEN UP HOPE!!

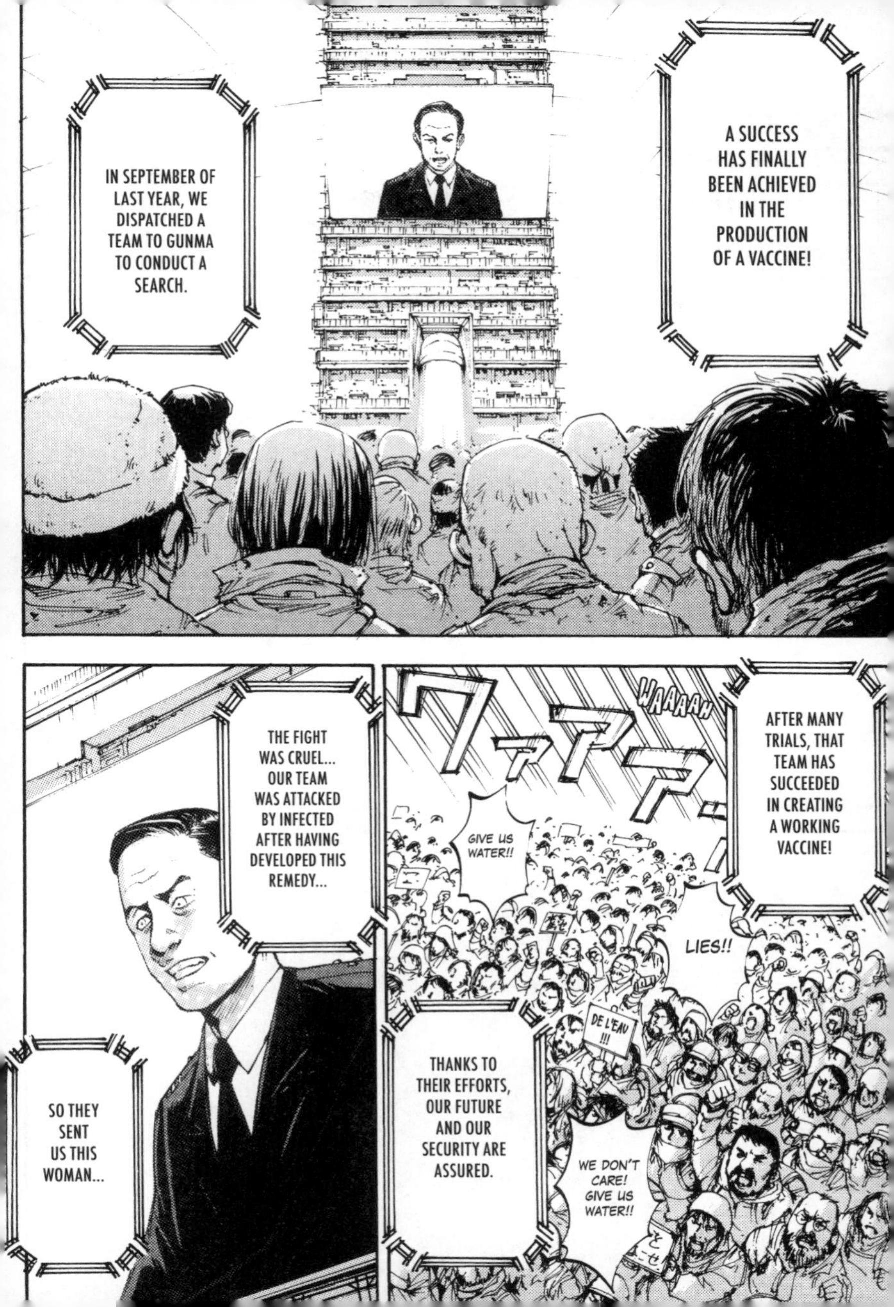
A SUCCESS HAS FINALLY BEEN ACHIEVED IN THE PRODUCTION OF A VACCINE!
IN SEPTEMBER OF LAST YEAR, WE DISPATCHED A TEAM TO GUNMA TO CONDUCT A SEARCH.
WAAAAAH
AFTER MANY TRIALS, THAT TEAM HAS SUCCEEDED IN CREATING A WORKING VACCINE!
GIVE US WATER!!
LIES!!
DE L'EAU !!!
THANKS TO THEIR EFFORTS, OUR FUTURE AND OUR SECURITY ARE ASSURED.
WE DON'T CARE! GIVE US WATER!!
THE FIGHT WAS CRUEL... OUR TEAM WAS ATTACKED BY INFECTED AFTER HAVING DEVELOPED THIS REMEDY...
SO THEY SENT US THIS WOMAN...

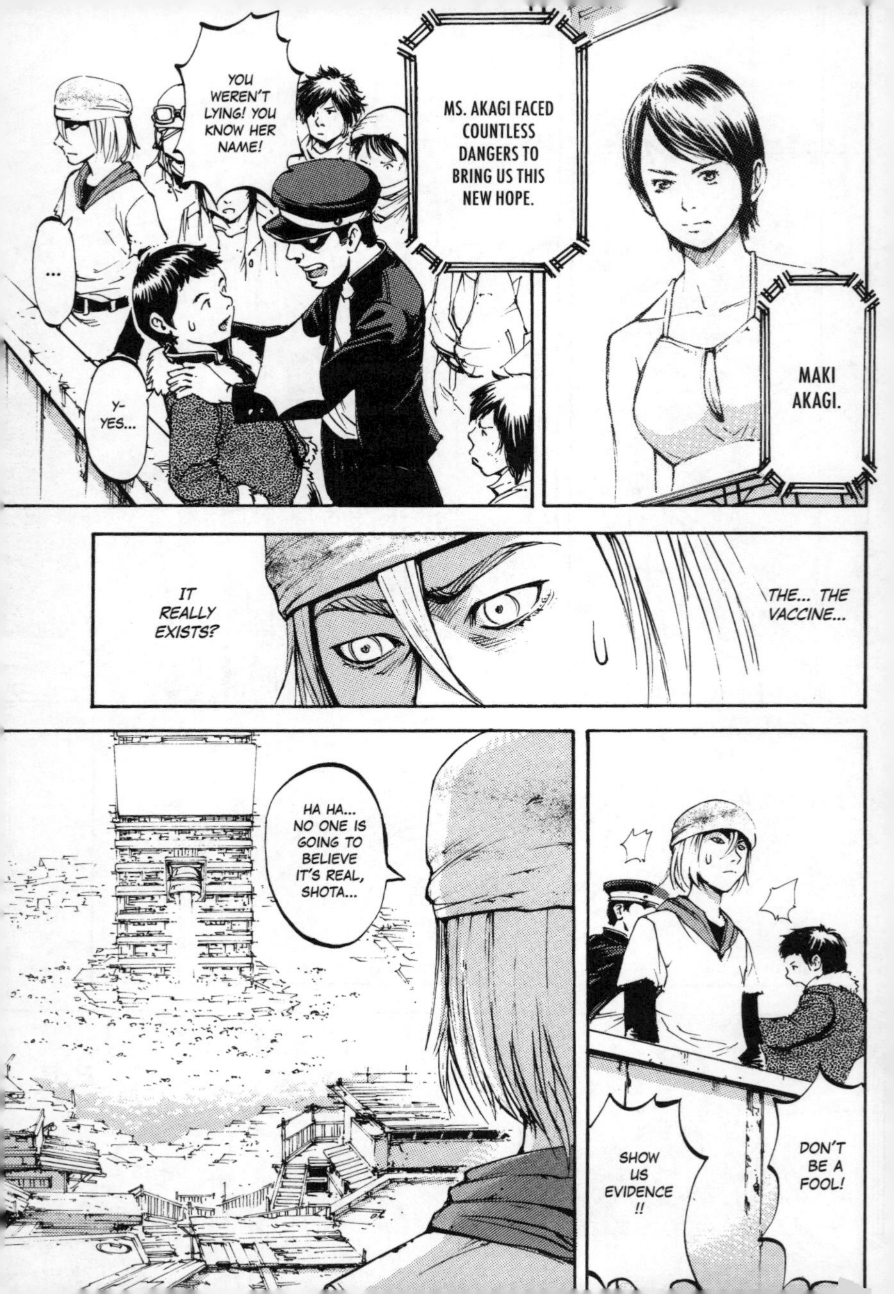
MS. AKAGI FACED COUNTLESS DANGERS TO BRING US THIS NEW HOPE.
MAKI AKAGI.
YOU WEREN'T LYING! YOU KNOW HER NAME!
...
Y-YES...
THE... THE VACCINE...
IT REALLY EXISTS?
DON'T BE A FOOL!
SHOW US EVIDENCE !!
HA HA... NO ONE IS GOING TO BELIEVE IT'S REAL, SHOTA...

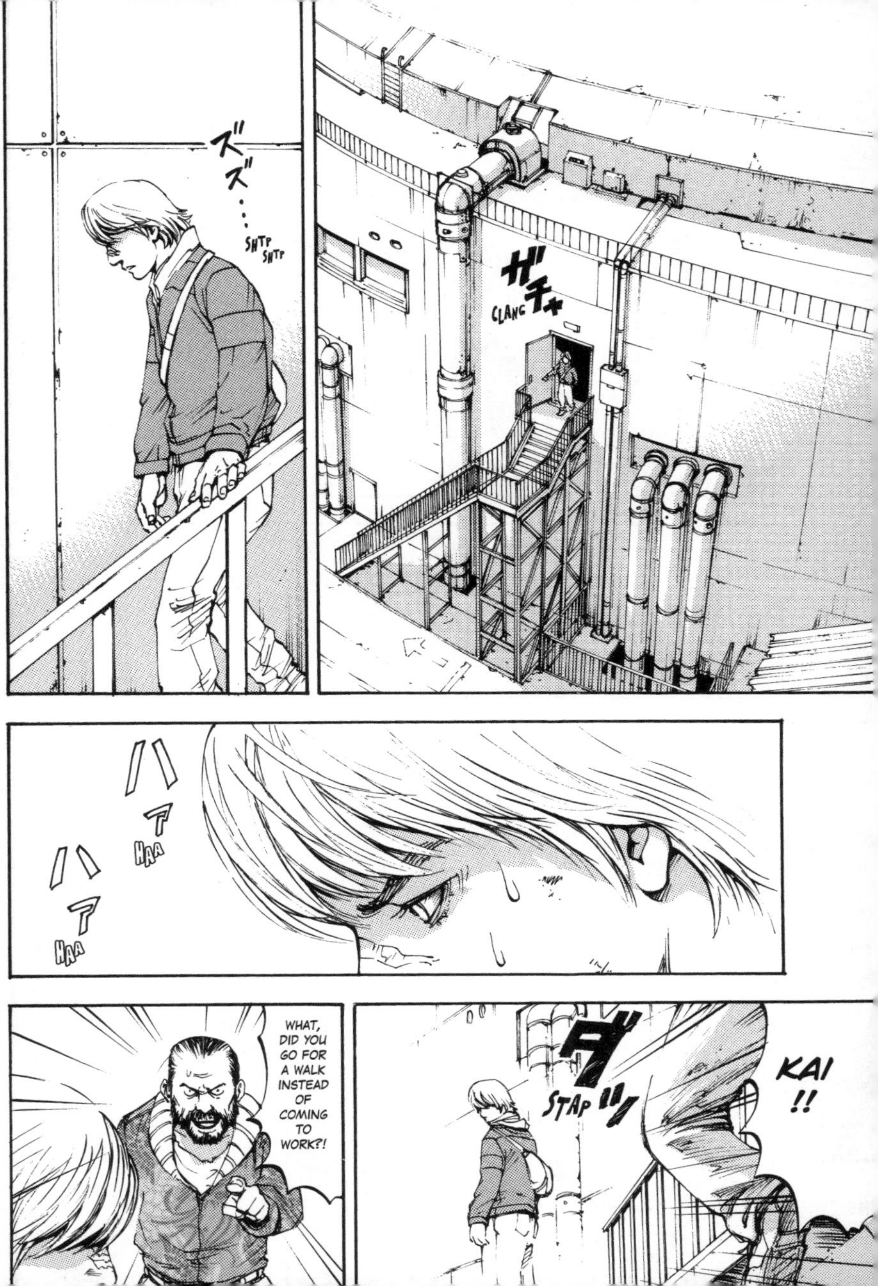
ガチャ
CLANG
ズズ…
SHTP SHTP
ハァ
HAA
ハァ
HAA
ダッ
STAP!!
KAI !!
WHAT, DID YOU GO FOR A WALK INSTEAD OF COMING TO WORK?!

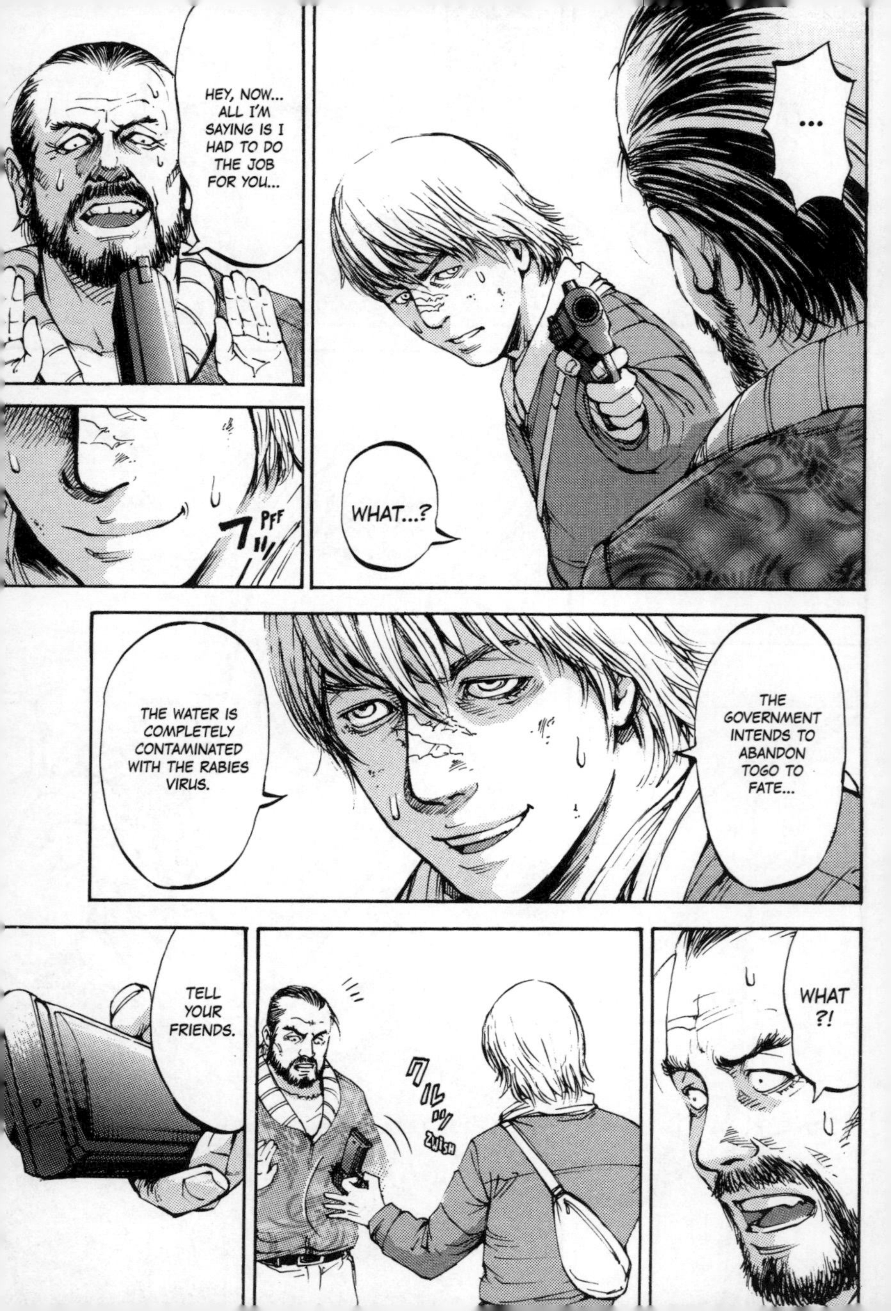
...
WHAT...?
HEY, NOW... ALL I'M SAYING IS I HAD TO DO THE JOB FOR YOU...
PFF
THE GOVERNMENT INTENDS TO ABANDON TOGO TO FATE...
THE WATER IS COMPLETELY CONTAMINATED WITH THE RABIES VIRUS.
WHAT ?!
ZWISH
TELL YOUR FRIENDS.

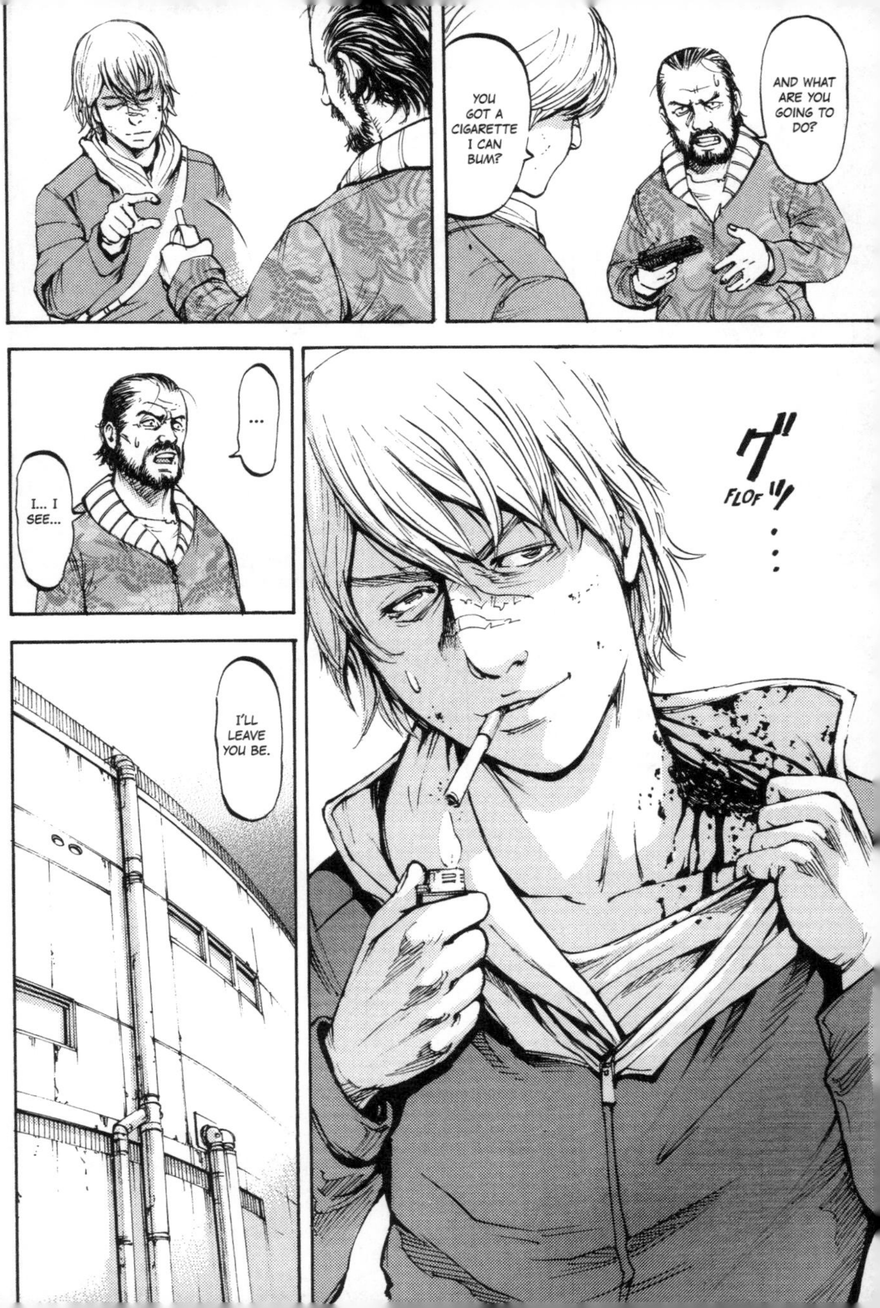
AND WHAT ARE YOU GOING TO DO?
YOU GOT A CIGARETTE I CAN BUM?
グッ
FLOF
...
...
I... I SEE...
I'LL LEAVE YOU BE.

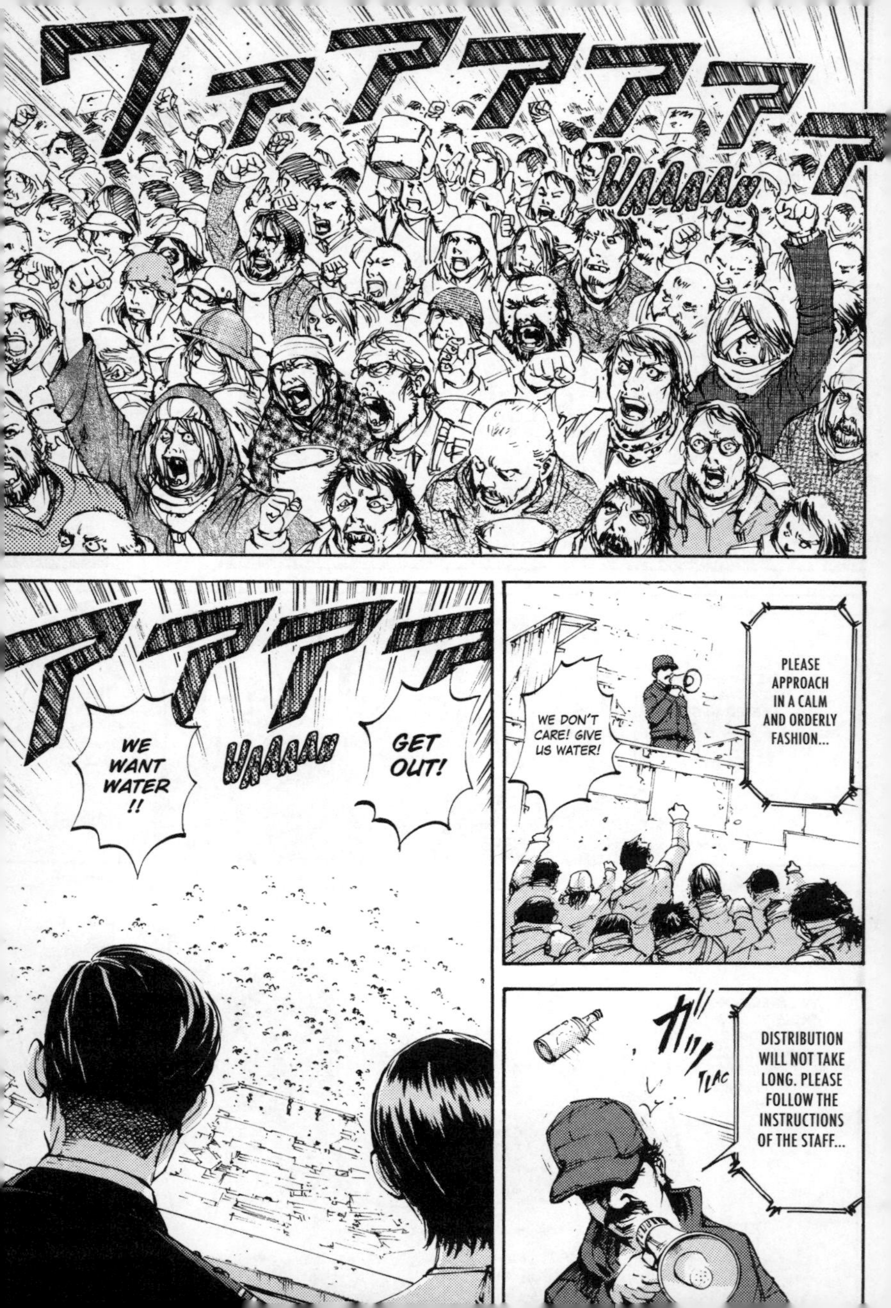
UAAAAH
PLEASE APPROACH IN A CALM AND ORDERLY FASHION...
WE DON'T CARE! GIVE US WATER!
DISTRIBUTION WILL NOT TAKE LONG. PLEASE FOLLOW THE INSTRUCTIONS OF THE STAFF...
TLAC
GET OUT!
UAAAAH
WE WANT WATER !!

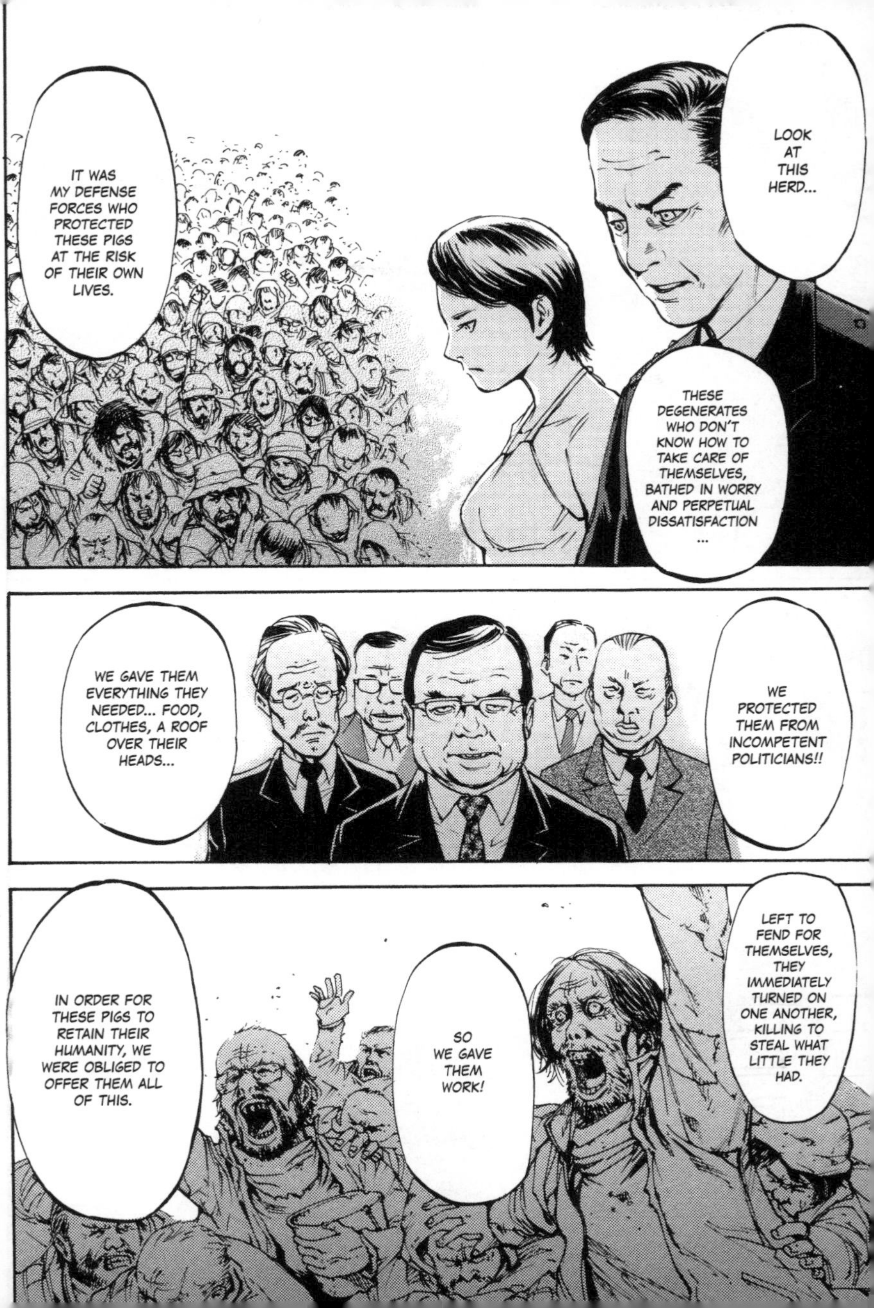
LOOK AT THIS HERD...
THESE DEGENERATES WHO DON'T KNOW HOW TO TAKE CARE OF THEMSELVES, BATHED IN WORRY AND PERPETUAL DISSATISFACTION ...
IT WAS MY DEFENSE FORCES WHO PROTECTED THESE PIGS AT THE RISK OF THEIR OWN LIVES.
WE PROTECTED THEM FROM INCOMPETENT POLITICIANS!!
WE GAVE THEM EVERYTHING THEY NEEDED... FOOD, CLOTHES, A ROOF OVER THEIR HEADS...
LEFT TO FEND FOR THEMSELVES, THEY IMMEDIATELY TURNED ON ONE ANOTHER, KILLING TO STEAL WHAT LITTLE THEY HAD.
SO WE GAVE THEM WORK!
IN ORDER FOR THESE PIGS TO RETAIN THEIR HUMANITY, WE WERE OBLIGED TO OFFER THEM ALL OF THIS.

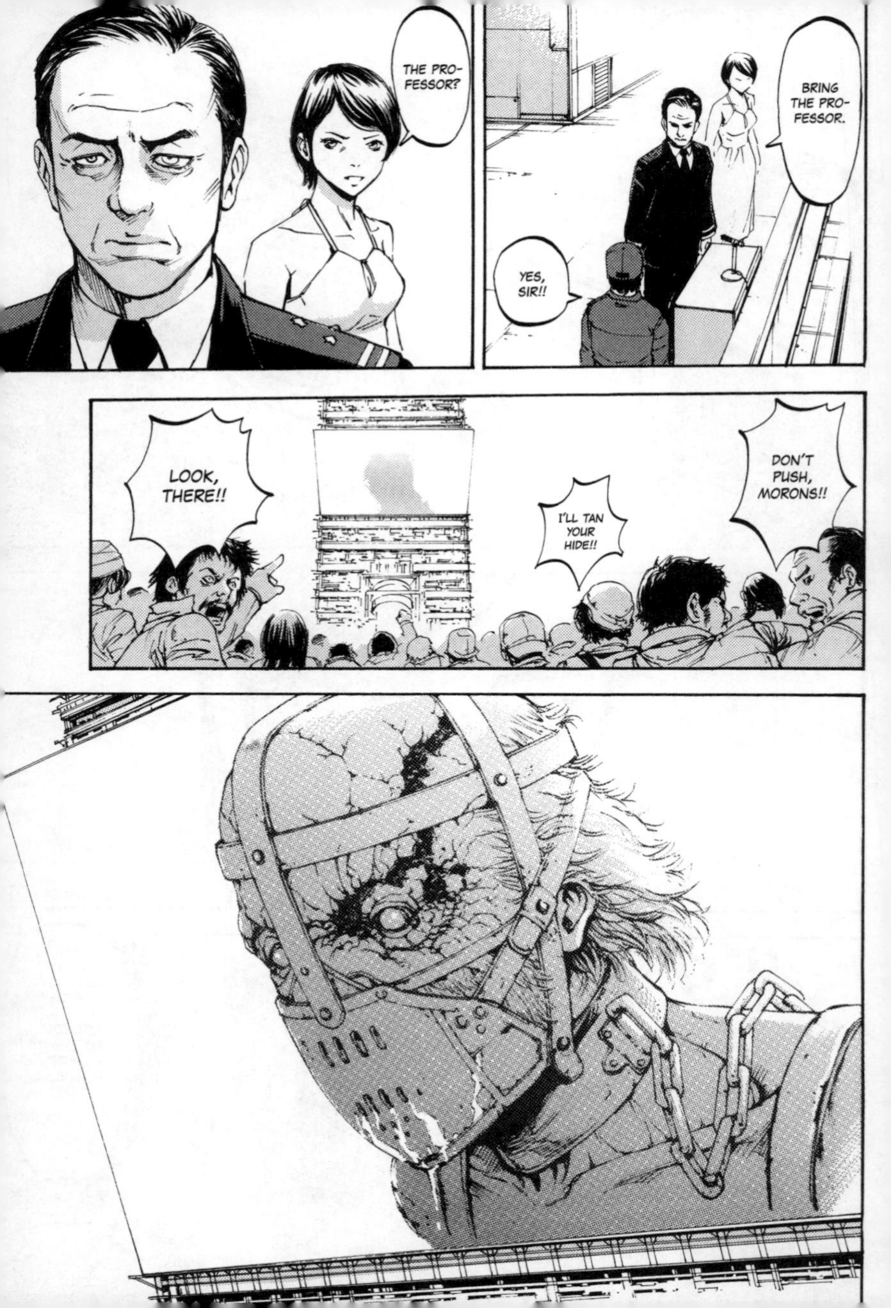
BRING THE PRO-FESSOR.
YES, SIR!!
THE PRO-FESSOR?
DON'T PUSH, MORONS!!
I'LL TAN YOUR HIDE!!
LOOK, THERE!!

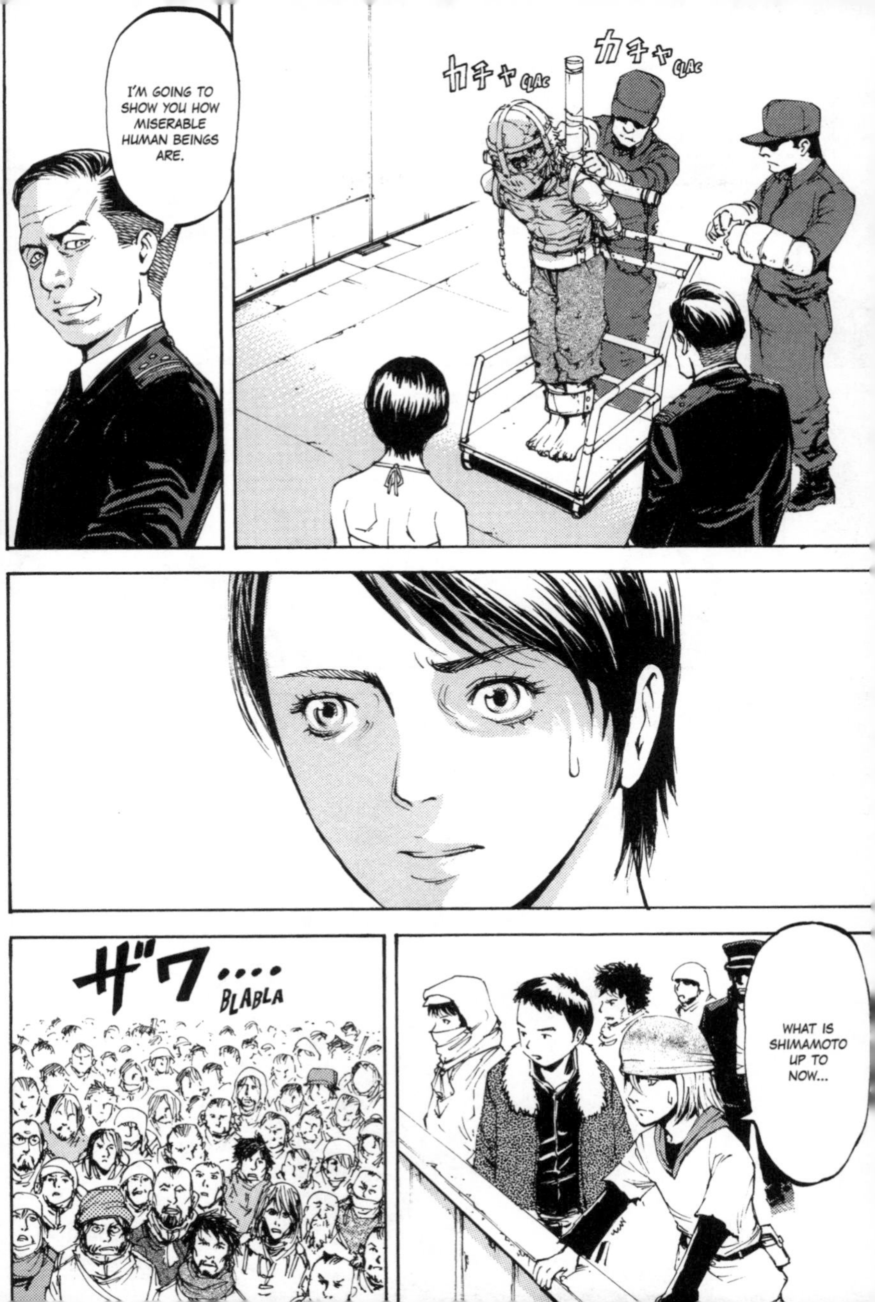
カチャ CLAC
カチャ CLAC
I'M GOING TO SHOW YOU HOW MISERABLE HUMAN BEINGS ARE.
WHAT IS SHIMAMOTO UP TO NOW...
ザワ.... BLABLA

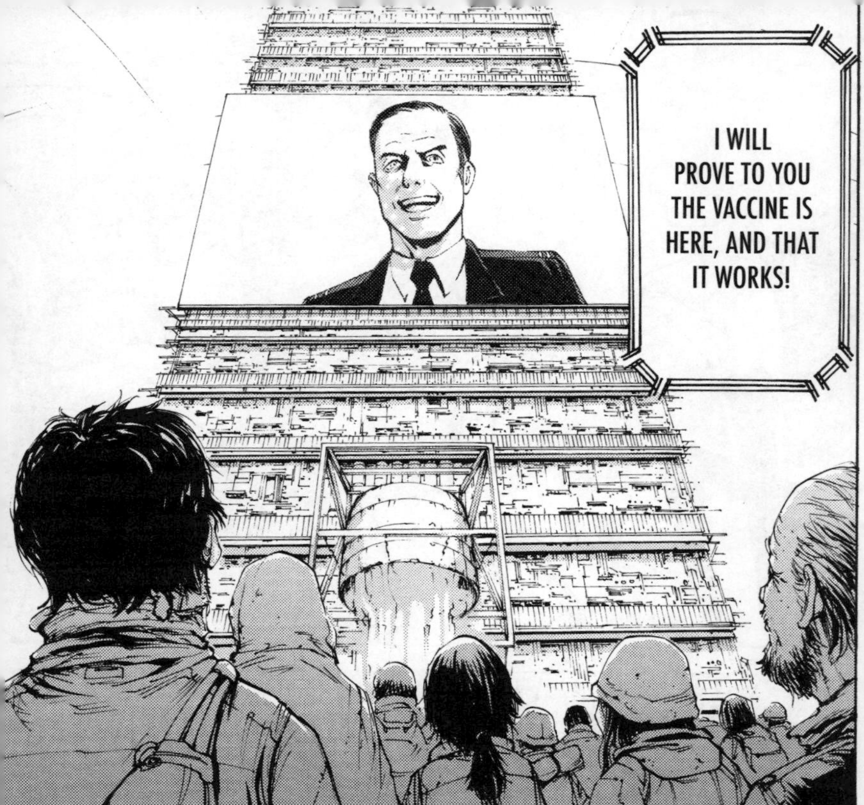
I WILL PROVE TO YOU THE VACCINE IS HERE, AND THAT IT WORKS!
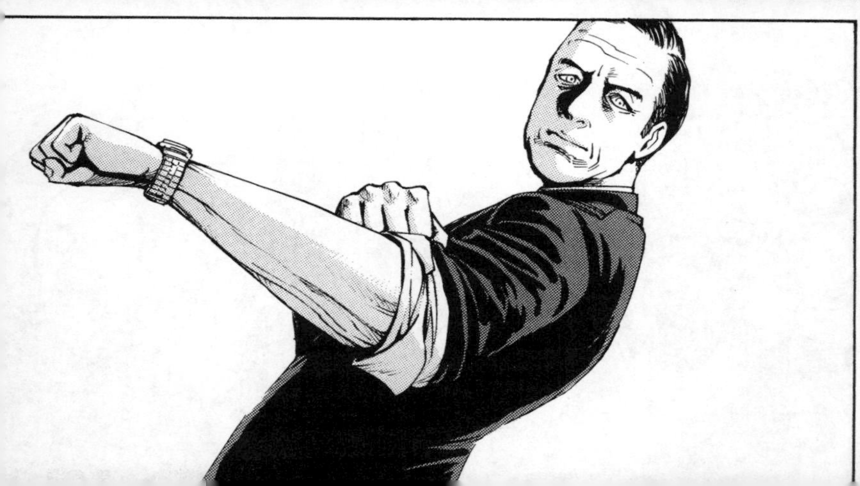

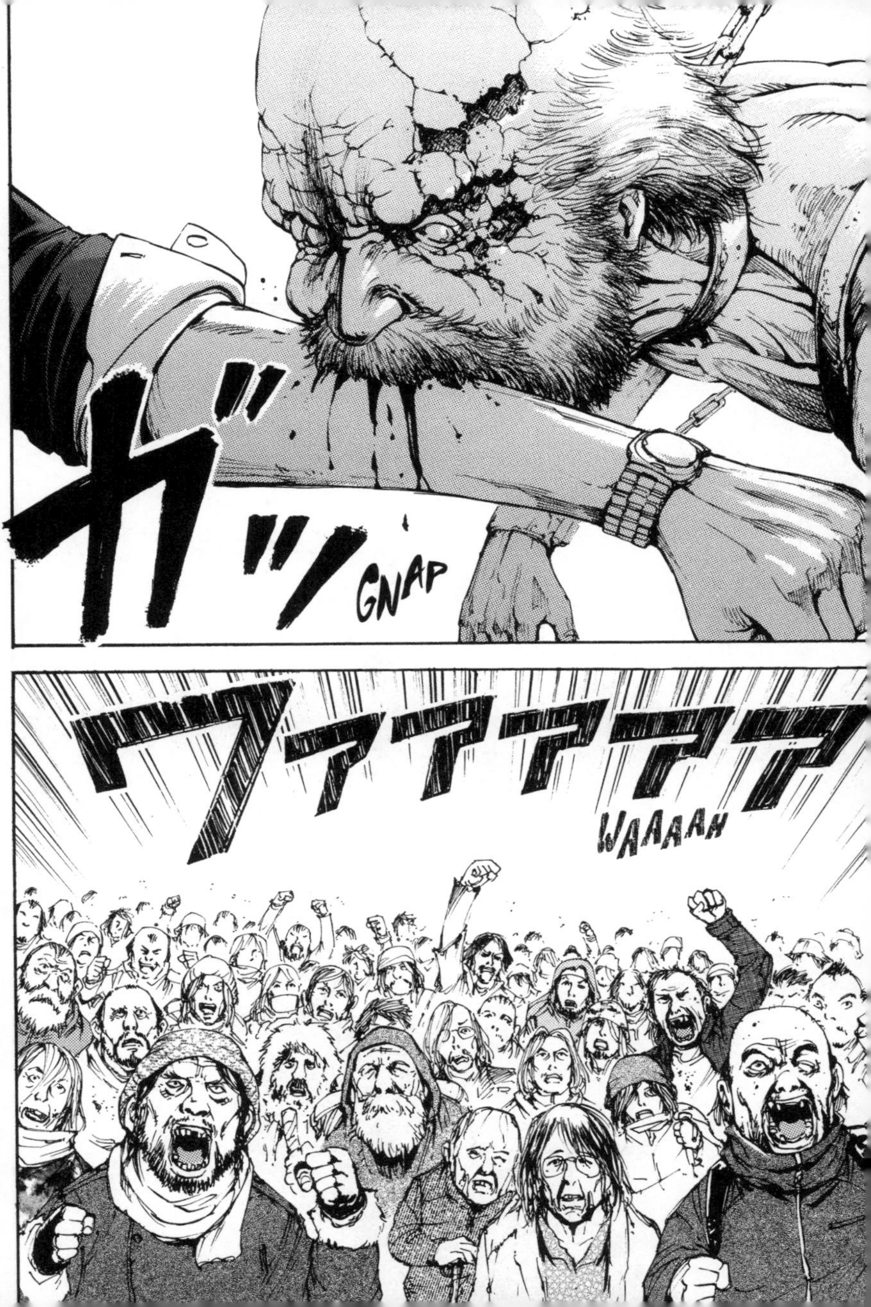
ガッ
GNAP
ワァアアアア
WAAAAH

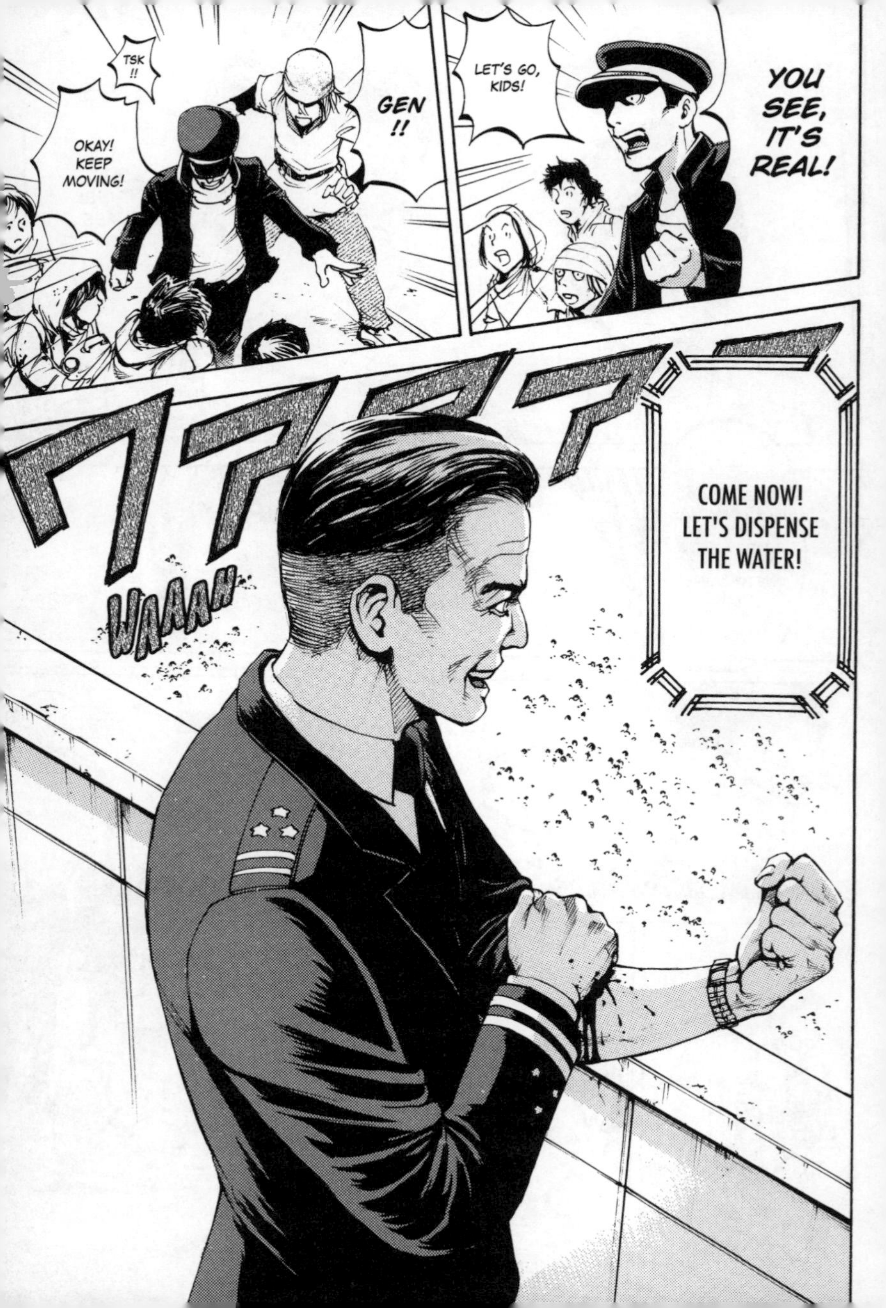
YOU SEE, IT'S REAL!
LET'S GO, KIDS!
GEN !!
TSK !!
OKAY! KEEP MOVING!
COME NOW! LET'S DISPENSE THE WATER!
WAAAH

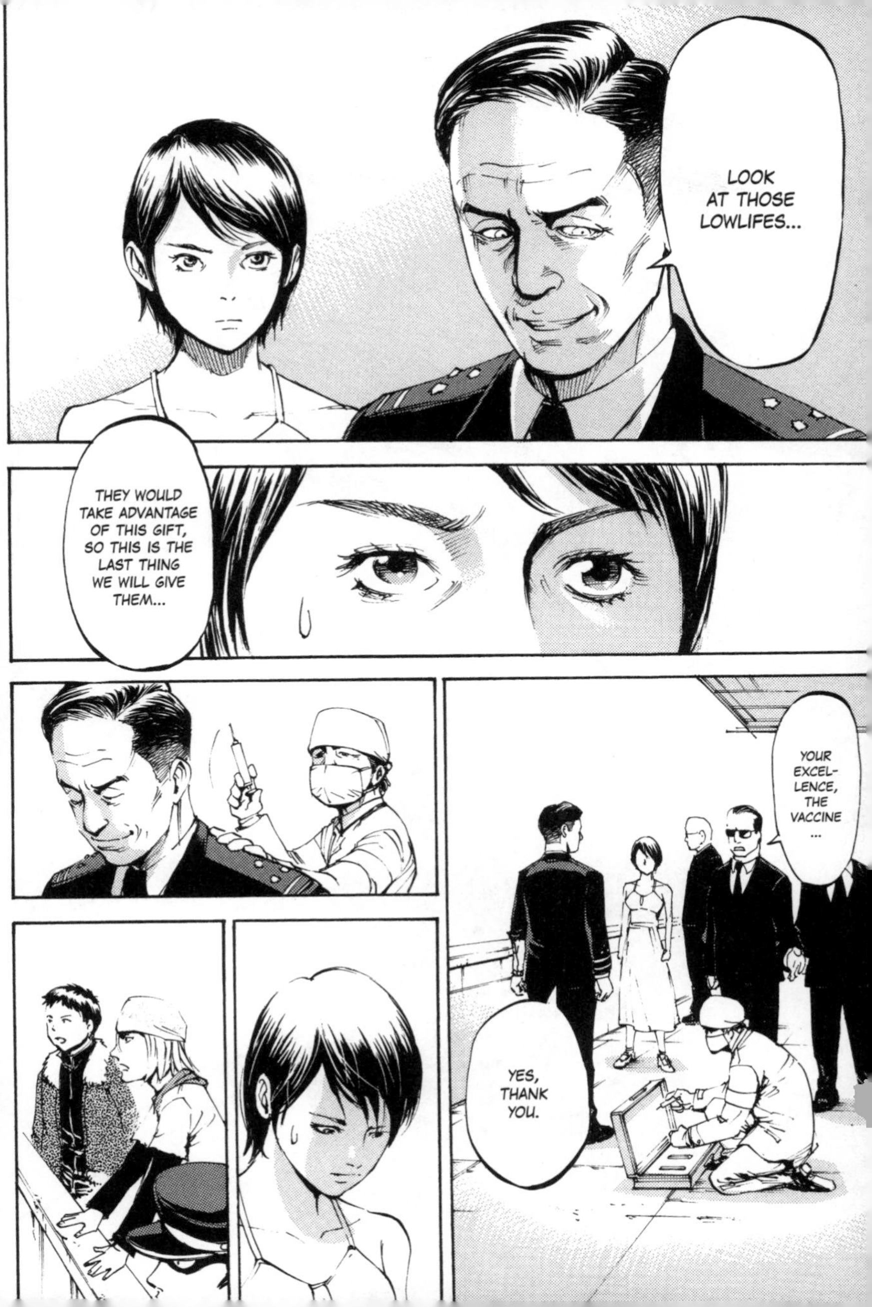
LOOK AT THOSE LOWLIFES...
THEY WOULD TAKE ADVANTAGE OF THIS GIFT, SO THIS IS THE LAST THING WE WILL GIVE THEM...
YOUR EXCEL-LENCE, THE VACCINE ...
YES, THANK YOU.

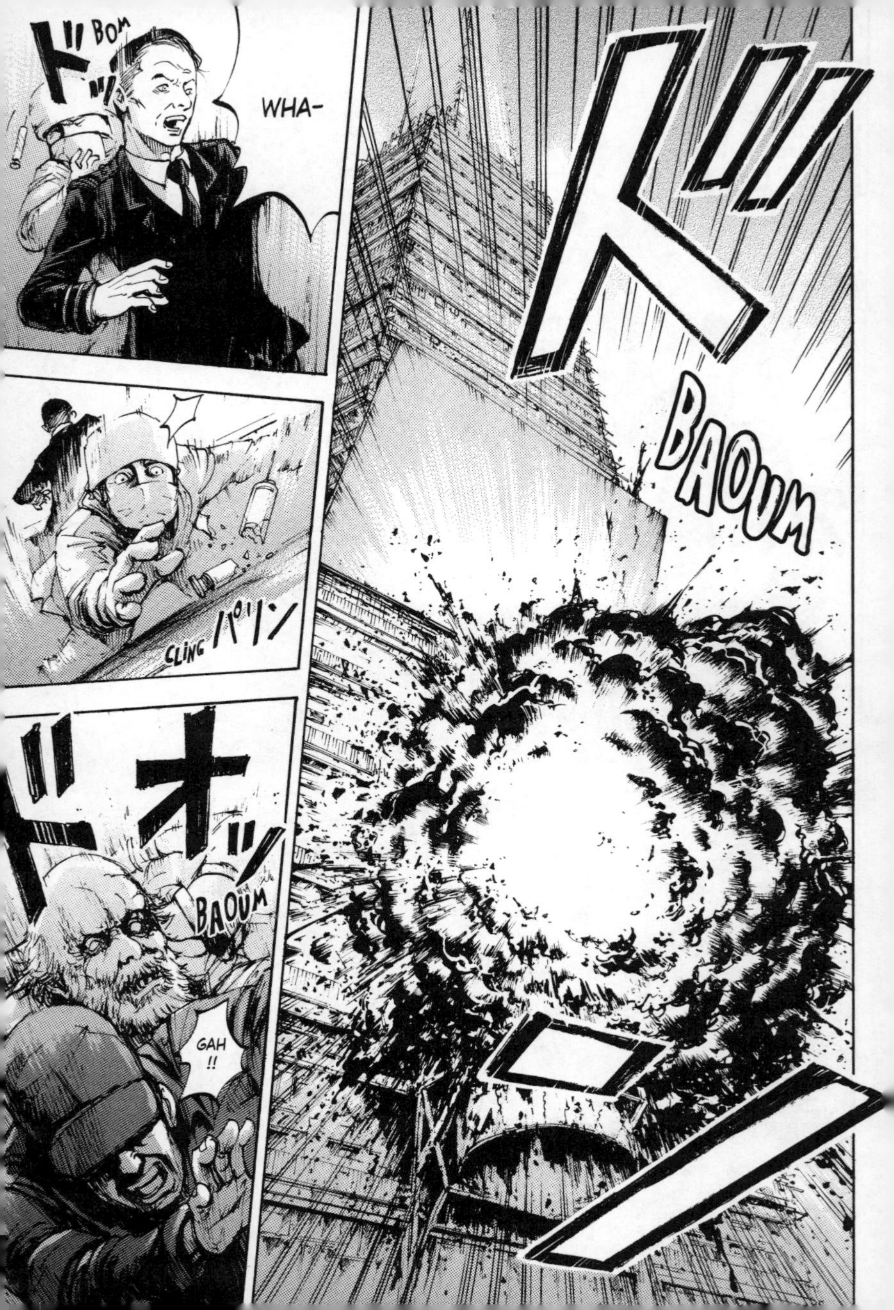
BAOUM
BOM
WHA-
CLING
パリン
BAOUM
GAH !!

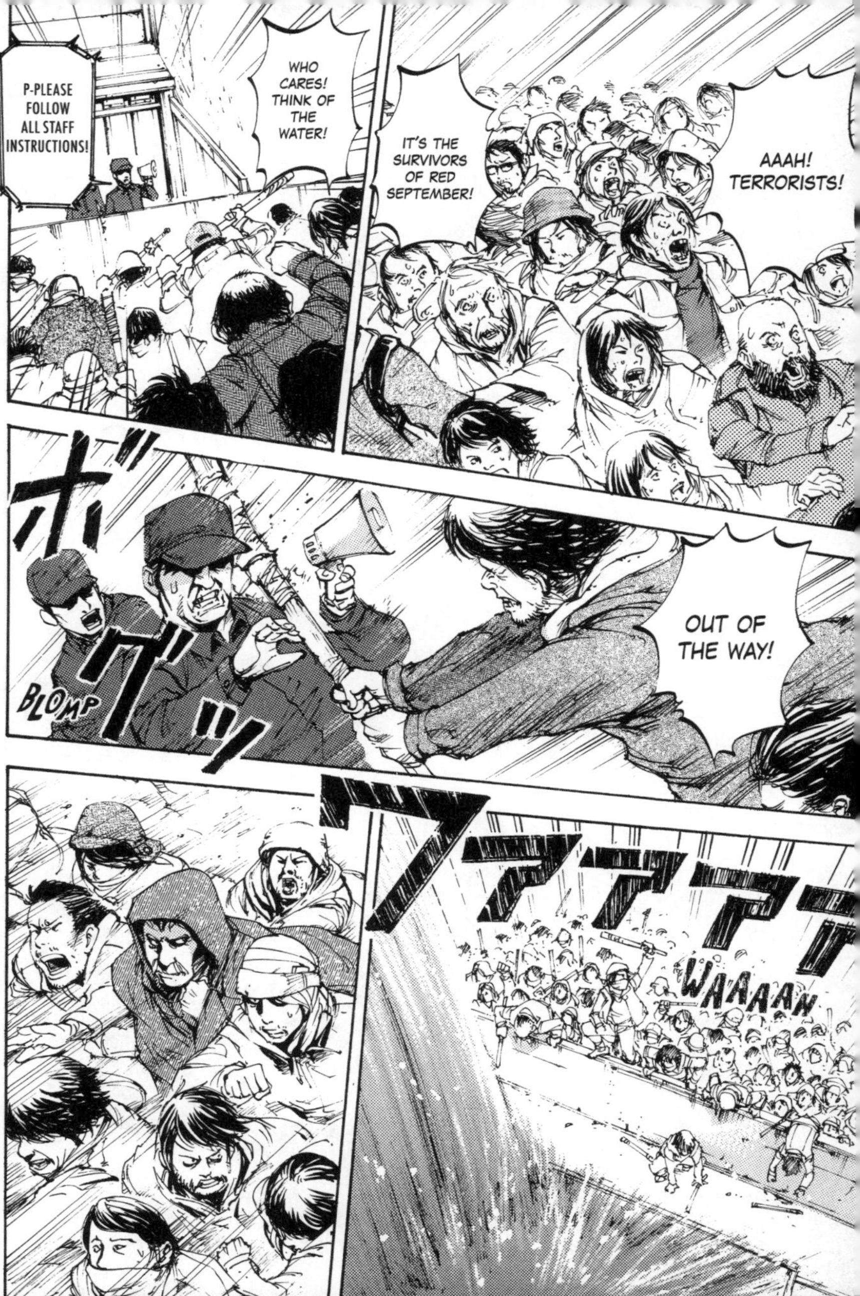
AAAH! TERRORISTS!
IT'S THE SURVIVORS OF RED SEPTEMBER!
WHO CARES! THINK OF THE WATER!
P-PLEASE FOLLOW ALL STAFF INSTRUCTIONS!
OUT OF THE WAY!
BLOMP
WAAAAN

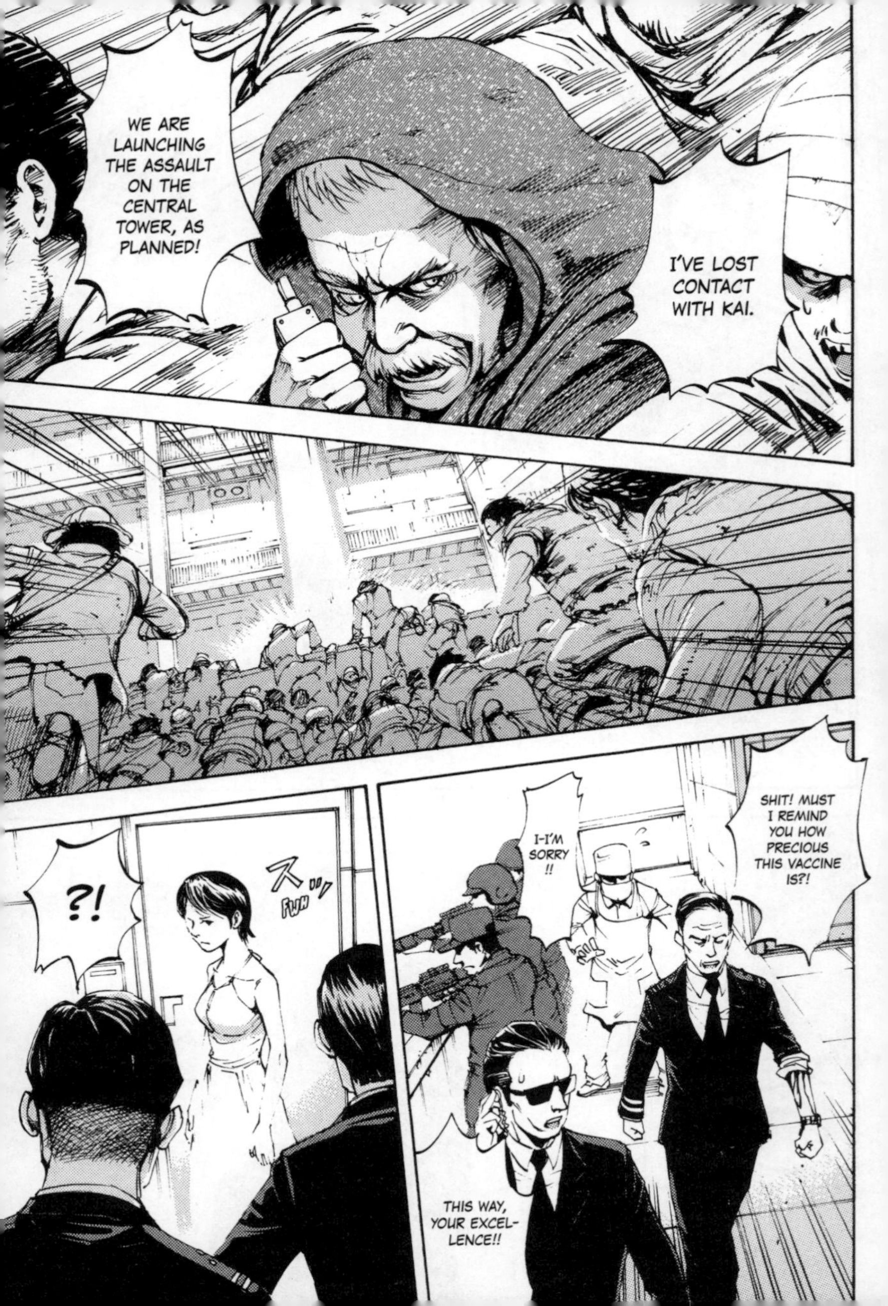
I'VE LOST CONTACT WITH KAI.
WE ARE LAUNCHING THE ASSAULT ON THE CENTRAL TOWER, AS PLANNED!
SHIT! MUST I REMIND YOU HOW PRECIOUS THIS VACCINE IS?!
I-I'M SORRY !!
THIS WAY, YOUR EXCEL-LENCE!!
ス
FWH
?!

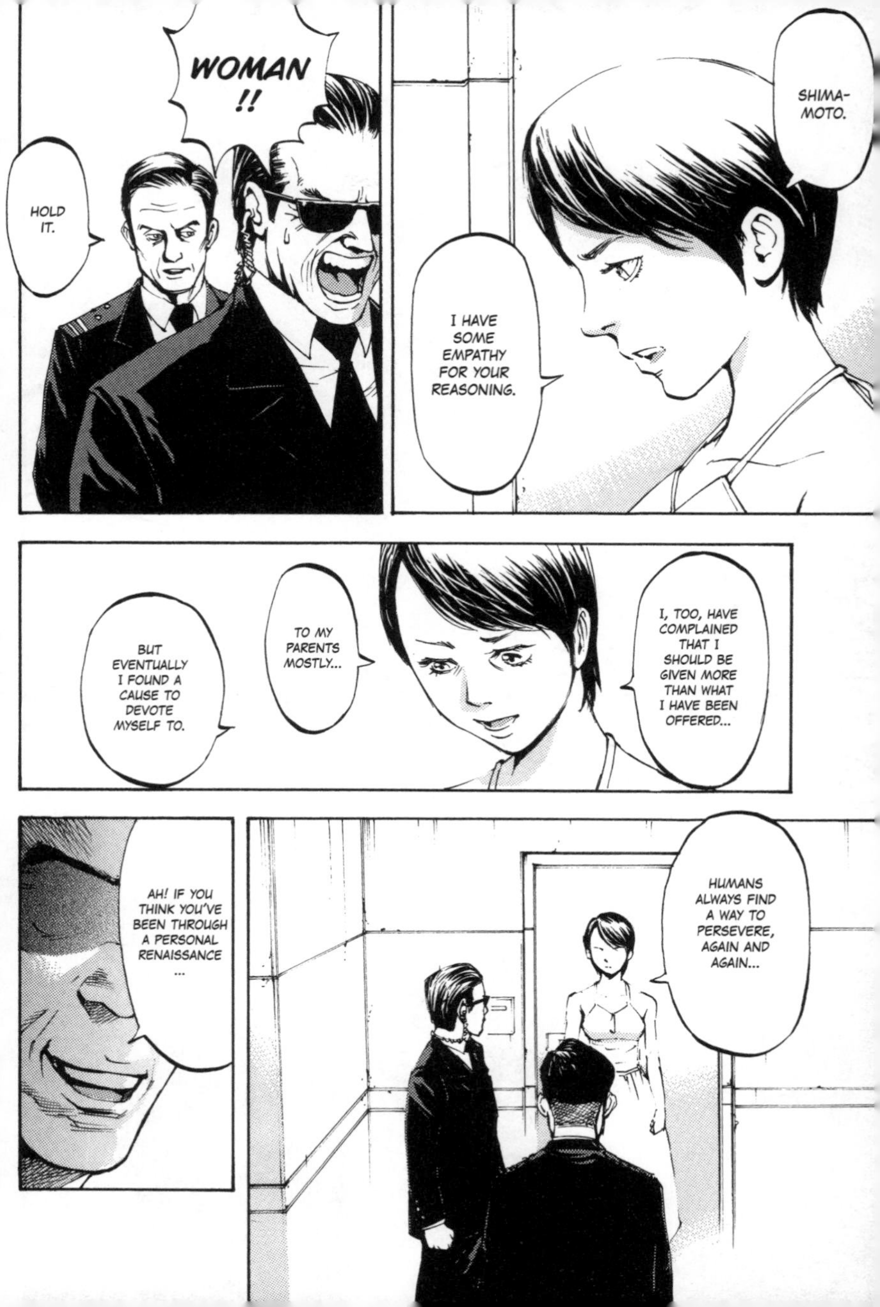
SHIMA-MOTO.
I HAVE SOME EMPATHY FOR YOUR REASONING.
WOMAN !!
HOLD IT.
I, TOO, HAVE COMPLAINED THAT I SHOULD BE GIVEN MORE THAN WHAT I HAVE BEEN OFFERED...
TO MY PARENTS MOSTLY...
BUT EVENTUALLY I FOUND A CAUSE TO DEVOTE MYSELF TO.
HUMANS ALWAYS FIND A WAY TO PERSEVERE, AGAIN AND AGAIN...
AH! IF YOU THINK YOU'VE BEEN THROUGH A PERSONAL RENAISSANCE ...

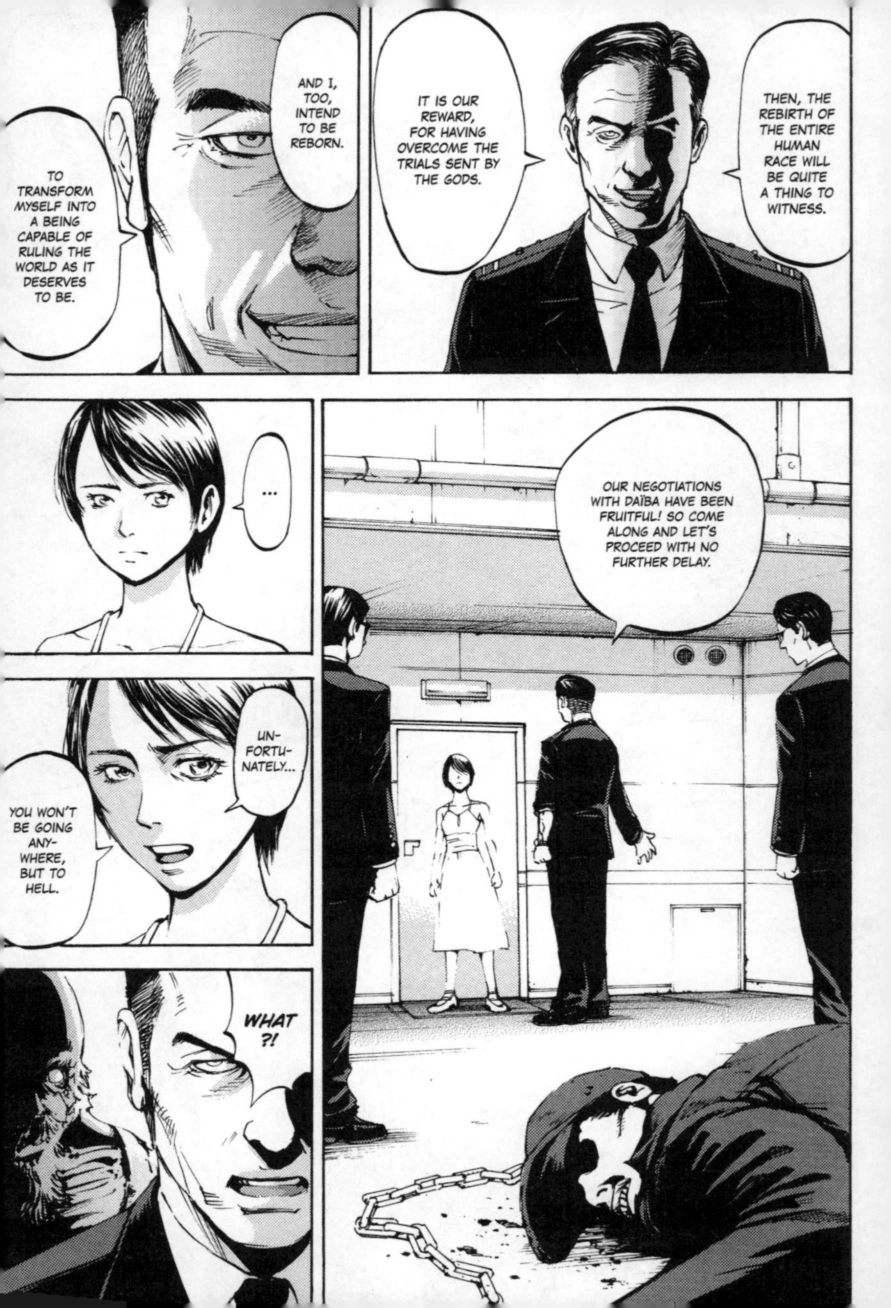
THEN, THE REBIRTH OF THE ENTIRE HUMAN RACE WILL BE QUITE A THING TO WITNESS.
IT IS OUR REWARD, FOR HAVING OVERCOME THE TRIALS SENT BY THE GODS.
AND I, TOO, INTEND TO BE REBORN.
TO TRANSFORM MYSELF INTO A BEING CAPABLE OF RULING THE WORLD AS IT DESERVES TO BE.
OUR NEGOTIATIONS WITH DAÏBA HAVE BEEN FRUITFUL! SO COME ALONG AND LET'S PROCEED WITH NO FURTHER DELAY.
...
UN-FORTU-NATELY...
YOU WON'T BE GOING ANY-WHERE, BUT TO HELL.
WHAT ?!

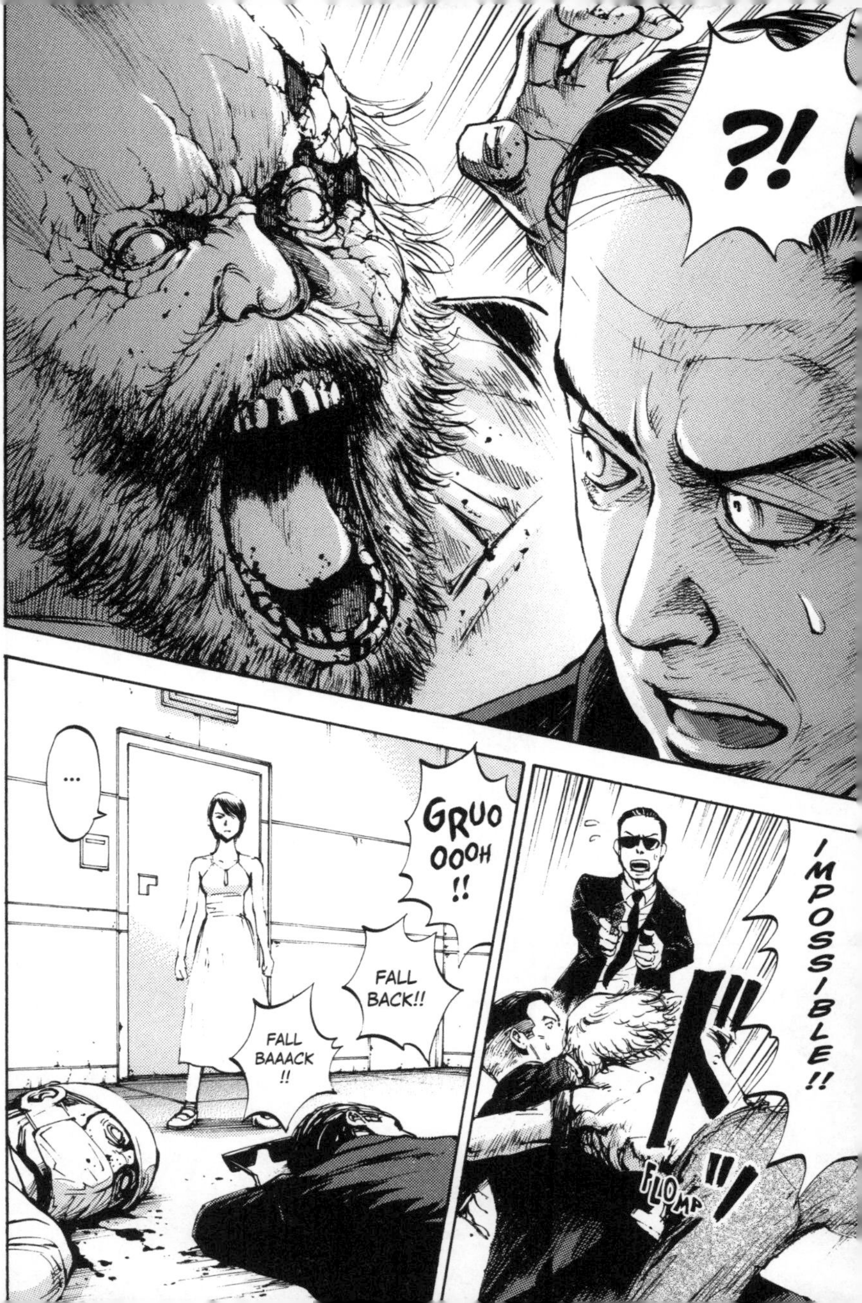
?!
IMPOSSIBLE!!
K!!
FLOMP
GRUO OOOH !!
...
FALL BACK!!
FALL BAAACK !!

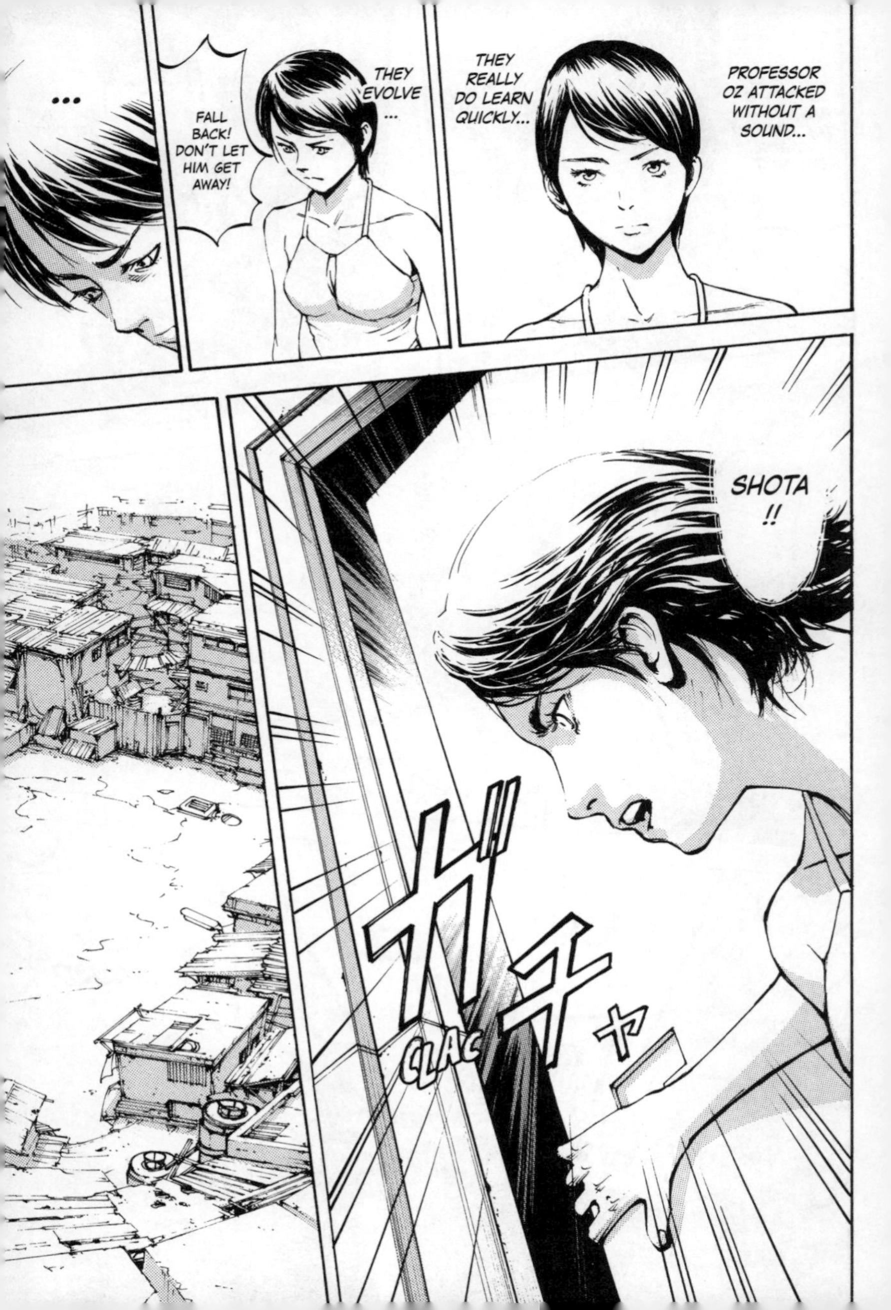
PROFESSOR OZ ATTACKED WITHOUT A SOUND...
THEY REALLY DO LEARN QUICKLY...
THEY EVOLVE ...
FALL BACK! DON'T LET HIM GET AWAY!
...
SHOTA !!
ガチャ
CLAC

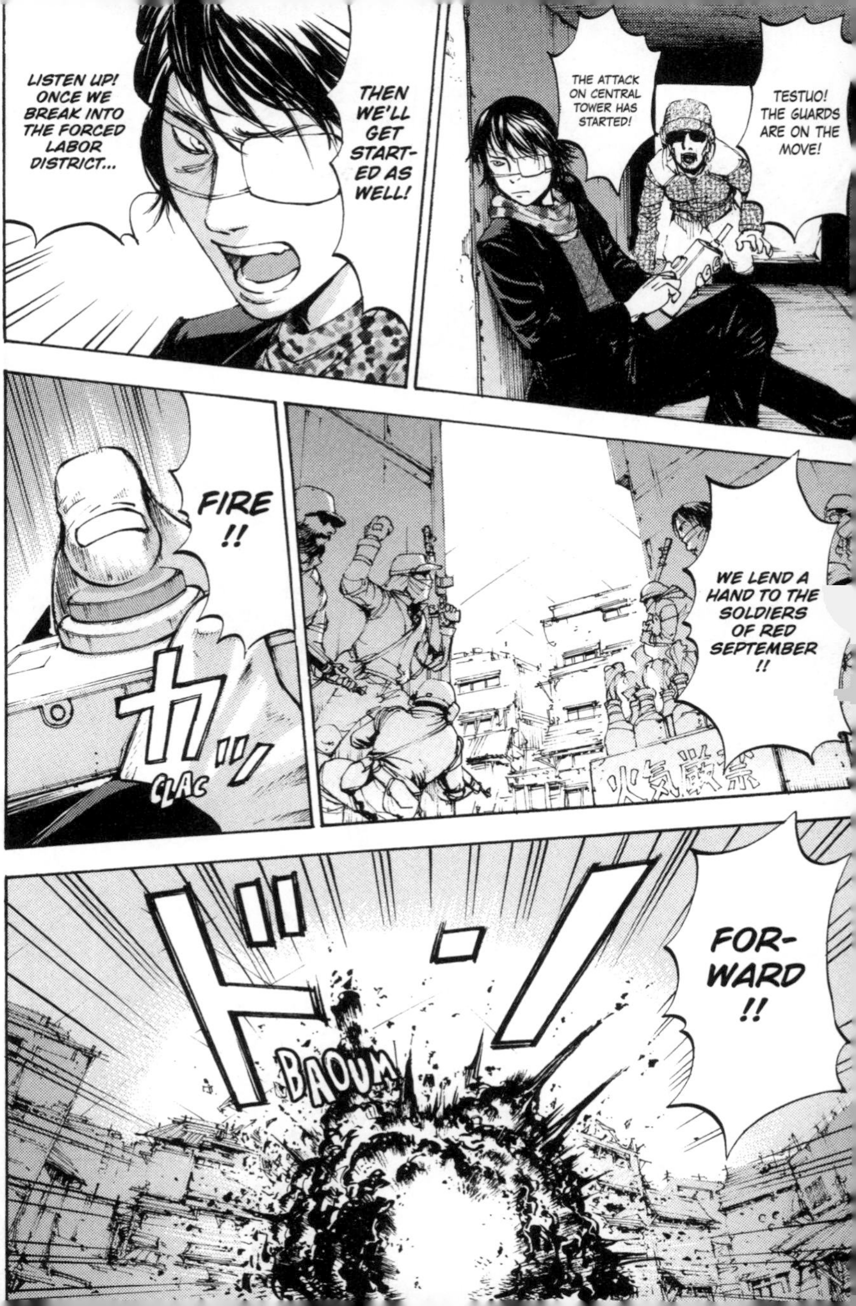
TESTUO! THE GUARDS ARE ON THE MOVE!
THE ATTACK ON CENTRAL TOWER HAS STARTED!
LISTEN UP! ONCE WE BREAK INTO THE FORCED LABOR DISTRICT...
THEN WE'LL GET START-ED AS WELL!
WE LEND A HAND TO THE SOLDIERS OF RED SEPTEMBER !!
FIRE !!
カッ
CLAC
FOR-WARD !!
ドーン
BAOUM

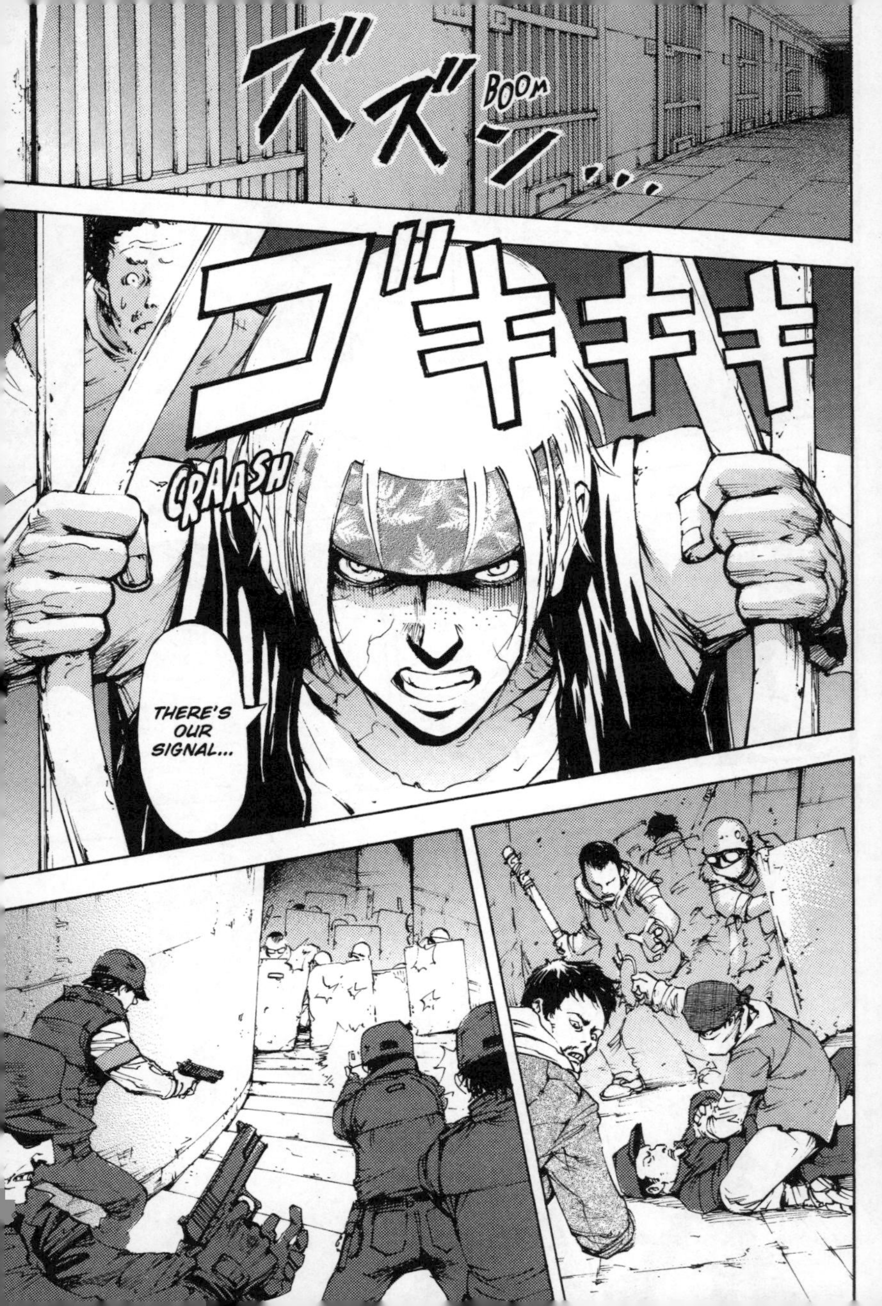
ズズン...
BOOM
ゴギギギ
CRAASH
THERE'S OUR SIGNAL...

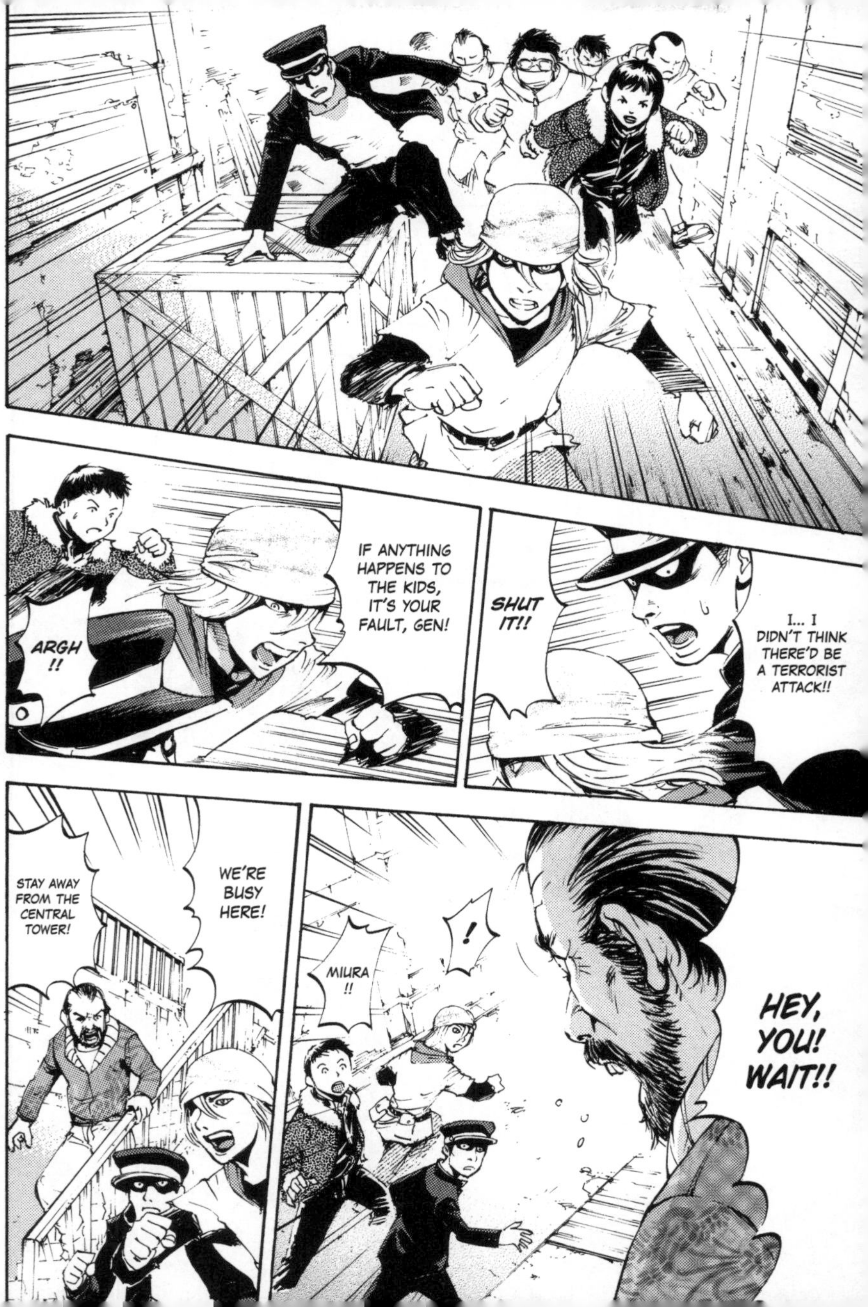
I... I DIDN'T THINK THERE'D BE A TERRORIST ATTACK!!
SHUT IT!!
IF ANYTHING HAPPENS TO THE KIDS, IT'S YOUR FAULT, GEN!
ARGH !!
HEY, YOU! WAIT!!
!
MIURA !!
WE'RE BUSY HERE!
STAY AWAY FROM THE CENTRAL TOWER!

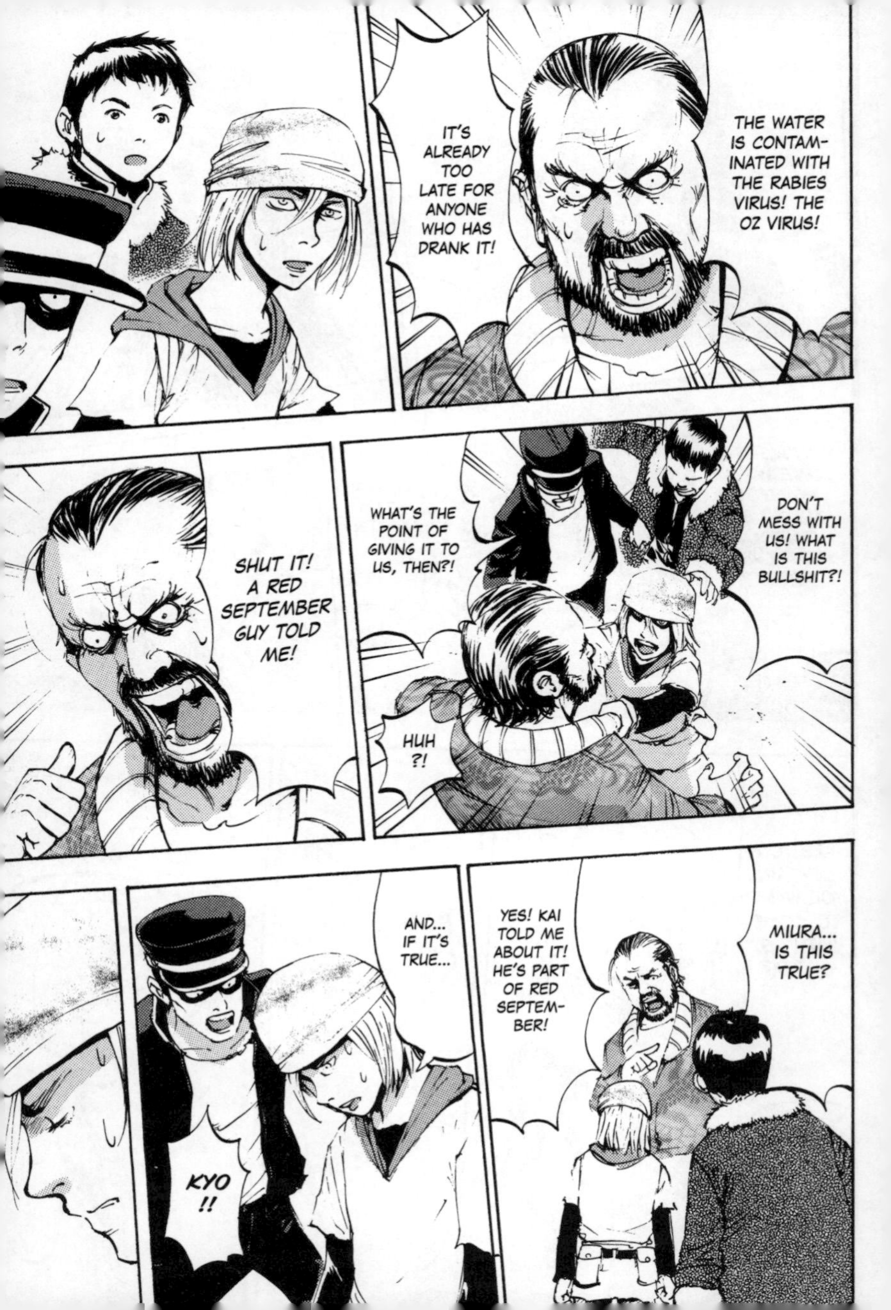
THE WATER IS CONTAMINATED WITH THE RABIES VIRUS! THE OZ VIRUS!
IT'S ALREADY TOO LATE FOR ANYONE WHO HAS DRANK IT!
DON'T MESS WITH US! WHAT IS THIS BULLSHIT?!
WHAT'S THE POINT OF GIVING IT TO US, THEN?!
HUH ?!
SHUT IT! A RED SEPTEMBER GUY TOLD ME!
MIURA... IS THIS TRUE?
YES! KAI TOLD ME ABOUT IT! HE'S PART OF RED SEPTEMBER!
AND... IF IT'S TRUE...
KYO !!

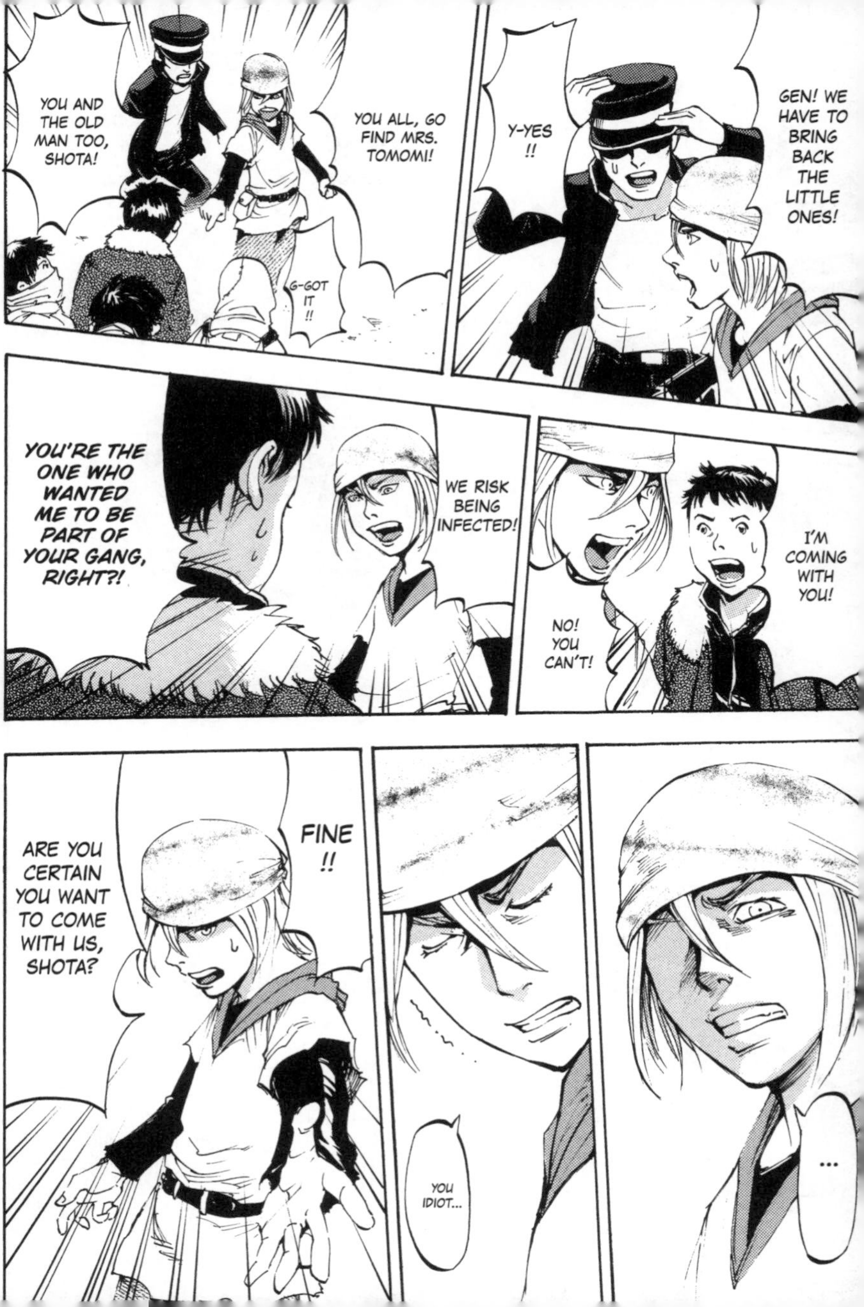
GEN! WE HAVE TO BRING BACK THE LITTLE ONES!
Y-YES !!
YOU ALL, GO FIND MRS. TOMOMI!
YOU AND THE OLD MAN TOO, SHOTA!
G-GOT IT !!
I'M COMING WITH YOU!
NO! YOU CAN'T!
WE RISK BEING INFECTED!
YOU'RE THE ONE WHO WANTED ME TO BE PART OF YOUR GANG, RIGHT?!
...
YOU IDIOT...
FINE !!
ARE YOU CERTAIN YOU WANT TO COME WITH US, SHOTA?

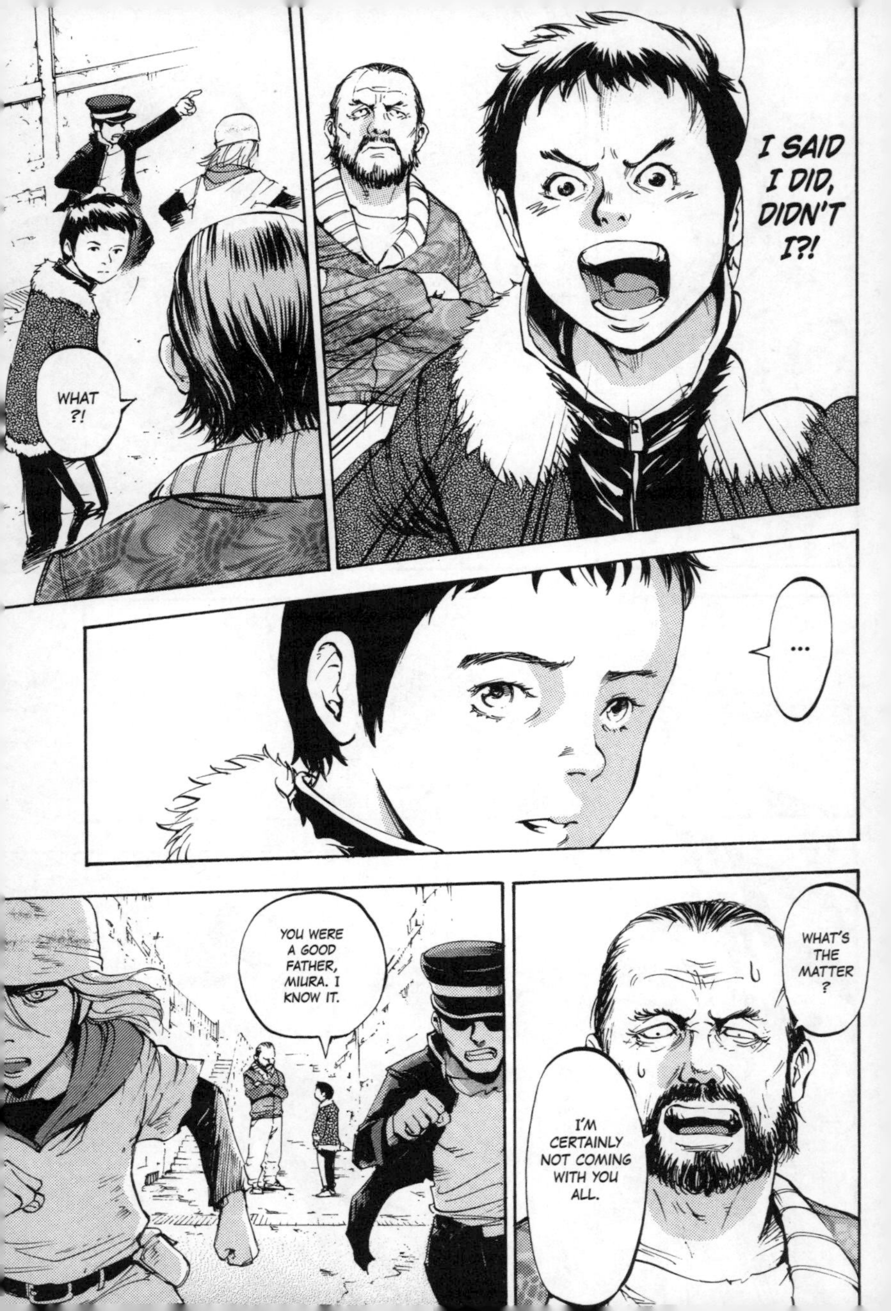
I SAID I DID, DIDN'T I?!
WHAT ?!
...
WHAT'S THE MATTER ?
I'M CERTAINLY NOT COMING WITH YOU ALL.
YOU WERE A GOOD FATHER, MIURA. I KNOW IT.

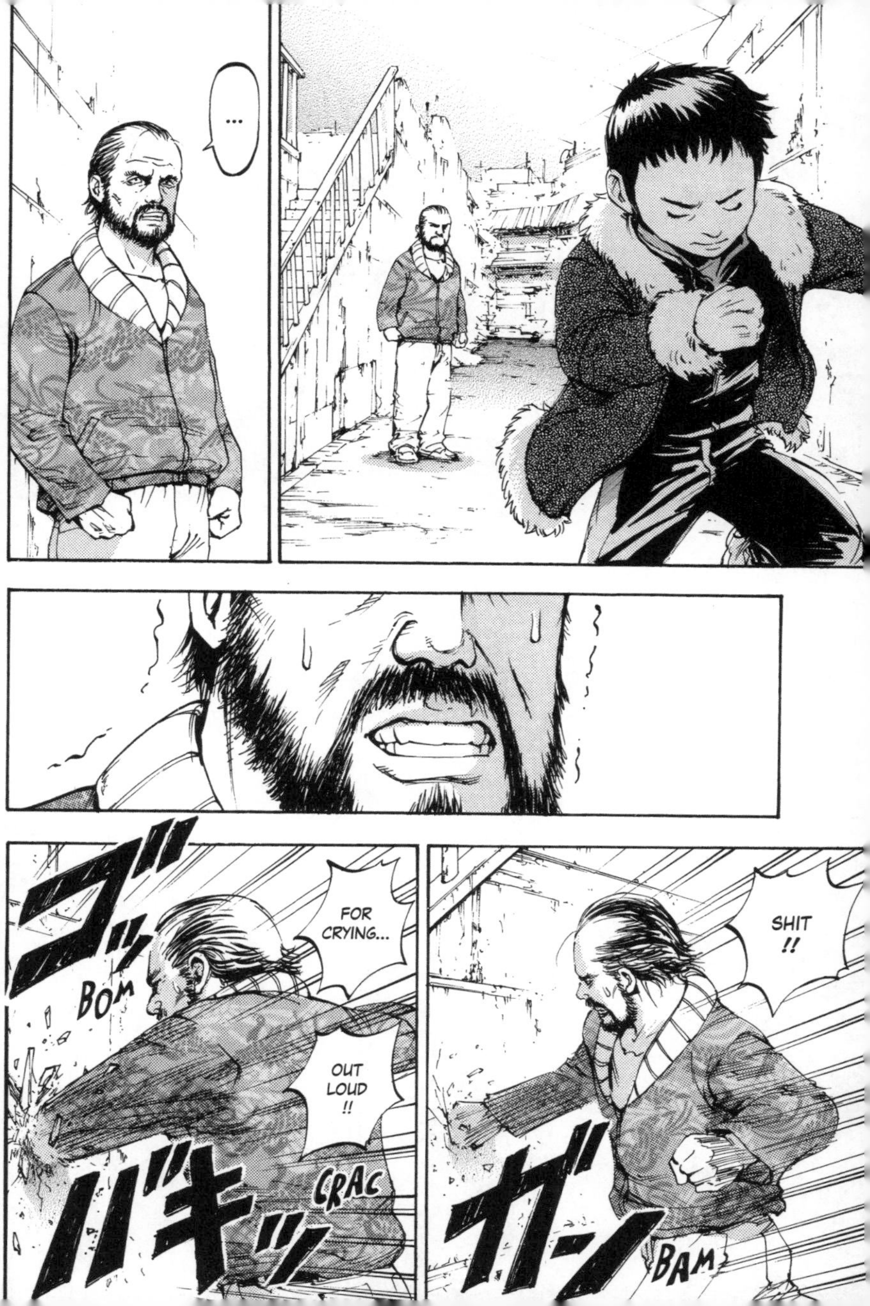
...
SHIT !!
ガーン
BAM
FOR CRYING...
ゴッ
BOM
OUT LOUD !!
CRAC
バキッ

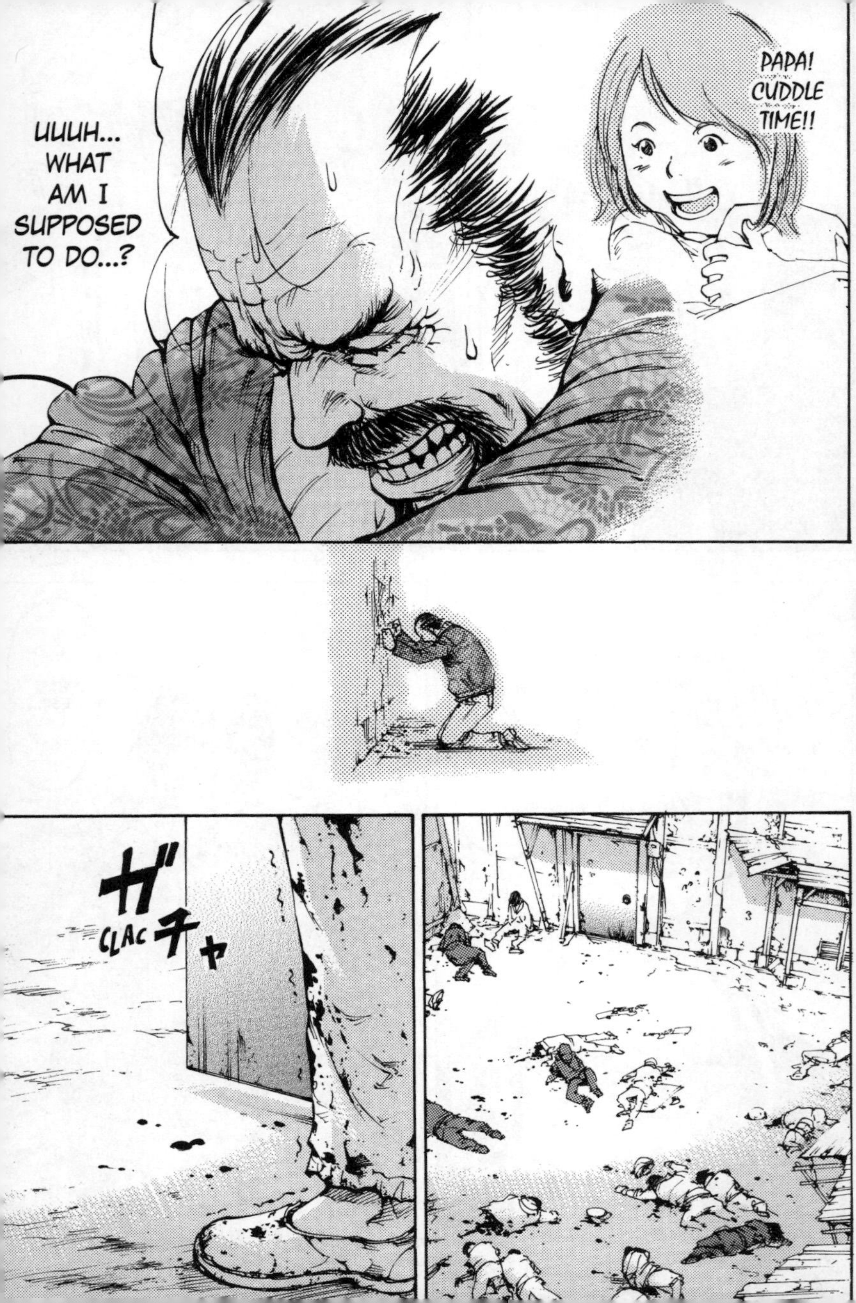
PAPA! CUDDLE TIME!!
UUUH... WHAT AM I SUPPOSED TO DO...?
ガチャ
CLAC

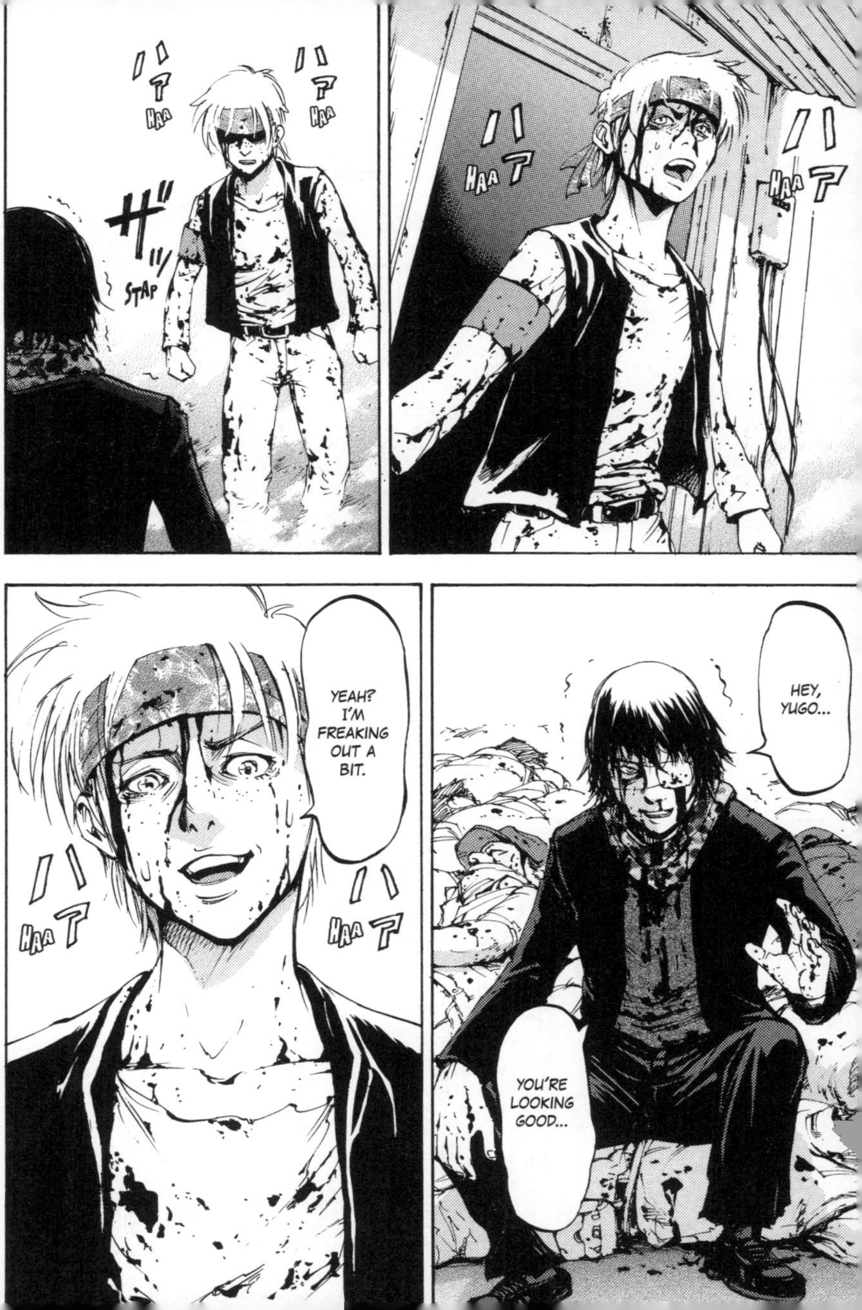
HAA
HAA
HAA
HAA
STAP
HEY, YUGO...
YOU'RE LOOKING GOOD...
YEAH? I'M FREAKING OUT A BIT.
HAA
HAA

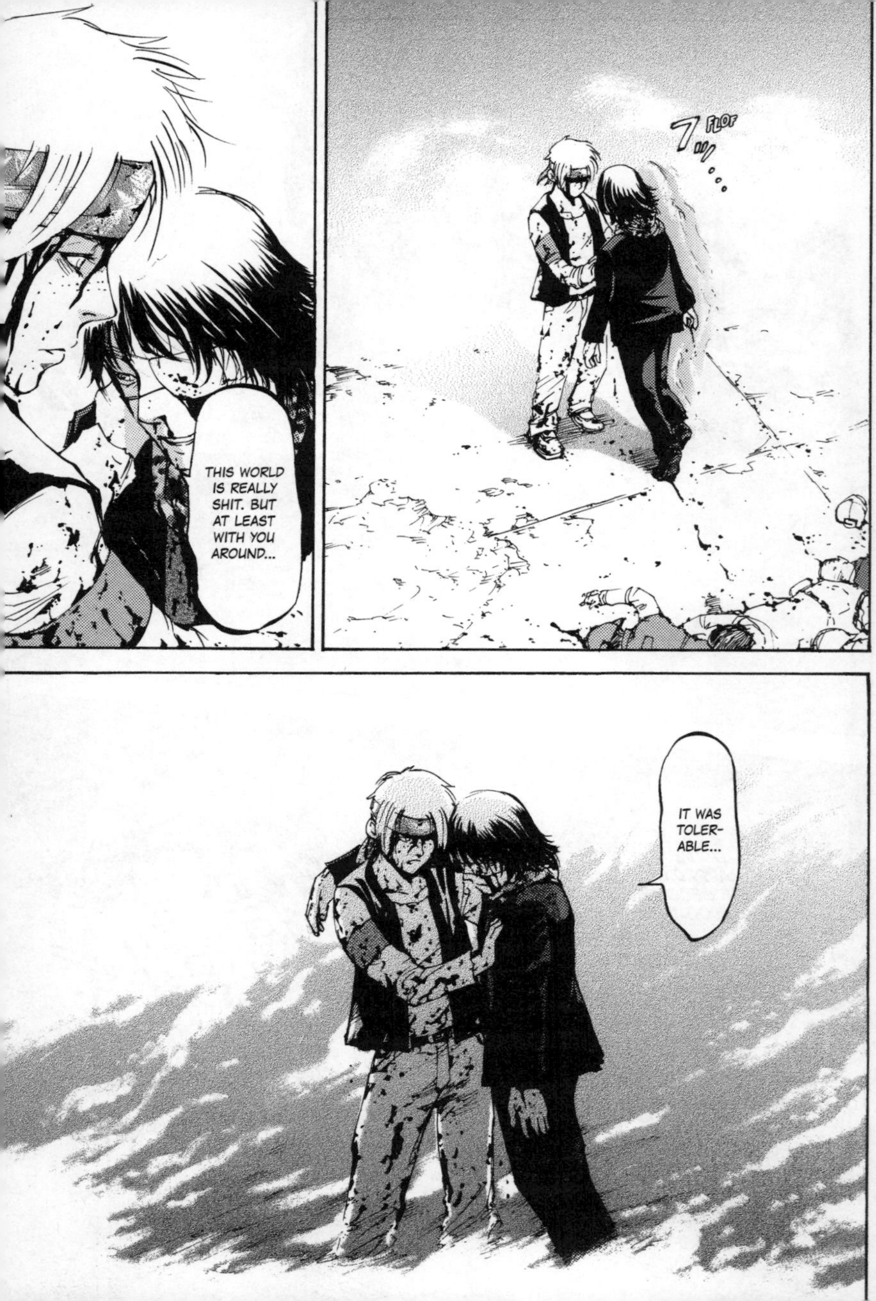
FLOP
THIS WORLD IS REALLY SHIT. BUT AT LEAST WITH YOU AROUND...
IT WAS TOLER-ABLE...

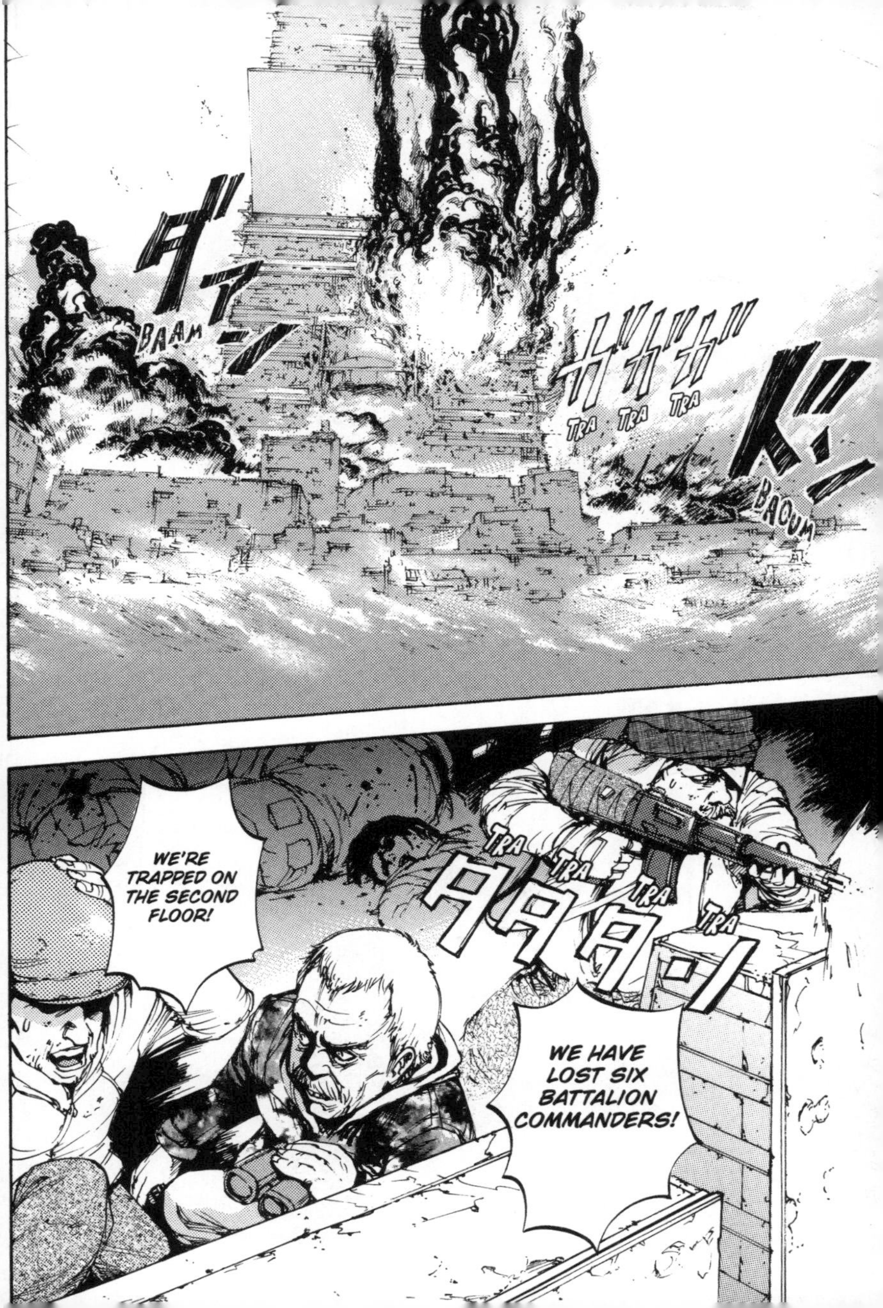
BAOUM
TRA TRA TRA
BAAM
TRA TRA TRA TRA
WE HAVE LOST SIX BATTALION COMMANDERS!
WE'RE TRAPPED ON THE SECOND FLOOR!

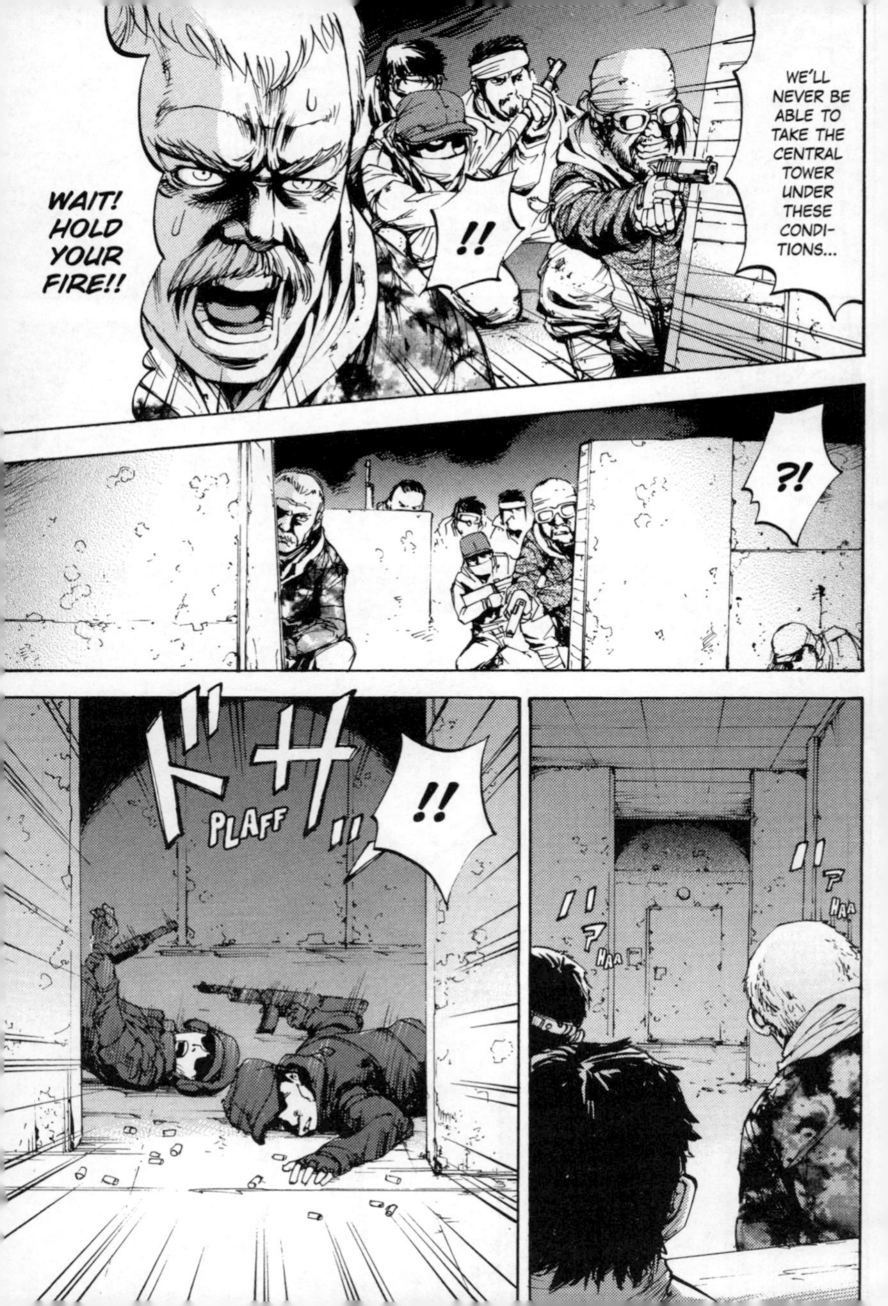
WE'LL NEVER BE ABLE TO TAKE THE CENTRAL TOWER UNDER THESE CONDI- TIONS...
!!
WAIT! HOLD YOUR FIRE!!
?!
ハァ HAA
ハァ HAA
!!
ドサッ
PLAFF

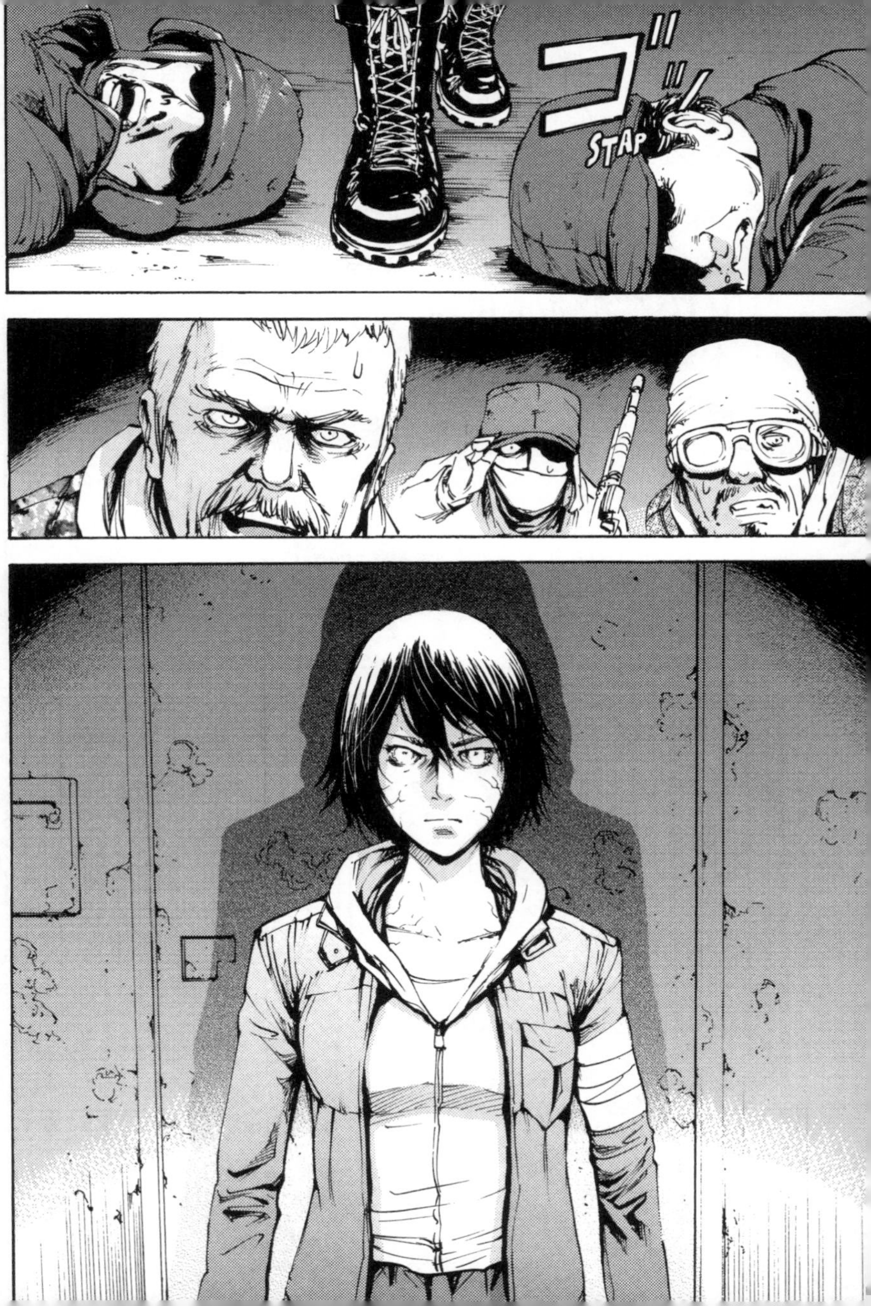
ゴ
STAP

CHAPTER 9

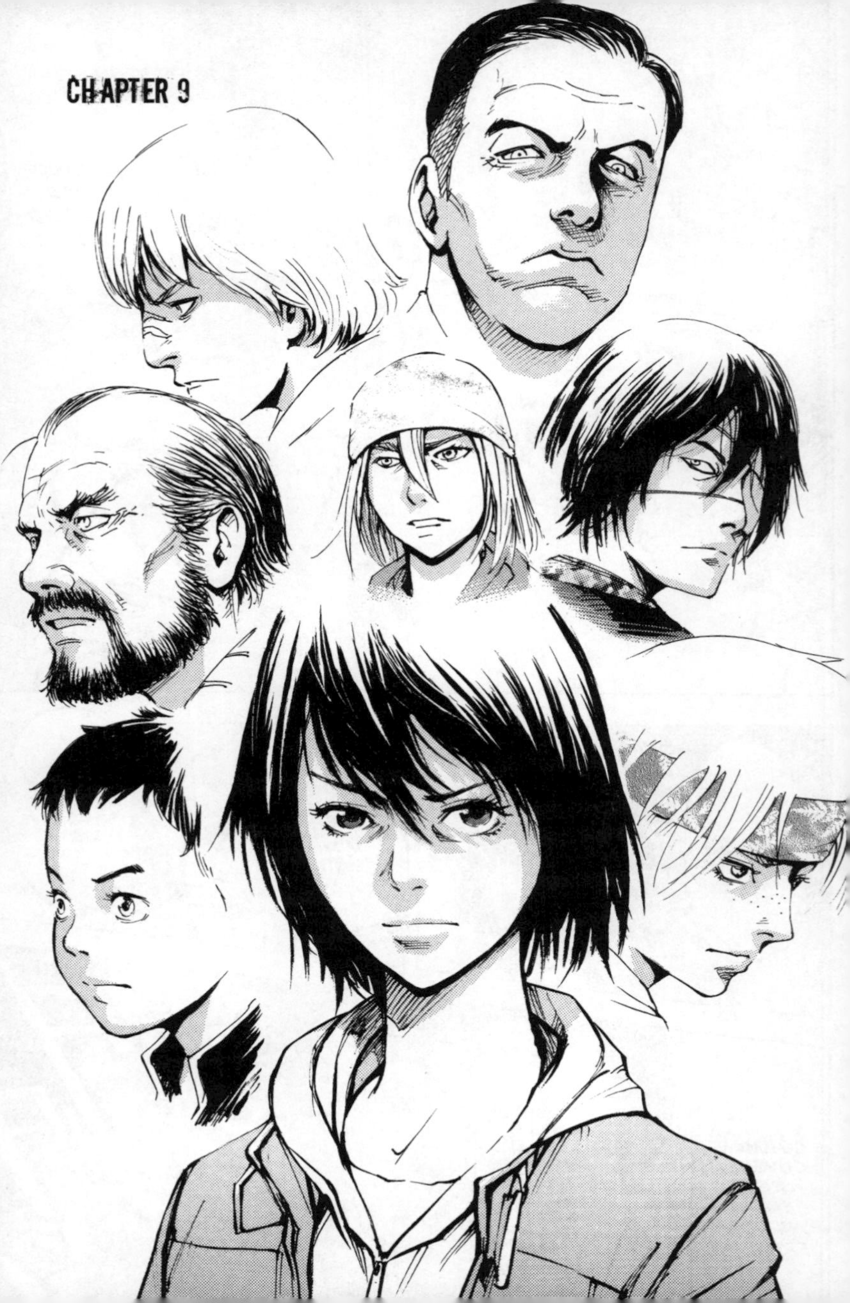

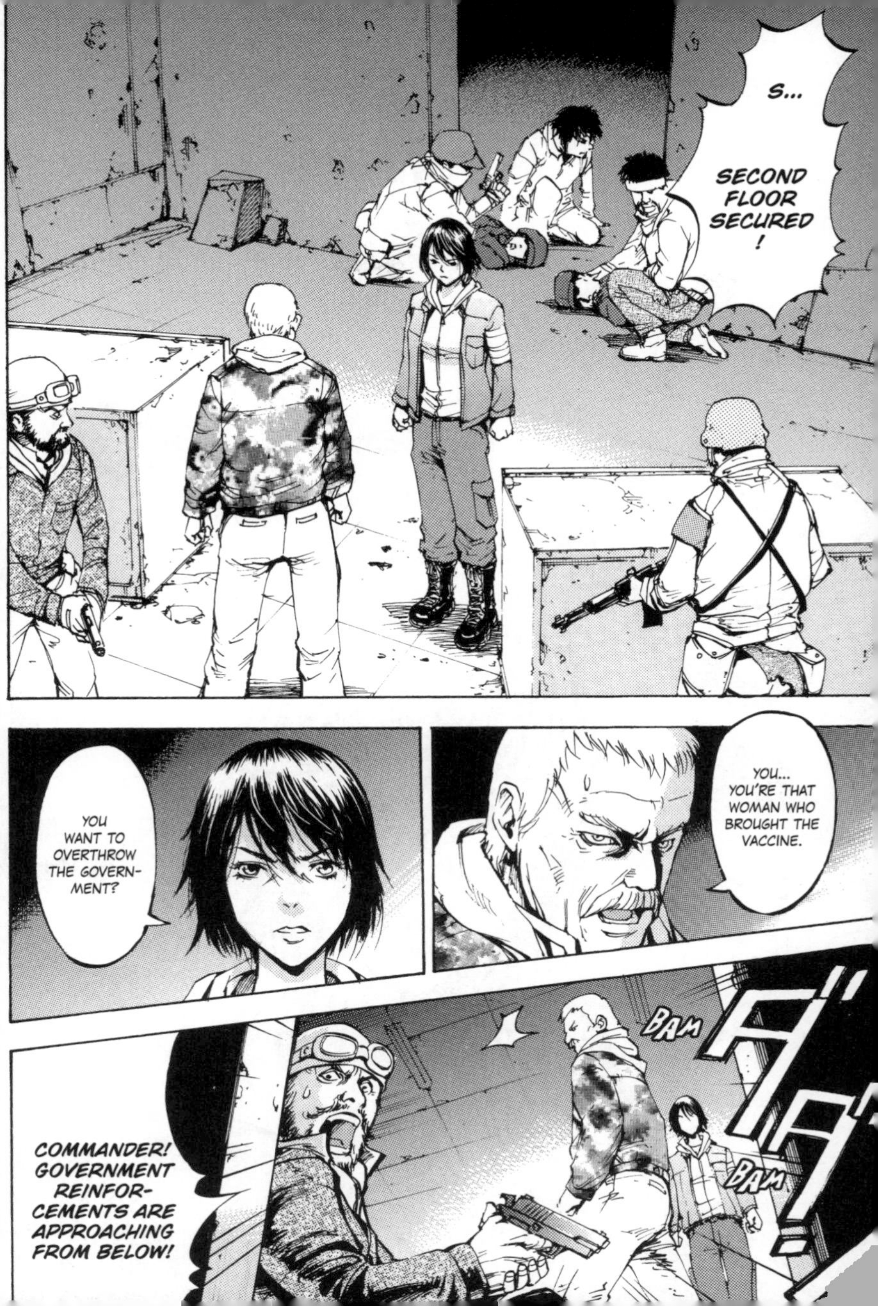
S...
SECOND FLOOR SECURED !
YOU... YOU'RE THAT WOMAN WHO BROUGHT THE VACCINE.
YOU WANT TO OVERTHROW THE GOVERN- MENT?
BAM
BAM
COMMANDER! GOVERNMENT REINFOR- CEMENTS ARE APPROACHING FROM BELOW!

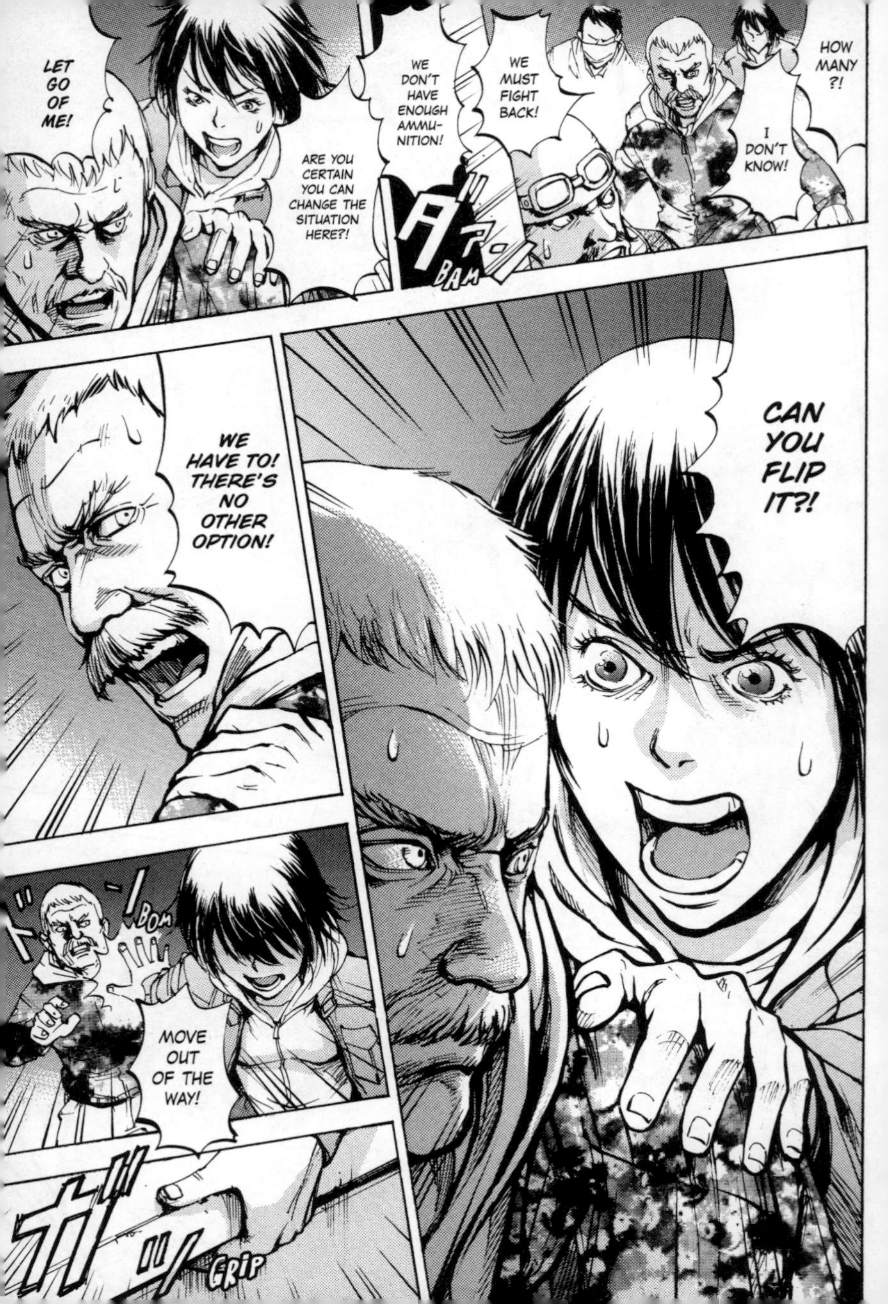

HOW MANY?!
I DON'T KNOW!
WE MUST FIGHT BACK!
WE DON'T HAVE ENOUGH AMMUNITION!
BAM
LET GO OF ME!
ARE YOU CERTAIN YOU CAN CHANGE THE SITUATION HERE?!
CAN YOU FLIP IT?!
WE HAVE TO! THERE'S NO OTHER OPTION!
BOM
MOVE OUT OF THE WAY!
GRIP

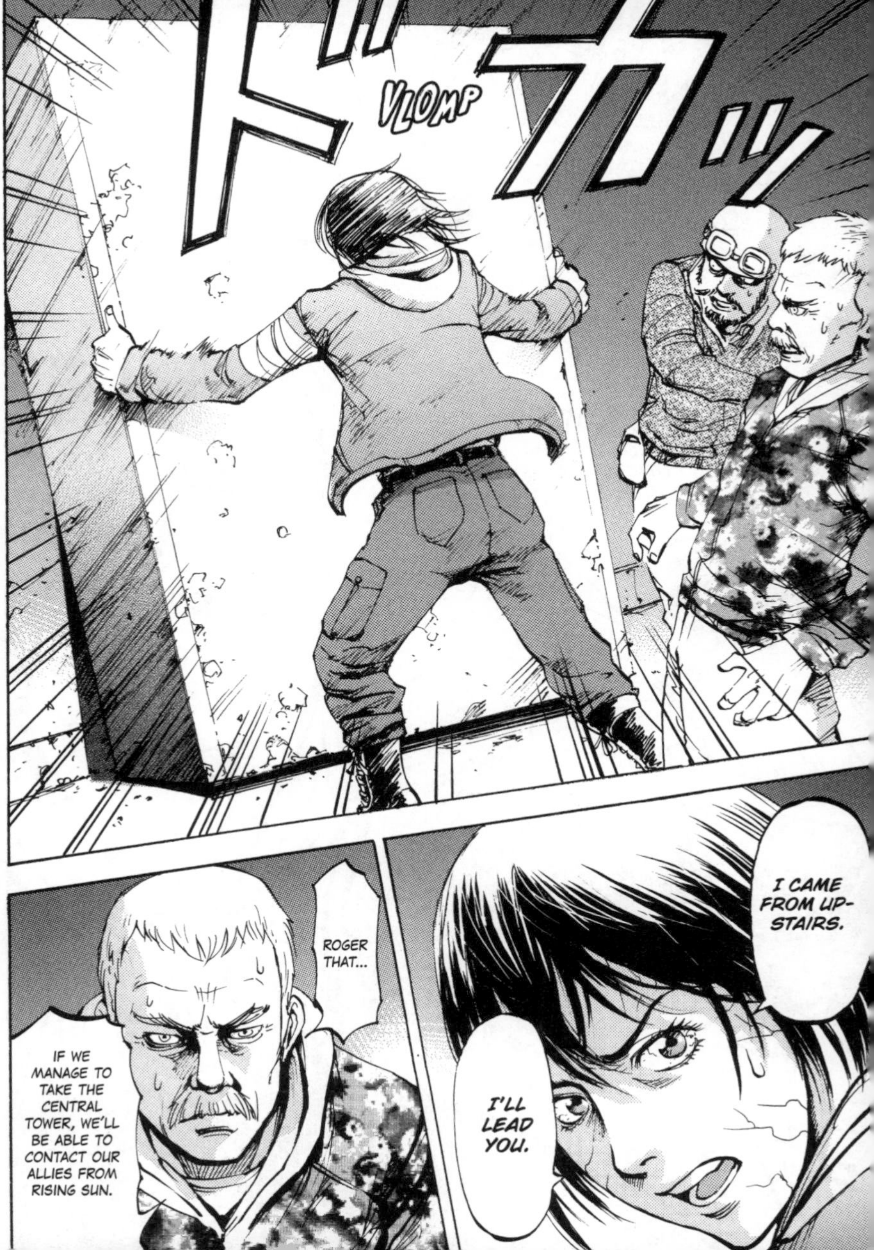
ドカッ
VLOMP
I CAME FROM UP-STAIRS.
I'LL LEAD YOU.
ROGER THAT...
IF WE MANAGE TO TAKE THE CENTRAL TOWER, WE'LL BE ABLE TO CONTACT OUR ALLIES FROM RISING SUN.

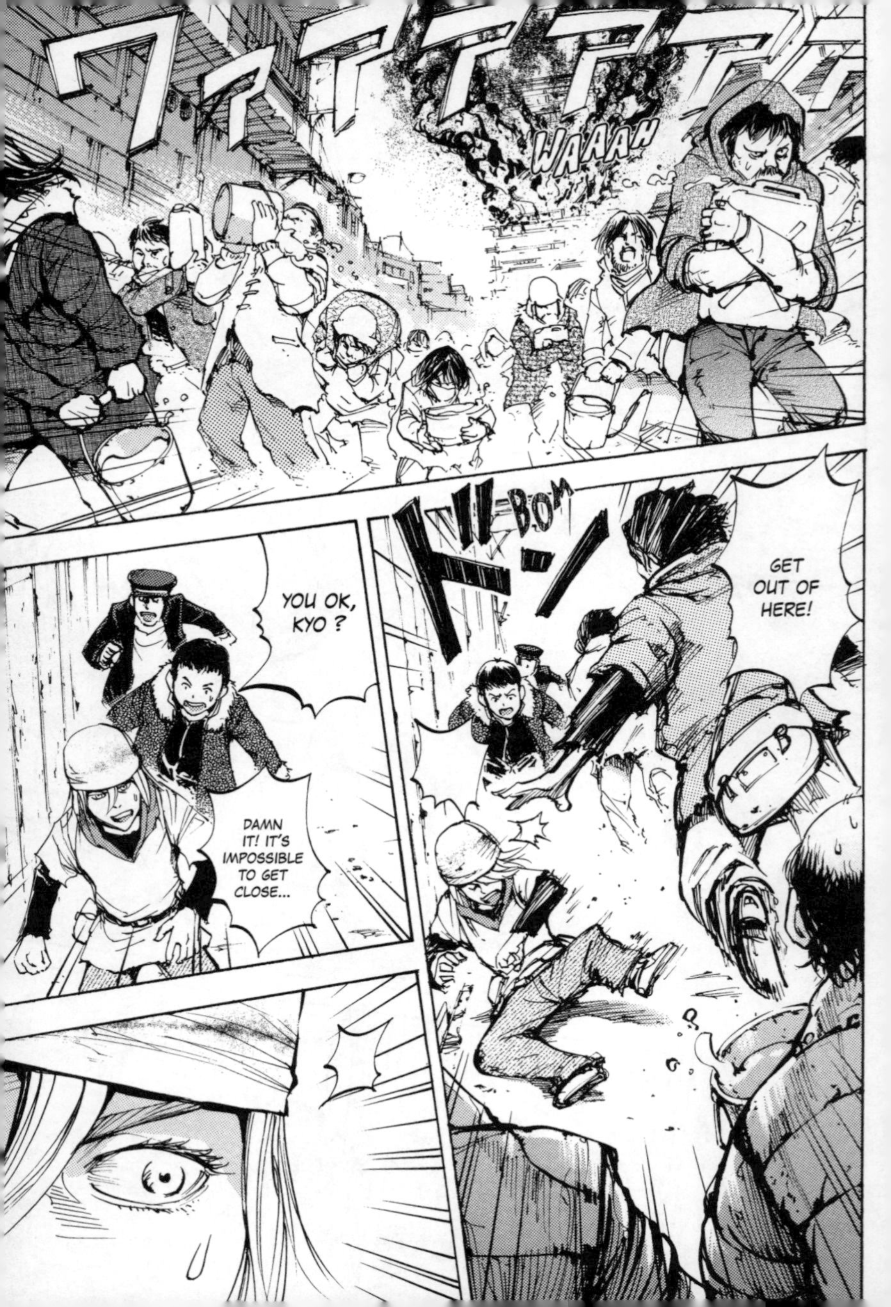
WAAAH
BOM
GET OUT OF HERE!
YOU OK, KYO ?
DAMN IT! IT'S IMPOSSIBLE TO GET CLOSE...

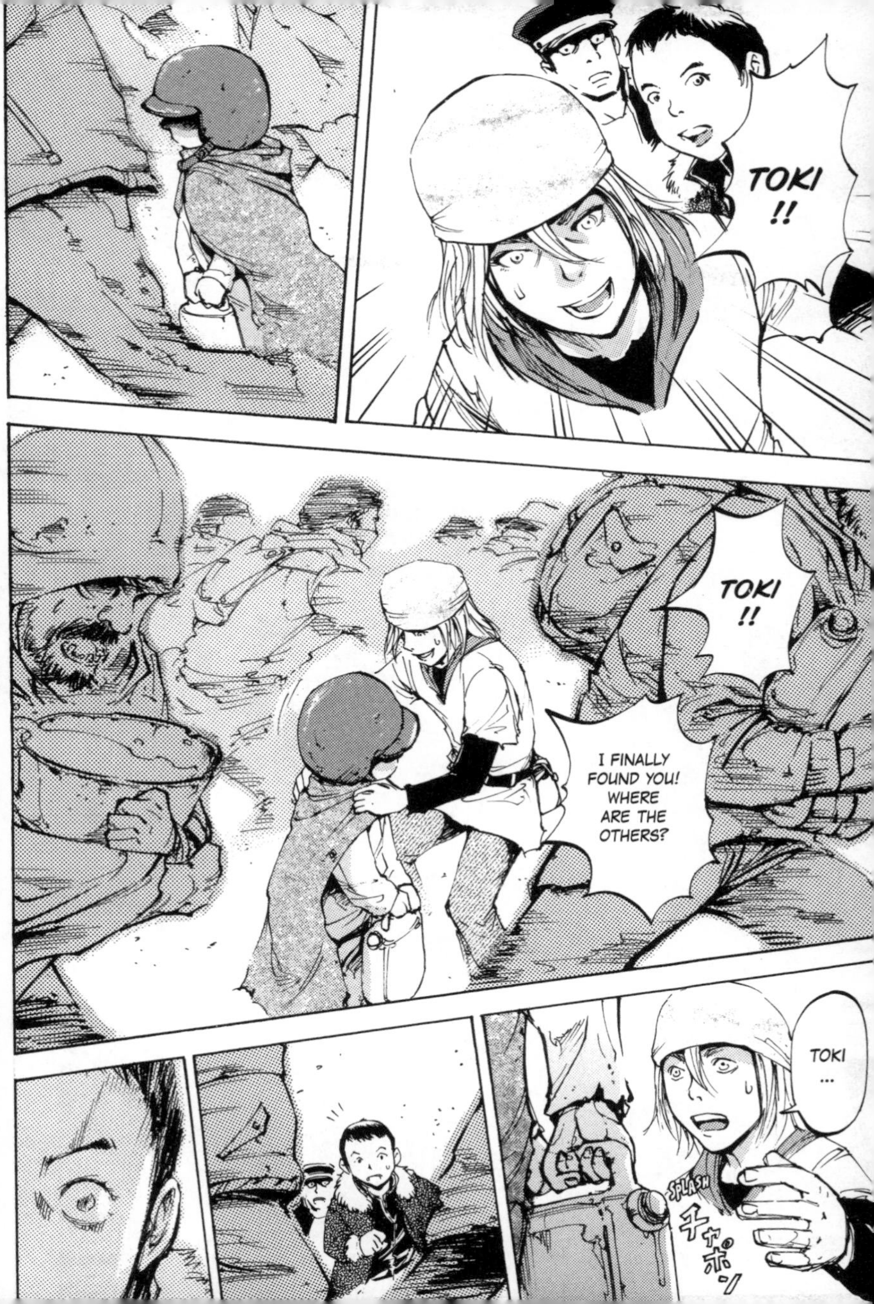
TOKI !!
TOKI !!
I FINALLY FOUND YOU! WHERE ARE THE OTHERS?
TOKI ...
SPLASH
チャポン

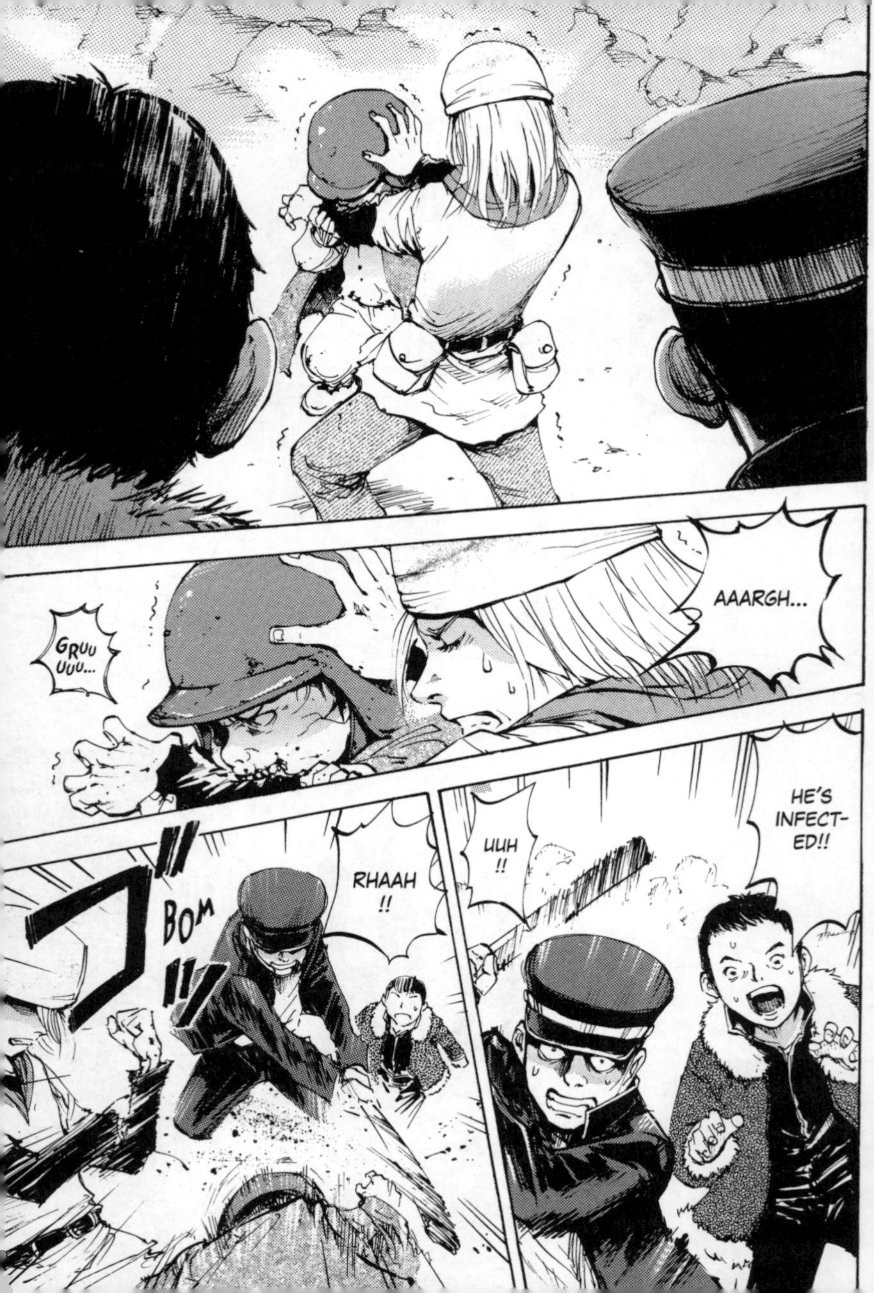
AAARGH...
GRUU UUU...
HE'S INFECTED!!
UUH !!
RHAAH !!
BOM

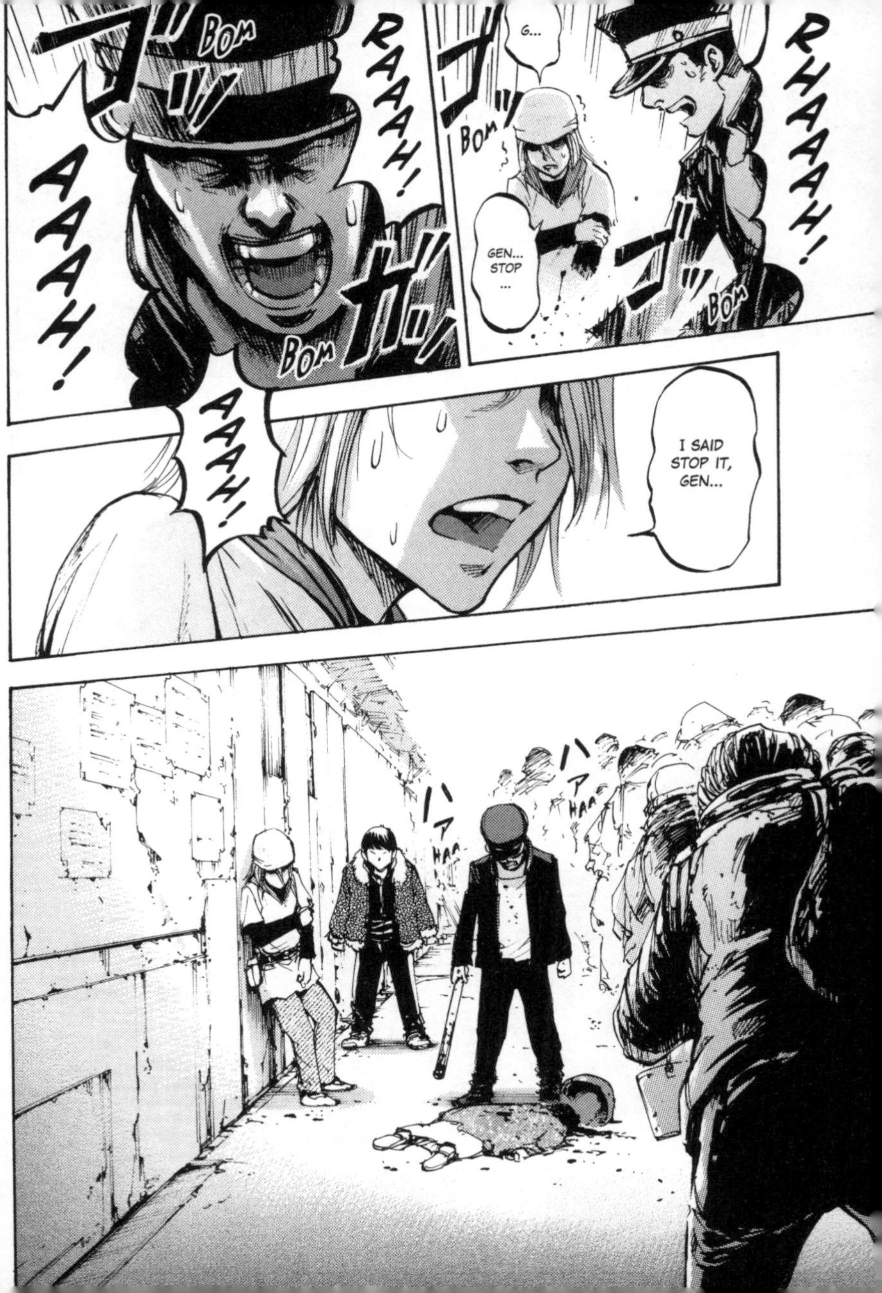
G...
RHAAAAH!
BOM
GEN... STOP ...
BOM
BOM
RAAAAH!
AAAAH!
BOM
AAAAH!
I SAID STOP IT, GEN...
HAA
HAA

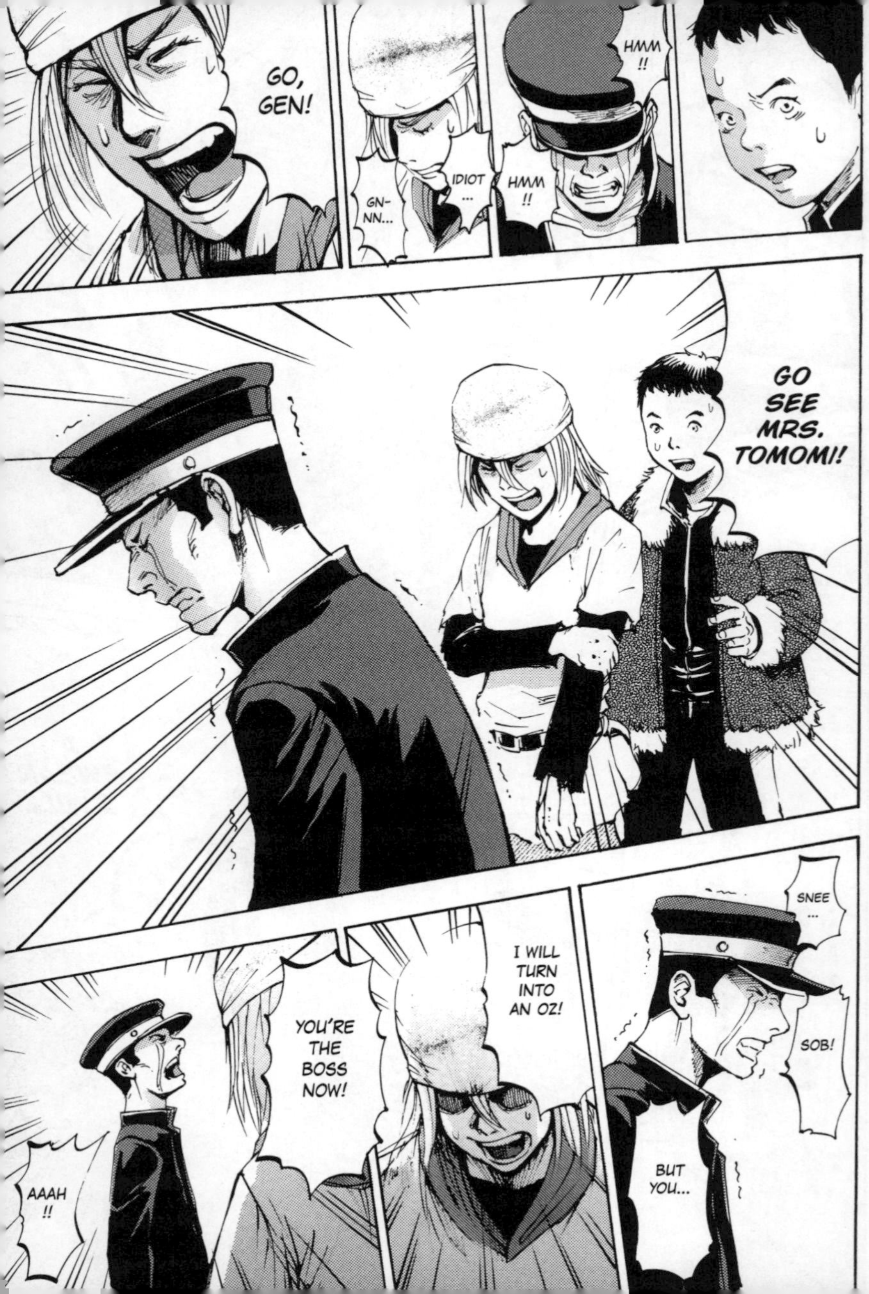
HMM !!
HMM !!
IDIOT ...
GN-NN...
GO, GEN!
GO SEE MRS. TOMOMI!
SNEE ...
SOB!
BUT YOU...
I WILL TURN INTO AN OZ!
YOU'RE THE BOSS NOW!
AAAH !!

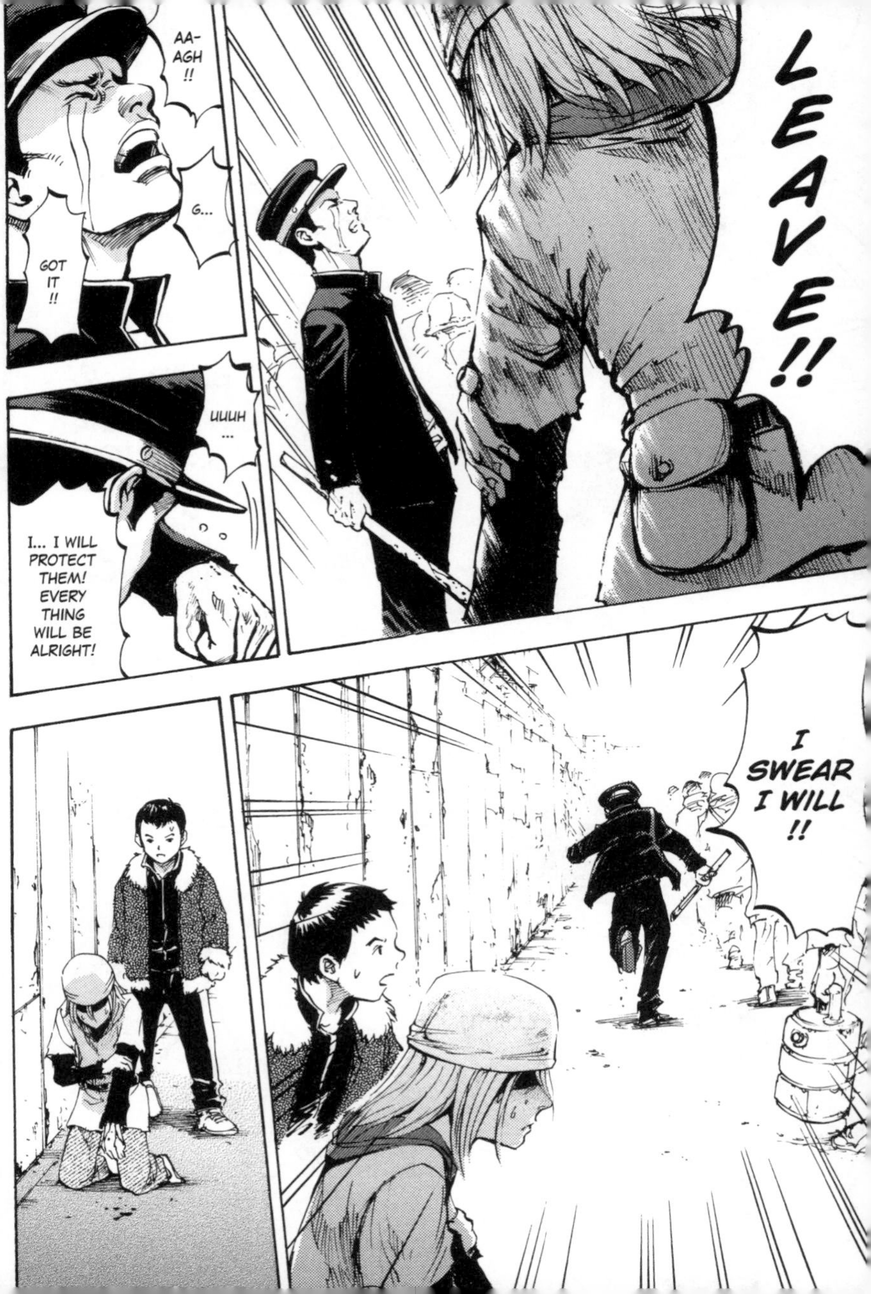
LEAVE!!
AA-AGH!!
G...
GOT IT!!
UUUH...
I... I WILL PROTECT THEM! EVERY THING WILL BE ALRIGHT!
I SWEAR I WILL!!

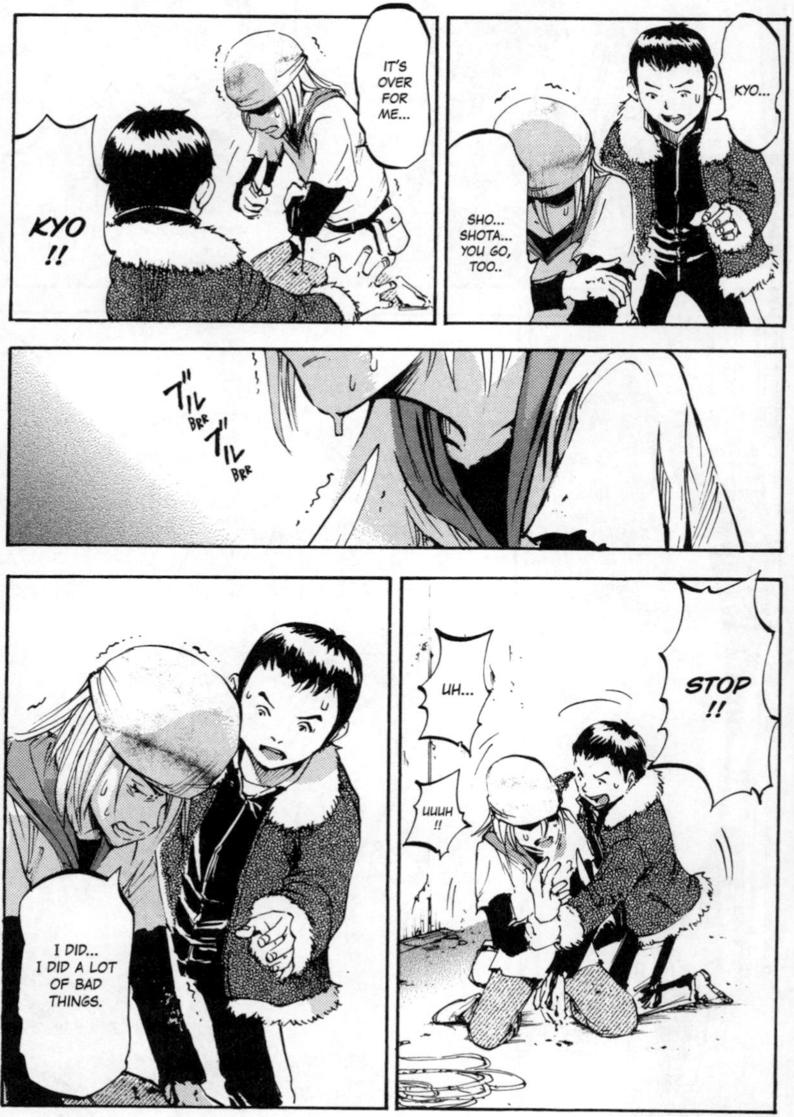
KYO...
SHO... SHOTA... YOU GO, TOO..
IT'S OVER FOR ME...
KYO !!
ブル BRR ブル BRR
STOP !!
UH...
UUUH !!
I DID... I DID A LOT OF BAD THINGS.

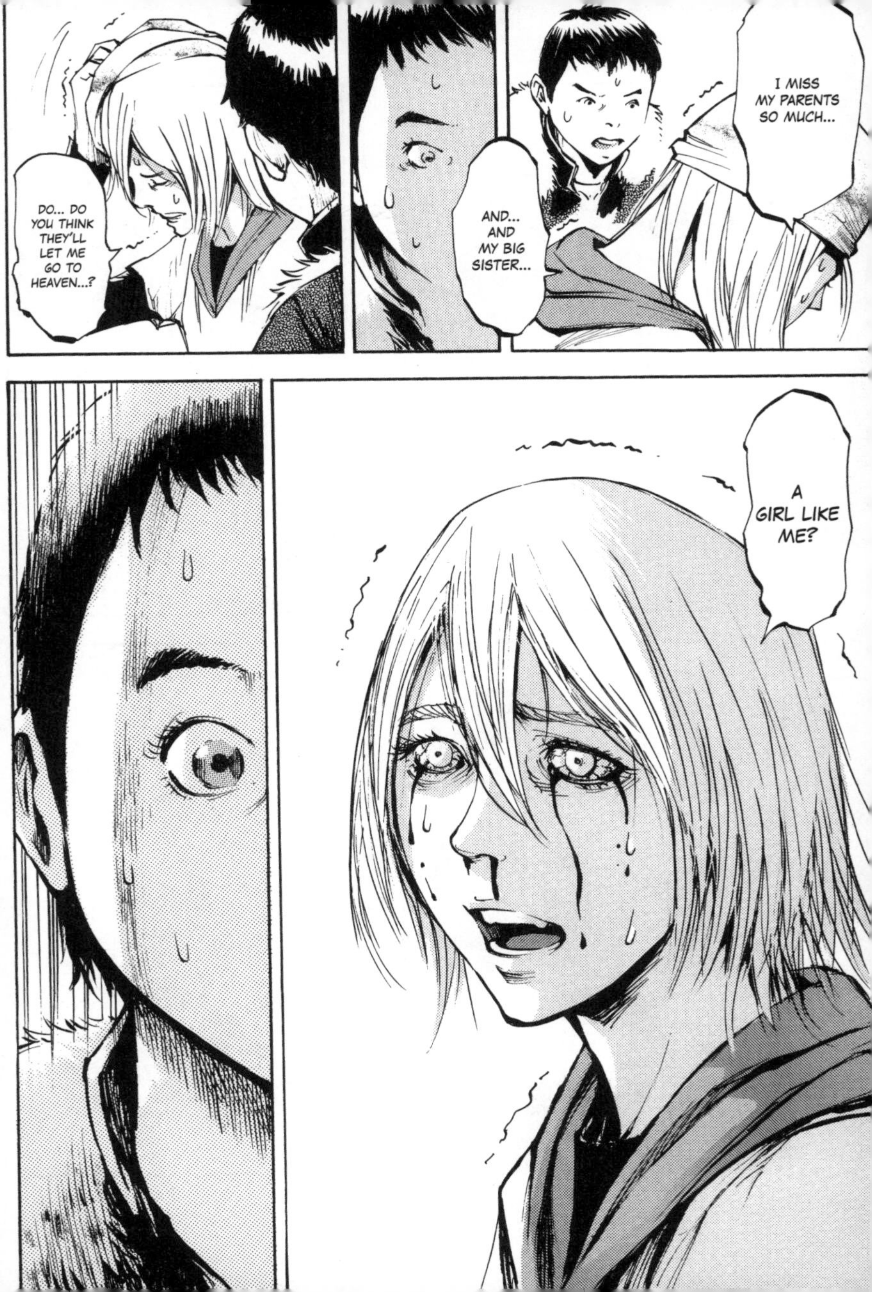
I MISS MY PARENTS SO MUCH...
AND... AND MY BIG SISTER...
DO... DO YOU THINK THEY'LL LET ME GO TO HEAVEN...?
A GIRL LIKE ME?

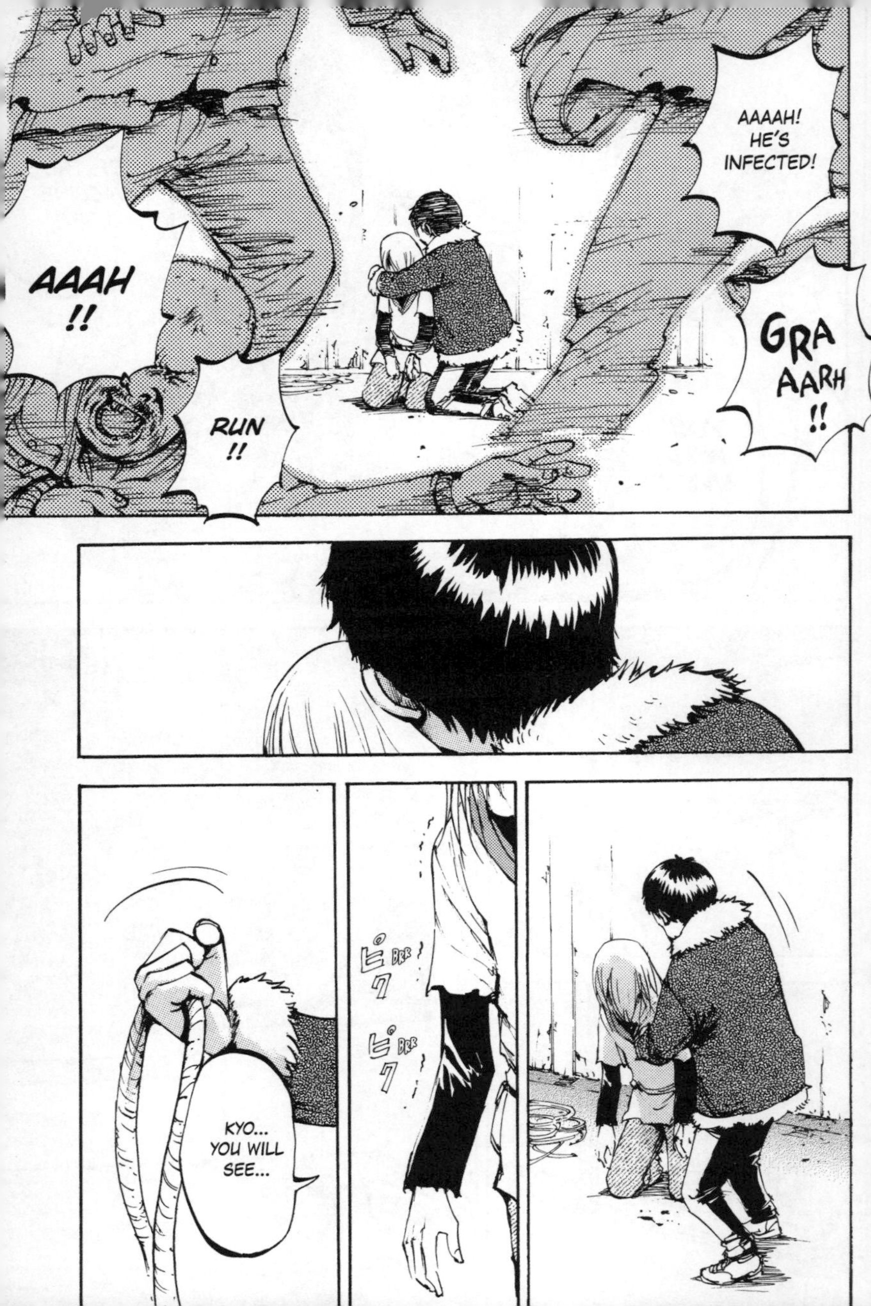
AAAAH! HE'S INFECTED!
GRA AARH !!
AAAH !!
RUN !!
ピク BRR
ピク BRR
KYO... YOU WILL SEE...

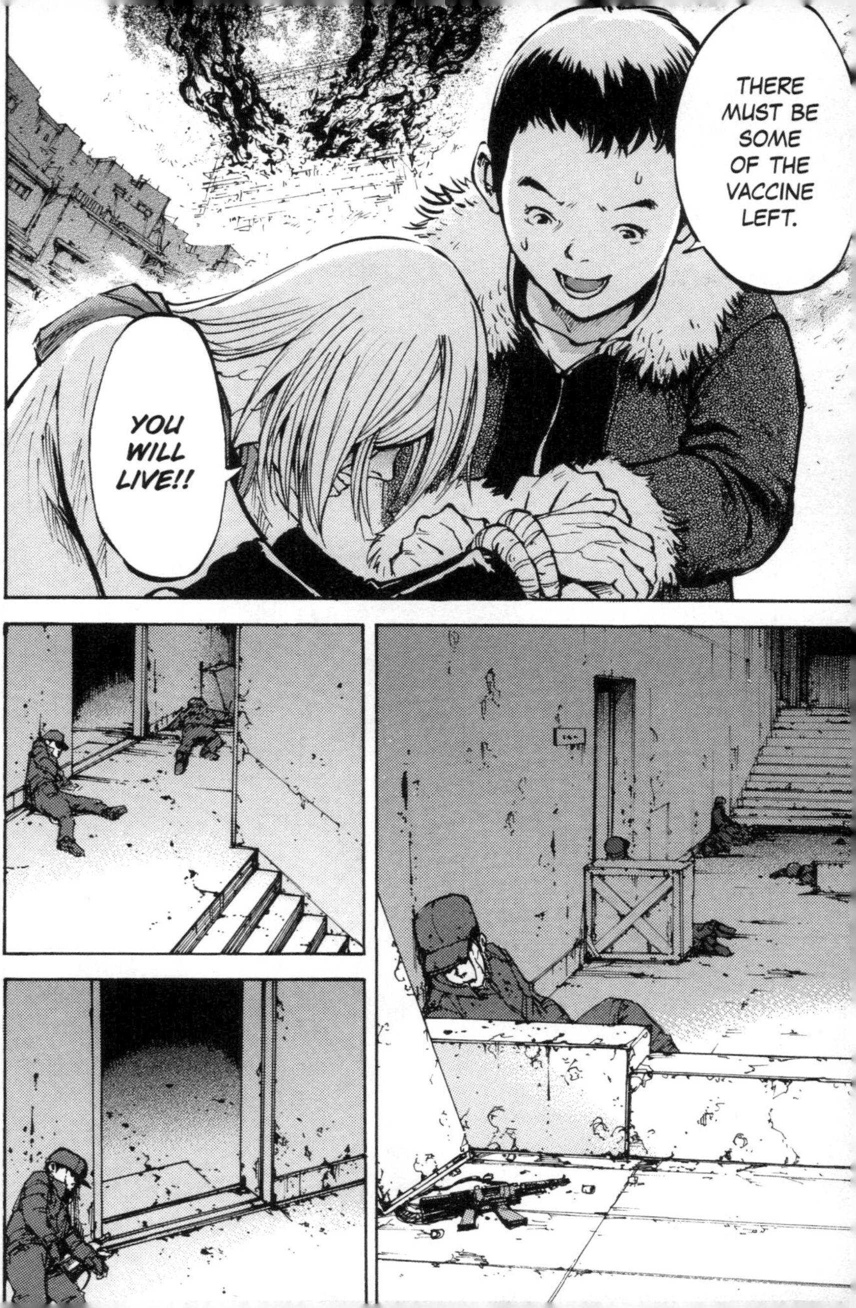
THERE MUST BE SOME OF THE VACCINE LEFT.
YOU WILL LIVE!!

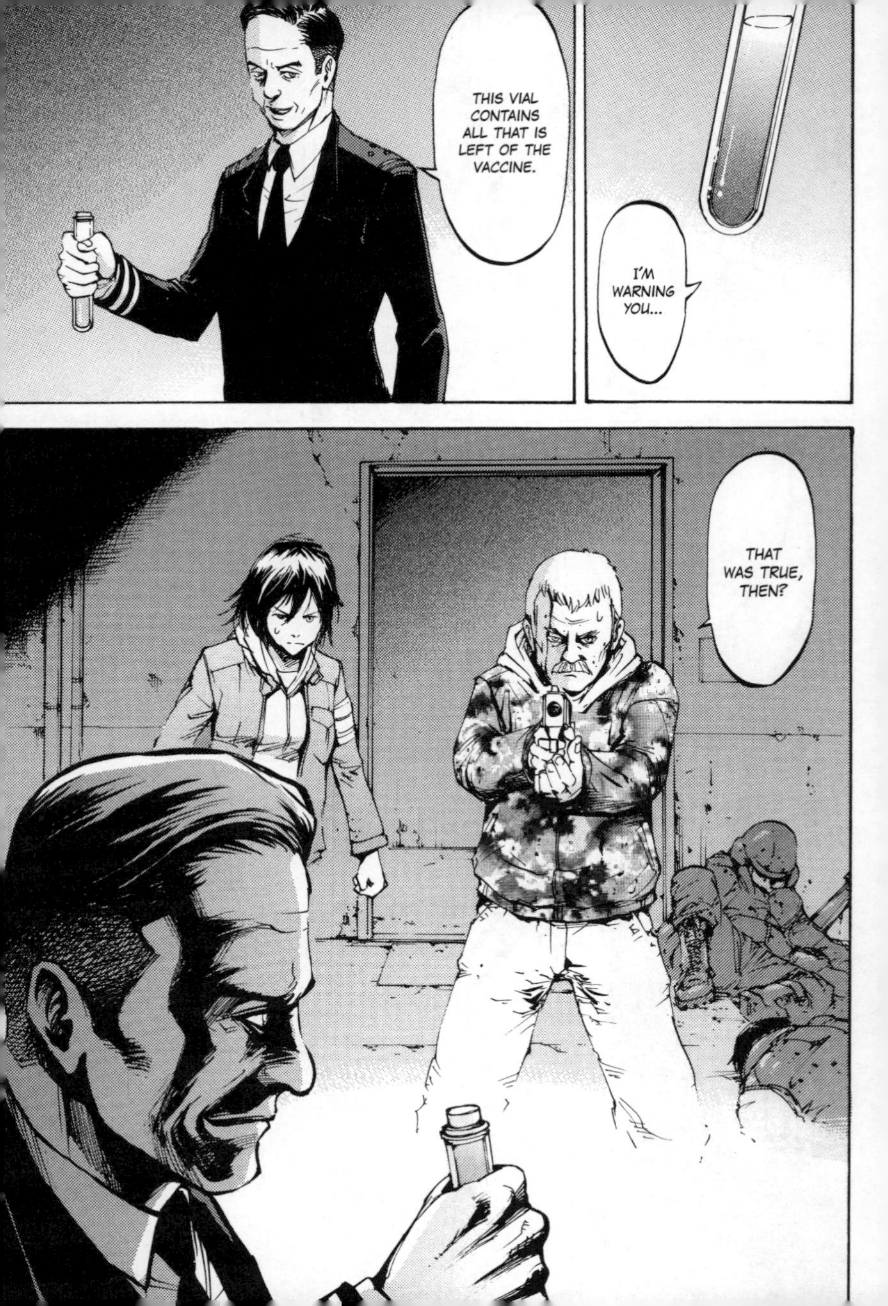
I'M WARNING YOU...
THIS VIAL CONTAINS ALL THAT IS LEFT OF THE VACCINE.
THAT WAS TRUE, THEN?

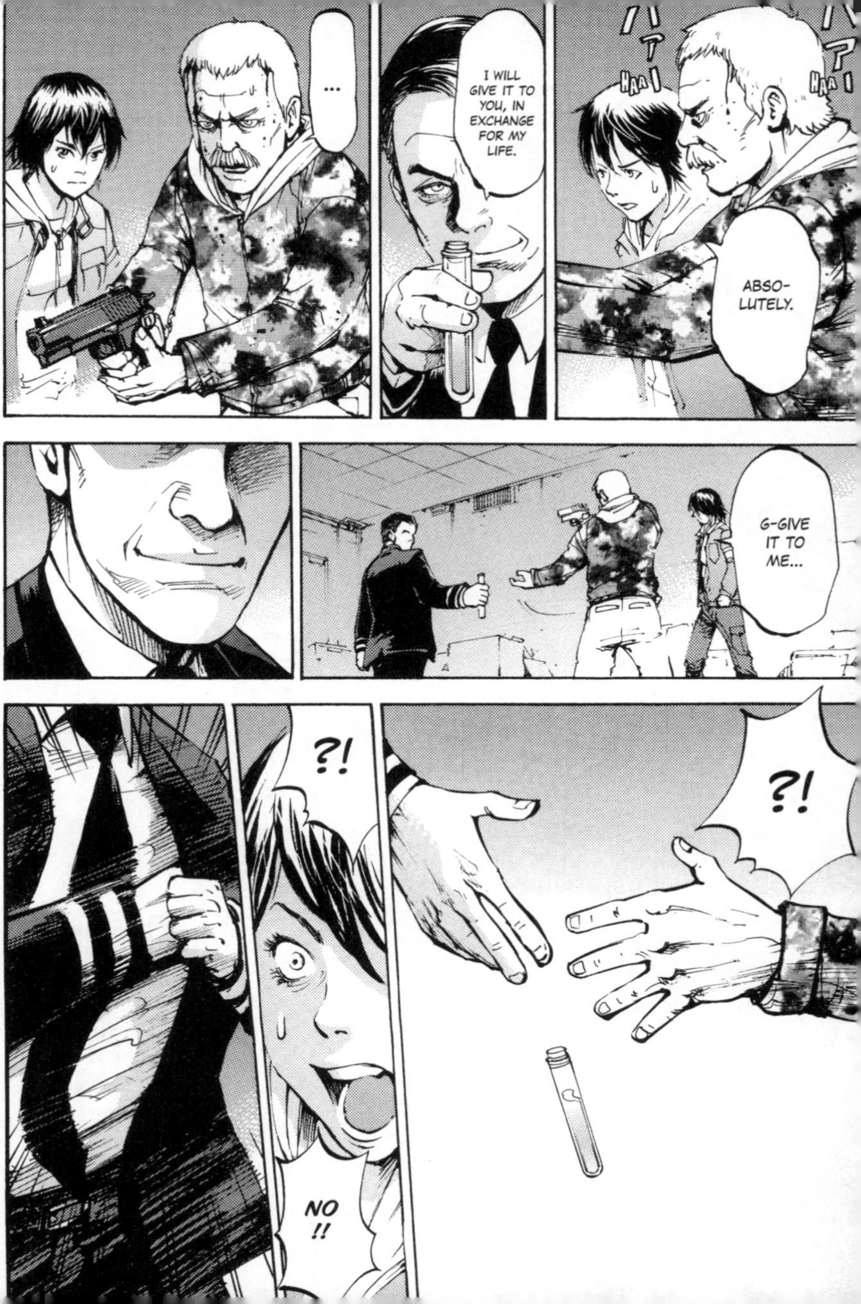

ハァ
HAA
ハァ
HAA
ABSO-LUTELY.
I WILL GIVE IT TO YOU, IN EXCHANGE FOR MY LIFE.
...
G-GIVE IT TO ME...
?!
?!
NO !!

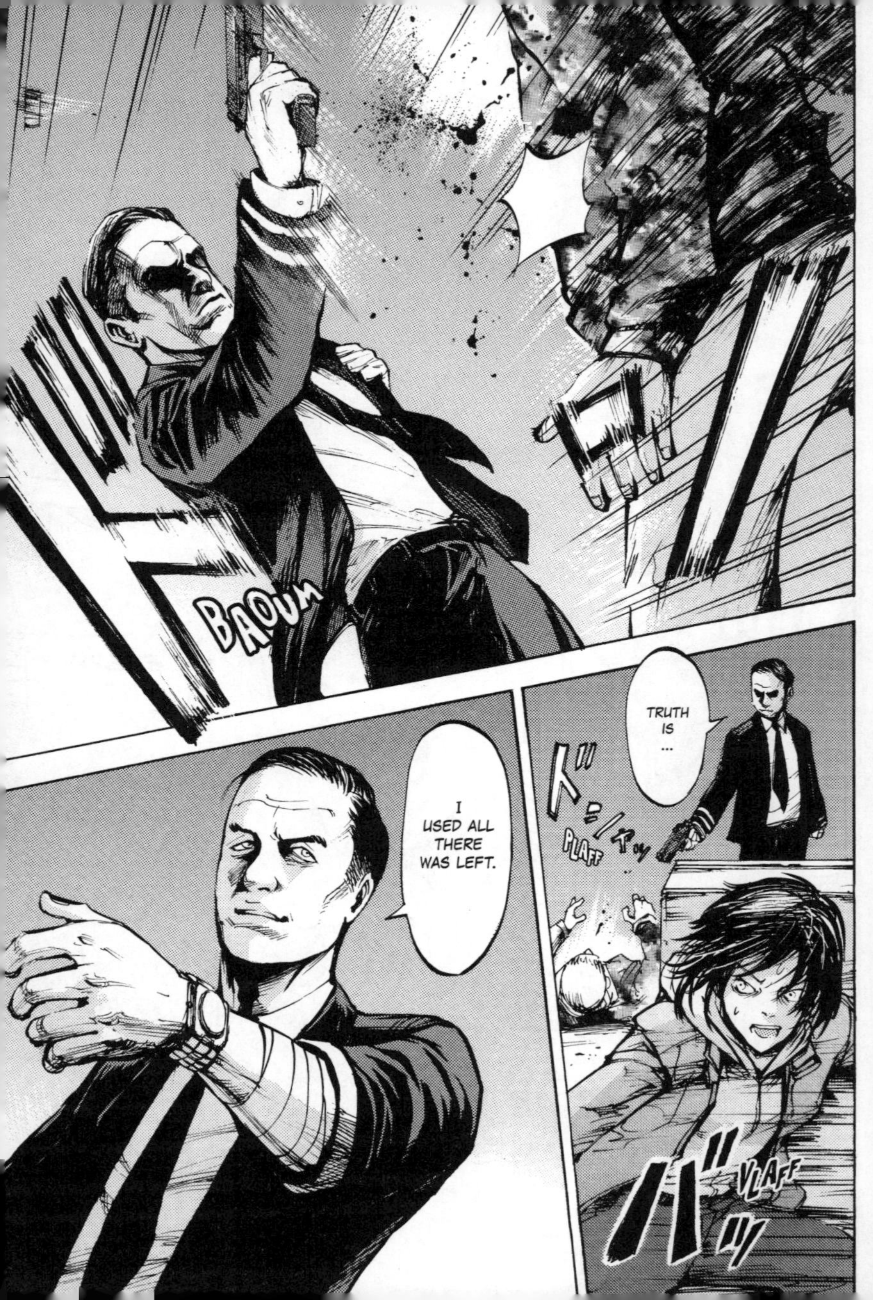
BAOUM
TRUTH IS ...
PLAFF
VLAFF
I USED ALL THERE WAS LEFT.

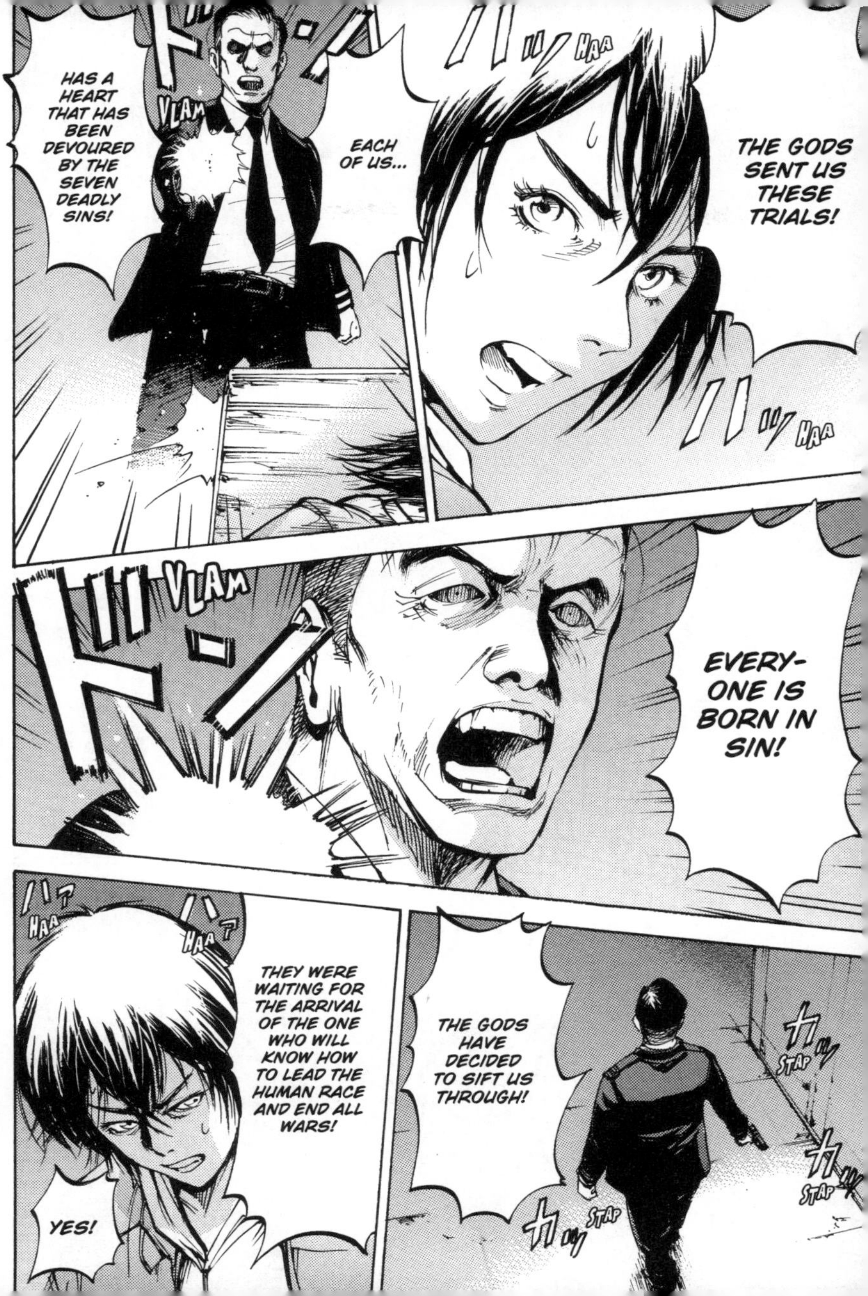
HAA
THE GODS SENT US THESE TRIALS!
HAA
EACH OF US...
HAS A HEART THAT HAS BEEN DEVOURED BY THE SEVEN DEADLY SINS!
VLAM
EVERY-ONE IS BORN IN SIN!
VLAM
STAP
STAP
STAP
THE GODS HAVE DECIDED TO SIFT US THROUGH!
HAA
HAA
THEY WERE WAITING FOR THE ARRIVAL OF THE ONE WHO WILL KNOW HOW TO LEAD THE HUMAN RACE AND END ALL WARS!
YES!

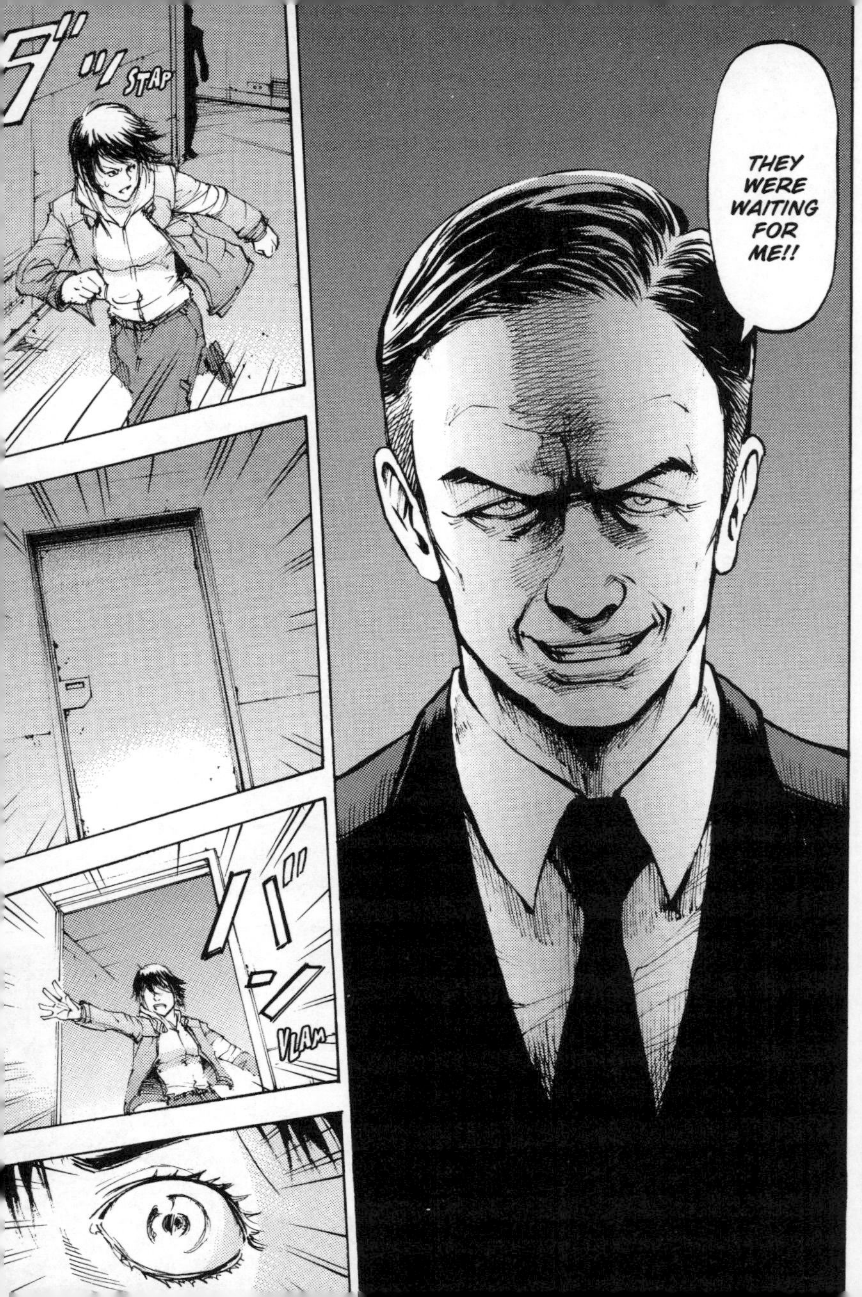
THEY WERE WAITING FOR ME!!
STAP
VLAM

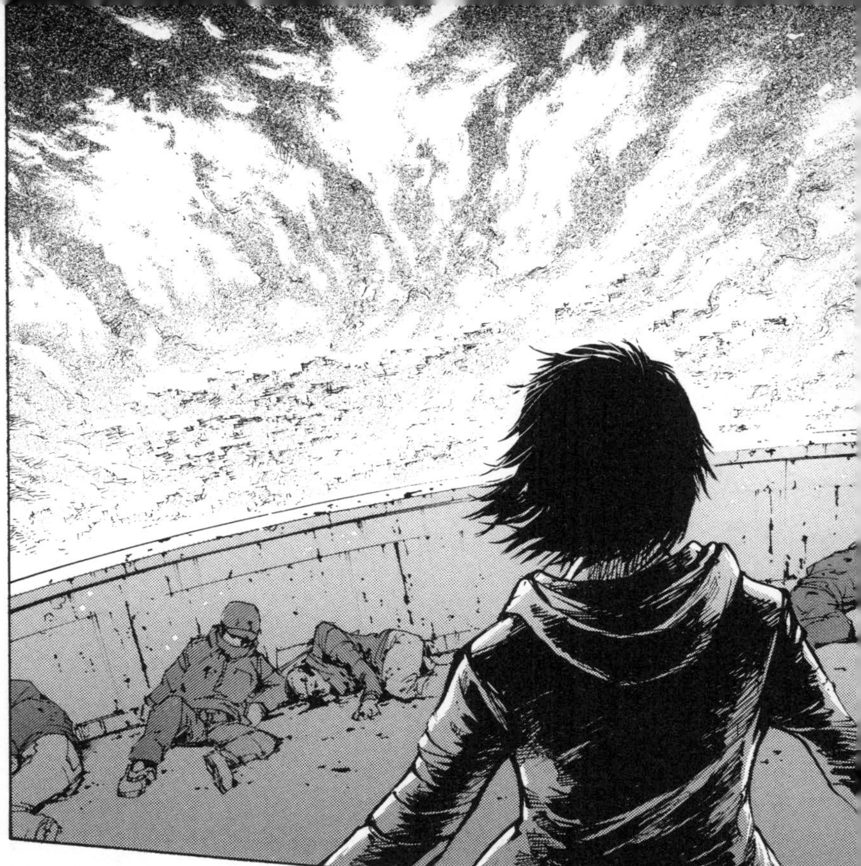
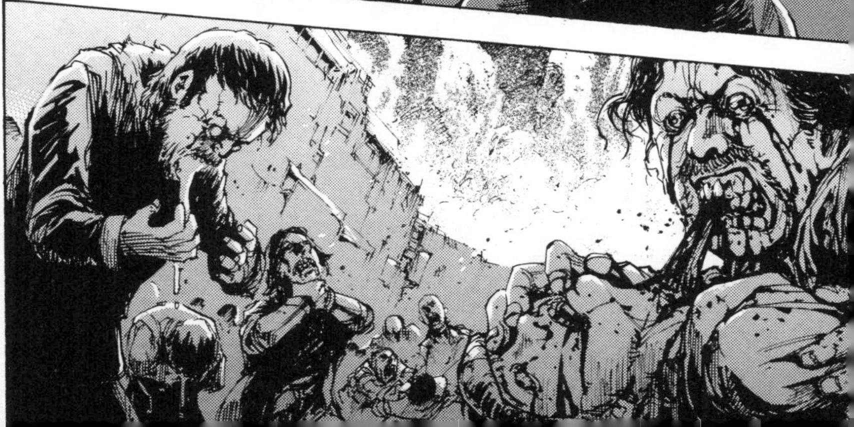

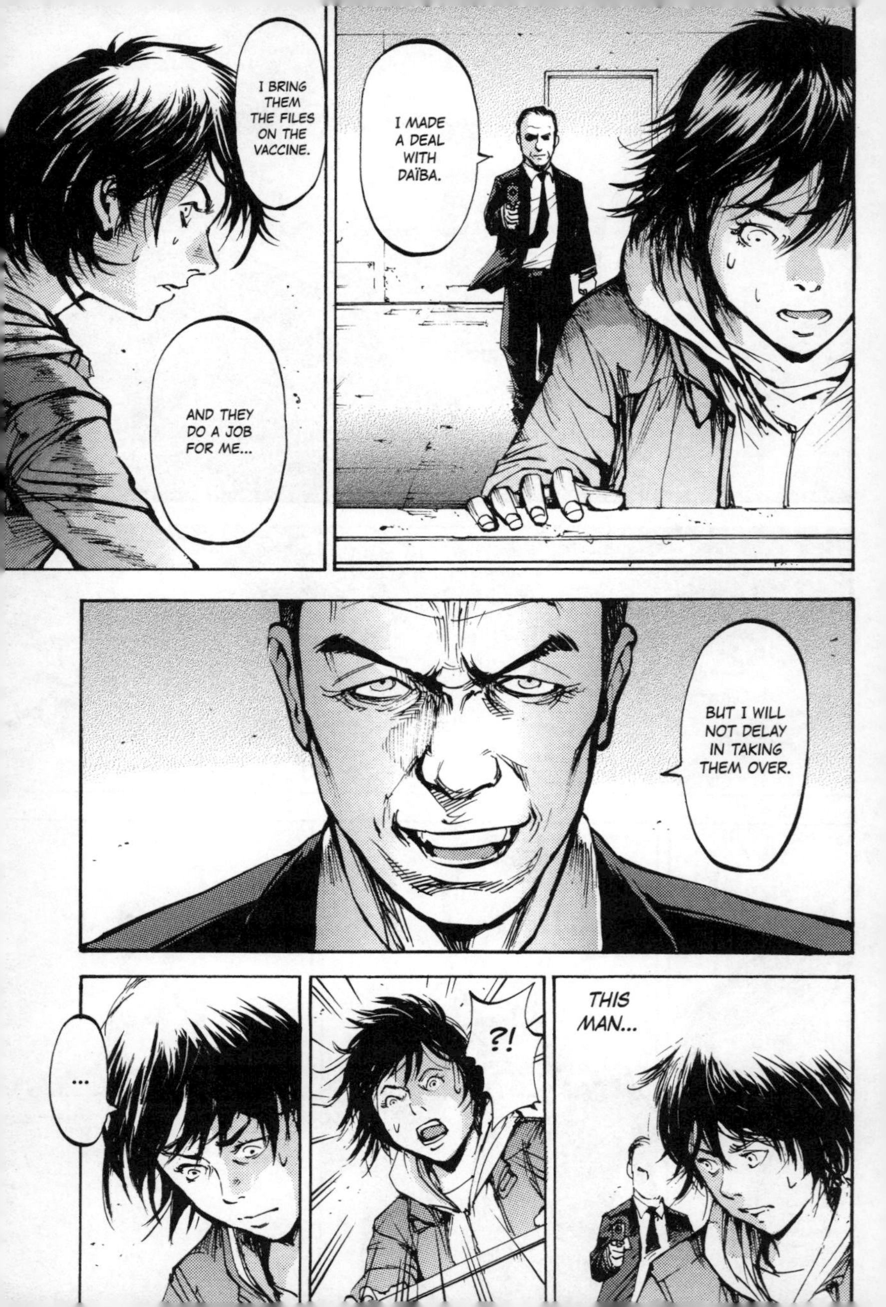
I MADE A DEAL WITH DAÏBA.
I BRING THEM THE FILES ON THE VACCINE.
AND THEY DO A JOB FOR ME...
BUT I WILL NOT DELAY IN TAKING THEM OVER.
THIS MAN...
?!
...

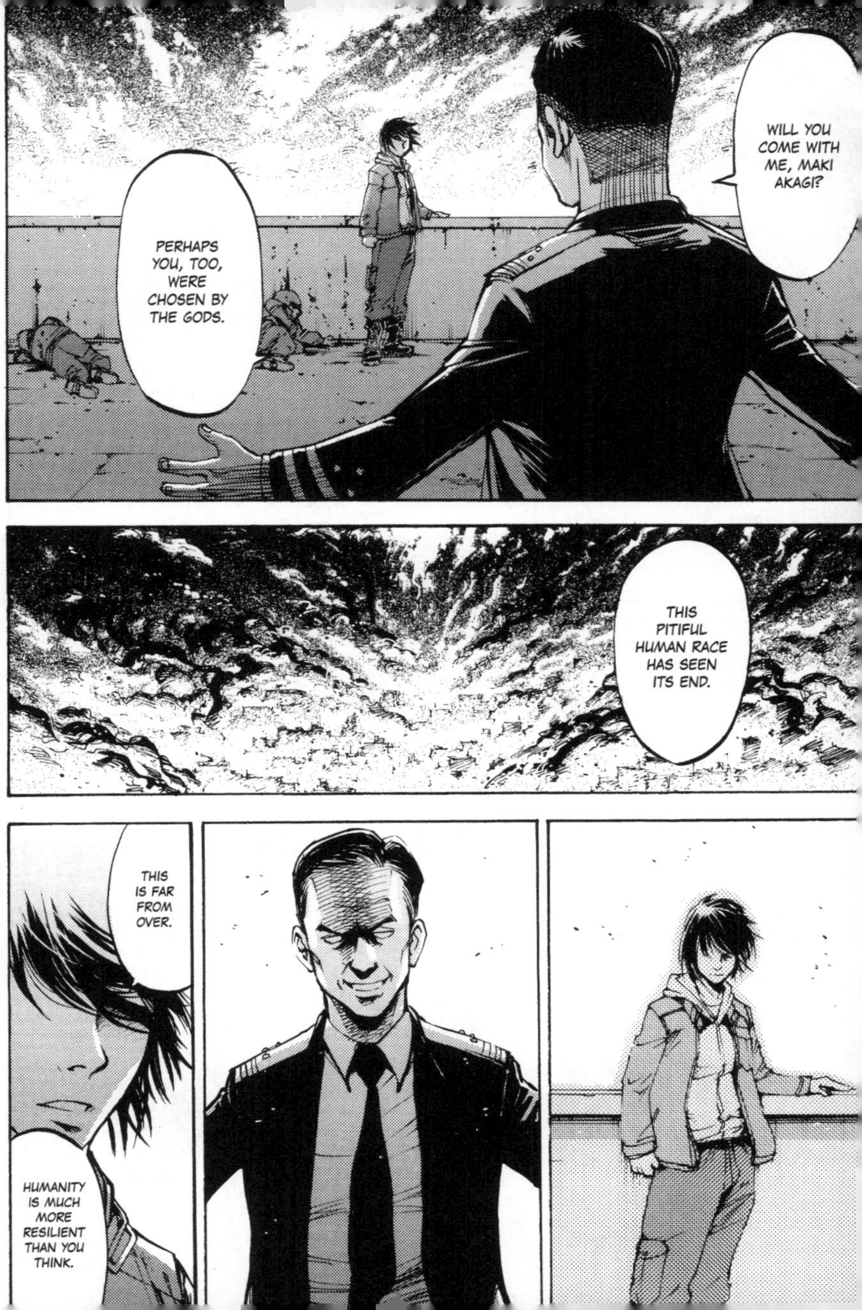
WILL YOU COME WITH ME, MAKI AKAGI?
PERHAPS YOU, TOO, WERE CHOSEN BY THE GODS.
THIS PITIFUL HUMAN RACE HAS SEEN ITS END.
THIS IS FAR FROM OVER.
HUMANITY IS MUCH MORE RESILIENT THAN YOU THINK.

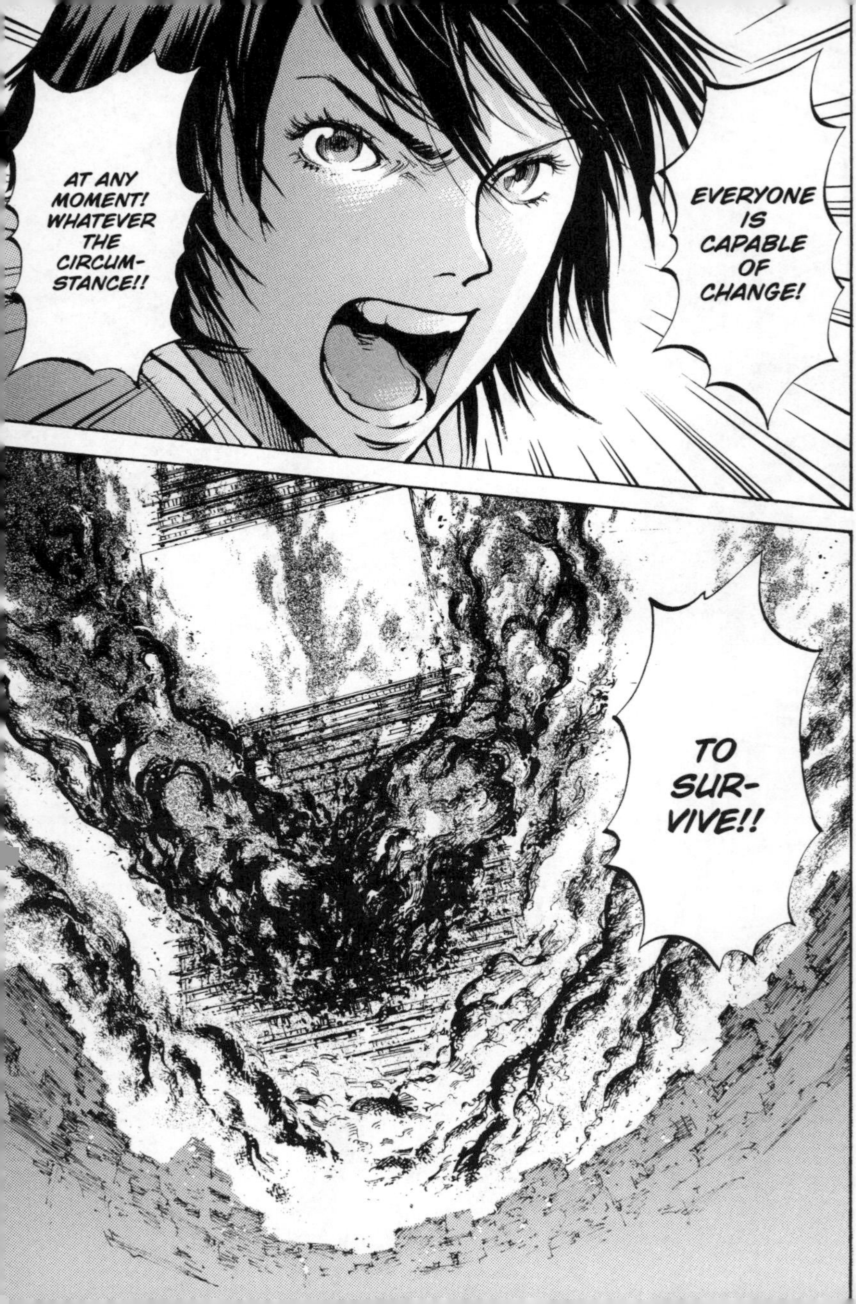
EVERYONE IS CAPABLE OF CHANGE!
AT ANY MOMENT! WHATEVER THE CIRCUM-STANCE!!
TO SUR-VIVE!!

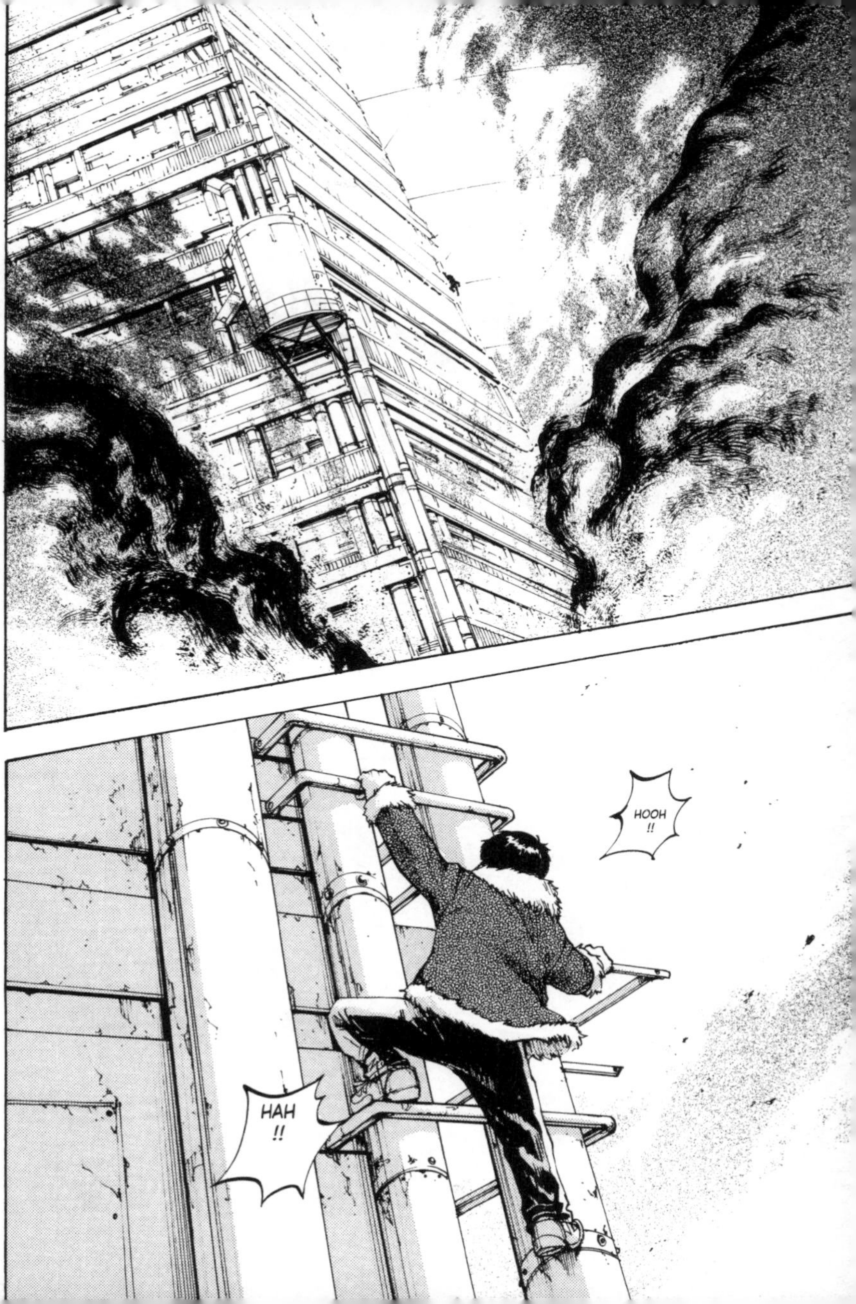
HOOH !!
HAH !!

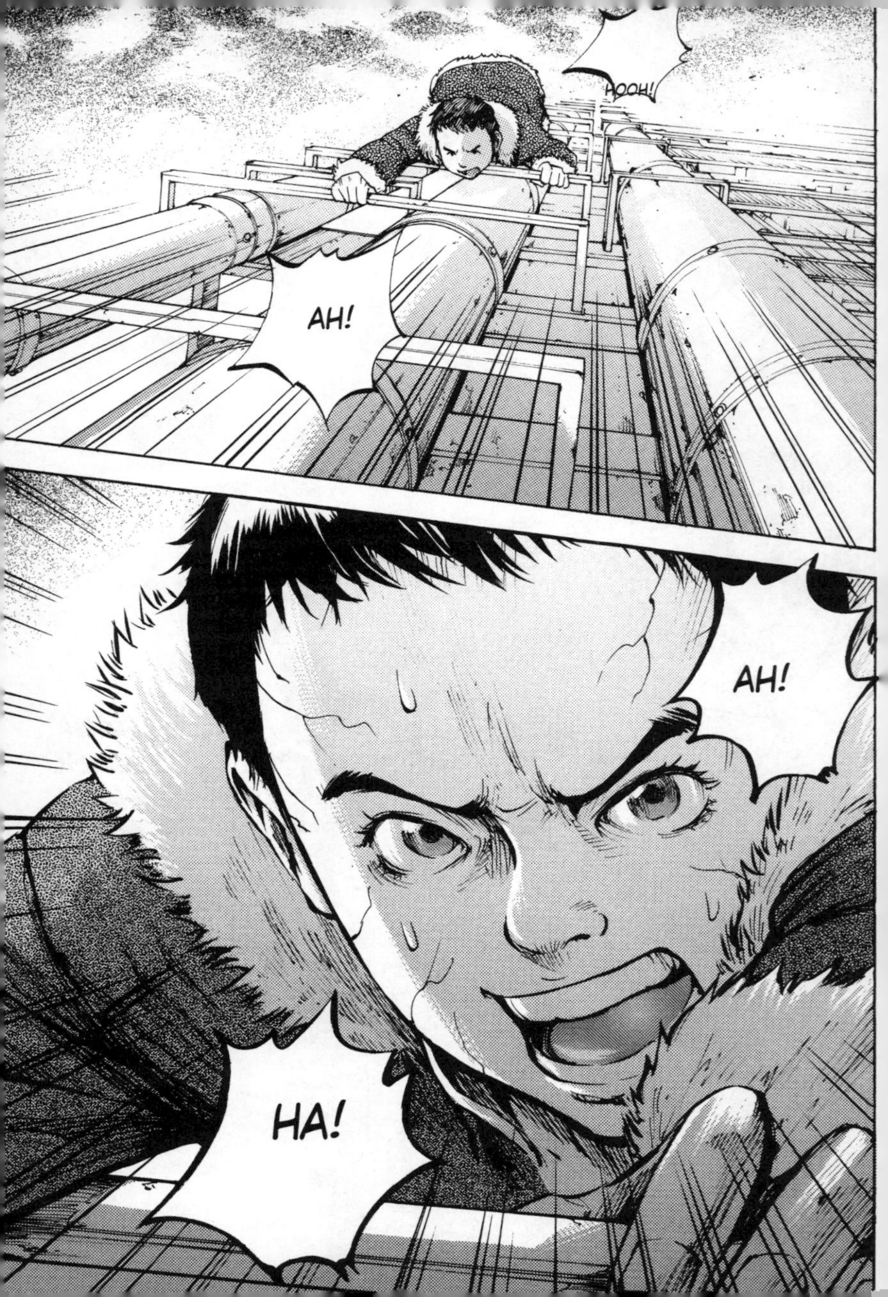
HOOH!
AH!
AH!
HA!

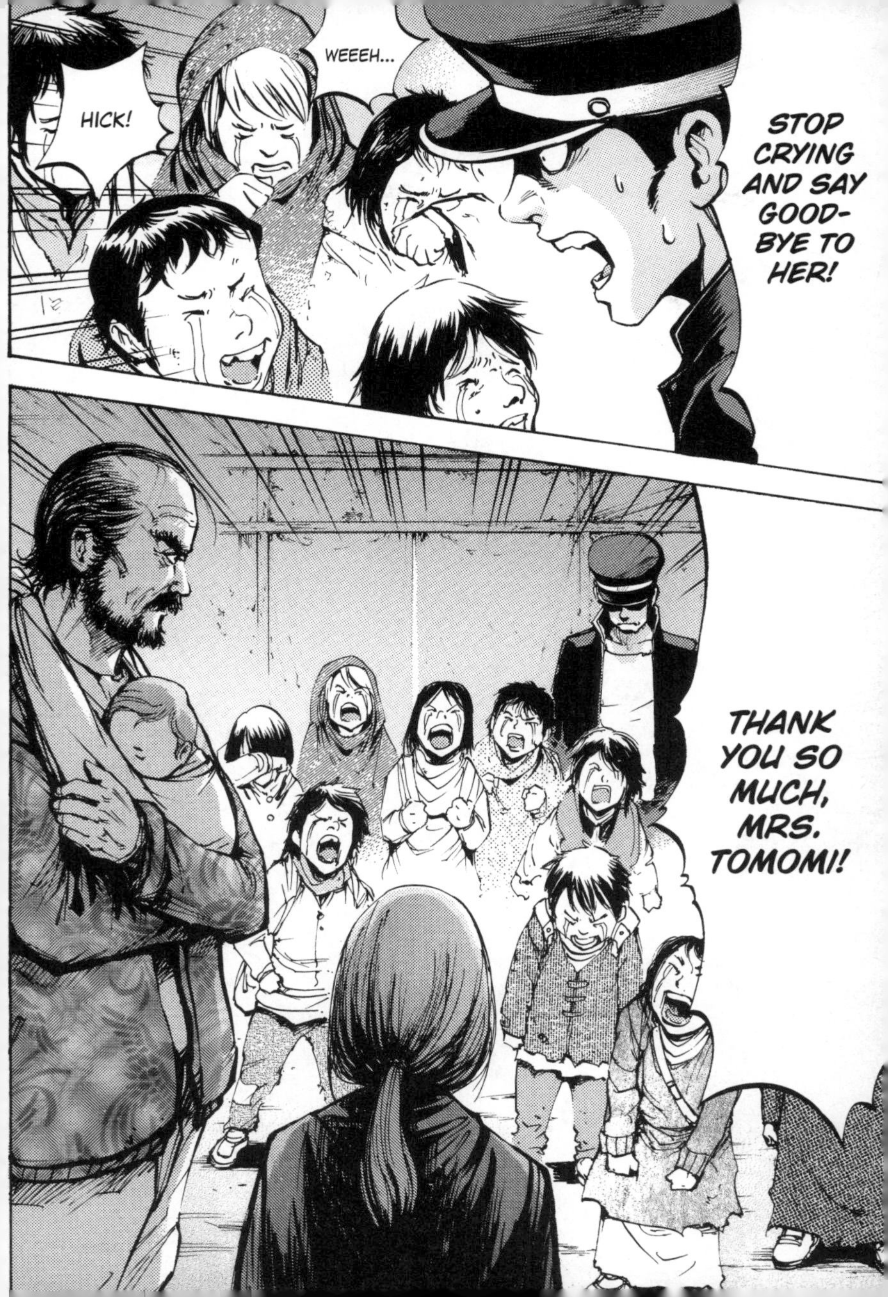
STOP CRYING AND SAY GOOD-BYE TO HER!
WEEEH...
HICK!
THANK YOU SO MUCH, MRS. TOMOMI!

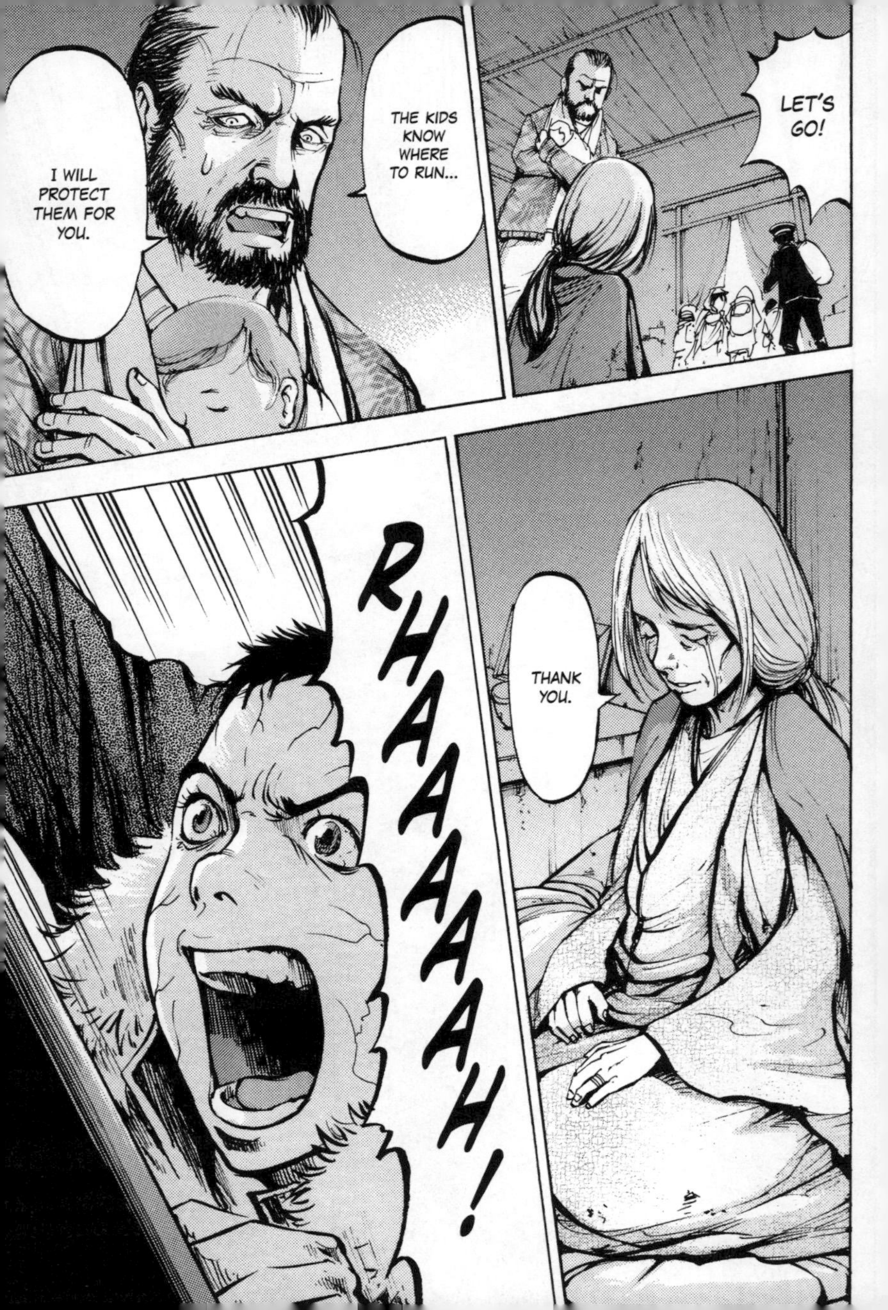
LET'S GO!
THE KIDS KNOW WHERE TO RUN...
I WILL PROTECT THEM FOR YOU.
THANK YOU.
RHAAAAAH!

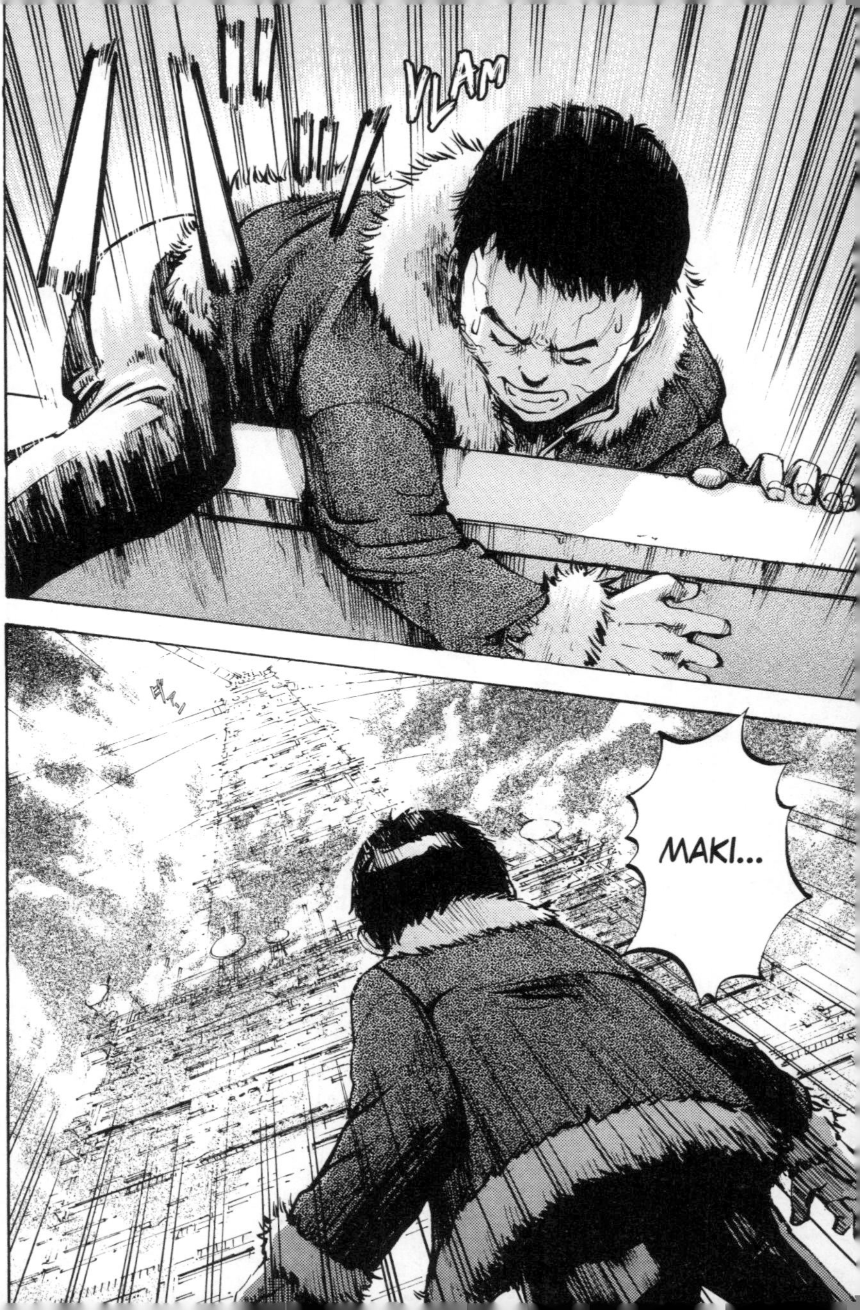
VLAM
MAKI...

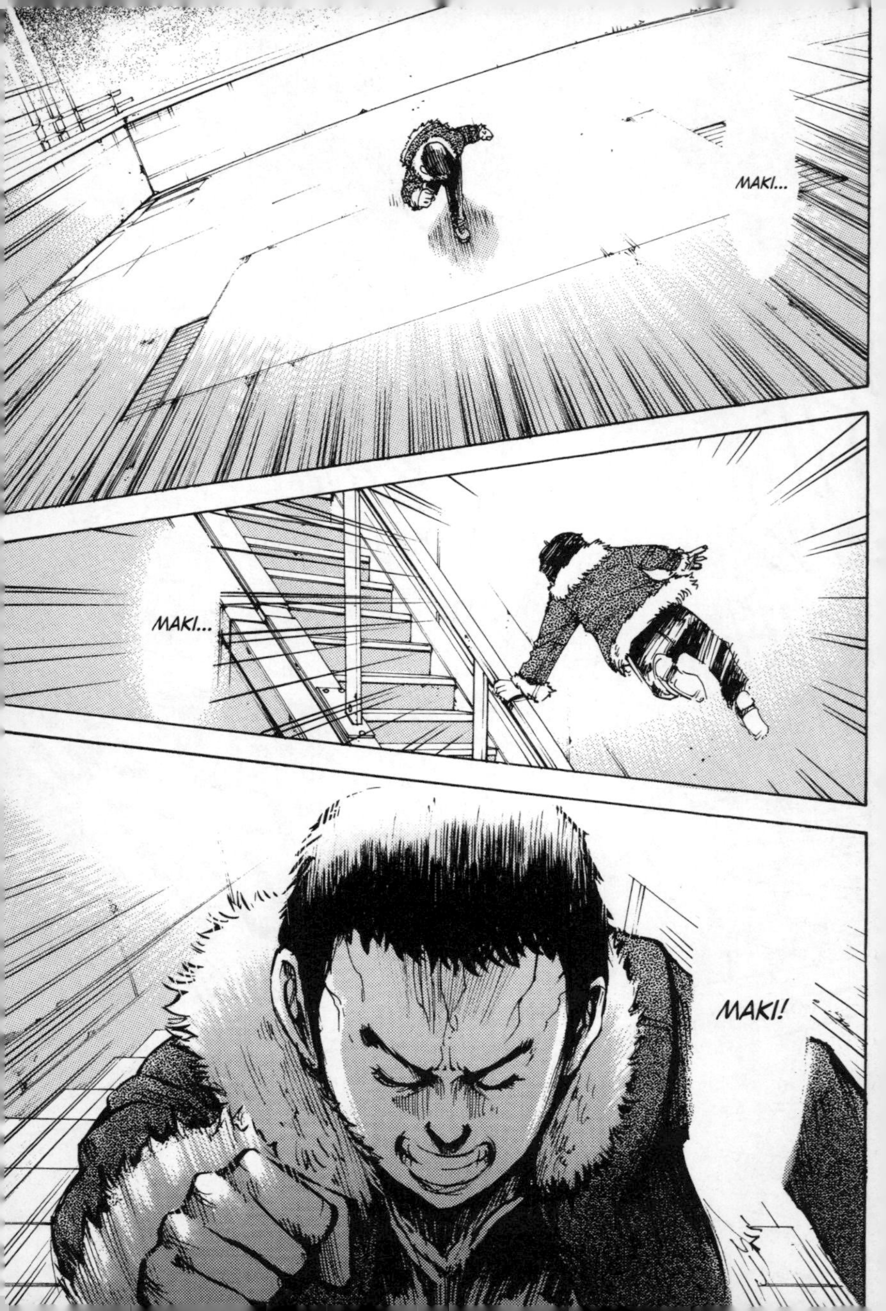
MAKI...
MAKI...
MAKI!

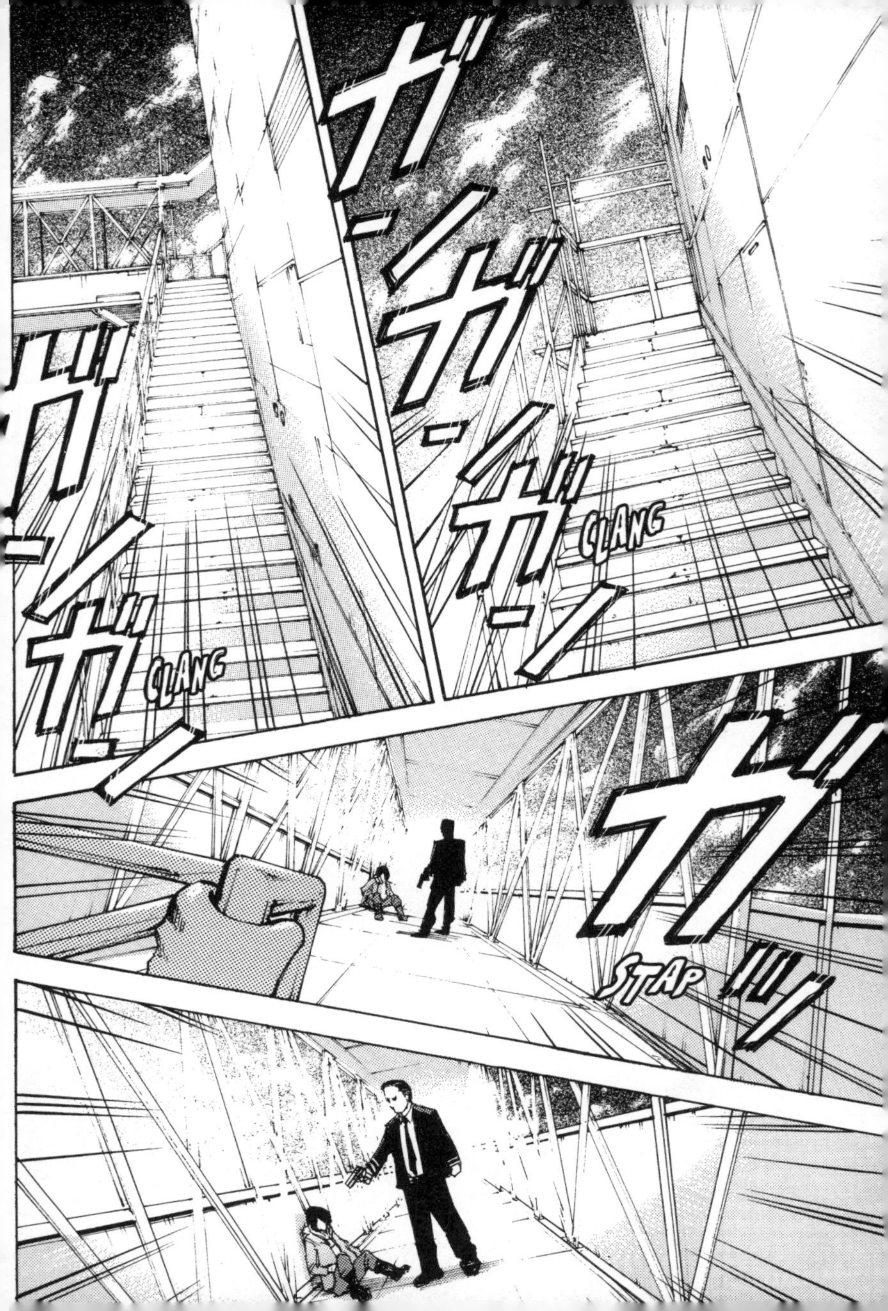
ガーンガーンガーン
CLANG
ガーンガーン
CLANG
ダッ
STAP

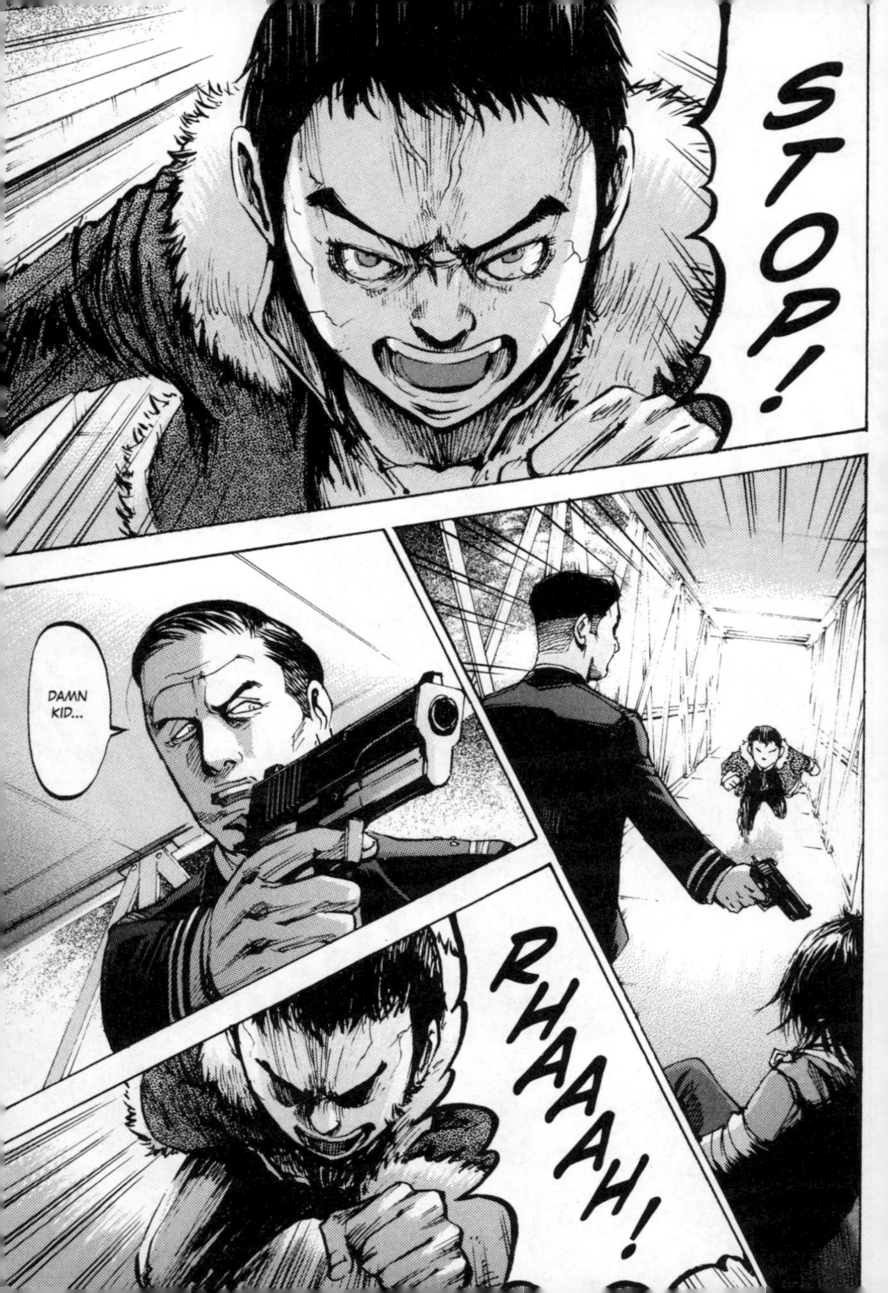
STOP!
RHAAAH!
DAMN KID...

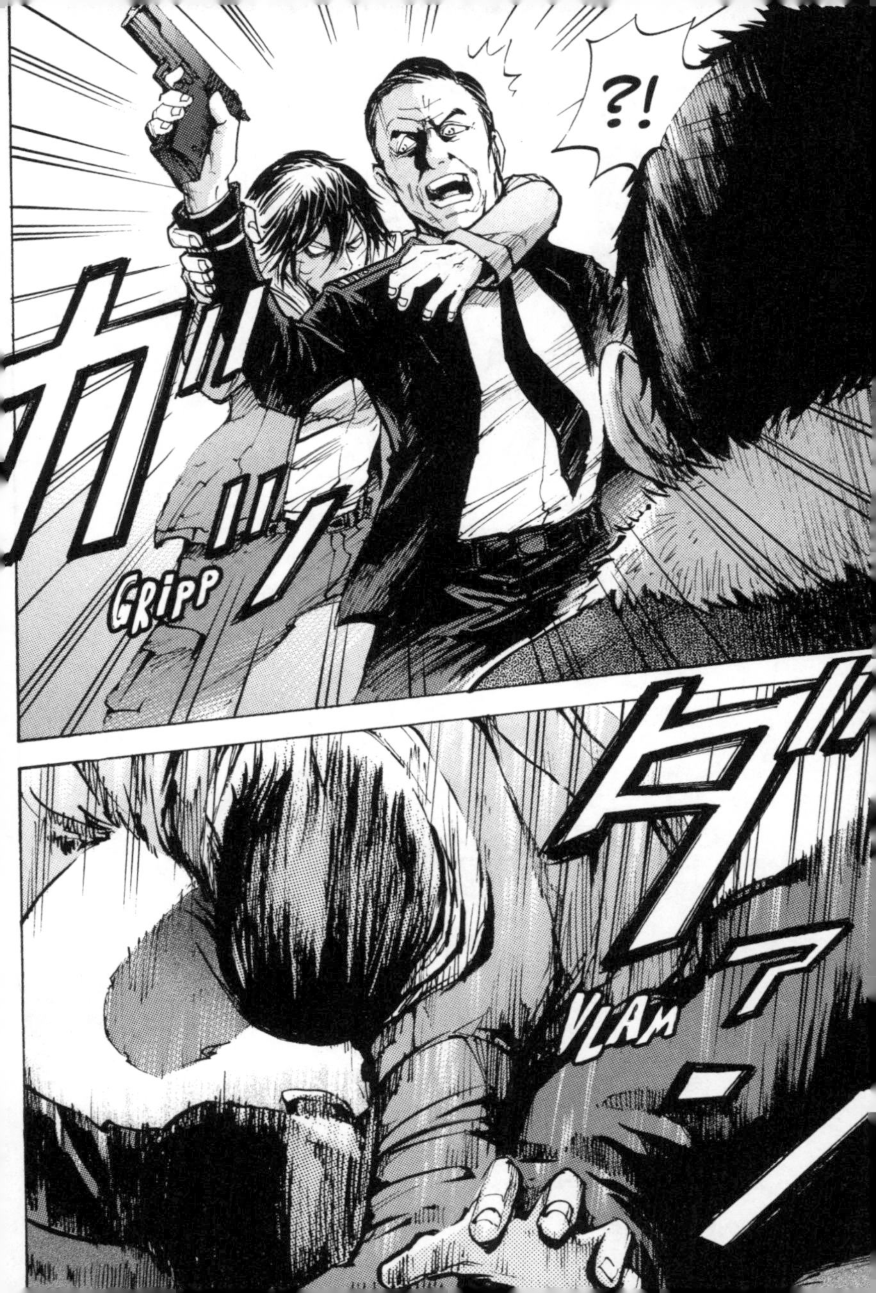
?!
GRIPP
VLAM

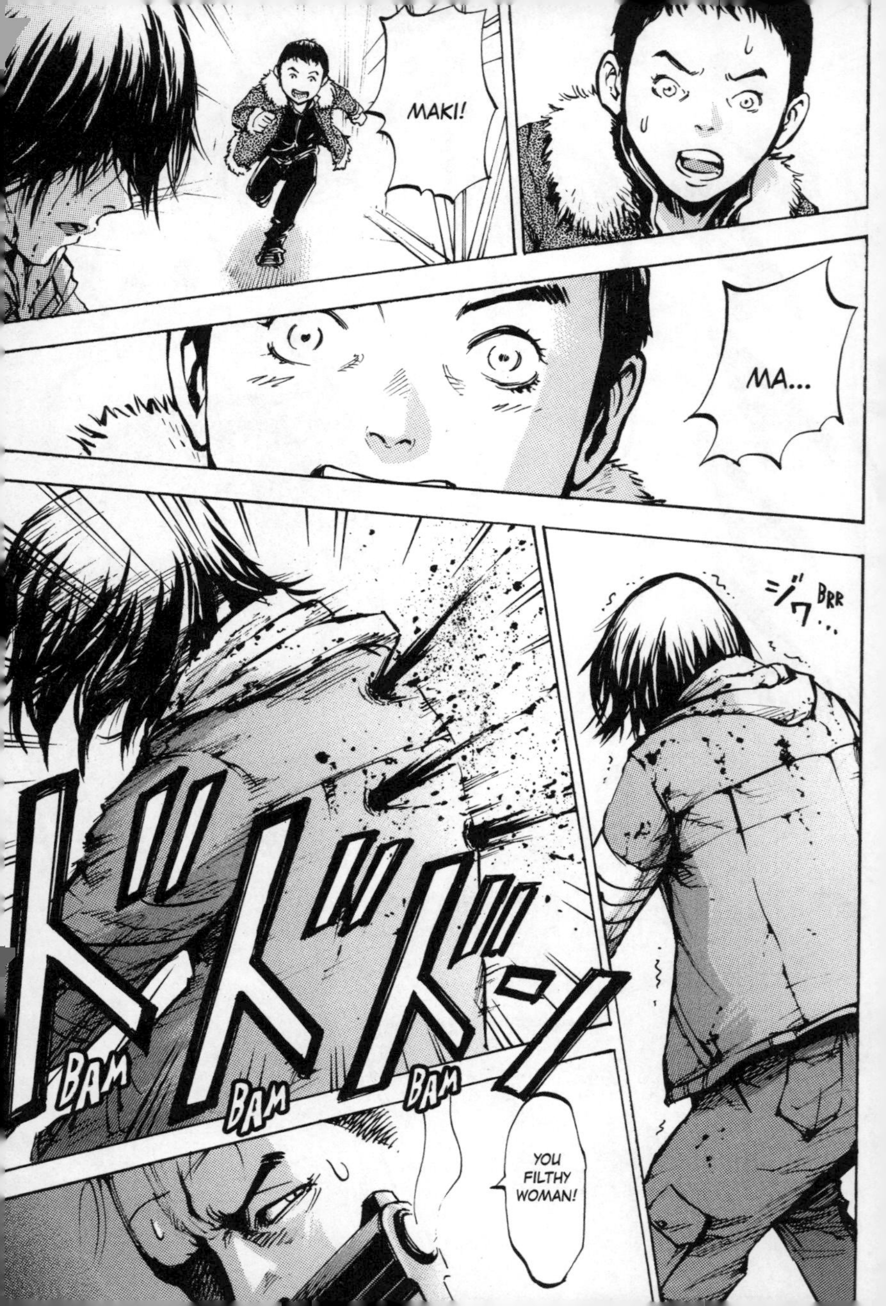
MAKI!
MA...
ジワ... BRR
ドドドーッ
BAM
BAM
BAM
YOU FILTHY WOMAN!

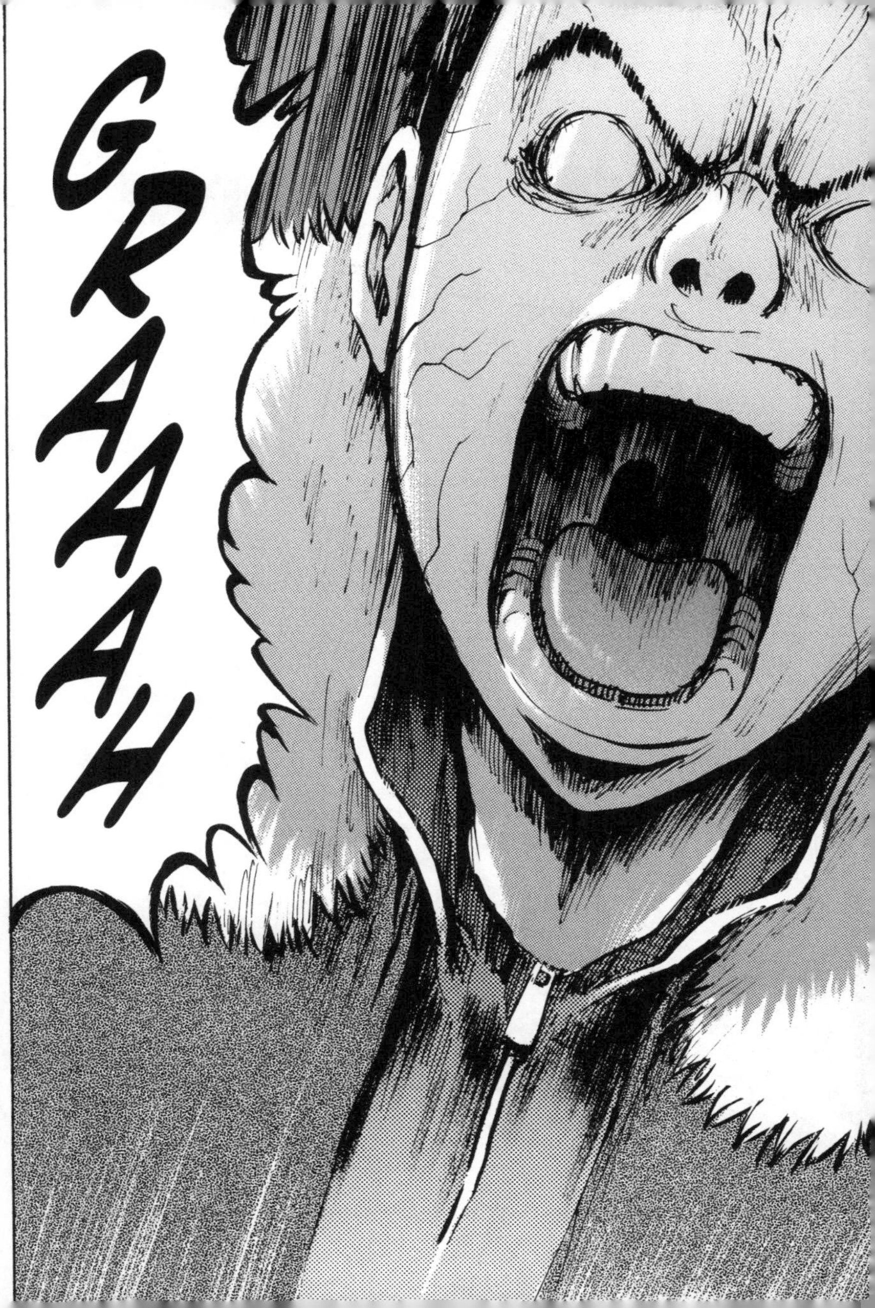
GRAAAAH

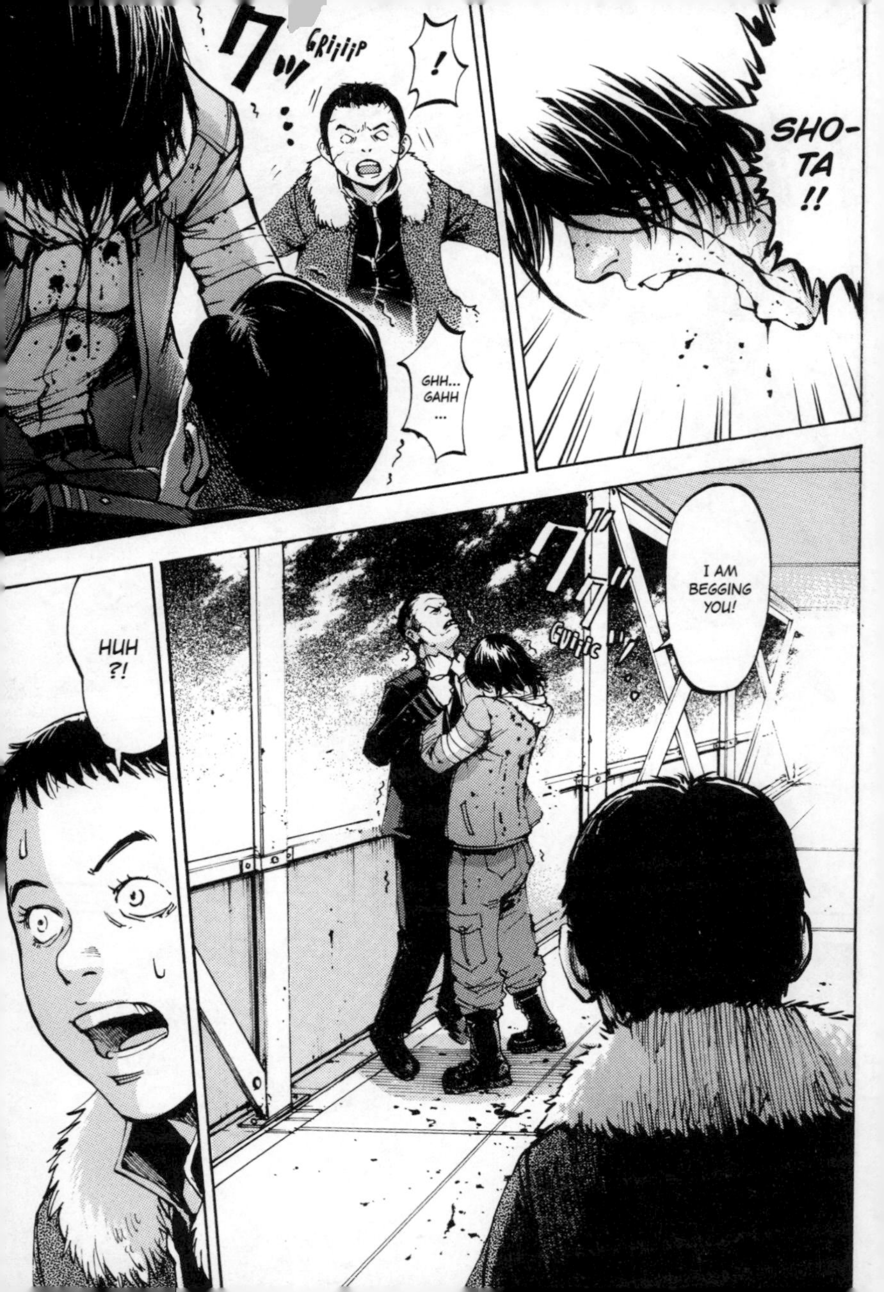
SHO-TA!!
GRIIIIP
!
GHH... GAHH ...
I AM BEGGING YOU!
GUIIIC
HUH?!

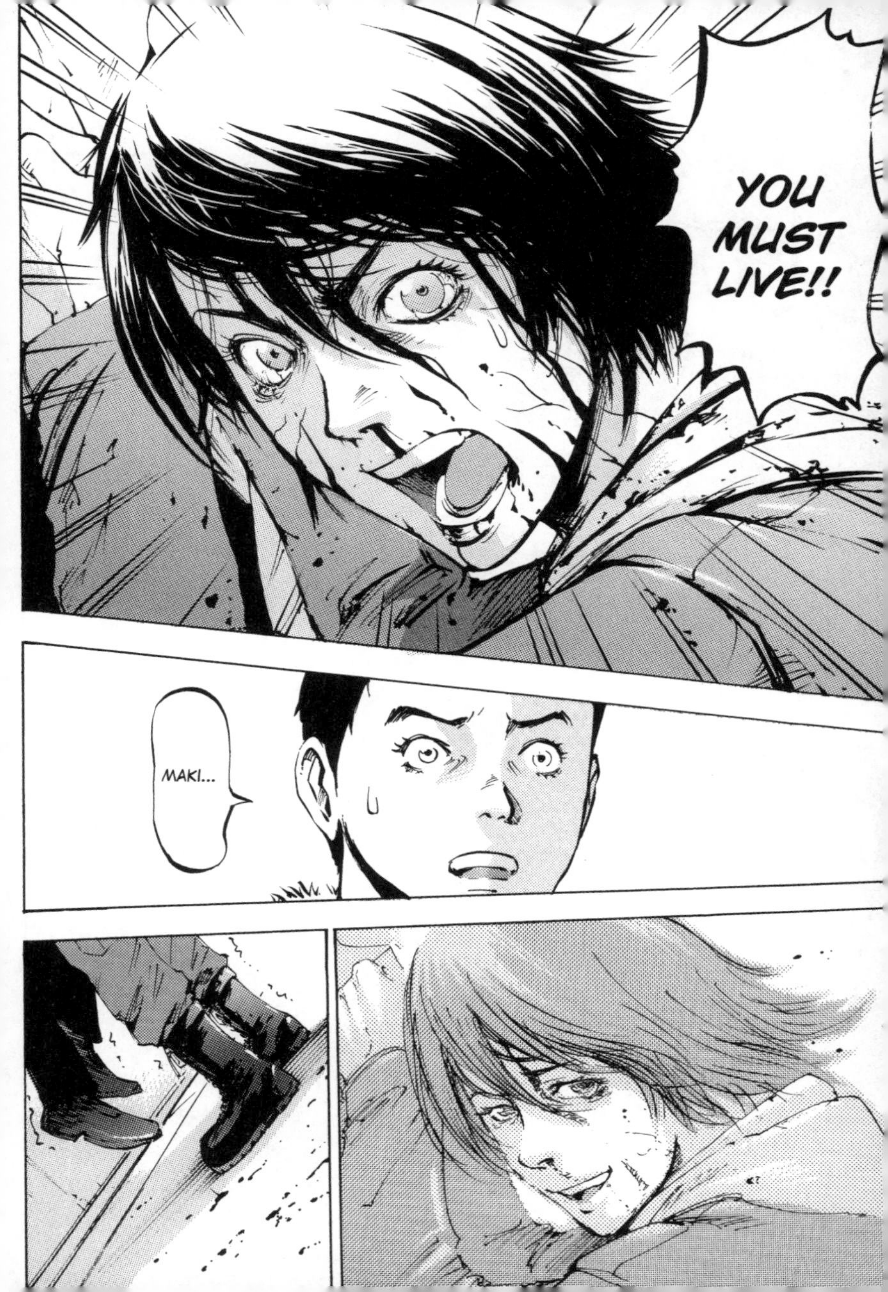
YOU MUST LIVE!!
MAKI...

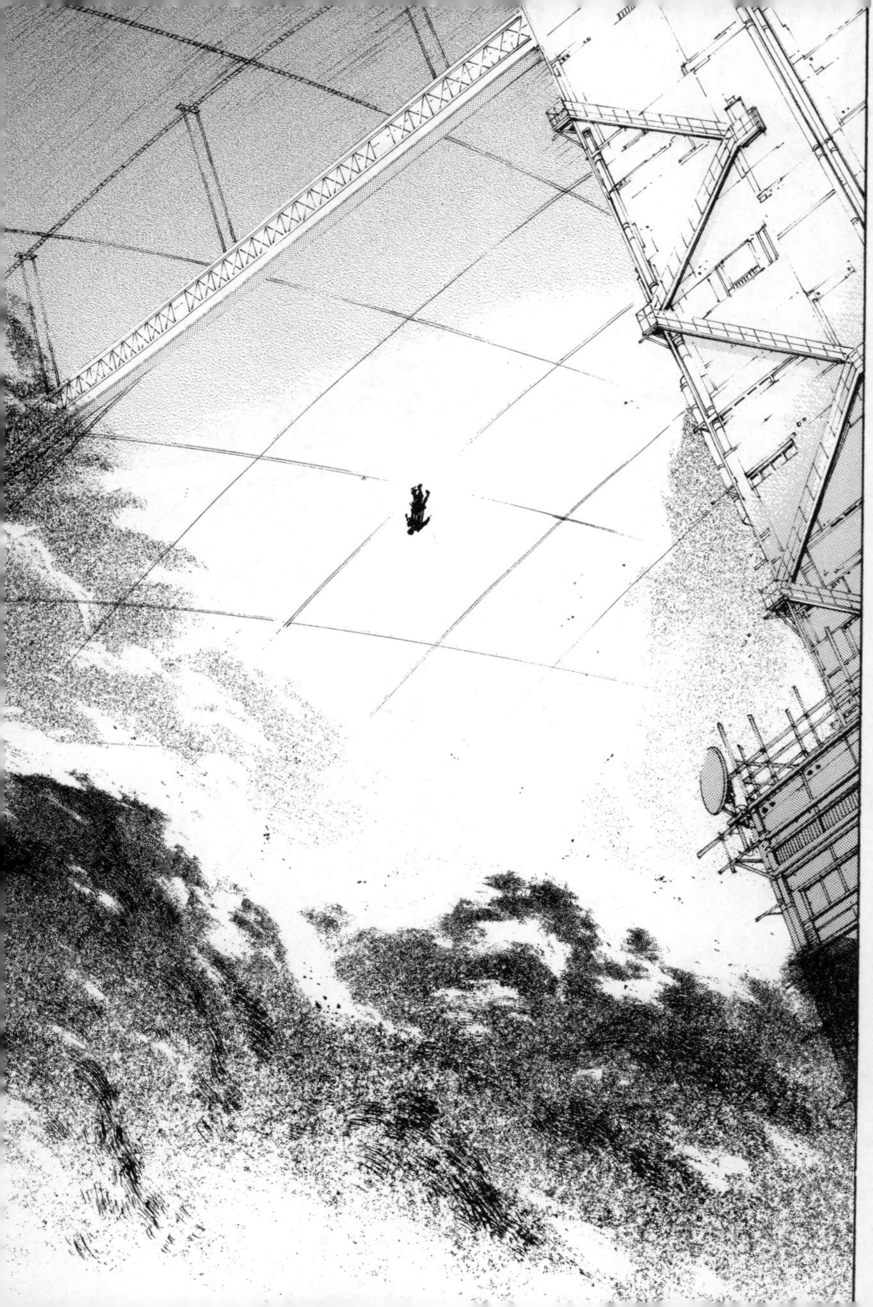

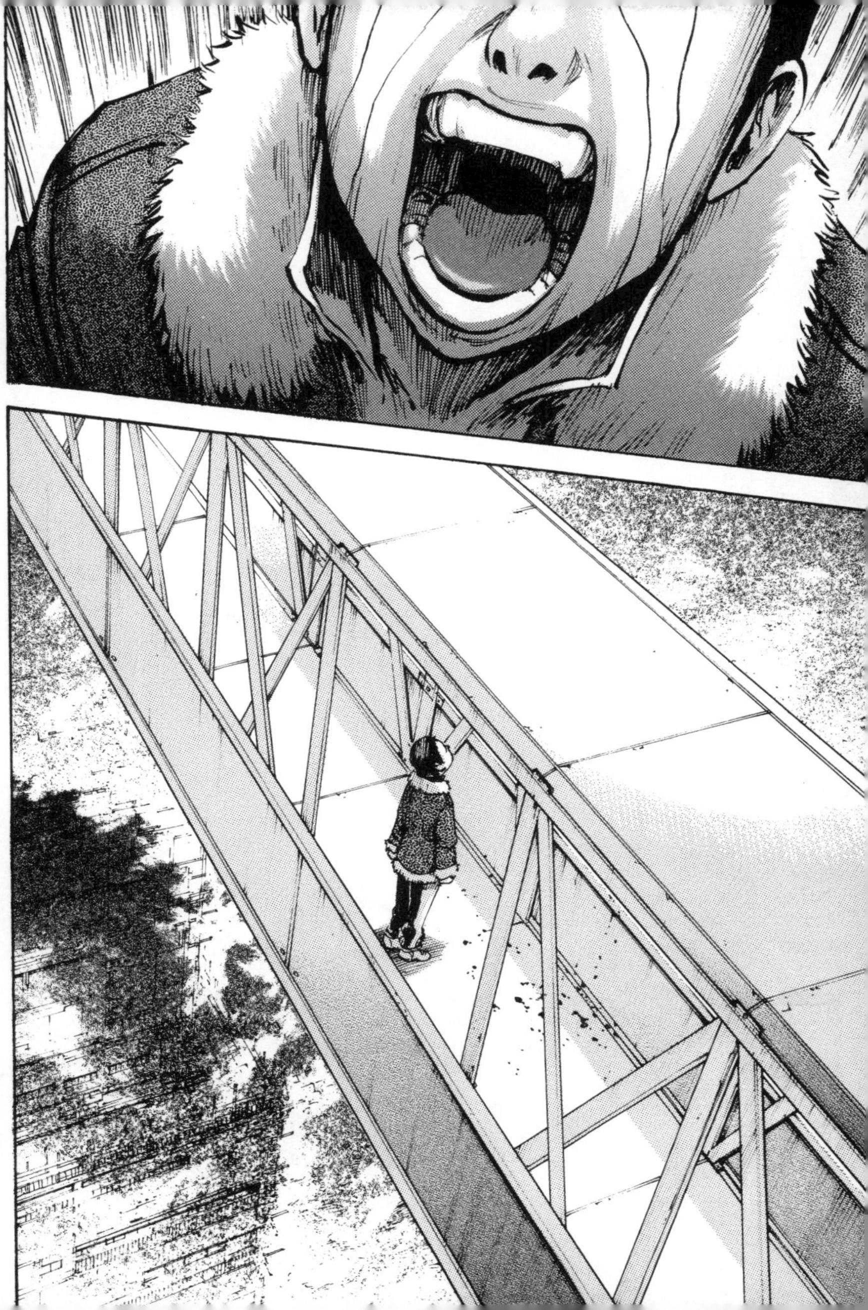

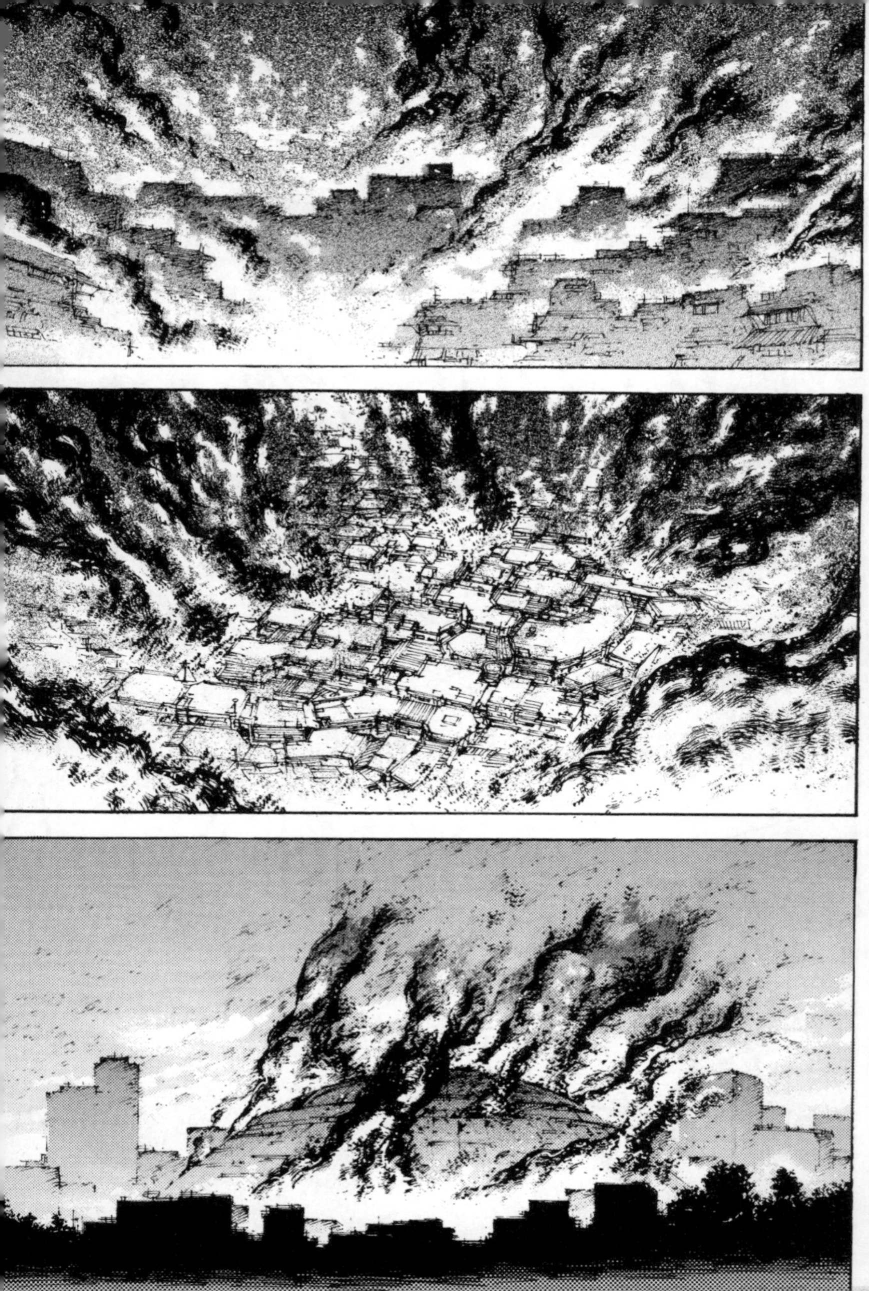

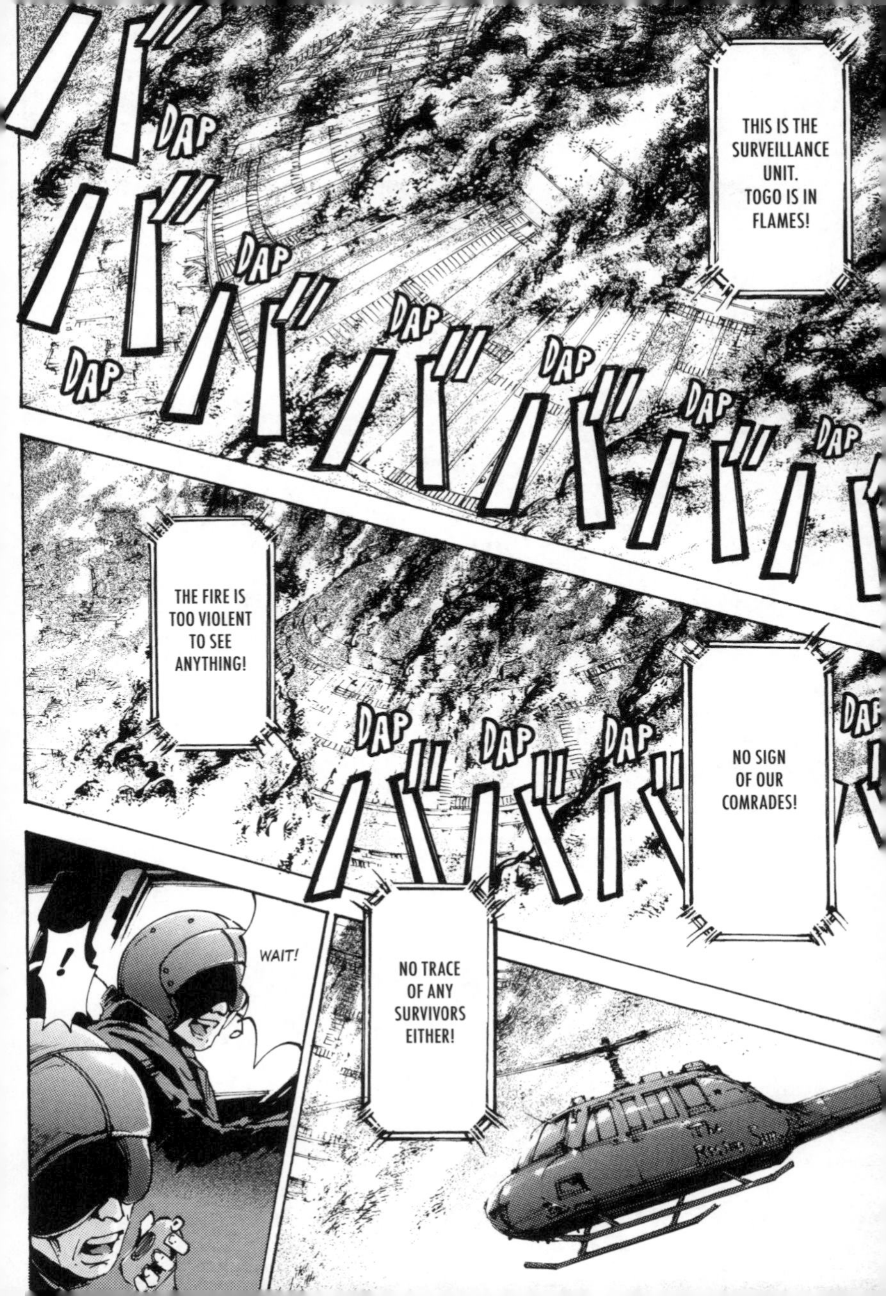
THIS IS THE SURVEILLANCE UNIT. TOGO IS IN FLAMES!
DAP DAP DAP DAP DAP DAP DAP
NO SIGN OF OUR COMRADES!
DAP DAP DAP
THE FIRE IS TOO VIOLENT TO SEE ANYTHING!
NO TRACE OF ANY SURVIVORS EITHER!
WAIT!
!

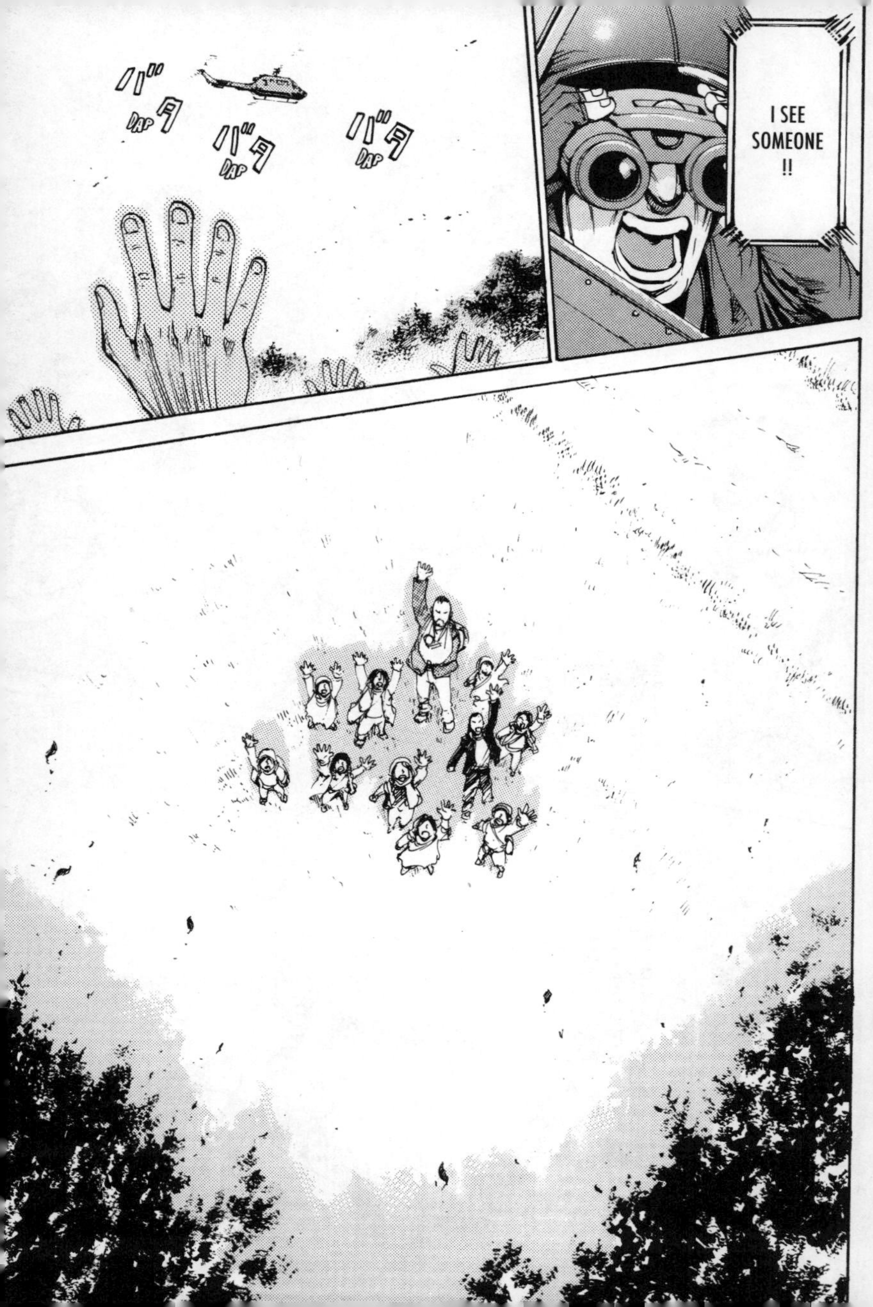
I SEE SOMEONE !!
バタ
DAP
バタ
DAP
バタ
DAP

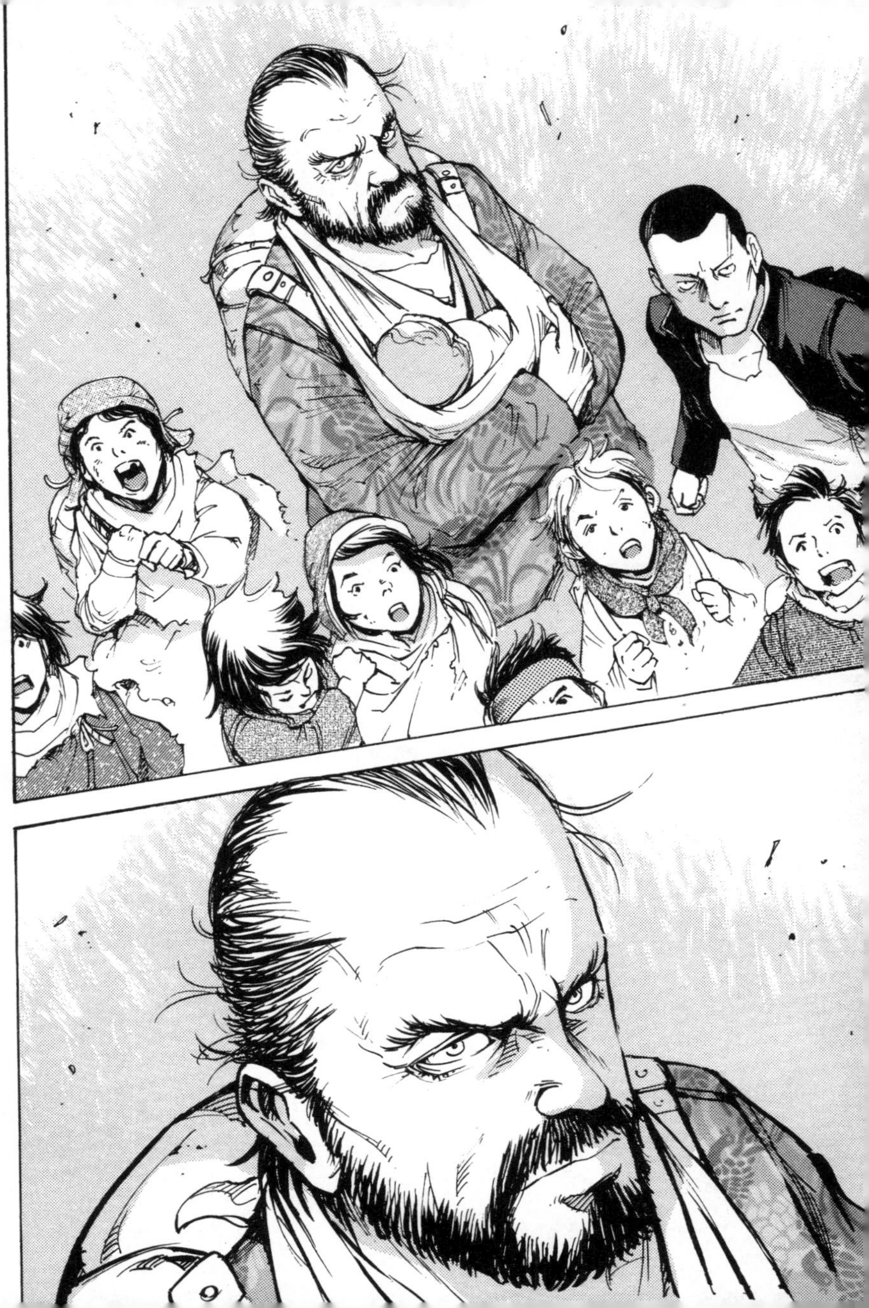

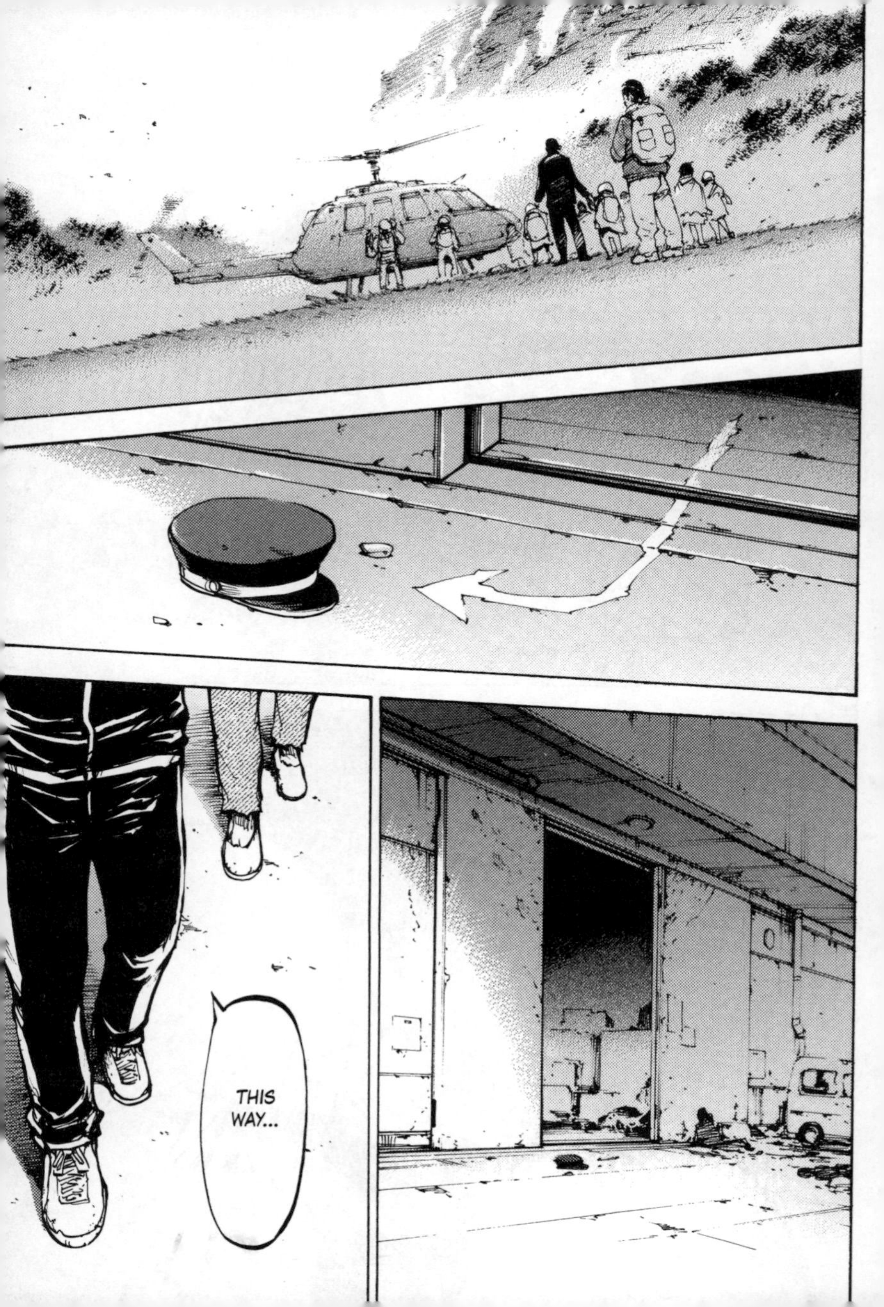
THIS WAY...

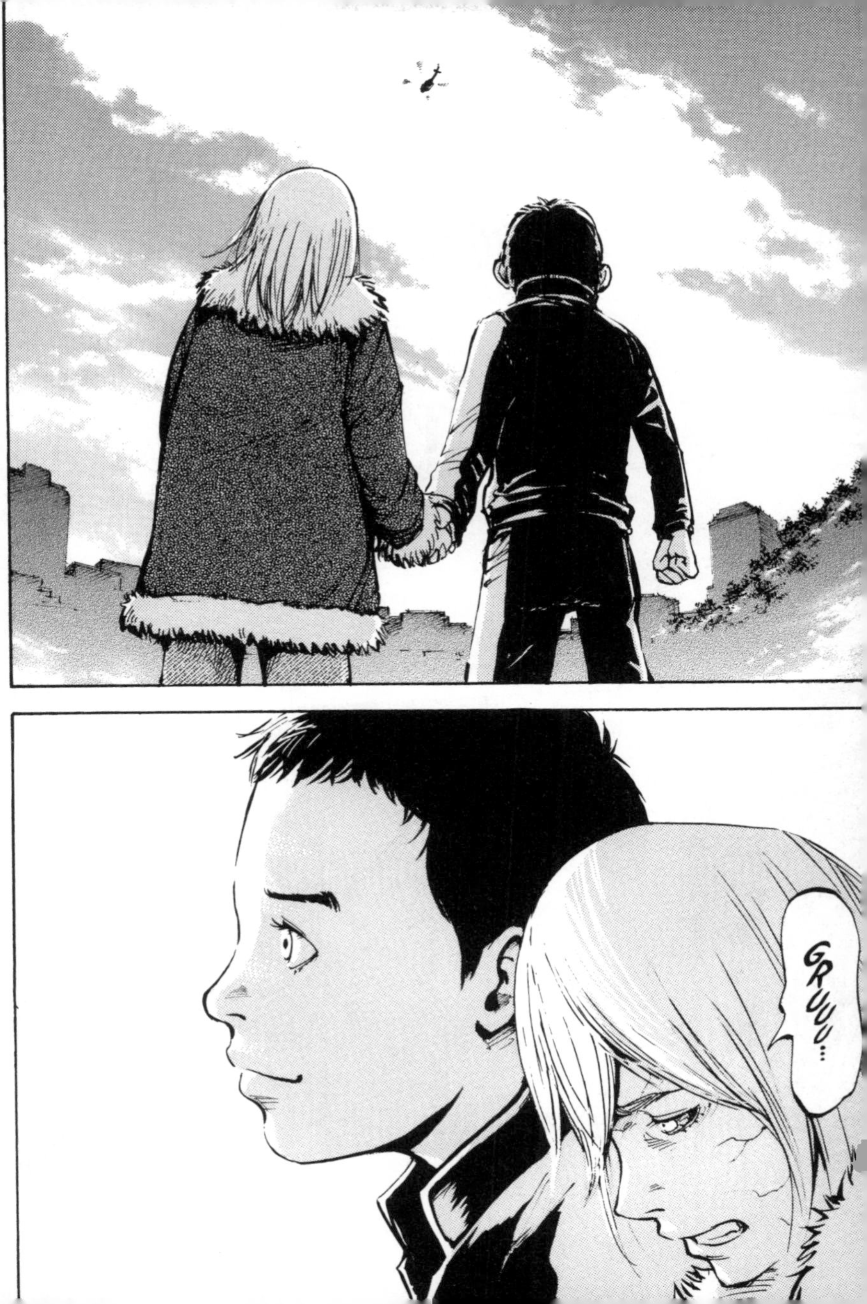
GRUUU...

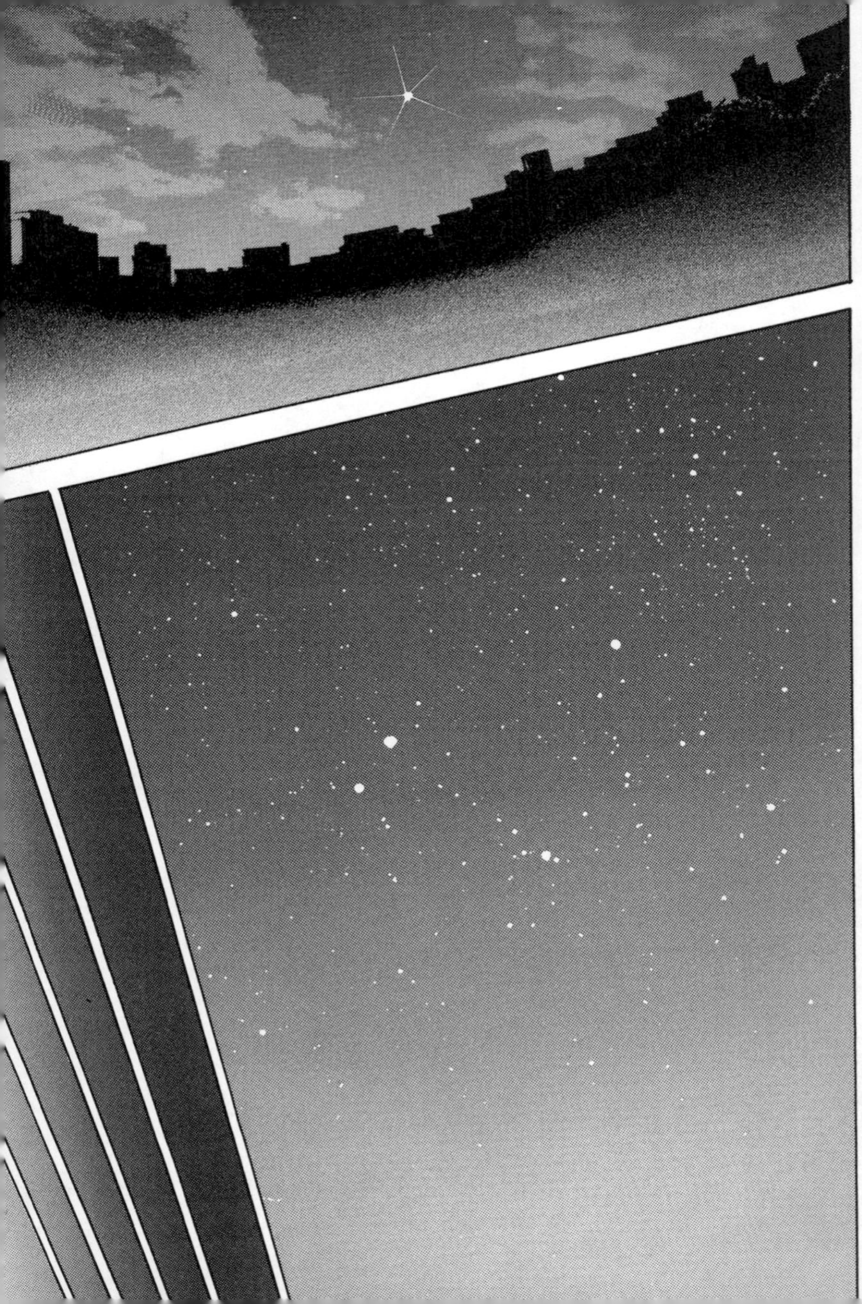

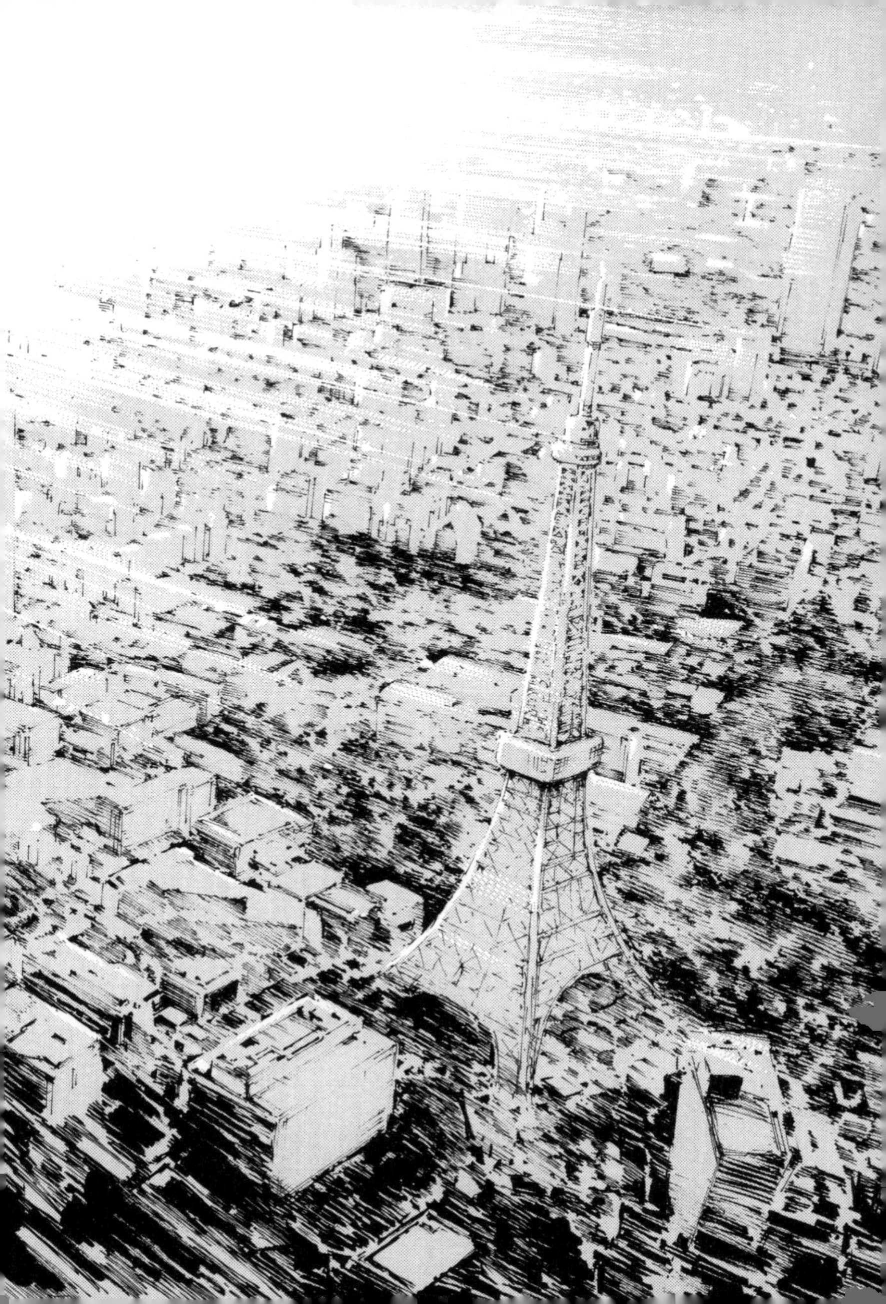

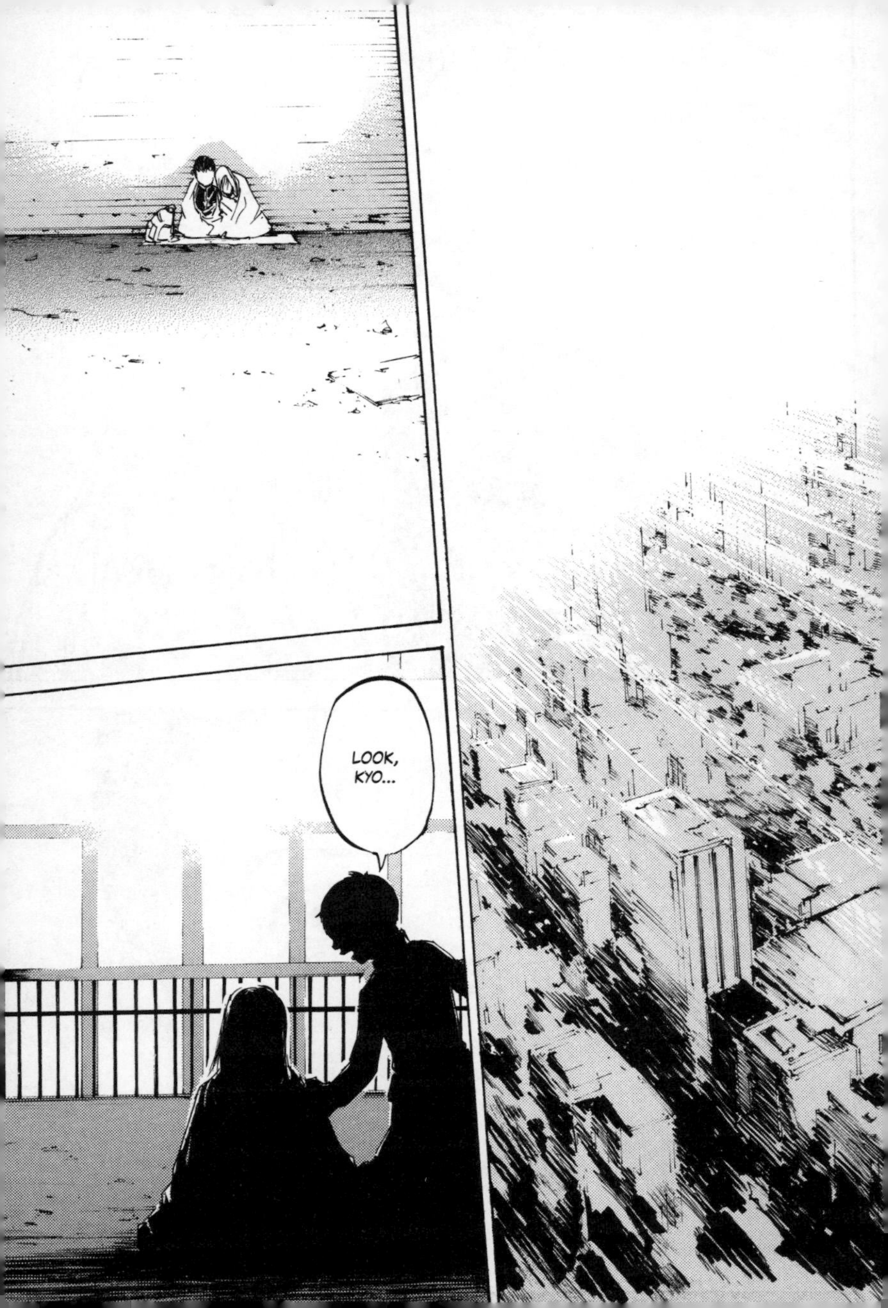
LOOK, KYO...

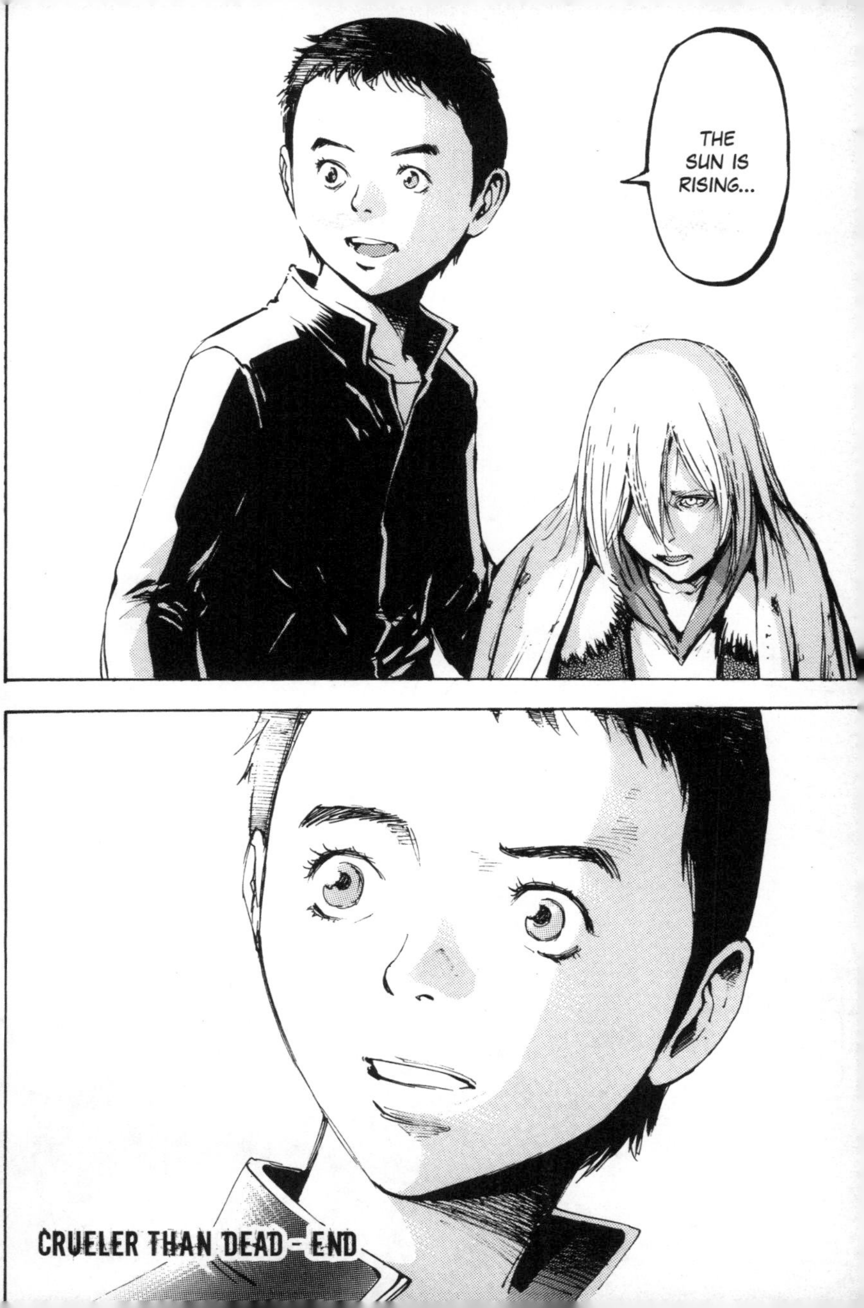
THE SUN IS RISING...
CRUELER THAN DEAD - END

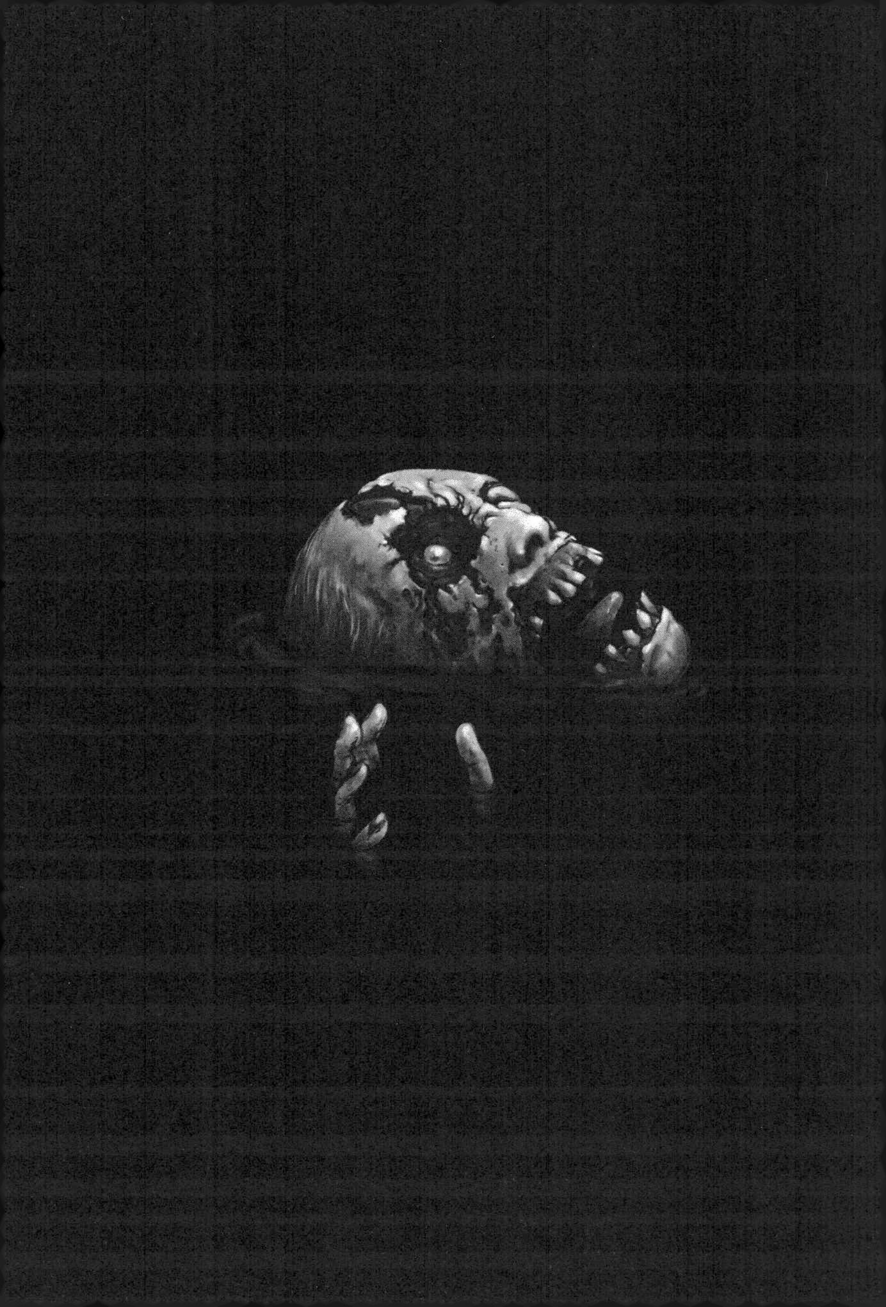

CRUELER THAN DEAD
by Tsukasa Saimura and Kozo Takahashi

Translated and lettered by:
FairSquare Comics (Fabrice Sapolsky, Lilliah Campagna)

FOR ABLAZE

Managing Editor:
Rich Young

Editor:
Kevin Ketner

Designer:
Rodolfo Muraguchi

Publisher's Cataloging-in-Publication data

Names: Saimura, Tsukasa, author. | Takahashi, Kozo, illustrator.
Title: Crueler than Dead , vol. 2 / Tsukasa Saimura; Kozo Takahashi.
Description: Portland, OR: Ablaze Publishing, 2022.
Identifiers: ISBN 978-1-950912-55-1
Subjects: LCSH Zombies—Fiction. | Tokyo—Fiction. | Horror. | Graphic novels. | BISAC COMICS & GRAPHIC NOVELS / Manga / Horror | COMICS & GRAPHIC NOVELS / Horror
Classification: LCC PN6790.J33 .S25 v. 2 2022 | DDC 741.5—dc23

 /ablazepub @AblazePub @AblazePub

ablazepublishing.com

To find a comics shop in your area go to:
www.comicshoplocator.com

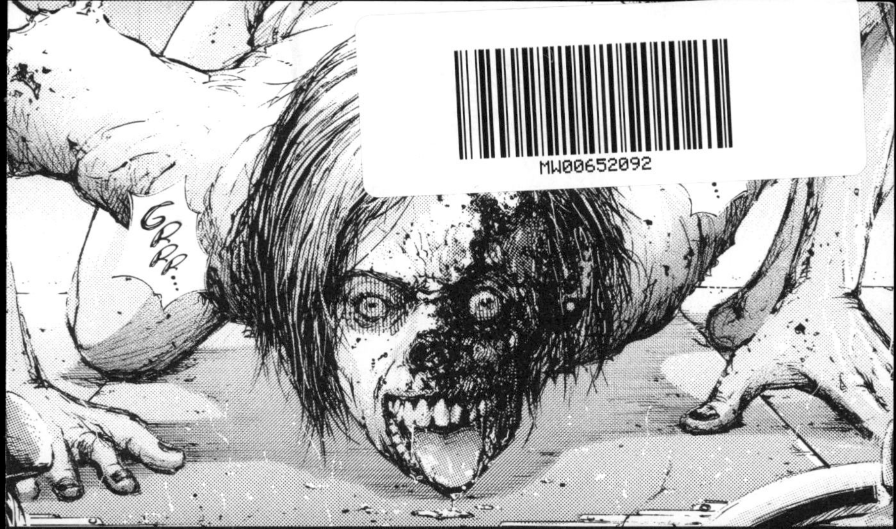
GRRR...

STOP!

THIS IS THE BACK OF THE BOOK!

his manga collection is
ranslated into English, but
rranged in right-to-left
eading format to maintain
he artwork's visual
rientation as originally
rawn and published in
apan. Start in the upper
ight-hand corner and
ead each word balloon
nd panel right-to-left.

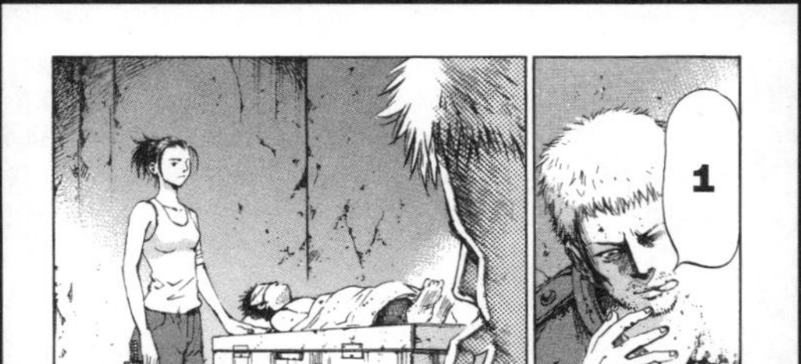
1
2
3
4
5

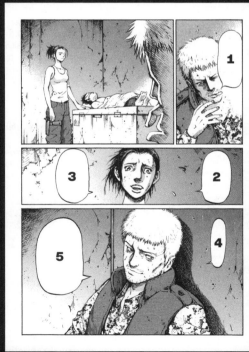